SAGE was founded in 1965 by Sara Miller McCune to support the dissemination of usable knowledge by publishing innovative and high-quality research and teaching content. Today, we publish over 900 journals, including those of more than 400 learned societies, more than 800 new books per year, and a growing range of library products including archives, data, case studies, reports, and video. SAGE remains majority-owned by our founder, and after Sara's lifetime will become owned by a charitable trust that secures our continued independence.

Los Angeles | London | New Delhi | Singapore | Washington DC | Melbourne

Sociology of India

Thank you for choosing a SAGE product!
If you have any comment, observation or feedback,
I would like to personally hear from you.

Please write to me at **contactceo@sagepub.in**

Vivek Mehra, Managing Director and CEO, SAGE India.

Bulk Sales

SAGE India offers special discounts
for bulk institutional purchases.

For queries/orders/inspection copy requests,
write to **textbooksales@sagepub.in**

Publishing

Would you like to publish a textbook with SAGE?
Please send your proposal to **publishtextbook@sagepub.in**

Subscribe to our mailing list

Write to **marketing@sagepub.in**

This book is also available as an e-book.

Sociology of India

Abhijit Kundu
*Faculty, Sociology Department, Sri Venkateswara College,
University of Delhi, New Delhi*

Nupurnima Yadav
*Faculty, Sociology Department, Sri Venkateswara College,
University of Delhi, New Delhi*

Los Angeles | London | New Delhi
Singapore | Washington DC | Melbourne

Copyright © Abhijit Kundu and Nupurima Yadav, 2021

All rights reserved. No part of this book may be reproduced or utilized in any form or by any means, electronic or mechanical, including photocopying, recording or by any information storage or retrieval system, without permission in writing from the publisher.

First published in 2021 by

SAGE Publications India Pvt Ltd
B1/I-1 Mohan Cooperative Industrial Area
Mathura Road, New Delhi 110 044, India
www.sagepub.in

SAGE Publications Inc
2455 Teller Road
Thousand Oaks, California 91320, USA

SAGE Publications Ltd
1 Oliver's Yard, 55 City Road
London EC1Y 1SP, United Kingdom

SAGE Publications Asia-Pacific Pte Ltd
18 Cross Street #10-10/11/12
China Square Central
Singapore 048423

Published by Vivek Mehra for SAGE Publications India Pvt Ltd. Typeset in 9.5/11.5 pt Bookman Old Style by AG Infographics, Delhi.

Library of Congress Control Number: 2021936025

ISBN: 978-93-5388-765-0 (PB)

SAGE Team: Amit Kumar, Indrani Dutta, Aishna Bhatt, Sudeshna Nandy and Rajinder Kaur

CONTENTS

List of Illustrations   xi
List of Boxes   xiii
Preface   xv
About the Authors   xvii

SECTION A. SOCIOLOGY AND SOCIAL ANTHROPOLOGY: DEVELOPMENT AND APPROACHES

CHAPTER 1
Development of Sociology and Social Anthropology in India   3

CHAPTER 2
Approaches: Colonialist Construction, Nationalist Discourse and Subaltern Critique   20

CHAPTER 3
For a Sociology of India: Indological and Ethnographic Approaches   36

CHAPTER 4
Ideas of India: Gandhi and Ambedkar   53

SECTION B. SOCIAL STRUCTURE AND SOCIAL INSTITUTIONS

CHAPTER 5
Castes and Classes in Modern India   71

CHAPTER 6
Religion and Tribes in India: Questions of Identity   89

CHAPTER 7
Family, Marriage and Kinship: Changing Contours   105

SECTION C. RURAL AND URBAN WORLDS

CHAPTER 8
Panchayat Raj and Rural Development   123

CHAPTER 9
Urbanization, Urban Social Transformation and
the Right to the City 139

SECTION D. SOCIAL CHANGE

CHAPTER 10
Sanskritization, Westernization and Modernization 157

CHAPTER 11
Industrialism to Globalization and the Role of the Media ... 174

SECTION E. SOCIAL MOVEMENTS, RESISTANCE AND NATION BUILDING

CHAPTER 12
Peasant Movement and Middle-class Phenomenon 195

CHAPTER 13
Dalit Movement 216

CHAPTER 14
Women's Movement 231

CHAPTER 15
Ethnic Movements 249

SECTION F. SOCIAL CHALLENGES

CHAPTER 16
Population, Poverty and Illiteracy 267

CHAPTER 17
Child Labour, Delinquency and Social Disorganization 284

CHAPTER 18
Violence against Women and Children 296

SECTION G. CHALLENGES TO CIVILIZATION AND SOCIETY

CHAPTER 19
Nationalism and Citizenship 311

CHAPTER 20
Communalism and Secularism 326

Index I–1

DETAILED CONTENTS

List of Illustrations — xi
List of Boxes — xiii
Preface — xv
About the Authors — xvii

SECTION A. SOCIOLOGY AND SOCIAL ANTHROPOLOGY: DEVELOPMENT AND APPROACHES

CHAPTER 1
Development of Sociology and Social Anthropology in India — 3
- Introduction — 4
- 1.1. Context of Development Sociology and Social Anthropology — 4
- 1.2. Phases in the Development of Sociology and Social Anthropology — 7
- 1.3. The Stage of Professionalization — 10
- 1.4. The Post-Independence Phase — 14
- Conclusion — 17

CHAPTER 2
Approaches: Colonialist Construction, Nationalist Discourse and Subaltern Critique — 20
- Introduction — 21
- 2.1. Colonial Discourse — 21
- 2.2. The Nationalist Discourse — 26
- 2.3. The Subaltern School — 29
- Conclusion — 32

CHAPTER 3
For a Sociology of India: Indological and Ethnographic Approaches — 36
- Introduction — 37
- 3.1. Indology — 38
- 3.2. Ethnographic Approach — 43
- Conclusion — 49

CHAPTER 4
Ideas of India: Gandhi and Ambedkar — 53
- Introduction — 54
- 4.1. Mahatma Gandhi — 54

    4.2. Bhimrao Ambedkar   59
    Conclusion   66

SECTION B. SOCIAL STRUCTURE AND SOCIAL INSTITUTIONS

CHAPTER 5
Castes and Classes in Modern India   71
    Introduction   72
    5.1. Social Structure   73
    5.2. Caste   74
    5.3. Structural Changes   78
    5.4. Class   81
    Conclusion   85

CHAPTER 6
Religion and Tribes in India: Questions of Identity   89
    Introduction   90
    6.1. Religion in India   90
    6.2. Tribes in India   98
    Conclusion   102

CHAPTER 7
Family, Marriage and Kinship: Changing Contours   105
    Introduction   106
    7.1. Family   106
    7.2. Social Institution of Marriage   109
    7.3. Kinship   112
    Conclusion   117

SECTION C. RURAL AND URBAN WORLDS

CHAPTER 8
Panchayat Raj and Rural Development   123
    Introduction   124
    8.1. Village in India   124
    8.2. Political Identity in Villages   130
    8.3. Economic Development   131
    8.4. Rural–Urban Continuum   134
    Conclusion   137

CHAPTER 9
Urbanization, Urban Social Transformation and the Right to the City   139
    Introduction   140
    9.1. Urbanization   140
    9.2. City and Urbanism   146
    9.3. City and Space   150
    Conclusion   151

SECTION D. SOCIAL CHANGE

CHAPTER 10
Sanskritization, Westernization and Modernization   **157**
    Introduction   158
    10.1. Sanskritization   159
    10.2. Westernization   163
    10.3. Modernization   165
    10.4. Current Complex   168
    Conclusion   171

CHAPTER 11
Industrialism to Globalization and the Role of the Media   **174**
    Introduction   175
    11.1. Industrialization   176
    11.2. Post-Industrialism   180
    11.3. Globalization   181
    11.4. Media   187
    Conclusion   189

SECTION E. SOCIAL MOVEMENTS, RESISTANCE AND NATION BUILDING

CHAPTER 12
Peasant Movement and Middle-class Phenomenon   **195**
    Introduction   196
    12.1. The Peasant Movement in India   197
    12.2. Middle Class Phenomenon   205
    Conclusion   211

CHAPTER 13
Dalit Movement   **216**
    Introduction   216
    13.1. Dalit Politics: Identity and Assertions   217
    13.2. Dalit Movement in India   222
    Conclusion   228

CHAPTER 14
Women's Movement   **231**
    Introduction   231
    14.1. Women in India   232
    14.2. Contemporary Feminist Ideas   237
    Conclusion   246

CHAPTER 15
Ethnic Movements   **249**
    Introduction   249
    15.1. Politics of Ethnicity   250
    15.2. The Assam Movement   253
    Conclusion   261

SECTION F. SOCIAL CHALLENGES

CHAPTER 16
Population, Poverty and Illiteracy — **267**
Introduction — 268
16.1. Population — 269
16.2. Poverty — 272
16.3. Illiteracy — 276
Conclusion — 281

CHAPTER 17
Child Labour, Delinquency and Social Disorganization — **284**
Introduction — 284
17.1. Child Labour — 286
17.2. Childhood — 287
17.3. Social Disorganization — 292
Conclusion — 294

CHAPTER 18
Violence against Women and Children — **296**
Introduction — 297
18.1. Women and Violence — 298
18.2. Violence against Children — 303
18.3. Violence against the Elderly — 305
Conclusion — 306

SECTION G. CHALLENGES TO CIVILIZATION AND SOCIETY

CHAPTER 19
Nationalism and Citizenship — **311**
Introduction — 311
19.1. Nationalism — 312
19.2. Bases of Nationality — 319
Conclusion — 324

CHAPTER 20
Communalism and Secularism — **326**
Introduction — 326
20.1. Communalism — 327
20.2. Secularism — 332
Conclusion — 339

Index — I–1

LIST OF ILLUSTRATIONS

Figure

6.1 Distribution of ST Population by States (in %)   99

Tables

7.1 Families Based on the Locality or the Residence: Determined by the Prevailing Authority   109

9.1 National Poverty Estimates (% BPL) from 1993–1994 to 2011–2012   150

10.1 Paradigm of an Integrated Approach   159

16.1 Key Population Statistics of India 1901–1991   269
16.2 Vital Rates per 1,000 Population in India 1901–1990   270
16.3 State-wise Poverty Estimates (% Below Poverty Line; 2004–2005, 2011–2012)   276
16.4 The Literacy Rates of the Top and Bottom Five States   279

LIST OF BOXES

1.1	Professionalization of Sociology	10
1.2	Specialization in Sociology	16
2.1	Book View versus Field View	25
2.2	Nationalism and Tradition	27
2.3	The Project of Time	31
3.1	Govind Sadashiv Ghurye (1893–1983)	38
4.1	A Critique of Gandhi	59
4.2	Ambedkar on Chaturvarnya	62
4.3	Annihilation of Caste	64
5.1	Hierarchy and Difference	72
5.2	Problem of Studying Class	81
6.1	T. N. Madan	97
7.1	Concept of Marriage in Different Religions	110
8.1	Salient Features of the 73rd and 74th Constitution Amendment Acts	126
8.2	Rural Social Development Programmes	135
9.1	Thorstein Veblen (1857–1929)	146
10.1	M. N. Srinivas	160
10.2	Critique of Modernity	170
11.1	Phases of Industrial Revolution	176
11.2	Media Theories Overview	188
12.1	The Dominant Peasantry	203
12.2	The Shallow Middle Class	210
13.1	Self-image of a Dalit	220
14.1	Gender and Nation	234

15.1	Criticality of Ethnicity	256
17.1	Child Labour	285
18.1	Dowry	299
18.2	Child Marriage	301
19.1	Citizenship and Autonomy	318
19.2	Hindu Nationalism	320
20.1	Nehru's Lamenting Voice	335

PREFACE

From a layman to a specialist, the Indian society has been a fascinating object of curiosity or knowledge. The Indian society with all its diversities and dynamics has caught the attention of both insiders and outsiders. For a layman, common sense plays a key role in approaching the aspects of Indian social organizations. While such comprehensions have worth, sociology of the Indian society rests on application of relevant sociological concepts to explain the working of the Indian society. Beyond the curiosity and speculation on the Indian society, sociological studies rest on rigorous theoretical orientation as well as ideological underpinnings. Sociology of India as a university degree course tries to capture the vast range of research studies which explain the social structures, processes and cultural systems. The mandate of the learning outcome-based course curriculum is to eclectically acquaint the students to substantive research studies which make sense of the Indian society.

As an introductory course on sociology of India, it explores the images and ideas of India as well as the key concepts and institutions which are fundamental for shaping the Indian society. At the auspices of the University Grants Commission, different universities have invested their academic councils, from time to time, to develop the state-of-the-art syllabus design and relevant text materials. The idea of the present textbook, *Sociology of India*, is to attend to the need of a holistic reading of the course. As a text, it makes best use of readings referred by leading universities of the country. As a textbook catering to the inquisitive student of sociology, it builds every theme and topic, drawing upon an updated conceptual development of every subject topic. Referred original texts are used to inspire students to explore the world of sociology of India.

Meaningful inspiration has come from diverse sources to prepare the present exhaustive textbook aimed at not only university degree students of sociology but also a cross section of interested students preparing for sociology courses for all-India competitive examinations. We are fortunate and humbly acknowledge the first-hand classroom experiences with some of the stalwarts of Indian sociology, whose texts have been abundantly used in the preparation of the present work. We also acknowledge the Tirumala Tirupati Devasthanams Governing Body, Sri Venkateswara College, University of Delhi, for facilitating the task and allowing us to indulge in quality time for writing the manuscript. Our graceful thanks to Indrani Dutta, Commissioning Editor, SAGE, for providing us with the necessary inputs at crucial moments of developing the work, which would add to the thrill of teaching and learning. For meeting the deadline, Hridi owns the credit in speedily typing much of the manuscript. Finally, our years of learning experience through teaching young minds of the discipline have shaped much of the organization of this textbook.

ABOUT THE AUTHORS

Abhijit Kundu is Associate Professor in the Department of Sociology at Sri Venkateswara College, University of Delhi. His doctoral work is on cinema and gender studies from Jawaharlal Nehru University, New Delhi. His areas of interest are sociology of contemporary India and sociological theories and methods.

Prof. Kundu has been a guest faculty at Aarhus University, Denmark, as part of a European Union-funded project of Contemporary India Study Centre Aarhus, and has acted as a resource person in the state-level orientation programme on methodology and choice-based credit system syllabus of a number of Indian universities. He has been in the course revision committee of the Sociology Department, Delhi School of Economics, University of Delhi; Indira Gandhi National Open University, New Delhi; and Ambedkar University Delhi.

His published works include, *The Humanities: Methodology and Perspectives* (co-authored, 2009), *The Social Sciences: Methodology and Perspectives* (edited, 2009), *Sociological Theory* (2012) and *Ambedkar: An Overview* (edited with an Introduction, 2018). He has been a frequent contributor in the popular *Anandabazar* (vernacular) op-ed pages. He has contributed to the Publications Division, Government of India, *Anthology on Indian Cinema through the Century* (bilingual, Hindi and English, 2015).

Nupurnima Yadav did her PhD from the Centre for the Study of Social Systems, Jawaharlal Nehru University. She is currently working as Assistant Professor in the Department of Sociology at Sri Venkateswara College. She has also undertaken various research projects with UNICEF and Delhi government. Her publications include, Creative Destruction and Enterprising Economy, in the (eds) *Crisis of Social Transformation in India* (2015) and Fearsome Goddess Seetala and Faithful Communities, published in *Nidan: International Journal for the Study of Hinduism*.

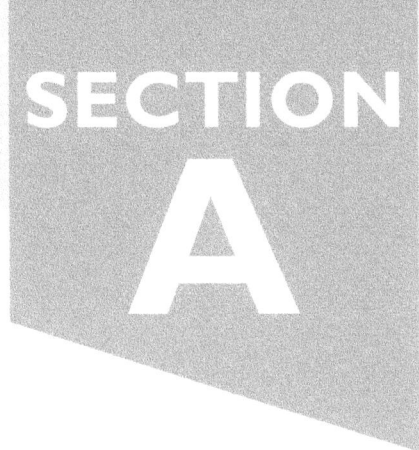

SECTION A

SOCIOLOGY AND SOCIAL ANTHROPOLOGY: DEVELOPMENT AND APPROACHES

Chapter 1
Development of Sociology and Social Anthropology in India

Chapter 2
Approaches: Colonialist Construction, Nationalist Discourse and Subaltern Critique

Chapter 3
For a Sociology of India: Indological and Ethnographic Approaches

Chapter 4
Ideas of India: Gandhi and Ambedkar

CHAPTER 1

Development of Sociology and Social Anthropology in India

LEARNING OUTCOMES

- To identify the various phases of the development of the disciplines
- To examine the formative years and the impact of socio-intellectual factors impacting the disciplines
- To comprehend the emergence of the disciplines as academic and professional
- To trace the changing contours of the disciplines and the aspects of specializations

Keywords: Age of Reason, functionalism, evolutionary, ethnology, Indology, professionalization, diversification

Indian sociology, like most other social sciences in India, has grown through an encounter with the Western philosophical and social scientific traditions.

—**Yogendra Singh**

INTRODUCTION

The nature and possibilities of any discipline are conditioned by not only the present but also its past. Especially for humanities, a discipline is intrinsically tied up with its socio-historical conditioning. Along its path of development, a discipline changes its course in terms of its perspectives as well as focal areas of study. For modern disciplines such as sociology and social anthropology, it will be fascinating to chart out the history. In the Indian context, the disciplines of sociology and social anthropology have shared not only common methods of study but also subject matter. The relationship between the two has elicited scholarly research papers. Growingly, the practice of doing sociology and social anthropology has converged to a great extent. While it is true that institutionally the two disciplines, anthropology and sociology, have remained separate in the Indian universities, the penchant for anthropological insights has been so strong among many leading sociologists that the possibility of their unification was even hypothesized from time to time. That was not to be, as the history of the development of the two disciplines has unfolded in particular ways. It is important for us to remember that the sociocultural climate that conditioned the development of the two disciplines has undergone significant changes over the years.

While it is true that the disciplines of sociology and social anthropology originated in India in a colonial context, they have passed through various phases of development. The Indian social milieu of anti-colonial and nationalist phases impacted the disciplines and its practitioners. The disciplines have flourished across universities, colleges and research institutes. Also, the disciplines have responded to the changing global conditions which have opened up new areas of macro as well as micro studies. While doing so, interfaces with related social science disciplines have deepened much, leading to interdisciplinarity among social sciences. Another significant aspect of development of sociology and social anthropology is that in the contemporary globalized world, there has been a growing interest in non-Western knowledge. Development of indigenous perspectives and models has gained attention in the research works of both the disciplines.

1.1. CONTEXT OF DEVELOPMENT SOCIOLOGY AND SOCIAL ANTHROPOLOGY

1.1.1. The Western Context

The context of development of sociology and social anthropology in India is quite different from the way they have developed in the West. As a social scientific discipline, sociology in the West was impacted by the social as well as the intellectual currents of Europe. The impact of the 18th-century industrial and democratic revolutions prepared the social background for the development of sociology. The Enlightenment ideas of the 18th century served as the intellectual milieu. At the level of ideas, the Enlightenment heralded a break from outdated, age-old ideas and values. We can say that the development of sociology signalled a celebration of the Age of Reason and rationality in order to understand society and promise newer modes of social progress. The philosophers of the Age of Reason prompted a modern way of looking at the world.

While sociology was conceived of as the discipline to explain modern civilized societies and their problems, social anthropology was considered in the beginning as one which explained primitive societies. In the West, as a separate discipline, social anthropology developed at the end of the 19th century. Sixteenth century onwards the colonial expansionist aspiration of Europe constituted the backdrop of the development of anthropology in general. The evolutionary scheme of tracing the development of human civilization dominated the early penchant for knowledge about people from the non-European world. The aim of anthropology underwent a change in the middle of the 19th century. The new perspective argued in favour of diffusion and spread of culture leading to mixture of people. The evolutionary model of a unilinear development of human society was refuted as conjectural. However, in the early 20th century the 'structural-functional' school replaced both the evolutionist and the diffusionist perspectives as instead of learning about society through a hypothetical reconstruction of their past, a functionalist anthropology insisted on an understanding of a society as a functioning system made up of constituent parts. Ultimately, this functional perspective of anthropology by and large came to be considered as social anthropology (Shah 1959).

In the early decades of the 20th century with the seminal contributions from Bronislaw Malinowski and Radcliffe-Brown, social anthropology attempted to explain pre-modern societies in terms of interrelations of its functioning parts. While the British social anthropological tradition focused on the real social relations among people to account for the real social structure, Robert Redfield in the USA, adopted a cross-disciplinary approach and used anthropological insights into sociological issues. Focusing on dynamics of social transition to examine civilization, Redfield supplemented the new field of social anthropology which originally developed in Britain. In direct contrast, Levi-Strauss forwarded the French structural school applying the structural linguistics of de Saussure. Instead of the real structure of interrelationships, he formulated the structuralist method of identification of the 'unconscious infrastructure' of the real world. The earlier anthropological insistence on the concept of 'function', inspired by Emile Durkheim's functional sociology, was permanently left aside in favour of the specific structural patterns which sustain different communities to a common fundamental thinking process.

1.1.2. The Indian Context

The initial phase of social anthropology was impacted by a colonial expansive mode of knowledge—to know the 'other' in the interest of the colonial power. The new turn of social anthropology was more to insist upon the universality of human experience. The historicity of the development of social anthropology in India could not escape the encounter with the Western theoretical tradition. On the one hand, the Western concepts impacted the development of social/cultural anthropology in India, on the other hand, the internal issues of a colonized country emerging as a sovereign independent nation governed the nature and development of the disciplines in India.

The British administrators were driven by an idea to grasp the Indian society as the 'other'. It was necessary to run the colonial government to understand the Indian society and its indigenous native ways. An overall evolutionary perspective and the Victorian idea of progress shaped the colonial exercise. For the colonial knowledge system, the native non-Western societies were merely the different forms of the earlier stages of development which the advanced European societies had already gone through. It is important to note that under the influence of Sir William Jones, the Asiatic Society of Bengal was founded in 1784.

Yogendra Singh has also raised the issue of 'social conditioning' of Indian sociology. He pointed out the historical forces of the colonial times that shaped the beginning of a new discipline like sociology (Singh 1986). Interestingly, he indicated that for societies like India, with deep civilizational roots, a general scientific view tried to estimate the coming of the present in evolutionary terms. It was in congruence with Western perspective that scholarship of early sociology in India prospered.

At the same time, sociology served as a critical scholarly tool to question the colonial rule. However, the initial evolutionary explanation of the Indian society and culture was questioned on the basis of faulty comparative evolutionary scheme. B. N. Seal and B. K. Sarkar responded to the all-pervading Western evolutionary scheme by portraying that a universal evolutionary path of development could not be projected for all, as institutions across different cultures were not historically coexistent (Singh 1986).

> Sociology, before it took its place as a teaching discipline in the academic institutions in India, had emerged as a generalized social ideology which viewed the social institutions of the societies from a scientific evolutionary viewpoint at a global level.... In the colonial context in which many such societies were ensnared, sociology became for the many intellectuals from these countries an ideology of revolutionary social and political movement for emancipation from the foreign rule. (Singh 2004, 136)

Overall speaking, both the colonial and the intellectual interests of the Western scholars were the background for a formal development of both sociology and social anthropology in India. At the same time, there were the reactions of the Indian scholars to the British administrative purpose to collect information about the customs and institutions of the colonized subject. A parallel and nationalist spirit emerged in the initial years of the development of the two related disciplines.

1.1.3. Alternative View

Some sociologists researching on the context of development and growth of sociology in India are of the opinion that the 18th-century European sociopolitical crisis provided a more authentic origin for its development. That is, the crisis of the society brought about by the industrial and political revolutions gave rise to an Enlightened way of explaining society. It was guided by a spirit of reconstruction and searching for a stable social order. However, the initial spirit was lost in the historical passage of the growth of the discipline.

In contrast, sociology is understood as a colonial implantation in India, which lacks such an authentic conditioning (Momin 2012). The colonial conditioning is seen as having detrimental consequences with respect to the image of India and its people. It is seen as a part of the colonial design to study and facilitate administrative policies. The policies were to create barriers between the Hindus and other marginal groups and to show India as a fragmented society. An uncritical acceptance of the Western conceptual categories marked the emergence of both sociology and social anthropology in India. This allowed the adoption of a methodology which was so congruent with the colonial purpose. The methodology focused on detailed in-depth studies of discrete castes and tribes.

1.2. PHASES IN THE DEVELOPMENT OF SOCIOLOGY AND SOCIAL ANTHROPOLOGY

1.2.1. The Foundation Years

The chronology of the development of sociology and social anthropology has received the attention of many sociologists since the 1970s. To trace the history in terms of historical phases was later on prompted by institutionalization of the disciplines aided by the all-India social sciences research body, Indian Council of Social Science Research (ICSSR). Professionalization as well as institutionalization of the disciplines required an evaluation of the historical growth and coverage of subject matter of the disciplines.

Two foremost attempts by eminent sociologists in India on the development of sociology and social anthropology were made in the early 1970s. One co-authored by M. N. Srinivas and M. N. Panini (1973) and the other was a result of the project sponsored by ICSSR, New Delhi (1974). M. S. A. Rao in his introduction to the project admitted the commonality between the subject area of sociological and social anthropological researches in India and the similar colonial administrative conditioning of both the disciplines.

A development timeline was put forward by Srinivas and Panini (1973) by identifying three broad periods: 1773–1900 AD as the foundation period, 1901–1950 AD as the period of professionalization and finally, post-1950s as the period of proliferation of research interests on the face of complex set of forces unleashed in post-Independence years and beyond. Yogendra Singh and Ramkrishna Mukherjee are the other two leading sociologists who worked on the passage of the disciplines to the present state of the art.

This phase could be marked as the one where sociology as a distinct branch of knowledge did not really emerge. Srinivas and Panini have traced the origin of sociology and social anthropology in India to the efforts of the missionaries and ethnographers at the behest of the British colonizers. The British interest was to understand the native society to deliver a smooth administration.

Ramkrishna Mukherjee (2012) prefers to call it 'proto-professional' stage of sociology to refer to the pre-20th-century period. This period according to him was marked by governmental findings, reports and surveys on the life of the people. Clearly, the colonial object was twofold. First was to learn about the people and their ways of life for an efficient state policy. And second was to know about itself. It was just a modern act of similar attempts made by rulers and kings in India's ancient and medieval history.

Yogendra Singh (2004) calls the period before development of sociology and social anthropology as academic disciplines 'the pre-sociological beginnings'. He identifies the social ideological components that marked this period. A progressive evolutionary prospective was pre-eminent in this period. He points out the role played by Shyamji Krishna Varma, who was influenced by Herbert Spencer in London and published a journal named *Indian Sociologist* in 1905.

In fact, the mid-19th-century intellectual tradition of cultural reawakening in India under the auspices of the leading figures of Ram Mohan Roy, Ishwar Chandra Vidyasagar, Swami Vivekananda, Swami Dayananda Saraswati, J. G. Phule, M. G. Ranade and many others laid the basis for many commentaries on India. Many of them were trained in European universities. Their reviews and criticisms of the European sociologists' and social anthropologists' explanation of the Indian society and culture had sociological elements in them.

1.2.2. Colonial Interface

The European studies on the Indian societies have to be seen as a continuum of the early colonial interests in India as pointed out by Srinivas and Panini. They pointed out that it was at the behest of the governor of Bengal and Bihar in 1769, Henry Verelst, that rigorous collection of information about the Indian families and customary ways were collected by revenue supervisors. British officials and missionaries devoted themselves to generate data on the Indian people. Elementary ethnographic studies were also conducted in the process. More consolidated attempts were made towards the end of the 19th century.

The consolidation was facilitated by the constitution of All-India Census Enumeration, initiated by the British Government in 1871. The exhaustive data collected in a more systematic way by the British officials were useful not only for smooth administrative purpose but also opened up social and cultural analysis.

In a way, Indian Civil Servant Herbert Risley pioneered ethnographic studies in India. He was posted in Bengal and authored *The Tribes and Castes of Bengal* in 1891. In his elementary ethnographies of caste, he showed the Brahmanical ideology of the caste system. His ethnography created a basis for distinguishing tribes from the caste Hindus. He also recorded meticulously the caste distinction among the Hindus. As the commissioner of the 1901 Census, Risley was instrumental in keeping the tribes out of the Hindu fold. This census exercise had significant sociological elements. According to Srinivas and Panini, the enumeration of caste divisions through census operations created caste awareness to the extent that each caste group started contesting any pre-assigned position in the caste hierarchy. Interestingly, the way social-cultural distinctions were recorded through census surveys, similar distinctions among other religious groups were not indicated.

> Finally, the recording of caste divisions among the Hindus at each census sharpened the self-awareness of each caste and gave rise to competitions amongst them to claim higher positions in the caste hierarchy than had been traditionally and locally conceded. (Srinivas and Panini 1973, 183)

1.2.3. Exploratory Phase

The colonial government's efforts to get familiarized with the native ways of life and the Indological works to gain insights into the Indian mind to understand its social institutions fed into each other. M. S. A. Rao in his introduction to the project of ICSSR (1974) used the term exploratory to name the foundation years. According to him, Indology constituted the primary area of sociological research in this period. Foreign scholars took keen interest in Sanskrit literature and made extensive translation of ancient texts into other Indo-European languages. Some of the important works were made by Sir William Jones (1746–1794), Henry Thomas Colebrooke (1765–1837), Max Müller (1823–1900) and W. D. Whitney (1827–1894). French philosopher-anthropologist Lucien Levy-Bruhl (1857–1939) and sociologist-cum-anthropologist Marcel Mauss (1872–1950) made extensive use of the classical Sanskrit texts in their phenomenal research works. Similarly, Henry Maine, a lawyer and the founder of comparative jurisprudence in England, made references to the Hindu legal system in his *Ancient Law* (1861) and to the village social life in his *Village-Communities in the East and West* (1871).

M. S. A. Rao also mentioned about the work done by the Indian Indologists such as R. G. Bhandarkar, P. V. Kane, Altekar and others. A. K. Coomaraswamy reacted against the foreign scholar interests on the Indian society. He indicated the danger of social conquest with such knowledge generation. While talking about social and cultural anthropology, the ICSSR survey (1974) recorded that historically in the exploratory phase, social anthropology was associated with tribal studies. The British civil servants made intensive and systematic studies of the tribes and castes of India, and the appointment of ethnologist Sir Risley as the commissioner of census operation in 1881 was in tune with the overall project. The first anthropological society was founded in Bombay in 1886 by Edward Leith.

Importantly, M. S. A. Rao noted that there was no clear-cut division between social anthropology and sociology in the exploratory phase. Ethnologists were concerned with both, tribes and castes. Among the other anthropologists, S. C. Roy in northern India and A. Iyer in the South were considered as the pioneers of the Indian ethnology. However, it needs to be remembered that during the foundation years, social anthropology did not develop as an academic subdiscipline. So the anthropological contribution during this phase was primarily informed by Indological literatures. Ajit K. Danda (1995) has pointed out that majority of the anthropological interests came from the European officials and Christian missionaries. According to Danda, the year 1784 was the most crucial for the growth of anthropology in India. The Asiatic Society of Bengal was founded by William Jones in this year. In the same year, the first research journal on Indological and anthropological subject was initiated.

So the preparatory years of the development of sociology and social anthropology were marked by a colonial interest. Detail and precise understanding of the Indian people was aided by Indological text as well as an interest in census surveys. Parallelly, social and religious reformism was stimulated by the 'social conquest' of the colonial dispensation. Nationalist sentiments prospered with a critical sense of understanding of the present in the light of a relook at the past. The social and intellectual conditioning for further development of the discipline was mainly located in the 19th century.

1.3. THE STAGE OF PROFESSIONALIZATION

1.3.1. Early Professionalization

The professionalization of sociology and social anthropology happened in the early decades of the 20th century. The 20th century saw the emergence of the disciplines as consolidated ones, but it was possible due to some preliminary proto-sociological works driven by nationalist feelings. The late 19th-century development of awareness among many Indian scholars and thinkers with respect to challenges to India's heritage, custom and society gave rise to a number of sociological writings. These writings served as a prelude to the subsequent formalization of the disciplines into the university system in the 1920s.

BOX 1.1
Professionalization of Sociology

The first half of the 20th century marks the period of academic professionalization of sociology. There were two trends—descriptive as well as explanatory sociology—developed in this period. The macro studies of the descriptive type dealt with the economic life of the people (exemplified by Radhakamal Mukerjee, K. P. Chattopadhyay and so on). The micro studies of the descriptive type adopted the anthropological method of small-scale intensive field study. Whereas explanatory sociology during this period exhibited a strong ideological orientation. The trend was to rationalize the Hindu way of life, which relied on ancient classical Indian/Sanskrit texts. The other trend, although weak, was to look beyond empiricism to idealism, bearing the imprint of Western idealist orientation.

Source: Mukherjee (2012).

The contributions of B. N. Seal (1864–1938) and B. K. Sarkar (1887–1949) are specially mentioned by Yogendra Singh (2004) to highlight the response from the Indian philosophers and thinkers to the Western sociologist's work on India. Seal questioned the evolutionary scheme of the Western sociology. The Indian reality had its own historicity which could not be easily compared with Western societies. B. K. Sarkar (1887–1949) took on the German Indologists and the orientalist biases which to large extent shaped the Western writings on the Indian society and culture. According to Yogendra Singh, many other thought-provoking writings by the Indian scholars in a rationalist-humanist mode gave rise to an academic background for formal teaching and researching the discipline.

> This was followed by the inauguration of early sociological writings by scholars in India, either as a sequel to, or in response to the writings of the western sociologists on India or in response to issues of epistemology and history. Most of this type of writing tends to be dialectical and exegetic. (Singh 2004, 137)

Srinivas and Panini noted the period of 1900–1920 as the introductory one for the subsequent establishment of sociology and social anthropology as academic disciplines in the Indian universities. In 1917, B. N. Seal was instrumental in the introduction of sociology in Calcutta University in the postgraduate council of arts and sciences. Seal left deep impression on his student Radhakamal Mukerjee, who went on to become the vice chancellor of Mysore University in 1917. Mukerjee was instrumental in the prosperity of Lucknow University as a centre of sociology. He was influenced by Thorstein Veblen, an American sociologist, on his visit to the States. He emphasized on values and traditions to understand the Indian society. Earlier, he was influenced by Patrick Geddes, who was the first professor of sociology, University of Bombay, 1919. Geddes propounded urban planning with emphasis on human geography.

1.3.2. Sociology as an Academic Discipline

A solid foundation of sociology as an academic discipline was laid by Patrick Geddes, G. S. Ghurye, Radhakamal Mukerjee, D. P. Mukerjee and D. N. Majumdar. Geddes and Ghurye were associated with Bombay University, the first university department to introduce sociology in the country. In 1914, the Government of India gave a grant to start the academic journey of sociology. Initially, a course of sociology and economics was introduced, which led to the establishment of a sociology and civics department. Geddes, who was the first professor, had an encyclopaedic expertise in sciences and humanities. He was against considering science devoid of moral question. Evidently, he was influenced by French sociologist August Comte's positivism. The relationship and integration of sociology with other related disciplines such as anthropology, ecology and statistics were also Geddes's area of interest.

The towering contribution of G. S. Ghurye is most important in the institutionalization of sociology in Bombay University. In Cambridge, he did his research in anthropology and came under the influence of W. H. R. Rivers. It had a lasting influence on Ghurye's sociology. Being a Sanskritist, he enriched the department in Bombay with his immense scholarship on Indology and anthropology. It had its bearing not only on the curricula for the teaching of sociology but also in all the researches undertaken by his students. He founded the Indian Sociological Society in 1952 and is also the founder editor of the foremost journal of the Society, *Sociological Bulletin*.

> Ghurye wrote several papers including one on 'Ethnic Theory of Caste' for his Ph.D, and this provided the basis for his book, Caste and Race in India (London, 1932).... Ghurye has written prolifically and over a wide range of theories. His studies include Rajput Architecture, Shakespeare and Kalidasa at one end and the sexual behaviour of American females at the other. His knowledge of Sanskrit enabled him to use the scriptures and epics in analyzing and interpreting Indian culture and society.
>
> (Srinivas and Panini 1973, 188)

Although sociology was first introduced at the postgraduate level in Bombay University, it was Mysore University which first introduced sociology at the undergraduate level in 1928–1929. The credit for that goes to A. R. Wadia, another product of Bombay University who did his postgraduation from Oxford.

Radhakamal Mukerjee, although was initially attached to Calcutta University (1917–1921), played a vital role in the development of the discipline in Lucknow. In fact, as far as the early days of the subject are concerned, Lucknow University played a glorious role with the contribution of outstanding scholars like D. P. Mukerjee and D. N. Majumdar.

According to Y. Singh, Radhakamal Mukerjee's outstanding contribution was to engage in critical theoretical analysis of the emergent socio-economic conditions of India at the beginning of the 20th century.

> Indeed, he is one of the earliest sociologist–economist in India to not only integrate the western theoretical and methodological paradigms in the studies of social and economic problems and issues in India but also the one who clearly lays down the foundation of a distinctive Indian sociological paradigm and theoretic structure. (Singh 2004, 141)

Mukerjee placed utmost primacy on the Indian philosophical traditions and tried to take the concept of dialectics out of the Western overwhelming philosophies. Away from the Western materialism and rationalist utilitarianism, he found dialectical method to be enriched more by the philosophical traditions of Vedanta, Buddhism and Taoism.

The other two leading figures of Lucknow school were D. P. Mukerjee and D. N. Majumdar. Although being receptive to the Marxian methodology in social sciences, popular during the early decades of the 20th century, Mukerjee campaigned for Marxology—a dialectical historical perspective which could use the Marxian categories in the specific Indian tradition and culture. According to his student Y. Singh, Mukerjee's teachings and research in sociology were the building blocks of the Lucknow School of Indian Sociology. It was innovative as well as grounded on solid philosophico-theoretical base.

D. P. Mukerjee had a master's degree in economics from Calcutta University and joined Lucknow University in 1922. He greatly inspired a whole lot of young researchers in the early years of sociology. He inspired the young scholars to ground their researches and methodology in tune with the Indian traditions and culture. Like D. P. Mukerjee, D. N. Majumdar was another star of the Lucknow School of Sociology. He was a trained anthropologist and a product of Calcutta University. He joined Lucknow University in 1928 before he left for England for his doctoral degree in cultural anthropology from Cambridge. He was greatly influenced by B. Malinowski.

> Mazumdar was instrumental in establishing the Ethnographic and Folk-Culture Society in Uttar Pradesh in 1945. Its quarterly journal, The Eastern Anthropologist, first published in 1947 has provided a welcome forum for anthropologist in India and outside. (Srinivas and Panini 1973, 190–191)

The other institutions where sociology as an academic discipline took shape were Deccan College of Post Graduate and Research Institute at Poona. In late 1930s, the department of sociology and anthropology at Poona started under the headship of Iravati Karve. Karve was a student of Ghurye and obtained her doctoral degree in anthropology from Germany.

Osmania University too introduced the study of sociology at the undergraduate level in 1928, but they started a separate department in 1946. Eminent scholars such as Christoph von F. Haimendorf and S. C. Dube illuminated the sociology department in Osmania.

1.3.3. Professionalization of Social Anthropology

The development of social anthropology in the early years of the 20th century was initially fraught with scepticism. The dominant nationalist sentiment considered anthropology and its related fieldwork method as a colonial design. It was understood as an official device to keep the tribes insulated from the mainstream anti-colonial nationalist feelings. Professional attention to ethnography started with W. H. R. Rivers' *The Todas* (1906). This work was based on intensive field study in the Nilgiris. It was a prelude to many fieldwork-based anthropology which subsequently took place in India. Radcliffe-Brown's research on the Andaman islanders (1922) set up a formidable base for development of social anthropology as an academic discipline. As far as the Indian anthropologists are concerned, the efforts of L. K. Ananthakrishna Iyer and S. C. Roy have to be noted. Iyer studied the caste and tribes of Mysore and the Syrian Christians of Kerala. Roy was prolific in his study of tribes of Bihar and in 1921 founded the foremost anthropological journal of India, *Man in India* (Srinivas and Panini 1973).

It is true that during the period of professionalization of the subject, the boundary of the academic discipline of social anthropology became more stable. Only after the 1920s, social anthropology started emerging with a separate identity, although from time to time practising sociologist in India indicated the difficulty of sustaining the distinction between the two disciplines (Beteille 1993). In its growing years, social/cultural anthropology had to face opposition from the nationalist thoughts. The steadfast contention of Verrier Elwin, a British ethnographer, to maintain and protect tribal habitat fuelled apprehensions against social anthropology. The pre-Independence period evoked quite a peculiar response towards social anthropology. It was marked by an unsympathetic attitude.

> Social/cultural anthropology as a branch of science was disliked during the pre-independence era for a different reason too.... The nationalist in particular resented them since according to their comprehension, subjects of anthropological studies were primitives who had been generally looked down upon because of their ascribed low status in social hierarchy. (Danda 1995, 72)

Recognition of anthropology as an academic discipline got a fillip with the establishment of the Department of Anthropology at the University of Calcutta in 1920. For more than two decades, the department remained as the only department of anthropology in India. It played a leading role in the future development of the discipline in terms of demarcating its specific subject areas, formulation of course syllabus and fostering research works. The second department of anthropology was founded in University of Delhi in 1946. While Calcutta University focused on social/cultural anthropology, the University of Delhi specialized in physical anthropology. Towards the end of this phase, the Anthropological Survey of India came to being in 1945.

It is to be noted that the anthropological researches of Great Britain impacted the Indian universities. Whereas the diffusionist approach of W. H. R. Rivers had its bearing on G. S. Ghurye and K. P. Chattopadhyay, the functionalist perspective of B. Malinowski and Raymond Firth influenced D. N. Majumdar and Aiyappan. During this phase, the boundary between sociology and anthropology did not really show up.

1.4. THE POST-INDEPENDENCE PHASE

1.4.1. The Initial Years

After Independence, sociology as well as social anthropology in India faced the unique challenge of nation-building for a newly independent state. Apparently, the freedom from the British exposed the practitioners of the disciplines to a wider theoretical influence, especially the American schools. As a result, the post-1950s period is often called the diversification phase. There was a considerable diversity in the theoretical approach in sociological and social anthropological fields of research. Many sociologists from time to time have raised the question of developing indigenous concepts and models of analysis. The self-awareness among researchers did affect the selection of research problems and conceptualization of the same to an extent. But overall speaking, the practice of the disciplines remained highly shaped by the British structural-functional approach.

According to Y. Singh (2012), it was only due to the pioneering role played by D. P. Mukerjee of the Lucknow School that sociology and social anthropology in India began to ground themselves in the Indian realities through indigenous models. Breaking away from the colonial framework of analysis, Mukerjee analysed the cultural challenges of colonialism by emphasizing a dialectical reading of the Indian tradition. A systematic dialectical analysis rooted in the Indian realities immensely appealed to the Indian students and scholars.

There has been a tremendous expansion of teaching of sociology in the Indian universities and colleges in the post-Independence phase. As a result of which there has been a proliferation of sociological researches on the Indian society. A number of professional journals led to the publication of significant research works. It is important to mention the role of *Sociological Bulletin*, the biannual journal of the Indian Sociological Society. The pioneering journal, *Contributions to Indian Sociology*, was founded in 1957. Its co-editors, Louis Dumont and D. F. Pocock, led important debates pertaining to the scope and nature of sociology in India. T. N. Madan carried forward the journal to newer heights.

The period between the attainment of Independence and the recognition of regional language as the medium of instruction is identified as the one which received encouragement from the central government for expansion of social sciences (Lakshmanna 2012). The establishment of ICSSR in 1969 served the purpose of expansion. Trend reports were commissioned by the Council under the editorship of leading sociologist M. S. A. Rao to identify the phases, trends and growth of the discipline. The first survey was conducted in 1974.

Recognizing change in the social order and trying to understand the conditions of change in the social order, research activities broadened their scope during the post-Independence phase. Newer methods of study were increasingly resorted to explain growing complexities of the modern social interactional orders. The development of research into different specialized areas of rural and urban sociology was accompanied by expansion of employment opportunities. Separate and independent departments of sociology and social anthropology emerged in many universities. Also, many research institutes came up which engaged trained sociologists and social anthropologists. Growing research interests also embraced intense professional interaction among different social sciences. Although there was consolidation of the two different disciplines, there was an interesting narrowing of the gaps between sociologists and social anthropologists. It was mainly due to the shared method of research techniques of the two disciplines. As far as teaching is concerned, both at the undergraduate and postgraduate levels, a diversified curriculum structure emerged. Beyond the broader division of rural and urban sociology, sociology of economic development, political sociology, sociology of social stratification, sociology of religion/kinship, social demography, medical sociology and so on made the discipline flourish to achieve greater academic status.

1.4.2. Diversification and Specializations

Having established itself as an academic discipline, sociology had to attend to the newer concerns of a newly developing nation state. Coming out of the colonial baggage, sociology had to confront the new historical forces that shaped the newly independent country. Planned development under the auspices of the National Planning Commission had its impact on the development of the social sciences. Economics enjoyed a hallowed status among all social sciences with respect to developmental planning. The community development programmes pushed forward by the different states since the 1950s realized after some time that the approach towards development had to address issues beyond the economistic matrix. The crucial implications of social, cultural and religious factors could only be addressed by sociologists and social anthropologists. The role of sociologists/social anthropologists in planning and development was finally taken note of, as intensive field study methods popularized by the two disciplines generated empirical knowledge about single village or community.

According to Srinivas and Panini (1973), the post-Independence scenario was marked by the application of structural-functional method in the studies of single villages/communities. The rigorous interplay of theory and data marked a break from understanding institutions and social practices of India through its sacred texts.

> The fruitfulness of the use of the 'structural-functional method' was demonstrated in the analysis of rural society and life, and others besides sociologists and anthropologists, begun to see that it provided intimate knowledge and new insights regarding such phenomena as land relations, factions, caste, family and religion. This was able to provide because of the new and high standards of fieldwork of the anthropologists and the holistic perspective they brought to bear on the analysis of social institutions. (Srinivas and Panini 1973, 200–201)

The popularity of village studies in the post-Independence period, however, was seen as dealing with fragmentary categories of the Indian social structure. The interacting, conflicting and dynamic aspects of the social categories were much neglected in this penchant for exhaustive and exclusive village studies (Singh 2012). The fancy of microscopic details of a single village or town prompted by socio-anthropological theories was contested in favour of structural studies. However, the need for a shift from culturological to structural studies had to be careful and avoid a simple replacement with concepts and models borrowed from the West.

For agricultural and community development, the American know-how and help was an obvious choice for the newly developing society. As a supplement, arrived the influence of American cultural anthropologists and rural sociologists in Indian sociology. As a result, the Indian sociologists followed the anthropological perspectives in their methods to conduct research as a problem-oriented exercise to understand and explain social change in local settings (D'Souza 1977). Policy-oriented researches received a stimulus around this time under the American influence.

Y. Singh noted that the diversification and specialization in the Indian sociology were characterized by the varied social, cultural and developmental issues that gained the attention of sociological researchers. Also, increasingly, sociologists and social anthropologists started using a variety of research methodologies and research tools.

BOX 1.2

Specialization in Sociology

In thematic terms, the first major differentiation in sociological studies in India was between rural and urban sociology. The decade of the 1950s witnessed a proliferation in the studies of the Indian villages. The pioneering work in this field was done by S. C. Dube, M. N. Srinivas, Ramkrishna Mukherjee, A. R. Desai and several other Indian sociologists. A large number of American and a few British and French social anthropologists also contributed to the village studies in various parts of the country.

Source: Singh (2004).

The study of social change during the 1950s and the 1960s was conducted from different theoretical perspectives. On the one hand, M. N. Srinivas explained caste profile of a particular village (Rampura, Karnataka) by focusing on the cumulative result of the rural status, economic status and political status, as well as the numerical strength to indicate a caste status. Also, he relied on culturological explanation to account for mobility and social change (Sanskritization and Westernization). The same culturological perspective is found in McKim Marriott's studies. Influenced by the Chicago anthropologists Robert Redfield and Milton Singer's conceptual distinction between folk and elite tradition/culture, Marriott studied social change of the Indian villages and towns.

On the other hand, sociologists such as Ramakrishna Mukherjee and A. R. Desai opted for a Marxist perspective to understand the Indian rural structure. Mukherjee used statistical data to develop the conceptual categories of the rural class structure. Desai stood for a systematic application of the historical-materialist method to unravel the rural dynamics. Along with this, many researchers were sponsored by the Planning Commission for urban studies. Beyond the limited scope of urban planning, pioneers of the discipline, such as N. K. Bose, G. S. Ghurye and M. S. A. Rao immensely contributed to urban sociology.

Apart from the popular micro-level studies, there have been attempts after the 1960s to view change and continuity in the Indian society from an all-India perspective. The works of D. Mandelbaum (*Society in India*, 1970, 2 vols) and Louis Dumont (*Homo Hierarchicus*, 1970) need to be mentioned in this context. Yogendra Singh's *Modernization of Indian Tradition* (1973) stands out as the seminal work that tried a synthesis of the conceptual schemes and methods to appreciate the integrative aspects of the varied conceptual categories. It throws a fresh look at the dynamics of modernity and tradition to analyse the processes of social change in India.

According to Ramakrishna Mukherjee (2012), along with the ahistorical, non-economic micro approach of social anthropology in the 1950s and the 1960s, the American influences of static 'system analysis', diffusionism and change dominated Indian sociology. However, from the later part of the 1960s, the Marxian perspective effected a diversification of the subject interest. From the village/community studies, interests shifted to the areas of agrarian relations, land reforms, peasants and social movements.

Apart from change, conflict and contradictions post-1970s saw a specialization in industrial and urban sociology. Studies on women gained momentum as new approaches and interests diversified the field of sociology and social anthropology. Studies of social movements, social stratification, backward classes, Dalits, minorities and women prospered more from the 1970s to the 1980s. Notable researches were contributed by Andre Beteille, T. K. Oommen, D. N. Dhanagare, Partha Nath Mukherjee, Anand Chakraverty, Dipankar Gupta and others. Studies on minorities, backward classes, Dalits and women were enriched by Neera Desai, Gail Omvedt, M. S. Gore and others. The 1980s saw a growing interest in historical sociology. Sociology of science, knowledge and technology was led by the prolific J. P. S. Uberoi.

The decisive economic, political and social changes under the global impact of liberalization policy impacted the Indian sociology in the 1990s and onwards. Issues of development, displacement and civil rights attracted sociologists, who opted for more reflexive, empathy-based objective studies of social realities. Ecological and environmental studies were the new turns experienced by the Indian sociology.

The discipline has also flourished with the recent debates on the crisis and the social construction of the Indian sociology. The issues of gender and feminine pedagogies are raised by Sharmila Rege, R. Palriwala, Maitrayee Chaudhuri, T. Niranjana and others. Rabindra Ray, Satish Deshpande, M. Thappan and Avijit Pathak have raised thoughtful questions from sociology of knowledge perspective. Veena Das has pointed out serious issues pertaining to the quality of sociological research in India by referring to the roles of institutions of university, University Grants Commission and professional bodies like the Indian Sociological Society. Overall speaking, the disciplines have moved forward through ebbs and tides of the changing face of the Indian society.

CONCLUSION

The theoretical and cognitive systems of both sociology and social anthropology are socially constructed. The development of the two disciplines in India is best located in the historicity of the social conditions from the colonial times onwards. From a curious exploratory phase, all disciplines develop into explanatory phase. In the exploratory phase, the discipline remains descriptive in nature essentially. As modern disciplines, sociology and social anthropology have evolved through progressive rationalization as well as differentiation—the paradigm set up by Western historical situation.

The Western colonialist interpretations and interests of the Indian societies shaped the formative stage of both sociology and social anthropology in India. The focus of studying India was from the administrative angle of the British who encouraged and prompted studies to understand the local culture of India. Their special focus on specific community, caste and tribal studies actively neglected integrative macro social processes of the society.

Indology as well as ethnography served the purpose of the colonial administration during the formative phase of sociology and social anthropology. At the same time, the nationalist feelings and movements for independence were also felt for the growth of the disciplines in the 19th and the 20th centuries.

As a distinct discipline, only in the early decades of the 20th century, sociology and social anthropology took shape with the establishment of university departments. The credit for the emergence of academic sociology goes to the establishment of the departments of sociology in Bombay and Lucknow. On the other hand, anthropology was initiated as an academic discipline in Calcutta University. The pioneers of the disciplines confronted the tension between reliance on Western perspectives and concepts to study the Indian society and the deep civilizational call of national awareness.

Post-Independence sociology and social anthropology were largely shaped by the demands of the newly emergent nation state. State institutions and research bodies encouraged a wider spread of the disciplines. Diversification of the disciplines took place along with their growing professionalization. To a large extent, diversification of the disciplines remained confined to micro-level studies dealing with fragmentary categories of the social structure.

The popularity and professionalization of the disciplines in recent times are a result of better institutional patronage by both government and non-governmental planning projects. To explore the crucial aspects of continuity and change in the India society, both the disciplines have tried to synthesize the text and the context. As cognate disciplines, sociology and social anthropology have come closer and signs of such integration is clear enough in teaching and research.

Points for Classroom Discussion

- Social conditioning of sociology and social anthropology
- A brief outline of different phases of development of sociology and social anthropology
- Development of sociology as an academic discipline
- Professionalization of sociology and social anthropology
- The post-Independence trajectory of sociology and social anthropology
- Major contributions to sociology/social anthropology towards specialization

GLOSSARY

Dialectical: A philosophical way of thinking to explain and understand any state of being as an expression of opposite factors.

Enlightenment: A philosophical-intellectual movement of the 17th- and the 18th-century Europe that emphasized the thought of applicability of reason and science in order to understand and improve humankind.

Epistemology: A branch of philosophy that studies the nature and grounds of knowledge, especially with reference to its limits and validity.
Ethnography: A method used traditionally in anthropology, where an anthropologist lives in a small community to learn the details of their daily life.
Evolutionary: A perspective in social sciences borrowed from biology, referring to development of complex societal form from simpler stages.
Functionalist: A sociological perspective that sees society as a complex system whose parts work together to promote solidarity and stability.
Historical-Materialist: Essentially a Marxist way of interpretation of the unfolding of historical stages of society. It explains society and its changes in terms of changing material forces of production.
Indology: An approach that relies on classical ancient texts, mainly Sanskrit, to understand the specific Indian ways of life.
Positivism: A philosophical position which rejects metaphysical epistemology and claims that authentic knowledge is that which is based on sense of experience and positive verification.
Structural-Functional: A perspective in sociology that considers society as constituted of different functioning parts, giving rise to a stable and systemic structure.
Structuralism: A method of analysis to examine how binary opposite parts relate to the whole structure of a society, language, myth and so on. Essentially, a linguistic theory applied and adopted in social anthropology by Levi-Strauss.
Utilitarianism: An ethical doctrine that values virtues in terms of utility by prescribing actions that maximize happiness and well-being for all individual.
Victorian: An ideal of morality characteristic of the time of Queen Victoria, which is stereotyped as work ethic, family values, religious observation and institutional faith.

REFERENCES

Beteille, A. 1993. 'Sociology and Anthropology: Their Relationship in One Person's Career.' *Contributions to Indian Sociology* 27, no. 2: 209–304.
D'Souza, V. 1977, December 22–24. Valedictory Address at the XXIV All India Sociological Conference, Osmania University, Hyderabad.
Danda, Ajit K. 1995. *Foundations of Anthropology: India*. New Delhi: Inter-India Publications.
Lakshmanna. C. 2012. 'Teaching and Research in Sociology in India.' In *Indian Sociology: Issues and Challenges*, edited by L. Thara Bhai. New Delhi: SAGE Publications.
Momin, A. R. 2012. 'Indian Sociology: Search for Authentic Identity.' In *Indian Sociology: Issues and Challenges*, edited by L. Thara Bhai. New Delhi: SAGE Publications.
Mukherjee, R. 2012. 'Indian Sociology: Historical Development and Present Problems.' In *Indian Sociology: Issues and Challenges*, edited by L. Thara Bhai. New Delhi: SAGE Publications.
Shah, A. M. 1959, July. 'Social Anthropology and the Study of Historical Societies.' *The Economic Weekly*, Special Number.
Singh, Y. 1986. *Indian Sociology: Social Conditioning and Emerging Concerns*. New Delhi: Vistaar Publications.
Singh, Y. 2004. *Ideology and Theory in Indian Sociology*. New Delhi: Rawat Publications.
Srinivas, M. M., and M. M. Panini. 1973. 'The Development of Sociology and Social Anthropology in India.' *Sociological Bulletin* 22, no. 2: 179–215.

CHAPTER 2

Approaches: Colonialist Construction, Nationalist Discourse and Subaltern Critique

LEARNING OUTCOMES

- To conceptually identify the contending approaches to the study of Indian society
- To identify the methodological issues of each approach
- To understand the image of India as a matter of different approach towards the subject matter
- To examine the changing focus on the study of Indian society

Keywords: Indology, Orientalism, missionary, field study, nationalism, ruling elite, everyday protest, resistance

Nothing is more disorienting than when our fundamental taxonomies are turned around and we blink at a world in which things occupy entirely unaccustomed places.

—**Sudipta Kaviraj**

INTRODUCTION

Every given period of any society contains a set of relations that include ways of learning, understanding and knowledge. The Indian subcontinent has been under the British colonial rule for about 200 years. The period has its bearing on the ways the Indian society had been experienced and understood. When we say the colonial discourse about Indian society, we mean those statements, analyses, understandings and narratives about India (the colonized people) from the perspective of the dominant colonizers. It is not merely a matter of different method or theory that we have different views about any society. It is the specific institutional patronage as well as dominant forms of knowledge system that shape up a particular discourse. In this light we shall examine not only the colonial view of India but also the nationalist viewpoint as well as the subaltern intervention. It is needless to say that every epoch has its own spirit of knowing the unknown. The nationalist approach essentially developed as a critique to the colonial construction of India. As a part of the popular, multi-class mass movement nationalist discourse took shape under the colonial rule. It almost emerged as an alternative ideology to the colonial-imperial purpose of knowing India. The subaltern school in a way addressed the issue of 'knowing' India from the sociology of knowledge perspective. By dislocating the source of knowledge from mainstream texts, it prioritized the marginal texts and folk traditions to approach India 'from the below'.

2.1. COLONIAL DISCOURSE

The colonial view of the Indian society was largely impacted by Indological perspective. Indology means study of Indian society and culture, and the methodology of such an approach rests on studying the Indian society through religious texts, ancient historical texts and archaeological materials. Essentially, a dominant book view of the Indian society was attempted in which ancient Sanskrit texts were privileged and thus translated, for example, the works of William Jones, Max Müller and others. However, it would be wrong to suggest that the Indological approach only supplemented the colonial construction of India. We shall see later that even nationalist view contained a modified Indology, which tried to refute the orthodox understanding of the Indian society.

The Indian society since the days of Greek, Arab and Roman travellers continued to be a fascinating object of study for the British colonizers. Much before a systematic study of this land and its people, the accounts of the ancient travellers from the foreign lands were essentially impressionistic. For example, Megasthenes, a Greek traveller, created his travelogue on the basis of his keen observation. He lacked necessary knowledge of native languages to throw light on the deeper aspects of the people. Also, the early European travellers hardly accounted for the society and its people as they were more focused on the political and commercial aspects of the society.

The serious effort to understand the Indian people obviously was a result of the colonial rule. For administrative purpose, one had to go beyond the exotica or the impressionistic views. There were various trend in the administrative approach, but all were geared towards facilitating the colonial rule, especially with respect to property rights, inheritance acts, landholding and revenue issues. A greater focus on the empirical knowledge and a field view of the Indian society emerged as a result. They might have lacked the methodological rigour and the theoretical finesse to explain the Indian society but definitely attempted a different image of India from the other two popular approaches that emerged since the end of the 18th century—the Orientalist view and the missionary view.

2.1.1. The Orientalist View

As theorized by Palestinian-American scholar Edward Said (1978), Orientalism refers to an academic tradition that privileges an Eurocentric view over and against Arab-Islamic people and their society. It works with the presumption of the Western superiority and posits the Orient (non-Western society) as static and irrational. It involves a way of perceiving the Eastern society as unchanging. It exaggerates and distorts the differences between the East and the West. Hence, an Orientalist is one from the West who looks at the culture and history of the Orient through the prism of Orientalism.

The Orientalists relied exclusively on the classical Indian texts and other secondary sources to be assured of an image of the Indian society and culture. As discussed by Bernard S. Cohn (1990), the development of Sanskrit, Persian and the vernacular languages in the 18th century allowed the Europeans to have a wide-ranging knowledge about the life and history of the Indians. He cited the translated work, *The History of Hindustan* (1768–1771), of Alexander Dow. Dow was an officer of the East India Company, who not only translated the available Persian histories of India but added a few essays to this volume.

To Dow, customs and manners appeared to have largely meant Brahmanic prescriptions derived from his studies in Persian and 'through the vulgar tongue of the Hindus' of 'some of the principal *shastras*' (religious texts). This he did with the assistance of a pundit from Benaras (Cohn 1990, 142).

Such a text put forward the Brahmanical theory of the origin of the caste system that the four *varnas* (colour) originated from different parts of the body of Brahma. Apart from the caste system, the other relevant aspects of the Indian society dealt by Dow were astrological practices, early marriage, practice of sati, death rituals, the privileges of the Brahmans, *sanyasis* (the renunciator) as the principal preachers of Hinduism and various types of penances which the Hindus used to undertake.

Mainly the scholars of Sanskrit texts acted as the source for such Orientalist commentators. As a result, a textual understanding emerged that foregrounded the Brahmans in social relations. In terms of the culture and customs as normatively prescribed in the Brahmanical texts, the Indian society was imagined through the colonial construction. As a consequence, a fossilized picture of the Indian society with its idyllic village life was drawn up. An unchanging, static society was conceived of, leaving out the actual behaviour, relations and variations of the people.

Interestingly, the 'unchangeableness' of India's village society figured in Karl Marx's explanation of Asiatic mode of production. Many find a resonance of Orientalist voice in Marx's observation of remarkable structural resilience of the Indian village community. That is to say, Indian villages were historically unchanging in character. The stagnating character of such village community was pointed out by Marx in a few journalistic articles written for the *New York Daily Tribune* in 1853. He argued that such an idyllic and static state was due to the exclusive role of despotic administration and the centralizing public works system like irrigation (Marx [1853] 1969). It can, however, be said that such a conclusion made by Marx lacked his otherwise methodological rigour to capture the structural specifics of a non-Western society. Hardly, he has made any rigorous analysis of the particular mode of production for such non-Western societies. Rather, he overemphasized the resistant social basis of the community life in India which could not get revolutionized in the face of colonial rule.

2.1.2. The Role of the Missionary

The missionaries were in league with the Orientalists in their basic understanding of the Indian society. Both the groups accepted that the structure of the society was premised on religious values and practices. As both of them privileged the Sanskrit texts and their interpretations by the Brahman scholars, they shared a similar image of India where caste and religion were the central organizing principles of the society. The difference between them was that the missionaries considered the central texts as full of evils and dehumanizing. The practices of widow burning, restrictions on widow remarriage and untouchability are all glaring instances of such dehumanization. They wished to save the society from the degradation of the Hindu religious system. The overwhelming role of the Brahmans coupled with the caste system was identified as the root cause behind the dehumanizing condition of the Hindu society. Such a depiction served the evangelical missions of commentators like Charles Grant or William Hard.

The purpose of the missionary view was clearly to condemn the Hindu society and its practices so that they could entice caste Hindus to embrace Christianity. Listening to the people and keenly observing the behaviours of the people brought the missionaries close to the lives of the common people. The everyday experiences of many subjugated castes were graphically narrated through various missionary texts. The task of translation of the Bible into Indian vernaculars was the logical offshoot of the same process. As noted by Cohn, the most significant aspect of this missionary endeavour to understand the Indian society presented us, by default, with some invaluable texts. Protestant missionary William Carey's contribution to this cause was the most noteworthy.

> Perhaps the first sociolinguistic study we have of an Indian language is William Carey's Dialogues Intended to Facilitate the Acquiring of the Bengali Language, published at the Press at Serampore in 1801. This work, which reads like a forerunner of modern language teaching materials for learning a language through the oral-aural method, is a series of dialogues between various types of Indians. (Cohn 1990, 145)

Interestingly, many of the missionaries subsequently got intimately involved with the Indian tribal population and some of them like Charles F. Andrews made meaningful contributions to interpret the tribal society vis-à-vis the British forest land policies.

Another early missionary Charles Grant, who served the East India Company as an officer, came out with a scathing observation of the erstwhile Indian society. Bernard Cohn went on to quote Grant to highlight missionary project for the Indian people.

> Upon the whole, then, we cannot avoid recognizing in the people of Hindustan, a race of men lamentably degenerate and base, retaining but a feeble sense of moral obligation, yet obstinate in their disregard of what they know to be right, governed by malevolent and licentious passions, strongly exemplifying the effects produced on society by great and general corruption of manners, and sunk in misery by their vices. (Cohn 1990, 144).

The condemnation of the Hindu society (used interchangeably with the Indian society) was a motivated one. It was not only limited to providing them with an alternative religion as a succour, but the missionaries also had to shoulder the responsibility of providing the converts socio-economic security, as most of them were from the vulnerable social groups. Unlike the Orientalists who never bothered to reform the Indian society but only to gather knowledge through diligent studies of the ancient texts and collaborating with their native scholars, the missionary objective was 'emancipatory'. In reality, the missionaries had worked towards the 'upliftment' of the society.

2.1.3. Administrative Approach and the Field View

The three major institutions of the Indian society—caste, tribe and village—were to be studied empirically if the colonial power had to rule the colonized society politically. For sheer administrative purpose, the empirical ground realities of the three major aspects of the Indian society had to be explored by the British administration. The Orientalist as well as the missionary views either romanticized the natives or made the Indian society exotic. But the ultimate objective of the British administration was to gain knowledge of the operational ground reality of the people so that the revenue collection, land acquisition and surveillance purposes could be conducted with ease.

As a result of the empirical studies, the images of caste, tribe and village underwent a change. That caste is much more than an ideological justification of the *Varnashrama*. The functional category of *jaat/jatis* and the associated behaviour are crucial for the administrative system to understand the sociopolitical implications of the caste system. *Jaatis* are usually localized operational endogamous units of caste. Bound by kinship and marriage ties, these functional units are embedded with respective myths and stories of their origins. Field-based studies were the penchant for the British survey tradition, hence, a proliferation of empirical studies followed.

The British tradition of survey studies was put into practice to devise strategies to govern the bewildering variety of people. To know the local practices, customary laws and indigenous cultures, categorization of people was also felt necessary. The practice of introducing census count for every 10 years was a unique administrative measure. In fact, the very classification of the Indian population into various categories was a corollary of the search for objective knowledge about the Indian society. The census exercise was first published in 1872 on an all-India basis. A definite quantifiable material about the Indian society was made available, thereby. For the first time, caste came close to be an entity which could be quantified to an extent. Bernard Cohn calls this an 'official view' of caste with definable characteristics such as endogamy, commensality rules, occupational specialization and common ritual practices. Such typification made things easy for the colonizers to objectify and rule.

BOX 2.1
Book View versus Field View

The 'book view' of India is the direct contribution of Indologists and Orientalists. The exclusive sources of the 'book view' are ancient Hindi texts, scriptures and certain historical records. Such a view was contested with the 'field view', trying to know the society through a direct study of the people's lives. It started with the development of survey method and finally prospered with the development of ethnographic method based on participant observation. Indian village communities were understood in new terms. The tranquillity of the village was demystified as the question of caste and political faction was examined in dynamic terms. The interdependence and interconnection of India's villages with the wider economy and broader society were indicated with this 'field view'. Although the colonial purpose was to treat village communities as discrete entities amenable for objectification, the result of 'field view' was far reaching. It served a latent function beyond the administrative purpose of empirical knowledge of the native people.

While talking about the role of census counting in his analysis of the relationship between tribe and peasantry, Andre Beteille observes,

> A notable feature of British administration in India was the task assigned to the decennial census operations. This included not only the counting of heads but the classification of the population into various categories. The successive census operations resulted in the creation of an enormously complex system of categories for dividing the population into tribes, castes, sects, and occupation. (Gupta 2005, 119)

The British official ethnographers' work generated enormous data which was administratively useful for the British rule. The survey exercise also provided the official ethnographers like H. H. Risley to indulge in classifications through typifications of caste practices, behaviours and customs (Risley 1915). The 'field view' to a large extent could not go much beyond the Brahmanical theory. However, different interpretations and observations kept pouring in on the basis of such raw data collected. More and more in terms of functional explanation, the history of caste was understood and explained.

Along with this, a parallel image of village India emerged during the colonial period. An idyllic and unchanging village society appeared as the circumscribed subject matter for the anthropologists. Village as a self-sufficient community was an appropriate object of study for conventional anthropology. An image of a static village republic as a political society was developed which was also considered as the repository of all the customs and tradition. As a custodian of traditional values, it was marked by tranquil social relations of even ownership of land as well. Such a view was not so different from the Orientalists' assumption of Indian the society as immutable. Overall speaking, it is the method of study as well as the purpose of study which gave rise to a specific picture of India's society during the colonial period.

2.2. THE NATIONALIST DISCOURSE

Evidently, the streams of the anti-colonial sentiments across the country, along with the rise of an educated middle class, created a consciousness to challenge the colonial construction of India. Especially since the early 20th century, a new social wave fostered a national sentiment against colonial domination in every sphere of social life. The impulse of the anti-colonial movement did shape the nationalist discourse on the Indian society, but definitely not in an undifferentiated way.

2.2.1. Indigenous Knowledge

The mainstream of nationalist thinking was a direct corollary to the political slogan of *swaraj* and swadeshi. The leading figures of anti-colonial struggle—be it Mahatma Gandhi, Rabindranath Tagore or Bal Gangadhar Tilak—all were pushing forward a critical look at the British education system. Of course, Tagore was promising a more nuanced criticism of the West, without a total rejection of the same. The modernizing elite of the pre-Independence period impacted the pioneers of Indian sociology, not only with respect to their selection of the proper subject matter of the discipline but also the appropriate methodological perspective for Indian sociology.

What is popularly known as the Lucknow School—the Department of Sociology, Lucknow University—played a leading role in shaping Indian sociology towards the cause of nation-building process. When the dominant strand of nationalism was revolving around a cultural criticism of the colonial rule, Radhakamal Mukerjee focused his study on the question of land issues in an agrarian society like India. The question of rural poverty and land was put as the central theme in Indian sociology. Radhakamal Mukerjee brought to light the problems of the peasantry as a result of the laws and custom of the land tenure. His book elaborated the welfare of the peasants and the reasons for the reforms for agricultural efficiency (Mukerjee 1933).

A typical strand of nationalism was to revert to cultural routes to reorient the Marxian perspective with self-reflection. D. P. Mukherji was curious to adapt the Marxist method to Indian situation. Instead of using the method as a dogma, he advocated Marxiology which could trace the Indianness of an impoverished society. That the national movement had to get rid of unthinking borrowing from the West. The gap between theory and practice had robbed personality development and meaningfulness of social life. A synthetic view of the Indian culture was D. P. Mukerji's response to successive challenges to the Indian civilization and culture.

> We talk of India's vivisection, but what about the vivisection of knowledge which has been going on these years in the name of learning, scholarship and specialization? A 'subject'

has been cut off from knowledge, knowledge has been excised from life, and life has been amputed from living social conditions. It is really high time for Sociology to come to its own. It may not offer the Truth.... We may as well be occupied with the discipline which is most truthful to the wholeness and the dynamics of the objective human reality. (Mukerji 1946, 11)

The nationalist discourse on the Indian society had its anthropological inputs from the leading Gandhian anthropologist Nirmal Kumar Bose of Calcutta University. Gandhi's ideas on the creation of a new India had a bearing on Bose's anthropology. As a quintessential fieldworker, he was an unrelenting listener and observer of living human beings. An authentic anthropology of the Indian civilization and culture, he thought, could result by combining the approaches of ethnographers, Indologists and social historians. Such an inclusive framework, he thought, was best suited to present a civilizational view of the Indian society. While using the traditional textual categories in the classification of diverse Indian culture, he was critical at the same time about their random application without contextualizing them in the material world (Bose 1975).

BOX 2.2
Nationalism and Tradition

The first task for us, therefore, is to study the social traditions to which we have been born and in which we have had our being. This task includes the study of the changes in traditions by internal and external pressures. The latter are mostly economic. Unless the economic force is extraordinarily strong—and it is that only when the modes of production are altered—traditions survive by adjustments. The capacity for adjustment is the measure of the vitality of traditions. One can have a full measure of this vitality only by immediate experience. Thus, it is that I give top priority to the understanding (in Dilthey's sense) of traditions even for the study of their changes. In other words, the study of Indian traditions should precede the socialist interpretations of changes in Indian traditions in terms of economic forces.

Source: Mukerji (1958).

G. S. Ghurye's study of caste resorted to Indological sources, while M. N. Srinivas's analysis rested on empirical village studies. The continuity of Indian society was an unstated domain background for the nationalist discourse. As observed by T. K. Oommen (2007), the sociology which emerged in the heyday of the anti-imperialist struggle was primarily to Indianize and not to professionalize sociology.

It is obvious that the nationalist discourse was essentially an exercise in nervousness as well as confidence. A leading role had to be played by the newly emergent Indian intelligentsia, who were definitely the product of the English education and values. Parallel to that was a cultural assertion that critiqued the unfiltered embrace of the Western modernity.

2.2.2. Ideology of Nationalist Discourse

Sudipta Kaviraj (2010) in his essay 'On the Structure of Nationalist Discourse' brings out the complexity of the nationalist response to the colonial construction. That the nationalist world was hardly a coherent and unifocal one as it was internally divided on the question of modernist project for India. He discerns the internal order of the world of ideas, arguments, documents as well as ideologies that made up the nationalist discourse in India.

According to Kaviraj, it was an intellectual process, over a period of time, that India as a nation was formed. The discourse that stands for India as a nation could be understood as a nationalist discourse factoring in the questions of elites and non-elites, the lower order of the society and the regional/vernacular. He could see that there were serious neglected cultural processes which failed the nationalist project as a unified ideological narrative.

The modernist elite invoked a kind of nationalism that could celebrate a replay of the European rationality on the Indian soil. The lower orders were decisively out of the orbit of this modernist elites. The other crucial dimension of the nationalist response was that initially it only posited itself against the political cultural domination of the colonial power without addressing the economic motives of colonization. It was the overwhelming success of an imagined crystalizing model of European modernity that the colonial education system thrived on. The newly emergent nationalist elite appeared as a vanguard social group disconnected with the traditional social groups speaking a 'language' that was alienating. The emergence of autonomous individual was not at all organic in the Indian scenario with the strong sense of community identity implicated with the territorial and linguistic factors.

However, technology-backed superiority of the rational modernist European model that inspired the initial burst of the nationalist elites was gradually debunked and contested with the alternative intellectual strands within European modernity. The ideas of romanticism and idealism impacted the later development of nationalist discourse.

> The sentiments, emotions, symbolic political acts and, finally, the pressure of its popular movements must be directed politically at an object-the territory and its people-through various contingent and complex processes, ultimately constituted by their collective imagination as the nation. Nationalism is an intensely poetic and dramatic affair, and at the heart of its historical initiatives stands the acts of an entire people, or acts initiated on their behalf. (Kaviraj 2010, 106)

The anti-colonial consciousness, therefore, ran on parallel multiple streams. The unilinear utilitarian justification worked for the colonizer. The British found the utilitarian framework useful to justify its rule and effect sociopolitical transformation of its colony. The domination of this instrumentalist model was undermined subsequently by the parallel alternative modes of modernity. The very notion of nation and nationalism underwent significant transformation. The role of Mahatma Gandhi, Rabindranath Tagore and a whole lot of popular figures of freedom struggle added to the dynamics of the nationalist discourse. Invoking a curious mix of compliance and defiance, Gandhi took up a unique discursive position to bridge the gulf between the elite and the non-elite (the lower orders). This astute political strategy effectively allowed Gandhi to act as a mediator between the worlds of the elite and the lower orders of the society.

Social radicalism came to affect mainstream nationalism by raising the question of social inequality and poverty, which largely escaped the attention of initial burst of nationalism. The larger agenda of nationalism subsumed many important issues like that had significant bearing on the lives of the populace. However, the fractious and unstable nature of the Left and socialist groups could not provide a viable alternative. Much of their theorization failed as an alternative, and they failed to come out of the dominant modernist scheme of the Western rationalism. Post-Independence, the Nehruvian model of social democracy was pushed forward with an excessive focus on instrumentalist and economistic aspects of development. Growing centralization of politics marked the subsequent development of the Indian nationalism.

Keeping the European history as its guiding foundational spirit and with the fancy for socialism and secularism, the nationalist discourse took shape under the tutelage of Nehru. From different social scientific disciplines, the pervasive nationalist model, however, is criticized. Sociologist T. N. Madan (1987), political scientist Partha Chatterjee (1986) and social-psychologist Ashis Nandy (1986) argued from different disciplinary grids that the dominant nationalist discourse foregrounded the state and the ruling elite who failed to be the voice of the popular. The elite fell into the Orientalist trap and the vernacular communities were left to the margin. The aspirations and the voices of the lower order of a highly stratified and unequal society were left unattended.

2.3. THE SUBALTERN SCHOOL

The subaltern critique of Indian nationalism is essentially an epistemological question-that is, how do we know what we know. There is a common adage that the story of the jungle is that of the lion and not that of the hunted. The conventional history is the history of the victor and not of the vanquished. The subaltern historiography attempts to alter the conventional method and source of knowledge.

The colonialist historiography as well as the nationalist one has fed into each other to constitute the dominant view of the Indian history and society. Hence, nationalism in India and the very imagination of the nation are exclusively an elite idea. The subalterns—those who are ranked low or outside the dominant discourse in the social hierarchy—are left 'voiceless' or their interpretations of history and society are unaccounted in the elitist construction of the nation. The rise of the native elite is just a device to give an appearance of anti-colonial struggle, while the essence of their rise was a collaborationist venture (Guha 1982).

2.3.1. Alternative History

Ranajit Guha, the pioneer of subaltern studies, along with a group of scholars/historians from South Asian countries mainly constituted the subaltern studies school to challenge the 'Cambridge School', which presented a statist history. Evidently, history as told by statist power was based on sources which had colonial, imperial imprints. Colonial administrative data as well as nationalist project of reconstructing history, without searching for alternative sources, resulted in hegemony of an imperial statist history. In the early 1980s, the group of historians led by Ranajit Guha compiled 'Subaltern Studies' by taking out publication through Oxford University Press, Delhi and Australia. The term subaltern is taken from Italian Marxist Antonio Gramsci's (1891–1937) work. For him the subjected underclass constitutes the subaltern of a society, on whom the dominant power exercises absolute hegemony. Traditional history neglected the voice of the subaltern in the making of history, thus, the ordinary and the everyday which do not fit into the version of the state are left out of the nationalist discourse. The other leading figures of the subaltern studies are Eric Stokes, David Arnold, Dipesh Chakrabarty, Partha Chatterjee, Gayatri Spivak, Shahid Amin and others. Guha's *The Elementary Aspects of Peasant Insurgency in Colonial India* (1983) serves us almost as an exclusive entry point of doing the alternative history of India.

Everyday protests which were derived from grand narratives of anti-colonial nationalism never found any serious attention and explanation in the traditional historiography. This left many events and happenings unprobed and unexplained in the Indian history. It hardly explains how the nationalist programmes and agitations of Gandhi at many crucial points deviated into legalist and constitutionalist mode. The language and the institutions of the colonizer and their administration continued to be the medium of nationalist expressions and shaped spectacular retreats on the face of indigenous 'free' participation of the masses.

> ...that all mass struggles after 1920 led by the Congress with Gandhi as its most important leader, became at some point or the other violent. Clearly, both the colonialist and the nationalist historiography had a lot of explaining to do. Why? Because, if 'politics' during the nationalist period is the creation of the elites (administrative elites, or nationalist elites), then how is it that this politics, at crucial moments during the nation's onward march to freedom, behaves in such uncharacteristic and wayward manner? (Amin 2002, 11)

Any control of the spontaneity of the masses is by definition statist/elitist. Clearly, the domain of politics in the 20th-century colonial India was not a homogeneous unitary field. On the one hand, there was the elitist historiography which analysed politics through the parameters set up by the institutions that were made to facilitate the colonial administration. While on the other, the Marxist scholarship used orthodox concepts to analyse history in a top-down model. This view left out the voices of the people, the other domain of politics in colonial India. This was the people's domain, autonomous and not a derived one from the top. Therefore, the principles of agitation and mobilization of the two domains also differed. The mobilization of the popular domain was not in a top-down manner, it was not a vertical leadership based organized struggle, but a diffused horizontal one. Instead of being constitutionalist or legalist, the people's mobilization was more spontaneous and, at times, violent. The very existential condition of the subaltern classes and the diversity of their social composition made their outlook less crystallized and unified. Yet the idea of defiance and resistance was at the core of popular subaltern responses.

However, Guha is clear in his understanding that despite 'the failure of Indian bourgeoisie to speak for the nation', the two dichotomous dominance of politics—the elite and the subaltern—were not split in an air-tight manner. There had been attempts from some sections of the native elite to integrate the voices of the masses into the mainstream, which from time to time blurred the boundaries of the two separate domains (Guha 1982).

The subaltern view, which subsequently developed in studies of the Indian society and history, attempted to retrieve all the voices which were at the margins of the mainstream narrative. It was an attempt to reclaim history in favour of the underprivileged. The subalternity was acknowledged in terms of class, caste, gender, race, language and culture. In order to reclaim the subaltern history, the subaltern theorists have to highlight the failure of the nationalist movement to effect a national liberation. The failure of the working class, too, has been poignantly acknowledged.

> ...the initiatives which originated from the domain of the subaltern politics were not, on their part, powerful enough to develop the nationalist movement into a full-fledged struggle for national liberation... it could do nothing to takeover and complete the mission which the bourgeoisie had failed to realize. The outcome of it all was that the numerous peasant uprisings of the period, some of them massive in scope and rich in anti-colonialist consciousness waited in vain for a leadership to raise them above localism and generalized them into a nationwide anti-imperialist struggle. (Guha 1982, 6)

2.3.2. Debates within Subaltern School

The subaltern study as a critique of national discourse is well alerted by one of its leading proponent Partho Chatterjee. The radical social histories of European historians have impacted the subaltern studies significantly, but the Indian history is different. Its path of development is handicapped by an incomplete transition to capitalist modernity. So historicizing the subaltern method is called for. Even while talking about the 'history from below', we need to free ourselves from any universalizing notion of historical development.

> In countries such as India, it was difficult to confine 'History from below' without any such given narrative limits. It was not possible to write the history of capitalism or modernity in India with an ending so clear and definite. (Chatterjee 1998)

BOX 2.3
The Project of Time

It has often been observed that Subaltern Studies was a product of its time. Speaking at a meeting of the Latin American Subaltern Studies Collective in 1993, Ranajit Guha said: Our project belongs to our time. It made its debut at a time of turbulence marked by the difficulties that faced India's new nation state, by acute civil disturbances which threatened occasionally to tear it apart, by a common anxiety in which the frustration of the Midnight's Children born since Independence blended with the disillusionment of older generations to produce an explosive discontent.

Source: Chatterjee (2012).

The moot point remains that 'what is historic and what is an historical deed cannot be left crafted, judged and certified by any form of statist knowledge, be it colonialist, nationalist or even Marxist'.

Sumit Sarkar, one of the early participants in subaltern studies dissented on the project at a later stage (Sarkar 1997). It is true that a widespread disillusionment in the Left academic circle with respect to the possibility of orthodox Marxist ideology to reclaim and resurrect the subject class led to the rise of the subaltern studies. The intermittent popular upsurges, especially the peasant uprising during the decades of the 1960s and the 1970s fuelled the imagination of many Leftist social scientists to expand the scope of orthodox Marxist theories. The binary of the elites versus the subalterns which was theorized with a qualified understanding of class and the mass gradually shifted to focus on the binary of colonial and indigenous community. The socio-economic conditions of subalternity were systematically replaced by an understanding of domination in discursive terms. The power–knowledge system had taken the central determining condition. As a consequence, the rationality principle of the enlightenment had become the villain. Eurocentric knowledge system has been identified as a hegemonic, encompassing discourse, whereby all foundational theories of people's liberation have lost their edges to cultural studies and discourse analysis.

CONCLUSION

The colonial construct of India essentially was guided by an apprehension. That is, the Indian society was different from European society. So the colonial rulers had to seek for indigenous sources of knowledge. The Indological approach immensely served the colonial system of knowledge. Indology exclusively focused on studying the Indian society through ancient historical religious texts as well as archaeological evidence. The ultimate conclusion drawn by studies that relied on Indological texts of William Jones of Asiatic Society or Sanskrit scholar Max Müller was that the Indian society was unique in terms of its culture and values. Such a view of India overlapped with the Orientalist view of India. Accordingly, India was considered as a conglomerate of scattered and static villages. Villages were self-sufficient and governed by orthodox practices.

The colonial construct of India had three different components: the Orientalist, the missionary and the administrative field view. The need for fieldwork tradition which emerged as the demand for empirical data about the Indian society was growingly felt by the colonial administrators. The administrative field view of India promoted by the colonial rule was an interesting exercise as it shifted the focus from the book view to a survey-based field view and to an extent deep insiders' view of early ethnographers. It was primarily directed by the consideration of governing the subject better by the colonial administrators. The field study based material generated about the Indian society indicated that necessary corrections were needed as anthropological assumptions about the Indian society were derived from the traditions of study of India initiated and governed by colonial interests. The entire exercise of census enumeration and developing objective indicators for carrying out colonial administration was useful and purposive for the British colonial power. To an extent, the Christian missionaries also contributed to generate ground view of the 'natives', mainly the tribal population of India.

However, post-Independence, the orthodox Indology was much modified by G. S. Ghurye, who reviewed the Indian historical texts to develop a qualified book view of the Indian caste system. Order as well as change of the Indian traditional system was important to Ghurye. Although he focused more on the Hindu tradition, forwarded a dynamic picture of India from the past. The nationalist discourse basically was informed by emergent sociological perspectives to study the Indian society. Social anthropological field study method of M. N. Srinivas stood out to refute the conservative static picture of India. The ideology of the nationalist discourse was primarily in reaction to the colonial project.

The national discourse was much more than a simple case of anti-colonial, anxiety-prone assertions of Indianhood. The Orientalist elements of thought spilled over from colonial understandings to the nationalist thoughts and the nationalist elites lapped them up as long as they documented upper Gangetic Hindu achievements in various social-cultural fields. By and large, it has been masqueraded as classical Indian culture. Many social anthropological works while studying the various social forms and institutions, beyond the site of the 'amalgam' of different cultures so conducive for 'secular politics' of Nehru, indicated the incompleteness of the model.

The methodological question of developing a people's history was the impetus for the formulation of the subaltern critique to the nationalist discourse. Against elitist historiographies, Ranajit Guha foregrounded the agency of the people as they make their own history, which is independent from elite intervention. The nationalist discourse was severely criticized for its idealist role of liberating the subjugated people by an enlightened elite class. Instead, the subaltern critique pointed out the compromising role of the leadership of any mass movement.

The subaltern critique came close to offer a corrective. They explored the fundamental question of whether the unheard voice of those sections of the society who were marginalized could be retrieved. They probed whether the everyday practices, protests and resistances could be documented to reconstruct a fresh history of India. To appreciate history from the depths of the crowd, from the instincts of the people was the stated objective of the subaltern critique. Questioning the relaying down of leadership for mass mobilization, so elemental for national independence, the subaltern scholars attempted to get rid of the purposiveness of the colonialist, the elitism of the nationalist and the disconnect of the orthodox Marxist. The subsequent tendency of the critique to lapse into a discursive exercise drifting away from foundational analysis of material contradictions keeps the issue alive for an appropriate approach for understanding the Indian society.

Points for Classroom Discussion

- Importance of identifying approaches to the study of the Indian society
- Identifying the different approaches to study the Indian society
- Analysing the impact of Indology on the colonial construction of India
- Examining the components of colonial construction of the Indian society
- The major contributions to the nationalist discourse
- The subaltern studies as a critique of the colonial and the nationalist construction of the Indian society

GLOSSARY

Discourse: The way of thinking and constitution of meaning as generated by debates and exchange of ideas, talks of a particular period of time.

Endogamy: Also called in-marriage is the custom of marrying within one's own social group, be it caste, ethnic community and so on.

Epistemological: Anything that pertains to the theory and study of knowledge with respect to its method, validity and scope.

Historiography: It is the art and science of writing history that essentially tries to explore the process, method and intention of doing history.

Indology: A method of studying the Indian society with the help of ancient history, epics, religious manuscripts and texts and so on which embody the Indian value and belief system.

Instrumentalism: A methodological strategy that weighs the worth of any idea or action in terms of its success in explaining a given phenomenon or achieving a stated end.

Marxiology: The term used by D. P. Mukerji as his method of applying Marxian dialectics for a synthetic understanding of the Indian tradition and culture.

Modernist: One who acknowledges modernity as an era that values scientific thought, individualism, technological advancement and inter-subjective appreciation.

Orientalism: A style of prejudiced thought that privileges the institutions and worldviews of the 'Occident' (mainly England, France and the USA) over the backwardness of the 'Orient' (the Middle East and the Far East Asia).

Secularism: A principle of statecraft that keeps the affairs of the state and public functions separate from any religious beliefs and practices.

Socialism: A socio-economic system that rests on collective, social ownership of the means of production.

Subaltern: In critical social sciences, the term refers to the underprivileged and depressed sections of the population who are kept away from the centre of resources.

Utilitarian: A blend of normative ethics and moral philosophy propounded by English philosophers Jeremy Bentham and John Stuart Mill that suggests that people should act so that the best possible consequences follow.

Varnashrama: The scriptural Hindu social structure made up of four *varnas*—Brahman, Kshatriya, Vaishyas and Shudras—and the four *asramas* (stages) of life—*Brahmachari, Grihastha, Vanaprastha* and *Sanyasi*.

REFERENCES

Amin, S. 2002. *Alternative Histories: A View from India*. Calcutta: SEPHSIS-CSSSC.

Bose, N. K. 1975. *The Structure of Hindu Society*. Translated by Andre Beteille from Bengali with an introduction and notes. New Delhi: Orient Longman.

Chatterjee, P. 1986. *Nationalist Thought and the Colonial World: A Derivative Discourse*. New Delhi: Oxford University Press.

———. 1998. 'A Brief History of Subaltern Studies.' Paper presented at the VIth Subaltern Studies Conference on 'Fractured Societies, Fractured Histories', Giri Institute of Development Studies, Lucknow.

———. 2012, September 1. 'After Subaltern Studies'. *Economic & Political Weekly* XLVII, no. 35.

Cohn, B. S. 1990. *An Anthropologist among the Historians and Other Essays*. New Delhi: Oxford University Press.

Guha, R. 1982. *Subaltern Studies*. Vol. 1. New Delhi: Oxford University Press.
———. 1983. *The Elementary Aspects of Peasant Insurgency in Colonial India*. New Delhi: Oxford University Press.
Gupta, D., ed. 2005. *Anti-utopia: Essential Writings of Andre Beteille*. New Delhi: Oxford University Press.
Kaviraj, S. 2010. *The Imaginary Institution of India*. Ranikhet: Permanent Black.
Madan, T. N. 1987. 'Secularism in Its Place.' *Journal of Asian Studies* 46, no. 4: 747–759.
Marx, K. (1853, June 25) 1969. 'The British Rule in India.' In *Karl Marx on Colonialism and Modernization*, edited and introduction by S. Avineri. New York, NY: Anchor.
Mukerji, D. P. 1946. *Views and Counterviews*. Lucknow: Universal.
———. 1958. *Diversities*. Delhi: People's Publishing House.
Mukerjee, R. 1933. *Land Reforms of India*. London: Longmans.
Nandy, A. 1986. *The Intimate Enemy*. New Delhi: Oxford University Press.
Oommen, T. K. 2007. *Knowledge and Society: Situating Sociology and Social Anthropology*. New Delhi: Oxford University Press.
Risley, H. H. 1915. *The People of India*. 2nd edition. London: W. Thacker.
Said, E. 1978. *Orientalism*. New York, NY: Pantheon Books.
Sarkar, S. 1997. 'The Decline of the Subaltern in Subaltern Studies.' In *Writing Social History*. New Delhi: Oxford University Press.

CHAPTER 3

For a Sociology of India: Indological and Ethnographic Approaches

LEARNING OUTCOMES

- To familiarize the students with the epistemological question of studying the Indian society
- To critically evaluate the Indological approach to study the Indian society
- To assess the strengths of fieldwork method
- To examine the contentious issues and themes of social anthropological researches on the Indian society

Keywords: Social anthropology, ethnography, fieldwork, Indology, ethnology, purity and pollution, hierarchical structure, comparative sociology, village studies

Sociology for me is the systematic study of nature and forms of social life, with the emphasis now more on social institutions.

—**Andre Beteille**

INTRODUCTION

'For a Sociology of India' as a discourse constitutes the most significant discussion and debate over the nature and character of sociology in India. It is all about what could be the appropriate way to approach the Indian society. Sociology/social anthropology is quite a new discipline which attempts to explore and explain a society with great civilizational depth. More so, the discipline has strong Western root and its implications for the constitution of proper subject matter are direct. The choice and selection of perspectives as well as methods of study are crucial, given the unique social formation of a very diverse society.

The major concern for early practitioners of the discipline, specially at its phase of evolving as an academic discipline, revolved around the claims for a 'sociology for India' vis-à-vis 'sociology of India'. What are the contentions of such claims and counter claims? The proponents of 'sociology for India' were guided by the idea that doing sociology in India required to be rooted in its historico-specific cultural setting of the society. That is to suggest that India has a culturally specific social structure which needs to be studied with respect to its cultural specifics.

'Sociology of India', on the other hand, stood for the validity of a generalized social science model. So universally valid sociological categories are equally applicable in the explanation of the Indian society. The debate was initiated by French social anthropologist Louis Dumont in the late 1950s, with the establishment of the leading professional journal *Contributions to Indian Sociology* (old series). Dumont co-edited the journal with David Pocock.

In this major discourse in Indian sociology, the journal *Contributions* (as popularly called, both old and new series) played a vital role, which continued for all the subsequent decades. This debate was substantially enriched by scholarly participation from T. N. Madan, J. P. S. Uberoi, Yogendra Singh, Satish Saberwal, Veena Das, R. S. Khare, Anil Bhat, Imtiaz Ahmad and others. For all the participants, the most relevant task was to identify the appropriate sources for teaching and research of sociology. Linked to this is the question of proper applicability of concepts and categories of analysis. The cardinal issue is that of how to develop a sociology for India which embodies the experiences and thoughts of the real people. The strand represented by Dumont and Pocock emphasized the importance of the ideas and values embodied by the specific Indian social structure. To tap these ideas and values, they indicated an exhaustive use of the huge body of ancient classical sacred texts of India. They endorsed the use of Indology for sociological understanding of the Indian society.

On the other hand, Indian sociology was impacted by American and British social anthropologists who upheld the validity of the universality of theories and concepts for sociological analysis. So instead of reliance on classical texts prompted by the Indological approach, ethnography was thought to be the approach best suited to account for the lived experiences of the people. So the local practices, vernacular ideas and culture-specific values could be subjected to analytical abstractions for a universally valid sociology. Instead of a 'text view' of the Indian society, a 'field view' was promoted and argued for. Indology and ethnology served as the two contrasting approaches that largely marked the initial years of academic practice of sociology in India.

3.1. INDOLOGY

3.1.1. The Use of Classical Texts

Indology is a method of studying the Indian society with the help of ancient history, epics, religious manuscripts, classical Sanskrit texts and so on, which were considered as embodying the Indian values and belief system. Renowned German Sanskrit scholar Max Müller is popularly considered to have played the lead role in popularizing the Indological method among the European scholars. The Indological tradition also inspired many Indian thinkers and researchers. Classically speaking, as a discipline, Indology studies traditional values, ideas, cultural norms and practices as embedded in the Hindu classical texts.

Evidently, culture is given central attention in the understanding of the Indian society. Hence, to understand the Indian society, it was felt pertinent to decipher classical texts as sources of reconstructing cultural and behavioural practices. Interested European intellectuals took to studying the texts by learning Sanskrit language and many resorted to translating the Vedas and other Sanskrit texts. One can say that it was a book-view approach of the Indian society. Useful to remember here is the role played by Sir William Jones, who laid the foundation of the Asiatic Society in Calcutta in 1784. The orthodox Indological approach was adopted by early sociologists in India. Sociological perspectives were combined with the Indological approach during the initial years of development of sociology as an academic discipline. G. S. Ghurye is considered the father of modern Indology.

BOX 3.1

Govind Sadashiv Ghurye (1893–1983)

Ghurye remains the foremost Indian sociologist who made a remarkable synthesis of Indological and sociological perspectives. His initial training as a Sanskrit scholar helped him immensely in his approach. His most important work is *Caste and Race in India* (1932). This is a foundational text for sociology of India, where we find a blend of historical anthropological and sociological approaches. Ghurye not only elaborated upon the characteristics of caste system in India but also demonstrated caste dynamics by referring to the textual evidences only.

3.1.2. Louis Dumont and David Pocock

In their seminal piece, 'For a Sociology of India' in *Contributions to Indian Sociology* (1957, Vol. 1), Louis Dumont and D. Pocock initiated the cause for a proper relation between sociology and classical Indology. They provided a general perspective to locate sociology of India at the confluence of sociology and Indology. They made references to the works of such scholars who successfully combined the two disciplines. For instance, the German sociologist and ethnologist Marcel Mauss who abundantly used Sanskrit knowledge to reconstruct history of sacrifice of the Brahmanas. The work qualified as a sociological analysis of the practice of sacrifice.

To appreciate the Indian society as one whole and as an object of study, we need to attend to the encompassing Sanskrit civilization. The unity of India is not only made possible by such a higher order of values and thoughts but can be easily demonstrated by such texts. Hence, the Indological approach provides a vantage position to a sociologist who aspires to grasp the Indian society and its complexities. The realm of ideas and values was thought to constitute the subject matter of sociologists who sought unity of India among its diversity. So the anthropological/ethnographic details of disparate particular communities/villages/castes would be insufficient to understand the pan-Indian existence of caste as a system. Dumont and Pocock referred to Jawaharlal Nehru's *Discovery of India* (1946, 49) and quoted him, 'The unity of India was no longer merely an intellectual conception of me: it was an emotional experience which overpowered me'. They were sceptical about researches of the Indian anthropologists who overlooked pan-Indian patterns and concentrated more on their specific field-based studies of diversities.

> The nature of Indian unity immediately confronts us with a problem of method. It is not merely a cultural unity such is known in other parts of the world, as let us say among a number of neighbouring African tribes.... As has been remarked, unity is found here above all in ideas and values, it is therefore deeper and less easily defined: on the one hand it is social in the strictest sense, and this justifies our sociological perspective, it makes *Indian society as a whole* the true object of our study. (Dumont 1957, 9–10)

A unique complementariness of opposites in the higher thought process marks the Indian society. Dumont and Pocock held, with reference to caste system, the fundamental opposition is between purity and pollution, which is distinctively embedded in the religious elaboration of the idea. They further exemplified that the Indian thought could not be approximated keeping it insulated from its relation with society. The transcendence of the man of earth to become a *sanyasi* (the renunciator) was examined in support of the argument. In a compartmentalized society, one reaches a stage not only to leave the material world but also enjoys the right to leave/renounce the social order (de facto the caste order). Now, this is a typical Indian thought, where one renounces by negating the social order and in the process denounces the caste system altogether.

Basically, the complementarity of thought and social categories was posited by Dumont and Pocock to apprehend the specificity of the Indian society. One continues to live in this world of caste order yet seeks the thought of the spiritual *sanyasi* (who has negated the caste order). While on the one hand, the Indian spirituality is much sought after expressing a moral revulsion against caste, on the other hand, one continues to live within the same caste order. It shows a blend of worldly wisdom with thoughts of the higher spiritual accomplishment. This way the complementarity of the society and spirituality is shown as the clue to understand the Indian society. It is here, around the dialogue of the *sanyasi* and the man of the world, that religio-philosophical speculation revolves, concealing a contradiction or a dichotomy. Nehru has rightly noted that the thought of the *sanyasi* is much closer to our own than that of the man within the caste, because the *sanyasi* like us exists as an individual (Dumont 1957, 17).

Louis Dumont's fundamental work on India, *Homo Hierarchicus* (1970), advanced the method of structuralism to explain the Indian caste system. Ideology and tradition are the crucial aspects of Dumont's concept of structure. To explain caste as a pan-Indian system, Dumont had to seek its justification in the ideology which could be best attested by Indological researches. In fact, the unity of Indian civilization was thought of as a result of a unified set of ideas and values. The set of values resulted in an ideological structure that rested on a binary opposition to that of the West. The opposition in the thought structure is along many axes—individualism against holism, modern against traditional, equality against hierarchy and power against status. All such oppositions are ramification of the fundamental principle of opposition between purity and pollution. The principle of hierarchy is typical to the Indian society. The pure encompasses the impure, which was forwarded by Dumont as the basic structure of the Indian society. To understand this typical structure, it is obligatory to refer to the normative classical texts of India. Apart from the caste system, it was argued that complementarities mark the field of kinship too. The baseline of Dumont and Pocock's understanding is that traditional India did not recognize the individual as he/she appears in the modern Western society.

There is no doubt that Indian society has exhibited a hierarchical structure and it has shown great resilience too. But changes in the structure are also historically valid ever since the mid-19th century. The problematic blending of Indology with sociology has been incisively commented upon by Andre Beteille. While appreciating the rigour of Louis Dumont, Beteille has observed that by concentrating exclusively on traditional texts to reconstruct history, Dumont has privileged an enduring traditional structure. This has led to a typifying approach to the study of the Indian society as against a classifying approach of a comparative sociology.

Critiquing Dumont, Beteille observed:

> The typifying approach used by Dumont has put all its emphasis on the enduring traditional structures, and paid little attention to newness and change. It has had a great appeal for those who have watched contemporary India from afar. But it has been out of tune with the perceptions of many Indian sociologist engaged in the study of their own society, for whom disorder and change have been a part of everyday experience. (Gupta 2005, 85–86)

3.1.3. Debates for a Sociology of India

Louis Dumont had argued that the rich body of classical Hindu texts needed to blend with sociological researches. Pure ethnological studies, it was thought, would give rise to ideas and beliefs through vernacular categories only. Universalistic concepts of sociology/social anthropology would be inappropriate to grasp the local nuances. F. G. Bailey, representing the Manchester School of Social Anthropology, refuted the position of Dumont and Pocock. Bailey (1959), who had made intensive village-level studies based on fieldwork method in Orissa in the early 1950s, insisted on making abstractions from field data and conceptualizing the local behaviour by applying the broader universal sociological/social anthropological categories of analysis.

Reliance on Indological texts would lead to a hypothetical image of the Indian village communities. Much of the 'higher texts' would generate false village solidarity as expressed through sharing common values and beliefs. Bailey strongly opposed the textual renditions of kinship system as enshrined with Hindu religious codes. The historical and cultural specificities of India were wrongly indicated by Dumont and doing sociology in India had to be seen as a part sociology as practised across the world.

It is to be noted that much prior to the formulation by Dumont and Pocock in favour of resorting to classical texts to interpret the 'present', S. V. Ketkar (*History of Caste in India*, 1909), A. S. Altekar (*A History of Village Communities in Western India*, 1927), S. V. Karandikar (*Hindu Exogamy*, 1929) and a few others had extensively resorted to source materials from the ancient acclaimed texts. But the strong theoretical implications of Dumont's work actually fuelled the debate. Sociologists such as T. N. Madan, Yogendra Singh and A. K. Saran were all inspired by the Lucknow School of Sociology. They did not outrightly rejected the use of the classical texts. But they were apprehensive of any emphasis in the study of Indian sociology from external point of view, focusing on particular ideo-structural categories. They attempted to make Indian sociology simultaneously particularistic as well as universalistic. Some categories which are apparently ethno-sociological could as well be abstracted further for universal cross-cultural studies.

The debate on 'For a Sociology of India' was furthered by the journal *Contributions to Indian Sociology* in its new series under the editorship of T. N. Madan. Madan (1967) outrightly rejected any external objectivist point of view of a sociologist, like that of a natural scientist. He questioned whether an observer could acquire any understanding of an 'other' culture without understanding the actors of such cultures through their words, languages, directly or through intermediaries.

What should be then the appropriate theoretical approach for studying the Indian society? Yogendra Singh made the most useful intervention in this debate. He agreed to the importance of the typical Indian institution and understanding of such typicality as significant for any explanation and theorization in sociology. But he was less convinced about the theoretical promises of sociological/social anthropological theories without empirical grounding. He offered to appreciate sociology's theoretic structure only when researches are based on empirical data resulting from fieldwork, which adhere to self-awareness of one's own society and scientific objectivity within their own ideological setting (Singh 2004).

An obvious shortcoming of an exclusive use of Indology was that the Indian society had been equated with the Hindu society. In fact, a major deficiency of not only the Indological approach but also of the ensuing debate is that the entire discourse overlooked societies and institutions which were outside the ambit of the majority Hindu society. This issue has been pertinently raised by Imtiaz Ahmad (1972). Evidently, the Indological approach could not do justice to the religio-cultural diversity of the Indian society.

J. P. S. Uberoi, Satish Saberwal, A. M. Shah and Veena Das are among the other leading practitioners of the discipline who enriched the debate on Indology vis-à-vis ethnology. Both J. P. S. Uberoi and Veena Das argued in favour of structural anthropology for understanding marriage and kinship. The general principles of the structural model of Levi-Strauss were upheld as trans-disciplinary to account for the culture of India. They thought that through the method of structuralism, the universal significance of the Indian thought and social categories could be enumerated. As such, J. P. S. Uberoi was not at all comfortable with a simplistic application of general universal categories of the disciplines to examine the Indian society (Uberoi and Das 1971).

However, the question remains as to the use of history in sociological analysis. Without reducing the study of the Indian society to a complete reliance on classical ancient texts, A. M. Shah admitted the use of historical records and texts with a clear validation of such in the light of fresh empirical research. Shah was careful to the problem of whether the classical texts compiled in ancient times could be used blindly for historical reconstruction. Classical texts have been interpreted in multiple ways and with the passage of time, they go through many twists and turns as they change hands. So even meticulously worked out researches exclusively premised on ancient classical texts could not be considered a viable alternative to rigorous historical method (Shah 1974).

Whereas Satish Saberwal (1982) argued in favour of historicizing the sociocultural life to the colonial past. The Indological approach of interpreting the contemporary with reference to the totalizing categories of the ancient classical texts was considered a misplaced theoretical exercise. Most often than not, classical texts depict and enumerate an 'ideal' past or, at best, mystify the past. Disciplines like sociology essentially are an exercise in demystifying the reality.

3.1.4. Qualified Use of Indology

The classical Indological approach rested on translating the Sanskrit texts which were essential religio-normative ones. Such ancient religious texts as well as archaeological findings were accepted as the reliable primary source material for understanding the Indian society. Since religion was accorded the primary importance to approach the Indian society, a narrow and lopsided view of the Indian society emerged. The Indian society was depicted and understood as something of a closed system immune to social change and lacking egalitarian principles or structures.

After the emergence of sociology/social anthropology as professional and academic discipline and, especially after Independence, the classical orthodox Indology was much qualified. It tried to blend Indology with other sociological/anthropological perspectives. The foremost appeal to synthesize Indology with sociology was made by Dumont and Pocock (Section 3.1.1). From the Indian scholars, the researches of G. S. Ghurye, Iravati Karve, Veena Das and T. N. Madan stand out as some leading examples of modern usage of Indology.

Ghurye's seminal work on caste system in India (*Caste and Race in India*, 1969) relied heavily on Indological texts. Trained in anthropology for his doctoral work at Cambridge with W. H. R. Rivers, Ghurye applied anthropometry to explain race and caste in India. Six features of caste system were elaborated by him by considering caste as a Brahmanical child of the Indo-Aryan culture. It was nurtured in the land of Ganga and Yamuna, therefrom it spread to other parts of India. The race and colour formed the basis of the caste system, as *varna* the Sanskrit term for colour, formed the initial basis of the divisions.

Without any primary data generated through field study, Ghurye relied on data from secondary sources. The problem of such an approach was aptly noted by D. N. Dhanagare (2014, 261).

> However, Ghurye's Indological probing and frequent excursions in anthropometry cannot be mistaken as systematic reconstruction of history or historical analysis of structure and

change in Indian society. Paradoxical as it may sound, Ghurye tried to generate historical explanation and perspective (historiography) without systematic 'use of history' in the sense this expression is understood today.

Classical texts were interpreted and abundantly used by Iravati Karve to study kinship organization in India. She used it in combination with ethnological data to reconstruct history, especially the linguistic data on kinship terminologies (Karve 1953; 1961). Although both Ghurye and Karve used Indological texts, Karve refuted the diffusionist explanation of Ghurye on the spread of caste system. She refuted the thesis that the caste and *varna* systems were a product of the Indo-Aryan culture. Still her 'historical survey' relied heavily on only ancient texts, whereby her research also cannot be accorded a proper status of historical reconstruction of a living system like caste. Classical texts cannot entirely and exclusively be taken as historical data. Such texts remain as a Brahmanical normative ordering of the society.

Using Levi-Straussian structural analysis, Veena Das made the most incisive intervention with regard to the use of Indological sources. Raising the epistemological question of how sociological knowledge could be gained, Das took a position against positivist anthropology. While ethnographic details are felt to be necessary, social reality is enmeshed with cultural categories which are circumscribed by normative texts. Between the observable social reality and sociological understanding, conceptual categories play the most crucial role. To understand that, one needs to refer not only to the religious scriptures but more to the mythologies that the ancient texts contain. Mythologies are crucial elements of the Indian culture, so for Das, caste Puranas are to be decoded whereby one could examine how every caste ritually seeks its origin to a mythical origin. This would lead to a completely different understanding of the hierarchy of the system. Thus, every caste claims ritually superior status than what an imposing or totalizing normative structure conferred to it once for all (Das 1987).

T. N. Madan (1989) also took exclusive recourse to the 12th-century test of Kalhana's *Rajatarangini*—the Sanskrit text which chronicled the history of Kashmir from the earliest times—to conduct his sociological research of family and kinship among the Hindu pundits of Kashmir.

3.2. ETHNOGRAPHIC APPROACH

3.2.1. Field View versus Book View

We have seen that the Indological approach refers to exclusive use of the literature of ancient India to the study of the Indian society. Such a text-based method naturally gave rise to a textual view of the Indian society. Also, it is popularly called the book view of the Indian society. Against this textual understanding, we find the field view of the Indian society. The field view is a direct result of the ethnographic approach to the study of society. Simply put, the ethnographic approach is guided by the anthropological objective for studying people taking into account the entire cultural setting, so that a first-hand narrative account of the particular culture and its people could be generated.

We may understand simply that ethnography is the documentation of the social/cultural anthropologists, which is a result of fieldwork. The ethnographic approach essentially uses the research method known as participant observation. It is driven by the desire for a holistic understanding of the people, achieved only through an intensive field-study method. The ethnographic method became very popular in the Indian sociology immediately after Independence. It served the purpose of orienting oneself to the real-life experiences of the people, with all its complexities and contradictions. The access and generation of rich field data allows an anthropologist to understand and interpret social reality in a round-about manner (Beteille 1972).

The ethnographic approach contends that the Indological approach is de facto a book view of the Indian society, which privileges the ancient past and even distorts the functioning of the society. The ideal has to be replaced with the real, and ethnography is best suited to accomplish this task. M. N. Srinivas in Indian sociology remains the pioneer, who promoted the field-study method leading to the prosperity of the ethnographic approach. A whole range of scholars was trained by Srinivas who produced the finest field-study based ethnographic researches on the Indian society. The proliferation of ethnographic studies took place with the works of McKim Marriott, Robert Redfield, Milton Singer, Kathleen Gough, F. G. Bailey, Andre Beteille, Bernard S. Cohn and so on. They creatively used ethnography with different theoretical orientations.

3.2.2. Ethnography and Theoretically Informed Fieldwork

Most ethnographers in colonial India dealt with those subjects which were understood as 'outside' the mainstream society. Such ethnographical studies tried to generate information about tribes or those people who were at the margins of the society. After the Second World War, the influence of the American universities along with the British anthropological tradition of structural functionalism breathed a fresh life into ethnographic research in India. From the 1950s onwards, we find a flood of 'village studies' that privileged grassroots empirical researches. The Indian society and civilization were theorized from micro-studies through such researches.

M. N. Srinivas was the foremost proponent of field study based researches. While foregrounding his insistence on intensive fieldwork in the structural-functional perspective, Srinivas accounted for social structure of the Indian villages (Srinivas 1955). His field view was backed up by a theoretic adaptation of the British ethnographic tradition. Through such an innovative approach, he presented a dynamic village system of caste. He studied the village structure as adaptive and fluid, while at the same time persistent. Without outrightly rejecting the macro-studies and historical reconstruction of the society, he argued for a rigorous method of participant observation. Such an ethnographic shift was to contest the Indological obsession with secondary texts.

In his inaugural address at the 20th All India Sociological Conference held in Mangalore, 29–31 December 1993, Srinivas expressed his views that just a compilation of empirical facts would not suffice for sociology. An appropriate sociological perspective had to be brought into the field data for a successful ethnographic research.

> It is when this perspective is brought to bear on empirical data that the kind of analysis and insights specific to sociology are produced.... Sociology is an empirical discipline, and

field-work is integral to it.... The important thing, however, is the need for methodological catholicity and resilience, and an ability to choose the appropriate method for tackling a particular problem. (Srinivas 2012, 182)

Along with M. N. Srinivas, S. C. Dube also has to be credited for establishing the trend of ethnographic social research in India. Dube (1955) showcased the way an Indian village, while rooted in tradition, changed with adaptation in his study of Shamirpet. To understand changes in traditional community life, the idea of progressive adaptation was floated by Dube, which impacted many other studies on the Indian villages. In the same year, McKim Marriott's (1955) edited work *Village India: Studies in the Little Community* signalled the arrival of the new interest in ethnography-based village studies in Indian sociology. Under the auspices of the University of Chicago, a seminar was held from which eight research papers were included in the symposium. Overall, the studies examined the relevance of holistic methods of analysis for micro-studies of India's villages. Robert Redfield and Milton Singer's thesis of 'great tradition' and 'little tradition' stands apart. Their thesis is to interpret the Indian villages within the matrix of the Indian civilization, which exhibit two distinctive but interrelated cultural traditions—the great tradition and the little tradition. The great tradition is the repertoire of the Sanskrit Vedic literature/ancient texts, and the little tradition is the life of the folk, life as prevails in the village local communities. The continuous interactions between the two formed the village social structure. In the backdrop of this thesis, contributions in *Village India* (1955) vividly portrayed a total picture of the Indian villages. These ethnographic details generated a wide range of rich data, which were thought to be useful for comparative sociology also.

Of course, not all the contributors exactly followed Redfield's formulation, neither did they share the same idea of village as a unit of study. Srinivas's study of Rampura village of Karnataka depicted how the local castes were divided by caste rules and united, on the other hand, due to occupational specialization. He applied the structural-functional perspectives to arrive at this conclusion. Interestingly, Cambridge-trained social anthropologist Kathleen Gough in her study of Kumbapettai village (Tanjore District, Tamil Nadu) came to conclude that the wider question of power and dominance were vital to understand the village structure. Beyond the village as a unit, one had to focus on the wider structures of the state and the government. This was in contrast to understanding village as exhibiting a stable social structure as indicated by Srinivas (Gough 1955). Such application of sociological theory we also find in the work of F. G. Bailey. He invoked the concept of 'para-political system' to his ethnographic study of Bissipara village in Orissa to understand caste dynamics (Bailey 1963). Hence, qualified use of ethnography in tandem with appropriate sociological perspective came to stay as the running spirit in sociological studies of the Indian society.

3.2.3. Wider Application of Ethnography

Essentially, the ethnographic approach in the Indian sociology concentrated mainly on village as unit of study. Caste had been the central subject of almost all ethnographic studies. Social anthropologists such as F. G. Bailey, Kathleen Gough and others started questioning this limited objective. No doubt, the ethnographic approach popularized 'village studies' as a model for doing sociological or social anthropological studies in India. But the vacuity of 'village studies' was felt quickly and the complexities and heterogeneities of changing India caught the attention of researchers subsequently. The 1970s saw a decline in the interest in village studies of the earlier decades. The larger structure and institutions of the society such as religion, class, industry and city gradually had to be brought under the scope of ethnographic focus. It is important to mention the edited work of C. J. Fuller and V. Benei, *The Everyday State and Society in Modern India* (2001). It is a rich compilation of ethnographic researches on everyday local politics in the Indian society.

The advanced use of ethnography was indicated by Andre Beteille much earlier in 1962. While studying the village of Sripuram (Tamil Nadu), he made it very clear that:

> ...The world of the village constitutes a sort of microcosm, and part of the interest of our study will be to see in what ways this microcosm is a reflection of the macrocosm which is the outside world. (Beteille 1962, 141)

The practice of ethnography in modern anthropology is varied. Peter Berger (2012) has made a critical evaluation of the theoretical developments of anthropology in India. If anthropological theory has to examine and analyse particular life worlds of sociocultural beings, the ethnographic reality has to be accepted as the most important ingredient to such theorization. Ethnography cannot remain as mere descriptions and anthropology operate as abstract thinking.

A popular opinion of the practice of ethnography in India is that it is largely imitative of and influenced by the British or American tradition of doing social or cultural anthropology. Without invoking the regular 'the West' versus 'the East' to appreciate the practice of ethnographic research in India, Patricia Uberoi, Nandini Sundar and Satish Deshpande (2007) in their joint work on the biographies of 12 leading anthropologists of India have made useful observation. The Ethnographic approach in India has to have a distinct style being impacted by the local conditions or exegesis. Something more than just the academic, ethnography has been part of a moral and political concern with the concurrent framework of development in India.

3.2.4. Anthropologist in the East

Patricia Uberoi, Nandini Sundar and Satish Deshpande in their co-edited work *Anthropology in the East* (2007) compiled 12 biographical essays on some of the pioneers of Indian sociology and social anthropology. The editors are less keen on building a conventional disciplinary history. Their emphasis is on the interface of knowledge, institutions and practices in the specific context of India. Instead of the regular expositions of the development of the disciplines in developmental phases or typological terms, an alternative approach is resorted to. It is not to refute the disciplinary history but to review the disciplinary tradition by focusing on the individual life stories, which are unifying as well as differentiating, of 12 different practitioners to examine the recurrent thematic concern. In this way, an alternative history of the disciplines is being suggested by drawing attention to the evolving discursive universe of Indian sociology and social anthropology.

The nature of the discipline and the methods of analysis put the practitioners in intimate relation with their 'field' of research. The life experiences are varied and embodied by the practitioners and, in turn, anthropology is embodied in their lives. The life histories of 12 stalwarts—Iravati Karve, Benoy Kumar Sarkar, S. C. Dube, Sarat Chandra Roy, Verrier Elwin, L. K. A. Iyer, A. R. Desai, P. Geddes, N. K. Bose, S. C. Ghurye, D. P. Mukherji and M. N. Srinivas—are enumerated to explore the transformation of the academic and professional practices of the disciplines which originated within the Western paradigm but were practised in a non-Western context.

Colonialism is complicit with institutionalization and professionalization of anthropology. Anthropology is implicated in the colonial experience, be it the British or the American. In the Indian context, post-colonial discursive formation about the discipline, the colonial includes the wider discourse of 'colonization of the non-Western mind'. The regular critics have pointed out how the unequal power relations between the West and the Third World have been reproduced in the practice of anthropology. It is not only the political but the same is seen at the theoretical level too. The crucial point is what Yogendra Singh noted about practising with conceptual tools which were culturally alien. The lack of originality, and imitative professional and scientific life have been underscored by J. P. S. Uberoi as the contentious issues. All these point to the colonization of the mind as popularly coined by Ashis Nandy. The point to be noted is that apart from the colonial-Westerner ways of 'othering', there are indigenous models of 'othering'. This is a crucial aspect of understanding the way the disciplines have been shaped in the post-colonial times.

The same point has been addressed by Surajit Sinha. In his incisive review of Nirmal Kumar Bose's ideas about the development of an Indian tradition of anthropology through the studies of emergent problems of post-Independence India, he indicated the dangers of using borrowed ideas from the West (Sinha 1967, 1707–1709). In his consistent critique of the colonial dependence of Indian anthropology, Sinha discussed 'the process of naturalization of the different strands of Western anthropological traditions'. In his chapter, 'India: A Western Apprentice' in *Anthropology: Ancestors and Heirs*, Sinha is less optimistic:

> For some time, the proliferation of trained manpower, random efforts at catching up with the latest developments in the West and a general increase in the number of publications will characterize the development of Indian anthropology. (Sinha 1980, 281)

3.2.5. Themes and Issues of Indian Anthropology and Sociology

While charting out an alternative reading of the professionalization of Indian anthropology and sociology, Uberoi et al. (2007) admitted two important points, namely the question of nationalism occupied a 'very wide spectrum' and no Indian anthropologist or sociologist could escape the hold of nationalist ideas. The authors listed the important and contentious themes and issues under the following heads:

1. **Science and modernity:** Overall speaking, as modern disciplines both anthropology and sociology have perched themselves on the achievements of modern scientific methods. However, in the colonial context, on the one hand, Indian pioneers tried to embrace it with a penchant for perfecting the

techniques to even surpass the colonizers by the virtue of enjoying the local knowledge. On the other hand, there was a trend to valourize Indian tradition of scientific reason by exploring Hindu classical texts to claim modernity to contest the Western model. One can locate this trend in the works of L. K. A. Iyer, S. C. Roy and Benoy Sarkar.

Against the grain, there were critiques of the Western paradigm as a whole, led by D. P. Mukerji, A. K. Coomaraswamy and their students. A drive for indigenous categories of sociological analysis was advanced by A. K. Saran and later we find the same spirit in J. P. S. Uberoi, Shiv Viswanathan and Ashis Nandy.

2. **Disciplinary boundaries:** Quite naturally with the growing professionalization and specialization of the disciplines, over the years, the disciplinary boundaries have become sharp. The boundaries have resulted as the disciplines had grown and established themselves. The earlier flavour was much eclectic in character. Initially, sociology tried to build a synthesis with Indology or searched for useful positivist categories of thought in Hindu classical texts. At the hands of the early practitioners, sociology tried to build itself with a potential to bring humanities and sciences closer. However, further institutional development of sociology tried to come out of its affinity with social philosophy or social work. It tried to build bridges with other social science disciplines like political science and history while moving away from its ties with cultural anthropology.

3. **Nationalism and the nation state:** Nationalism did impact the development of Indian sociology and social anthropology but not in an undifferentiated manner. The anti-colonial stance contained a wide spectrum from a Gandhian version of nationalism represented by N. K. Bose to somewhat Hindu nationalism of G. S. Ghurye. Not to forget the Marxist anti-imperialism guided nationalism of A. R. Desai or the more indigenous swadeshi spirit of Benoy Kumar Sarkar. Overall, narrow or bigoted interpretations of nationalism never shaped up the frontrunners of the disciplines.

4. **Questions of methodology:** Classical sociological texts were not empirical but with their close association with social philosophy, they were essentially synthetic, encyclopaedic and theoretical. Empirical methods adopted by Indian sociologists and social anthropologists have been based on various models of fieldwork. Often, instead of long-term participant observation based fieldwork, many contemporary works are based on survey methods. It is important to remind ourselves that irrespective of the self-assured researcher with respect to the methods of science, many researches have confronted resistance in the field situations. The objective of 'othering' the subject often resulted in irritation and non-cooperation from the subject.

5. **Sociology/anthropology for whom?** The question of English as the language medium for scientific communication has implication for the disciplines in their role of public policymaking and intervention. The gap between the practised language and the experiences and emotions of fieldworks among the indigenous people continues as an unresolved problem for the disciplines. A case of vernacularization of the research exercise poses a practical challenge to the disciplines.

6. **Study of the other:** Although classically speaking, studying 'other' societies is the theoretically proclaimed position for the disciplines but all Indian born sociologists and social anthropologists, barring a handful scholars like R. K. Jain, hardly studied societies outside the Indian subcontinent. Interestingly, Indian researchers placed in the Western universities continue to select Indian subject matter for their studies. This trend has contributed to the development of South Asian studies or contemporary Indian studies by many European centres. The ideal of comparative studies of concurrent societies has been not benefitted from this evolved trend.

Exploring the biographies of some of the pioneering figures of Indian sociology and social anthropology in their compilation, Patricia Uberoi, Nandini Sundar and Satish Deshpande (2007) are apprehensive of the neglect to reach out and communicate with the local indigenous populace. The professional knowledge acquired through meticulous research activities has failed on the vital question of 'reaching out' or 'participation'. The contemporary debates of the discipline have deep roots in the very history of the discipline. Instead of ancestor worship, we require self-conscious appreciation of the contributions from the pioneers of the discipline. The overwhelming subject of nation state and nationalism has taken a new turn. Incisively, the discipline has to negotiate whether political independence has really given rise to a 'rupture' in the 'power–knowledge' nexus or just simplistically raised the question while consolidating a professional expansion of the discipline.

CONCLUSION

Indology originally means an approach of understanding the Indian society and culture, considered as unique and different from Western societies. Therefore, the Indian social values, beliefs and practices are to be studied through Indian classical high texts only. However, with the coming of the modern discipline of sociology, the Indological approach was modified and used in tandem with various sociological perspectives. Classical use of Indology was quite impovised to synthesize with modern anthropological methods.

Two leading scholars of sociology/social anthropology, G. S. Ghurye and Louis Dumont prompted the use of Indology in the study of the Indian society. Ghurye in his most acclaimed work on caste and race in India relied more on Indological sources, the validity of which for historical reconstruction of the past is dubitable. Whereas Dumont heavily drew upon textual interpretation of classical texts to account for the values, belief systems and ideology underlying the caste system. The question remains as to whether such normative classical literature can be considered as historical evidence and data to account for the living present. Both Ghurye and Dumont did not exclusively confine themselves to the classical texts but have utilized primary and secondary sources produced by mainly other researchers.

The proliferation of studies from the field, primarily in the form of ethnographic monographs, indeed enriched and complicated the picture of an essentialized, coherent view of the Indian society generated by Indologists. The ethnographic approach which rests on field view, prior to the 1950s, was primarily initiated by the colonial administrators, scholars and census officials with a colonial objective in mind. Along with this, the prolific travel writers produced a great deal of empirical work on the Indian society. Such empirical details ran counter to the uniformity, conformity or placid character of the Indian society that the classical texts produced.

Ethnography was recognized as an essential component of doing sociology or social anthropology in India. The focus on intensive field-study method gave rise to a new thrust in Indian sociology. A detailed round-about view of a small unit of study (a village or a tribe in its entirety) enriched the discipline immensely. However, the initial village studies mainly focused on caste system and considered the village or community as a unit of sociological probing. Neglecting the inter-caste relations and multiple arrangements between them, the villages are studied as mere collection of blocks. It was felt by a qualified application of Indology that the relations between castes as well as the interconnections between various social groups could be grasped in terms of and in relation to an encompassing set of religious values. Such values could be in turn located in the Indological texts. Through such a research method, a confluence of sociology and Indology could yield a perspective on the structure of what appears to be discrete and as such making up a coherent system.

Modern Indian sociologists, more or less, acknowledged that Indological texts are not canonical authority, but the ideas are profound and need to be counterposed with the present living reality. Empirical research for generating data to account for that reality has to base itself in solid ethnography. Ethnography has moved beyond the earlier limiting interest for village studies to engage with the larger structure of the Indian society. A distinct style of ethnography in the Indian context has to come out of its restrictive baggage of earlier times.

Points for Classroom Discussion

- The use of Indology in Indian sociology
- The salient points of debate with respect to appropriate method of studying the Indian society
- The importance of qualified use of Indology in ethnographic research works
- The themes and issues of Indian sociology and anthropology as addressed by leading social anthropologists/sociologists

GLOSSARY

Anthropometry: It is the science of obtaining systematic measurements of the human body.

Comparative sociology: Comparison of the social processes across different types of society for arriving at universal principles by either seeking similarity across different countries and cultures or the variances.

Ethnographic: A method used traditionally in anthropology where an anthropologist lives in a small community to learn the details of their daily life.

Field view: As against the text view, field view means a first-hand collection of data by conducting field research relying on personal observation in detail.

Indological: Pertaining to the method of studying the Indian society with the help of ancient history, epics, religious manuscripts and texts, and so on which embody the Indian value and belief system.

Participant observation: An anthropological method of conducting research by staying and participating with the subject that one wishes to study.

Secondary sources: Data used by a researcher which are not personally collected by him/her, that is, retrieved from archives, classical texts, periodicals, journals and so on.

Text view: An approach in sociology that relies on textual perspective of social phenomenon, rather, on classical texts to interpret the present.

REFERENCES

Ahmad, I. 1972. 'For a sociology of India'. *Contributions to Indian Sociology* 6, no. 1: 172–178.
Bailey, F. G. 1959. 'For Sociology of India'. *Contributions to Indian Sociology* 3, no. 9: 88–101.
———. 1963. *Politics and Social Change: Orissa in 1959*. Berkeley, CA: University of California Press.
Berger, P. 2012. 'Theory and Ethnography in the Modern Anthropology of India'. *HAU: Journal of Ethnographic Theory* 2, no. 2: 325–357.
Beteille, A. 1962, February. 'Sripuram: A Village in Tanjore District'. *Economic & Political Weekly*, Annual Number.
———. 1972. 'The Tribulations of Fieldwork'. *Economic & Political Weekly* 7, no. 31–33.
Das, V. 1987. *Structure and Cognition: Aspects of Hindu Caste and Ritual*. New Delhi: Oxford University Press.
Dhanagare, D. N. 2014. *The Writings of D. N. Dhanagare: The Missing Tradition—Debates and Discourse in Indian Sociology*. With a foreword by Partha Nath Mukherji. New Delhi: Orient BlackSwan.
Dube, S. C. 1955. *Indian Village*. New York, NY: Harper Colophon Books.
Dumont, L. 1957. 'For a Sociology of India'. *Contributions to Indian Sociology* 1, 7–22.
———. 1970. *Homo Hierarchicus: The Caste System and Its Implications*. Delhi: Vikas Publications.
Fuller, C. J., and V. Benei. 2001. *The Everyday State and Society in Modern India*. London: Hurst and Co.
Gough, K. 1955. 'The Social Structure of a Tanjore Village'. In *Village India: Studies in the Little Communities*, edited by McKim Marriott, 36–52. Chicago, IL: University of Chicago Press.
Gupta, D. 2005. *Essential Writings of Andre Beteille*. Delhi: Oxford University Press.
Karve, I.1953. *Kinship Organisation in India*. Pune: Deccan College.
———. 1961. *Hindu Society: An Interpretation*. Pune: Deccan College.
Madan, T. N. 1967. 'For a Sociology of India: Some Clarifications'. *Contributions to Indian Sociology* (new series) 1, no. 1: 90–93.
———. 1989. *Family and Kinship: A Study of Pandits of Kashmir*. New Delhi: Oxford University Press.
Marriott, M. 1955. *Village India: Studies in the Little Communities*. Chicago, IL: University of Chicago Press.
Nehru, J. 1946. *The Discovery of India*, 49. Calcutta: The Signet Press.
Saberwal, S. 1982. 'For a Sociology of India: On Multiple Codes'. *Contributions to Indian Sociology* 16, no. 2: 289–294.
Shah, A. M. 1974. 'Historical Sociology: A Trend Report'. In *Survey of Sociology and Social Anthropology*, edited by M. N. Srinivas, 432–459. New Delhi: Indian Council of Social Science Research.

Singh, Y. 2004. *Ideology and Theory in Indian Sociology*. Delhi: Rawat Publications.
Sinha, S. 1967. 'Involvement in Social Change: A Plea for Own Ideas'. *Economic & Political Weekly* 2, no. 37: 1707–1709.
———. 1980. 'India: A Western Apprentice'. In *Anthropology: Ancestors and Heirs*, edited by Stanley Diamond. The Hague: Mouton Publishers.
Srinivas, M. N. 1955. *India's Villages*. Bombay: Asia Publishing House.
———. 2012. 'Sociology in India and Its Future'. In *Indian Sociology: Issues and Challenges*, edited by L. Thara Bhai. New Delhi: SAGE Publications.
Uberoi, J. P. S., and V. Das. 1971. 'The Elementary Structure of Caste'. *Contributions to Indian Sociology* 5: 33–47, 79–81.
Uberoi, P., N. Sundar, and S. Deshpande. 2007. 'Introduction: The Professionalization of Indian Anthropology and Sociology—Peoples, Places and Institutions'. In *Anthropology in the East: Founders of Indian Sociology and Anthropology*, edited by Patricia Uberoi, Nandini Sundar, and Satish Deshpande, 1–63. New Delhi: Permanent Black.

CHAPTER 4

Ideas of India: Gandhi and Ambedkar

LEARNING OUTCOMES

- To get familiarized with Gandhi's vision of India
- To critically examine Gandhi's view on the practice of untouchability
- To explore Ambedkar's sociological writings on Hindu *shastra*
- To appreciate the contrasting ideas of Gandhi and Ambedkar

Keywords: Western modernity, *Swaraj*, untouchability, depressed classes, Hindu *shastras*, caste, *Varnashrama*, conversion

*Democracy necessarily means a conflict of will and ideas,
involving sometimes a war of the knife between different ideas.*

—**M. K. Gandhi**

*Bhakti in religion may be a road to the salvation of the soul.
But in politics, Bhakti or hero worship is a sure road to degradation
and to eventual dictatorship.*

—**Bhimrao Ambedkar**

INTRODUCTION

Mohandas Karamchand Gandhi (1869–1948) and Babasaheb Bhimrao Ambedkar (1891–1956) represent two towering politico-intellectual figures of modern India. Gandhi intervened in India's freedom struggle as an unconventional voice. It was a voice for truth and love seeking to demystify the 'successes of Western thoughts of modernity'. Taking the freedom struggle to a philosophical height of challenging the very premise of Western rational order of development, he charted out a wholesome critique of Western paradigm of reason and rationality. Gandhi's conception of achieving the ideal society rested on the strength of two tools of truth and love.

Gandhi pursued for an ideal Indian society premised on the values of non-violence and a voluntary social order that balances individual freedom with social responsibility. He realized the Western modern development as a life-corroding competitive ethos. In contrast, he wished to retrieve the spirituality enshrined in the Indian civilization and tradition. On the practical front, he laid his emphasis on village uplift and a return to the concept of voluntary recognition of duty of all engaged in labour.

On the contrary, Ambedkar found in the liberal ideas of the West a succour to change the face of India. For him, the reality of caste oppression and social inequality was more immediate than the final goal of freedom from the colonial rule. As a liberal modernist, he took refuge in the power of reason and rationality to challenge the ideals of Hindu scriptures to envision a new India. Beyond his concern for nation-building and constitutionalism, Ambedkar was firmly committed to the cause of uplifting the downgraded castes from the brutal actualities of life. His real intellectual oeuvre is best captured in the role that he played in examining the ills of a caste society and struggled all his life for democratic and republican values.

The emergence and assertion of Dalits and Other Backward Castes (OBCs) in the Indian society gained strength from the incisive contribution of Ambedkar. Dalit texts and literature have prospered, holding aloft the seminal ideas of Ambedkar. The writings of Ambedkar are contrary to the mainstream Gandhian ideas of India. Gandhi through his life and works have impacted nationalist discourse. The goal of self-rule and the dream of independent India are all couched in his interpretation and propagation of *Hind Swaraj*. Ambedkar had made a critical assessment of the *Puranic* texts and Hindu *shastras* offering an alternate understanding of the Indian society. While the leading thoughts of Mahatma Gandhi could be traced in his *Hind Swaraj* (1909), Ambedkar's writings on the classical Hindu texts are scattered in his selected writings and speeches. His indictment of the caste ridden Indian society in *Annihilation of Caste* (1936) is worth sociological reading.

4.1. MAHATMA GANDHI

4.1.1. Gandhi's Vision of India

For all studies of modern India, the idea and roles played by Mohandas Karamchand Gandhi remain a point of departure on the course of India's emergence into the world of freedom. At a very critical juncture of India's history, Gandhi arrived on the national politico-intellectual scene. At a time when different strands of political and intellectual activities in India were grappling with the colonial rule, Gandhi breathed a fresh air of mass mobilization and participation into the body politic.

Raising the question of self-rule or self-governance to a philosophical level of self-awareness and self-reflection, he intervened into the politics of freedom movement. He raised it to a holistic critic of the colonial that included not only his opposition to the instrumentality of the Western modernity but also a refreshed engagement with one's own traditional values, norms and beliefs.

Gandhi forwarded a new vision of the social and the political at a very significant point of the Indian history of freedom struggle. As a participatory project, he ensured a coming together of all disparate sections of the society so that the nationalist movement could prosper into a liberating discourse in every sense. Like many of his predecessors, Gandhi critiqued the Western paradigm of modernity, but he also invoked the strength of morality in anti-colonial struggle. Interestingly, the turning point for the intellectual history of India's path to freedom was a total rejection by Gandhi of all the Western values of progress and reason. In a way, he spiritualized the movement for freedom, whose vision of India was unlike that of a traditionalist yet critically embedded strongly in India's great civilization and tradition.

A new identity for India that Gandhi imagined was built on a creative engagement and exploration of the Indian traditional thoughts. A refreshingly new ideal of an egalitarian society signalled a decisive departure from militant nationalists as well as modernist thoughts. As a fascinating leader and a seeker of truth, Gandhi remains the most enigmatic persona of the 20th century. He dreamt a vision of a new India and fell to the bullets for his conviction. Like a true transformative leader, his vision was unorthodox. It was a vision of India made up of self-sustaining village republics. For him, India had to be a morally enlightened non-violent state that rests on the principles of compassion-based equality. In *Hind Swaraj* (1909), one finds Gandhi's coherent views on the ideal society for India. Also, his *An Autobiography* (1927) gives us a clue to his journey to this awareness and realization of a morally liberating state of society.

4.1.2. Gandhi's Hind Swaraj

Hind Swaraj translated in English stands for Indian home rule. Originally written in Gujrati in 1909, Gandhi's *Hind Swaraj* in a self-critical mode challenged the 'civilizing mission' of the Englishman. Comprising 20 chapters, the text serves as an alternative paradigm for a new civilization—the condition for India's home rule. It starts with a scathing critique of the Western science-based modernity. He develops his ideas of the real character of Indian home rule, which abhors all forms of instrumentality and violence. The text has a unique style of positioning one's views in an interactive manner between the reader and the editor (proxy for Gandhi).

Gandhi's basic formulation for attaining true *Swaraj* is not just to drive away the colonial master. Self-rule demands unshackling the bondage of thoughts. It demands that every Indian becomes a self-ruling individual, which would serve as a premise for making India free. This calls for a refreshed thinking on 'what is civilization'.

> ...We rarely find people arguing against themselves. Those who are intoxicated by modern civilization are not likely to write against it. Their care will be to find out facts and arguments in support of it, and this they do unconsciously, believing it to be true. A man whilst he is

dreaming, believes in his dream; he is undeceived only when he is awakened from his sleep. A man labouring under the bane of civilization is like a dreaming man. What we usually read are the works of defenders of modern civilization, which undoubtedly claims among its votaries very brilliant and even some very good men. Their writings hypnotize us. (Gandhi 1938, 32)

By surrendering to the spirit of modern civilization, India had lost its freedom, according to Gandhi. So just by rejecting the colonial British, *Swaraj* could not be attained. The dictates of modern civilization revolved around material greed, acquisition, domination, competition and violence. Substantive self-rule rests on spiritual regeneration. An enlightened soul was the search for Gandhi, which primarily had to do away with the indoctrinated false ideals of progress and development. Be it the English education system, the system of law, the railways, state and government—all were argued as aspects of a hegemonic colonial modernity. Rejecting the Western civilizing project of modernity, he imagined India as a nation resurrected through *swadeshi* as an act of self-reliance. For which one has to tap the resources embedded deep into the Indian civilization and tradition.

...Civilization is that mode of conduct which points out to man the path of duty. Performance of duty and observance of morality are convertible terms. To observe morality is to attain mastery over our minds and our passions. So doing, we know ourselves. (Gandhi 1938, 54)

Gandhi had a unique way of appreciating true civilization. The modern instrumental civilization has subsumed the ethical and spiritual self. Gandhi identified this as the central problem which needs to be addressed by way of return to a foundational meaning of civilization. It demands a mode of self-reflection that ensures the emergence of a new man who on knowing his self, could seamlessly see the blend of morality with duty. The struggle for freedom from a colonial rule has to be firmly rooted in the struggle for advancing self-knowledge.

How to accomplish the objective of *Swaraj*? Self-knowledge and self-rule are entwined in Gandhi's understanding of the ontology of *Swaraj*. Duty has a composite meaning for him. It is a service to humanity, the sufficient condition for a moral uplifting and reawakening premised on self-awareness. Not through a transformation of the material structures that one could bring in the transformation of the industrial capitalist civilization, it calls for an ontological break with the idea of progress as designed by the Western thoughts.

Neither the violent methods of revolutionaries nor the methods of the moderates to petition before the ruler were endorsed by Gandhi. He abhorred violence on moral and ethical grounds. Instead, he called for soul force, a kind of passive resistance. It was the power of *Satyagraha* to secure rights through 'personal sufferings'. It was not a sign of weakness but of moral conviction and strength. As a unique transformative text, *Hind Swaraj* raises certain fundamental questions about reimagining the Indian society. It is interesting to note that in this text, he has talked about the Indian civilization instead of naming it as Hindu civilization. His reference to the Indian civilization, thus, signifies a confluence of different streams of cultures irrespective of religious denominations. The ideal India for Gandhi is *Hind Swaraj* where one practices religion by setting a limit to worldly pursuits. Here, religion becomes a syncretic one offering a religious outlook on life, without being a religion of confession. In doing so, he wished to see its relevance as the most decisive link between civilization and politics.

Self-regulation has been such an overwhelming conception for Gandhi that he denounced the presence of the modern state in the life of people. He envisioned an ideal state marked by absence of interfering political institutions and coercive political power. The backbone of such an ideal state will be the *Gram Swaraj* (village republic), where it is not the state but the self-rule that regulates the social order. The village community of self-rule and individual could control their needs and passion while delivering good to the community. Gandhi reposed his faith not among the leaders or the advance section of the society, but on the nameless people of India to take India to an alternative path of development.

John Middleton Murray in his 'A Spiritual Classic' in *Aryan Path* (September 1938, 437–438) made the most prolific observation that *Hind Swaraj* was one of the spiritual classics of the world. The new India envisioned by Gandhi rested on a vision that gave primacy to an ethical standard of evaluation of the Western model of modernization and development. Now, quite expectedly, the ideas of *Hind Swaraj* when tested against the practical realm of modern India would appear to be unpragmatic. The text is didactic, no doubt. But we could see Gandhi's political action and operationalization of his ideas in his political career. The lesson to take home from him is the critical challenge he put up against the violent methods of securing one's rights and freedom. That is, the method of voluntary suffering as a premise of any non-violent politics. Skilfully, he legitimized the concept of 'passive resistance'—the method of resisting domination and subjugation by personal suffering. When the materialistic pursuit of the modern world systematically legitimized the random use of violent means to realize the objective, Gandhi's utopic vision definitely provided us with an alternative.

4.1.3. Gandhi on Untouchability

Untouchability in the Indian context takes its meaning from the notion of 'pollution' associated with the caste system. Those at the lowest rung of the supposed hierarchy of caste are considered to be defiling. The caste ideology shows its worst face by legitimizing ostracization of low-caste Dalits and segregates them from the mainstream social prestige, customs and practices. Gandhi's ideas as the foremost thinker and visionary for a new India demand special attention on this question. How did the egalitarian and humane order visualized by Gandhi negotiate the practice of untouchability?

The use of the term *Harijan* for the ex-untouchables by Gandhi could serve us as the entry point for exploring his views on untouchability. From the 1920s onwards, Gandhi was campaigning against the practice of untouchability. He referred to them as *Antyaja* (last born) in the vernacular, while chose to term them as 'supressed classes' in English. After the contentious Poona Pact (1932), where Bhimrao Ambedkar had to yield to Gandhi's view on separate electorates for the depressed classes, Gandhi started using the term *Harijan*, meaning the 'children of god'. He invoked the term in opposition to the pejorative term of 'untouchable'. Also, he preferred the term over the colonial coinage of 'depressed classes'. To popularize the term, he renamed his weekly newspaper, *Young India*, as *Harijan*. In the ensuing vigorous campaign against the practice of untouchability, the term *Harijan* was used replacing the demeaning term untouchables.

Without outrightly rejecting the caste system, one can find Gandhi's opposition to the reproachable practice of untouchability in the following note, 'Dr Ambedkar and Caste', prepared by him for his edited weekly *Harijan*.

> ...caste has its limitations and its defects, but there is nothing sinful about it, as there is about untouchability, and, if it is a by-product of the caste system, it is only in the same sense that an ugly growth in a body, or weeds of a crop. It is as wrong to destroy caste because of the out-caste, as it would be to destroy a body because of an ugly growth. (Gandhi 1933, 3)

Remaining within the caste fold as prescribed by the ancient scriptures, Gandhi took up a most intriguing step of denouncing untouchability. His contention was that the 'caste ideal' as derived from the scriptures and as practised was just travesty of the original idea. There is no linear 'no saying' in his thought with respect to the complex question of caste and untouchability. He was a critic of untouchability as an insider to the caste system in an unconventional way. His profound ideas did give rise to critical observation.

> ...as a savarna Hindu, when I see that there are some Hindus called avarnas, it offends my sense of justice and truth...if I discover that Hindu shastras really countenance untouchability as it is seen today, I will renounce and denounce Hinduism. (Gandhi 1934, 7)

We find a trait of self-criticism and self-reflection in Gandhi's engagement with the degrading caste system. In a way, he was an orthodox to consider (caste system) as providing the principle of hereditary occupation as an eternal social order. Dharma was considered by him as a duty; *Varnashrama dharma* was endorsed as a system of distribution of men in different occupations to maintain the balance and complementarity of the social-economic order. It satisfied the need for religious, social and economic harmony of the society (Unnithan 1965).

Gandhi's defence of the *varnavyavastha* and denouncement of untouchability created an image of inconsistency and paradox, according to his critics. But researchers like Anthony J. Parel through substantive studies of Gandhi's wide range of writings and political activities concluded that it was possible to evaluate him from a different angle. He realized that caste as envisaged in the classical texts has lost its ideal and the *Varnashrama* could not be revived or restored (Parel 2006).

When we relate Gandhi's thoughts with his life, as he was essentially a man of action, we discover him as a consistent critic of untouchability. Through his engagement with political mobilization and 'experiments with truth', he stood out as an unorthodox and non-conformist (Gandhi [1927] 1983). Through the life he led and the symbols he used abundantly in his politico-intellectual activities, Gandhi proved himself as an enigma. He cannot be fully appreciated by the logic we have learnt from the Western thought paradigm, the paradigm he was essentially contesting.

Gandhi led a countrywide campaign to defy ban on temple entry by 'untouchables'. Such a popular mass action proves the salience of his political practice. As an astute

> **BOX 4.1**
> **A Critique of Gandhi**
>
> Gandhi has been by far the most consistent and savage critic of modernity and its best-known cultural product: the modern West. Gandhi called the modern culture Satanic and, though he changed his mind about many things, on this point he remained firm. Many Gandhians cannot gulp this part of him. Either they read him as a nation-builder who, beneath his spiritual façade, was a hard-headed modernist wedded to the nation-state system, or they say that he was a great man pursuing crazy civilizational goals.
>
> **Source:** Nandy (1984).

political strategist and a leader of the masses, he evolved through a trajectory of being an orthodox to a more liberal thinker. And he in an unorthodox manner turned out to be a revolutionary radical thinker and practitioner in the Indian context. The egalitarian vision of a new India can never escape the question of liberation from the evils of untouchability. In no uncertain terms, he rested his case:

> Untouchability as at present practiced is the greatest blot on Hinduism. It is (with apology to Sanatanists) against the Shastras. It is against the fundamental principles of humanity, it is against the dictates of reason that a man should by mere reason of birth, be ever regarded as an untouchable, even unapproachable and unseeable. (Gandhi as quoted in V. V. Ramana Murti 1970, 355–356)

4.2. BHIMRAO AMBEDKAR

4.2.1. Ambedkar's Idea of India

Liberty, equality and fraternity are the three cornerstones of Bhimrao Ambedkar's vision of a new India. Popularly referred to as Babasaheb Ambedkar, he was an academic, jurist, social reformer and a political activist—all rolled into one great persona. Ambedkar could overcome the handicap of being born in the Mahar caste, an erstwhile untouchable caste of Maharashtra, to excel in academic life and simultaneously articulate sociopolitical concerns. As a prolific writer and speaker, he intervened in a discursive field that remains so pertinent to the question of India's path to modernity.

The wide canvass of Ambedkar's thoughts and campaigns questioned the dominant views on the Indian society. Couched in liberal modernist thoughts, he agitated both politically and academically. Through his in-depth commentaries and erudite academic articles, he proposed an image of India, liberal and democratic, as opposed to the caste-ridden inegalitarian orthodox Indian society. He moved beyond the description of the evils of orthodox Indian tradition to empathically present the experiential world of the 'untouchables'. He compiled anecdotes from his personal life in a piece, satirically titled by him as 'Waiting for a Visa' (Ambedkar 2014a, 661–692). In the personal narratives, we find varied experiences that explored the particular aspects of the dehumanizing practice of untouchability in tradition-bound India. We find a caustic indictment of Hinduism as a religion that rests on certain inegalitarian exclusionary principles.

Politically as well as academically, Ambedkar led a relentless fight against the caste system. Forcefully, he argued and pleaded with the traditionalists to re-read the *shastras* and the Sanskrit texts and admit that they were all the legitimizing texts for an exclusionary social order.

Independent India generally understands Bhimrao Ambedkar as the 'maker' of the Indian Constitution. Ambedkar as a constitutional expert played a lead role in the drafting of the Indian Constitution as the chairman of the Drafting Committee of the Constituent Assembly. His wide range of involvement with India's freedom struggle has to be located in the Western empirical and liberal intellectual tradition to which he was exposed to in his academic career. He floated the idea of coming out of the Hindu fold as he found no hope for untouchables in any notion of Hinduism as divine dispensation. In the 1950s, after two decades of contemplation with the idea of conversion, he finally embraced Buddhism. Hinduism was a closed option for him. Beyond the agitating mode of a political activist, Ambedkar philosophized religion as a succour for the distressed lives of the common people. Reposing his faith on Buddhism, he found hope for progress and equality in it. With a deep commitment to the principle of justice, liberty and equality, he asserted that fraternity was the elementary condition for any sense of modernity.

Certainly, Ambedkar shaped the progressive, futuristic idea of a modern India. The Republic of India is the basis of the country's nationhood. The constitutional values of equality, freedom and justice were driving ideas of Ambedkar's polemical engagement in the freedom struggle. At the time of the freedom struggle, when most of the national leaders laid emphasis on political aspects of nationalism, he put the emphasis on social justice—securing equality for all. For uplifting the most degraded, his scheme of nationalism demanded freedom from internal serfdom, oppression, subjugation and exploitation. (Jefrrelot 2005)

4.2.2. Ambedkar: A Critique of Hindu Shastra

Exclusively based on his thorough readings of the Indian traditional texts on the caste system, Ambedkar developed a profound critique of the caste system. At Columbia University in 1916, he presented a research paper for an anthropology seminar of Dr A. A. Goldenweiser. The title of the paper was 'Castes in India: Their Mechanisms, Genesis and Development' (Ambedkar 2014b, 3–22). It represented a critical scholarship on the erstwhile anthropological and sociological literature on caste. In a lucid and argumentative fashion, the paper presents endogamy as the essence of caste system. Endogamy means the prohibition of inter-caste marriage.

Ambedkar looked at caste as a system in which each *jati* is part of the whole. Positioning against the popular argument, he refused to accept caste system as a system of 'division of labour' which minimized competition among occupational groups. For him, caste system was a division among the labouring classes rather than division of labour.

According to Ambedkar, endogamy was superimposed on a pre-existing exogamous society. In his view, India's religion was essentially primitive, and it functioned with its tribal code. Across the world, with the passage of time, the practice of restricting the field of marriage lost its efficacy, but it still operated in the Indian society. Not only the blood kin could not marry (*sapinda*) but marriage is also prohibited within the same *gotra*/clan (*sagotra*). The endogamy rule was superimposed on the original practice of exogamy. This was the germinating point for caste system.

Interestingly, in this mechanism of endogamy, Ambedkar located the uxorial Hindu customs of sati, enforced widowhood and child marriage. These three customs strengthened endogamy as the means for creating strict caste boundaries. Initially, it was the Brahmans who put these practices into place, which was subsequently taken up by others.

In the same paper, Ambedkar concluded that some of the social groups in ancient India which were classes turned into enclosed endogamous groups probably to ensure the privileges they enjoyed out of an elementary ancient class system. Since the Brahmans and the Kshatriyas were the most privileged classes, they took the lead in enclosing themselves as endogamous groups to secure their privileges. The other groups merely emulated the higher classes, and the system was naturalized across a wider region. So according to him, classes in India were forerunner to castes, and castes were analysed by Ambedkar as enclosed classes characterized by endogamy.

Using the tool of fierce rationalism, Ambedkar scrutinized the classical Hindu texts. He historicized the dehumanization of the Shudras. The Hindu texts served as the pillars of the most degrading social organization of caste. Without the absolute repudiation of Hinduism itself, one cannot meaningfully do away with the practice of untouchability. With a thorough scrutiny of all the varieties of Brahmanical texts—be it the Vedas, Upanishads, epics, Puranas, Smritis or Dharmashastras—Ambedkar exposed the Brahmanical theory of the status of the Shudras (Ambedkar 2014c). He refuted the very basis of *chaturvarna* or caste system and questioned the origin of the *chaturvarna* in the Indo-Aryan society.

Ambedkar examined the *Purusha Sukta*, the part of Vedas as fabricated by Brahmans to serve their dubious intent. It was Manu who created the social ideal of *chaturvarna* by invoking a sense of divinity and infallibility. It was a later-on addition to the Vedas. According to Ambedkar, it was the *chaturvarna* that served as the premise of the caste system. The *varna* system was harmful as it degraded the masses by denying equal opportunity to knowledge and resources. The concept of dharma as moral duty had been inserted in all Brahmanical texts with an ideological jugglery. The mischief was accomplished by dharma in preordaining compulsory duties and obligation of the different *varnas*. The religious prejudices and the sacred notions were implicated in the Hindu social organization, irrespective of whether one believed in *varna* or caste. A severe indictment of Gandhi we find in Ambedkar as he argued that an endorsement of the *varnashrama* for some imaginary utility of division of occupation as determined by principle of hereditary would be fictious.

> ...the idea of varna is the parent of the idea of caste. If the idea of caste is a pernicious idea, it is entirely because of the viciousness of the idea of varna. Both are evil ideas, and it matters very little whether one believes in varna or in caste ... Orthodox or the Sanatan Vedic Hindus had no rational defence to offer. All that they could say was that it was founded on the authority of the Vedas and that as the Vedas were infallible so was the varna system. (Ambedkar 2018, 300)

So Ambedkar was forthright in his politico-intellectual mission to challenge and discard the divine authority of the *shastras*. Demystifying the Brahmanic theory of Shudras, he made a passionate appeal to engage in rational examination of the received texts from the hallowed past. An original and offbeat perspective was forwarded by him to claim caste as a form of class arrangement.

4.2.3. The Annihilation of Caste

The text *Annihilation of Caste* stands as the most audacious statement by Ambedkar against the sacred texts of Hinduism. It was the content of a speech which Ambedkar was supposed to deliver in 1936. It was at the annual conference of Jat-Pat-Todak Mandal, a Hindu reformist group, which ultimately had to be cancelled under controversial circumstances. The text was already presented to the committee in advance. The volatile text was published subsequently as a booklet by Ambedkar (2000). In a way, it is a subversive text that called for a breach in the traditional and orthodox thinking in India.

How to bring about a breach in the system?

> ...you must not forget that if you wish to bring about a breach in the system, then you have got to apply the dynamite to the Vedas and the Shastras, which deny any part to reason; to the Vedas and Shastras, which deny any part to morality. You must destroy the religion of the Shrutis and the Smritis. Nothing else will avail. (Ambedkar 2000, 68)

BOX 4.2
Ambedkar on Chaturvarnya

To me this Chaturvarnya with its old labels is utterly repellent and my whole being rebels against it. But I do not wish to rest my objection to Chaturvarnya on mere grounds of sentiments ... as a system of social organization, Chaturvarnya is impracticable, harmful and has turned out to be a miserable failure ... The principle underlying caste is fundamentally different from the principle underlying Varna. Not only are they fundamentally different but they are also fundamentally opposed. The former is based on worth. How are you going to compel people who have acquired a higher status based on birth without reference to their worth to vacate the status? ... For this you must first break up the caste system, in order to be able to establish the Varna system. How are you going to reduce the four thousand castes, based on birth, to the four Varnas, based on worth? (Ambedkar 2000, 46–47)

Ambedkar even took exception to the socialist understanding of equality and justice in the Indian context. He expressed his doubts as to accomplishing equality with just an economic interpretation of history. He strongly believed that no economic reform could be successful without being preceded by a holistic social reform. That even after accomplishing economic equalization of property, there is no guarantee that discrimination on account of caste and creed would come to an end. A deeper commitment to equality demands a deeper understanding of the peculiar nature of injustice in the Indian society. To rectify such ills, one needs to develop a spirit of fraternity towards one another.

> Can you have economic reform without first bringing about a reform of the social order? ... It seems to me that, other things being equal, the only thing that will move man to take such an action is the feeling that other men with whom he is acting are actuated by a feeling of equality and fraternity and-above all-of justice ... I can't see how a Socialist State in Indian can function for a second without having to grapple with the problems created by the prejudices which make Indian people observe the distinctions of high and low, clean and unclean. (Ambedkar. Ibid. p 30–31)

Making a roundabout review of the world history of liberal and democratic discourses, Ambedkar located the peculiarity of the Indian caste system. The dogma of predestination denies any scope for an individual to change his/her occupation. Without rejecting the central propositions of socialism, he called out the fallacy of socialist theories. The economic interpretation of history would not allow one to effectively explain the unique case of caste inequality. Any socialist revolution demands unity—a feeling of equality, fraternity and justice—which is absolutely impossible without dismantling the caste system.

Reason and morality are the two most important weapons to dismantle the unreasonable and illogical edifice of caste. But the Brahmans guard their homeland of caste and have created an impregnable wall around it. Brahmans are the natural intellectual class who lead the Hindus. Hence, Ambedkar's call was to come out of that religion, revolt against it by defying it. It is not that Ambedkar was against religion per se. For him, religion stands for hope and that the distressed lives on hope. Such an understanding of religion, in the sense of universally acceptable spiritual principles, is not to be found in the Hindu religion, at least, such egalitarian principles do not govern the life of a practising Hindu. Instead, Ambedkar found Hinduism just an ensemble of a multitude of commands and prohibitions. It lacks the essential character of any universal religion, that is, the emancipatory potential.

According to Ambedkar, the Hindu religion is full of code of ordinances and it demands only conformity to its commands. There is no loyalty to any ideals of progress, equality or harmony in it. So Ambedkar was unabashed in his call for destroying such a religion. Through a critical examination of all the classical texts, he came to conclude that the texts do not allow the followers to apply reason and leave no room for them to reflect rationally on the very foundation of caste or *varna*. Ambedkar cited the occasions in one's life (e.g., when one takes up a rail journey or foreign travels and so on), where a Hindu cannot really follow all the caste commands, yet in an unreflexive manner follows all the caste considerations for the rest of one's life. No scope of this irregular behaviour is left for reason to ponder as the same Hindu religion invokes the concept of *prayaschitta* (penance), which very cleverly introduces a spirit of compromise so that the caste system could perpetuate eternally.

Ambedkar wrapped up the text appealing to the Hindus to consider four points. He made up his mind to leave the field of Hinduism; he decided to convert to Buddhism already. But he left behind the following critical questions as to:

1. Whether the Hindus would take the beliefs, habits, morals and views of life as given by their *shastras* as infallible and opaque to any scrutiny by reason or subject them to critical examination.

2. Whether the Hindus would be conservative to retain all the orthodoxies or be selective in choosing from the social heritage to pass on to future generation.
3. Whether the Hindus would continue the principles of the past as their ideals, which actually deny the present and are detrimental for any progress.
4. Whether the Hindus accept that there is nothing *Sanatan* or eternal. Change is constant, one must continually revolutionize old values and accept the changing standards of values over time.

Finally, Ambedkar rested his case with a conviction that the much sought-after *Swaraj* would be only possible if the Hindu people could defend it by uniting with all religions. He held that only a casteless society could accomplish it.

BOX 4.3
Annihilation of Caste

Caste is not a physical object like a wall of bricks or as like a barbed wire which prevents the Hindus from co-mingling and which has, therefore, to be pulled down. Caste is a notion, it is a state of the mind. The destruction of Caste does not therefore mean the destruction of a physical barrier. It means a notional change. (Ambedkar 2000, 59)

4.2.4. Debate with Gandhi

Caste system is a pernicious system, it dehumanizes the Indian society. Instead of touting about harmony of the social organization, it actually divides people in the most inegalitarian way. As a theoretical crusader against this caste practice, Ambedkar had to engage with Gandhi's ideas on the caste question. Both Gandhi and Ambedkar were concurrent politico-intellectual figures who contested untouchability. Gandhi, as an insider to the Hindu system, advocated a reform of the practices while acknowledging the *varnashramic* arrangement as potentially harmonious for the society. In the true spirit of a reformer, Gandhi through his life practices defied and broke all the dehumanizing practices of the caste system; however, he did not challenge the structure of the *Sanatan dharma.*

Through penance, self-suffering and moral awakening, one cannot do away with untouchability; as long as the caste system survives, no emancipation of the 'outcastes' is possible. Ambedkar contradicted Gandhi on this point and forwarded a scathing criticism of any attempt to integrate the 'untouchable' with the Hindu caste system. In a bitter critic of Gandhi's campaign against untouchability, Ambedkar wrote 'What Congress and Gandhi Have Done to the Untouchables' (1945).

> What hope can Gandhism offer to the Untouchables? To the Untouchables Hinduism is a veritable chamber of horrors. The sanctity and the infallibility of the Vedas, Smritis and Shastras, the iron law of caste, the heartless law of Karma and the senseless law of status by birth are to the Untouchables veritable instruments of torture which Hinduism has forged against the Untouchables. (Ambedkar [1945] 2014, 296–297)

Ambedkar was very clear that the Hindus observed caste as long as they were religious. It was the *shastras* that taught and imparted the religion of caste. So no amount of reform or self-awakening could conclusively deal with the issue. The lofty ideals of holding inter-caste dinners and celebrating inter-caste marriage were just sugar coating of a bitter reality and at best tokenism. The real remedy is to overthrow and denounce the sanctity of the *shastras*.

After the publication of *Annihilation of Caste*, quite expectedly Gandhi was outraged by Ambedkar's vitriolic attack on the Hindu religion. Gandhi took it up as a challenge to Hinduism. In 1936 only, he published his observations in the journal *Harijan*. Considering Ambedkar as one belonging to the Hindu fold, Gandhi argued that his selection of texts and interpretations were inappropriate. Defending the *varnashrama* system, Gandhi opined that *varna* and *ashrama* were institutions which had nothing to do with castes. He emphasized the divine calling of *varna* division. He found that every calling carried equal merit before God. Strongly, he asserted that the law of *varna* never professed untouchability (Gandhi 1936a). He indicated that Ambedkar chose the wrong interpretations of the religion to arrive at faulty understandings.

Gandhi even took exception to the note of Sant Ramji of the Jat-Pat-Todak Mandal, who invited Ambedkar for the conference. Sant Ramji, representing the reformist strand of the Hindu religion, did not subscribe to Ambedkar's radical position to quit Hinduism. Nevertheless, he endorsed Ambedkar's position that for all practical purpose, caste and *varna* are one and the same in the Hindu society. He too found Gandhi's support of the *varnavyavastha* as an ideal which is utopic and imaginary. Gandhi straightaway argued that by questioning the *shastras*, the Mandal too ceased to be Hindus (Gandhi 1936b).

Ambedkar replied to Gandhi's argument by questioning whether he had progressed from his earlier position of being a true blue-blooded *Sanatani* Hindu by suggesting the difference between *varna* and caste. Contrary to the Vedic conception of *varna* as the pursuit of one's calling governed by one's natural aptitude or choice, Gandhi understood *varna* as the ancestral calling irrespective of natural aptitude or choice. So *varna* appeared to be just a different name for caste for Gandhi, according to Ambedkar. Clearly, he repudiated the thesis of stability and harmony as floated by Gandhi in defence of the social organization sustained by the *varnavyavastha*. He acknowledged stability but not at the cost of equity and fluidity of the system. With regards to the accusation that only the worst representations of the Hindu *shastra* were picked up and indicated by him, Ambedkar had a cryptic response to it. Why were the worst examples so numerous and prevail upon the life practices of the Hindus all the while? He accused Gandhi of attempting to make the Hindu society tolerable without making any fundamental change to its central structure, so that it could perpetuate itself (Ambedkar [1945] 2014, 83–96).

It is apparent that Gandhi and Ambedkar were representing two world views epistemologically separate. Gandhi was profound in his critical examination of the modernist paradigm and Western mode of thought. As an insider to the Hindu society, he attempted to negotiate with it in a unique way through personal life practices. His crusade against untouchability had layers of meanings to debunk it while remaining within the Hindu religious fold. On the other hand, Ambedkar was fired by his exposure to Western academic ambience of liberal and modernist values. More importantly, he looked at the caste system as a victim of it. Evidently, he was passionate in his critical scholarship on the caste-divided Indian society.

CONCLUSION

One can find an important set of contrasting views on the Indian society in the Gandhi vis-à-vis Ambedkar discourse. Counterposing the ideas of Gandhi and Ambedkar, of late, has attracted attention from scholars researching on the modern Indian society. Especially, with the assertion of Dalit and Bahujan in Indian polity and social thought, the vision of Ambedkar has been retrieved to critically assess Gandhi's imagination of new India. The conflicting worldviews of the two are important inputs for Indian sociology for fresh researches on the emancipatory potential of ideas and thoughts.

From Mahatma Gandhi's two fundamental texts *Hind Swaraj* and *An Autobiography*, as well as from his pieces in the journal *Harijan* (*Young India*, renamed), we arrive at his understanding of the Indian society. We limit our scope mainly to Gandhi's exposition on the question of self-rule and amelioration of the caste-divided Hindu society. He tried to seek strength and guidance from the great civilizational depth of the Indian tradition. As a thorough critic of Western modernity, he built his visions for *Swaraj*. Freedom, he thought, has to be holistic in nature, so it was imperative to debunk the parameters of thought given by the West. Indigenous thinking and an alternative paradigm of development could only ensure self-rule in the real sense. On the question of fighting the degrading practice of untouchability, he spiritualized the exercise to do away with it in a non-conflicting harmonious model without a total rejection of the Hindu religious ideas. His model of refutation was full of critical bents that possibly were conditioned by his astute political strategies and actions.

Ideas of Babasaheb Ambedkar, as available from his selected writings and speeches and his most provocative and controversial pamphlet/booklet, *Annihilation of Caste*, show his unflinching faith in the modern liberal philosophy. Exclusive for Ambedkar are the tools of reason and rationality. As a social science researcher, Ambedkar analysed the Hindu *Puranic* texts to demystify the Hindu social order. The infallibility of the divine order that endorses the most disdainful practice of untouchability was his primary target. He questioned the *shastras* and argued that staying within the Hindu fold, one cannot undo the evil practices. His scholarly as well as polemical writings powerfully put up a case against the Gandhian method of countering untouchability. Also, he was sceptical of any meaningful self-rule for India; freedom has to be preceded by a social reform that fosters fraternity. These questions continue to have relevance in the contemporary times.

Points for Classroom Discussion

- India as envisioned by Gandhi
- Gandhi as a critic of Western modernity
- Ambedkar's critic of the Hindu *shastra*
- Contrasting views of Gandhi and Ambedkar on fighting untouchability

GLOSSARY

Endogamy: An upper-caste practice, also called in-marriage, is the custom of marrying within one's own social group, be it caste, ethnic community and so on.
Self-governance: It is self-rule, meaning control of the government of a state, community or other body by its own members.
Swadeshi: A Gandhian concept of insisting a practice of home-made products.
Varnavyavastha: The textual fourfold division of the Hindu society in terms of four fundamental *varnas*, each assigned with a particular calling.
Village republics: A Gandhian idea of village as a complete republic, independent of its neighbours for its own vital wants.

REFERENCES

Ambedkar, B. R. [1945] 2014. 'What Congress and Gandhi Have Done to the Untouchables'. In *Dr. Babasaheb Ambedkar Writings and Speeches (BAWS)*, edited by Vasant Moon, Vol. 9, 296–297. Bombay: The Education Department of Maharashtra.
———. 2000. *Annihilation of Caste*. New Delhi: Bluemoon Books.
———. 2014a. 'Waiting for a Visa'. In *Dr. Babasaheb Ambedkar Writings and Speeches (BAWS)*, edited by Vasant Moon, Vol. 12, pt. V. Bombay: The Education Department of Maharashtra.
———. 2014b. *Dr. Babasaheb Ambedkar Writings and Speeches (BAWS)*, Vol. 1. Bombay: The Education Department of Maharashtra.
———. 2014c. *Dr. Babasaheb Ambedkar Writings and Speeches (BAWS)*, Vol. 7. Bombay: The Education Department of Maharashtra.
———. 2018. *Ambedkar: An Overview*, with an introduction by A. Kundu. New Delhi: Rupa.
Gandhi, M. K. [1927] 1983. *An Autobiography: The Story of My Experiments with Truth*. Ahmedabad: Navajivan Publishing House.
———. 1933, February 11. *Harijan*.
———. 1934, February 2. *Harijan*.
———. 1936a, July 18. *Harijan*.
———. 1936b, August 15. *Harijan*.
———. 1938. *Hind Swaraj or Indian Home Rule*. Ahmedabad: Navajivan Publishing House.
Jefrrelot, C. 2005. *Dr. Ambedkar and Untouchability: Analyzing and Fighting Caste*. New Delhi: Orient BlackSwan.
Murti, V. V. Ramana, ed. *Gandhi: Essential Writings*. Delhi: Gandhi Peace Foundation.
Nandy, A. 1984. 'Cultural Frames for Social Intervention: A Personal Credo'. *Indian Philosophical Quarterly* XI, no. 4.
Parel, A. J. 2006. *Gandhi's Philosophy and the Quest for Harmony*. Cambridge: Cambridge University Press.
Unnithan, T. K. N. 1965. 'Gandhi's Views on Caste and the Untouchables'. In *Gandhi: Maker of Modern India?*, edited by M. D. Lewis. Boston, London: D.C. Heath and Co.

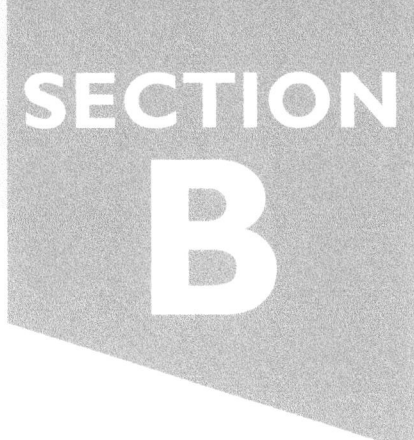

SECTION B

SOCIAL STRUCTURE AND SOCIAL INSTITUTIONS

Chapter 5
Castes and Classes in Modern India

Chapter 6
Religion and Tribes in India: Questions of Identity

Chapter 7
Family, Marriage and Kinship: Changing Contours

CHAPTER 5

Castes and Classes in Modern India

LEARNING OUTCOMES

- To facilitate the understanding of social structures and institutions in India
- To highlight various approaches in the study of caste and class
- To explore how variables of caste and class operate in modern India
- To examine agrarian classes in India
- To identify the composition and development of the class in industrial–urban society

Keywords: Social structure, social stratification, caste, class, middle class, professionals

Structures can be analysed as rules and resources, which can be treated as 'sets' in so far as transformations and mediations can be identified between the reproduced properties of social systems.

—**Giddens**

Caste system is such an obtrusive factor of Indian social organization that since the time of Megasthenes it has never failed to attract the attention of the foreigner –be he traveller, administrator, or student of Sanskrit literature.

—**G. S. Ghurye**

A class situation is one in which there is a shared typical probability of procuring goods, gaining a position in life, and finding inner satisfaction.

—**Weber**

INTRODUCTION

Social structure is one of the quintessential concepts in the discipline of sociology. The term 'social structure' implies patterns which are relatively immovable in social relations. A critical evaluation of social structure is essential pertaining to their appropriateness in various societies. In India, the social structure is characterized by unique social institutions of the caste system; this institution also stratifies society.

The following chapter grapples with the notion of social structure and how social structures of caste and class are established and operate in modern India. But first, it is important to explicate the concept of social structure. The word 'caste' is derived from the Portuguese word 'casta' meaning breed or race. The caste is a structure of social stratification in Indian society. Across India, castes and subcastes are referred to as *jati*, which derives its roots from Indo–Aryan concept meaning category of people related through the same physical and moral structure. The caste system is based on the *varna* model, that suggests that the society is divided into four *varnas*: Brahman, Kshatriya, Vaishya and Shudra. There was also a certain section of society which was considered outside of this *varna* model, referred to as untouchables, also known as the Dalits. They were considered permanently and hereditarily defiled. This *varna vyavastha* (arrangement) is based on Hinduism's divine decree that intends to organize society on the basis of occupation, which is mutually connected through structured inequality. Social stratification implies how individuals are positioned in different social categories. According to Gupta (1991), this stratification can take two forms; the first is based on a ranked scale, inequality; the second kind of social ordering is not about ranking or inequality. In the latter, people are separated on conception of differences. See Box 5.1 for better understanding.

BOX 5.1

Hierarchy and Difference

When inequality is the foundation of stratification in any society, it leads to hierarchy, whereas differences often create equal and horizontal groups. In a hierarchical system, there exists inequalities of income, status or rank, power and so on. For instance, in the hierarchy of wealth or income, there are rich and poor and many in between. In a power hierarchy, there are some at the top who wield most of the power, while people at the lower levels exercise lesser or no power at all. In social differentiation, the differences cannot be ranked in order; linguistic differences can be used as an example.

> There is a continuous intersection of hierarchy and difference; it becomes one of the reason for sociology to undertake a systematic study of the social stratification in society. However, it is pertinent to mention here that there are a few societies that are not stratified in one way or the other. The study of social stratification in society is useful not only to discuss the strata and order but also to direct analytical comprehension towards social mobility and social change; it tells us about social stasis and social dynamics.
>
> Social mobility is a recognized approach in an open system of stratification, whereas it is proscribed in a closed system of stratification. In a closed system of stratification, ascribed attributes are central, such as those of caste and race. The notion of hierarchy is central to the caste system. Dumont's *Homo Hierarchicus* is one of the most stimulating works published on the caste system; nonetheless, it reeks of colonial and Brahmanical legitimacy.

Although both caste and class are a status group (a collection of individuals who share a typical style of life and a certain consciousness). But caste is ascriptive, regulated by religious rituals and observance, and class is achieved status defined in terms of relations of productions. Class systems are fluid with less clear-cut boundaries, with no restrictions on marriage between people from different classes. There are arguably a few concepts, which are more contested in sociological theory than the concept of class.

5.1. SOCIAL STRUCTURE

5.1.1. Conceptualizing Social Structure

Spencer ([1873] 1896) attempted to explain social structure by juxtaposing it with living organisms. He believed in the functional necessity of social structures in society. Merton (1938) believed social structures to be the source of pressure; there were two elements of social and cultural structure to which he gave prominence. The first one was culturally defined goals, purpose and interests which are often integrated with aspiration with varying degrees of prestige and sentiments. The second important element of social structure is to regulate and control the acceptable modes of achieving these goals. Both these elements of cultural goals and institutional norms function collectively. Parsons (1961) stated that 'structures of social systems involves institutionalized patterns of normative culture.' Social roles are, thus, defined by certain norms that prescribe rules for behaviour. Every sociologist, however, conceptualizes social structure differently leading to varied contesting approaches.

Porpora (1989) conceptualizes 'four dominant approaches towards understanding social structure'. These views are as follows:

1. **Patterns of aggregate behaviour that are stable over time:** This view was associated with Homans and Collins; according to Homans (1975, 53)

'structure seems to refer first to those aspects of social behaviour that the investigator considers relatively enduring or persistent.' Collins (1981) defines social structure as 'micro-repetition in the physical world.' Under this view, the structure is defined in behavioural terms where it is perceived as a behaviour that is stable or repeated.
2. **Lawlike regularities that govern the behaviour of social facts:** This perception is associated with Durkheim and structural school, according to which, social facts are related to each other by an arrangement of lawlike uniformities which collectively constitute the social structure. The task of the sociologist is to identify these uniformities or regularities through empirical observation and describe the social structure accordingly. It allows for a quantitative and positivist approach.
3. **Systems of human relationships among social positions:** The aforementioned view is associated with Marxian tradition. The systems, here, are referred to as modes of production while social positions are class positions. These relationships between humans are characterized by domination, exploitation and competition. Not only economic modes of production, but also patriarchy, racial exclusion, caste hierarchies can also be integrated as systems of relationships among social positions.
4. **Collective rules and resources that structure behaviour:** This conception of social structure as rules and resources is associated with Anthony Giddens. Giddens believed patterns of relationship do not themselves constitute a social structure, but structure comprises of rules and resources associated with those relationships.

5.2. CASTE

5.2.1. Institution of Caste System

Caste is prevalent across the country but is operationalized through *jati*. These *jatis* do not operate on the popular models; instead, the customs and practices around the ordering of *jatis* vary from region to region. The most accepted reason for the persistence of the caste system is a religious sanction, based on ancient texts—the Rig Veda and Manusmriti. Dalits have sought to escape from the inhuman practices of untouchability by migrating to cities for economic and social freedom. However, individuals and families which converted to other religions, such as Christianity and Islam, continue to keep certain of their caste attributes even though their new religions did not have notions of caste (Searle-Chatterjee and Sharma 1994).

The following encompasses various attributes of the caste system in India:

1. **Ascription:** Caste of a person is determined by birth; it is a lifelong membership, revoked only under certain violations by other caste members.
2. **Occupational gradation:** Members of each caste mostly follow the certain pre-decided occupation, and restrictions were imposed on what could not be performed by certain caste.

3. **Purity and pollution:** The occupations were ranked on the degree of purity associated with each kind of occupation. Brahmans who performed religious rituals and teaching enjoyed higher status than other skilled workers from other castes.
4. **Hierarchy:** The hierarchy was based on occupation and other life patterns complying to the scale of purity and pollution.
5. **Commensality:** The restrictions are placed around eating and drinking with members of the other castes, based on their ranking in the caste order.
6. **Endogamy:** Marriage is also restricted within their own caste; however, marriage within the same *gotra* (subcaste) is prohibited.

5.2.2. Analytical Models

5.2.2.1. Caste and Race

Further, G. S. Ghurye (1969) attempted to sociologically study the origin and characteristic of the caste system on the basis of an ancient text. He borrowed from the works of Denzil Ibbetson and J. C. Nesfield; they explained the caste system to be occupational in origin, which gradually was organized into guilds and slowly stratified into castes. Ghurye's work on Indian caste is deeply influenced by Herbert Risley's work. Risley (1891) employed anthropometric data to analyse Indian provinces as a part of the ethnographic survey. Also in Sanskrit texts, there have been mention of the caste-like institution; Ghurye's understanding of Sanskrit enabled him to focus on much deeper roots.

According to Ghurye (1969), Aryans poured into India through the north–west around 2000 BC. Caste, thus, emerged due to the Indo–Aryan Brahmans to maintain their purity through endogamy and ritual restrictions. The classical writers developed concepts which were restricted by colonial understanding. Ghurye, with his Indological perspective, tried to explore the category of caste as an endogamous unit linked with the hierarchy of purity and pollution. He also believed caste to be the derivative of underlying racial differences, which were reassessed under ongoing intercultural interaction, assimilation and conflict. The caste groups were constantly changing as groups migrated and came in contact with others, creating complex structures. Ghurye highlighted the political cost of enumeration of caste in the Census of India; he condemned it as it promoted caste-based associations, leading to conflict and contestation. This understanding was later explored by Dumont (1970) for 'substantialization' of caste identities under modernity.

5.2.2.2. Dumotian Perspective

Dumont's approach was to explore the principle of hierarchy as the reason for underlying coherence of the caste system through Hindu rationale. Dumont constructed two opposing categories of purity and pollution to be the central principle of the caste hierarchy. Further, his structural analysis of caste system focused on the interrelationship between different castes. Dumont (1980) was critical of anthropologists who focused on the singular aspect of the caste system (*jajmani* system, food restrictions) and failed to address the inter-caste relations in totality. He stated 'the Indian caste system is not individualistic; it emphasizes its totality, not its individual members' (Dumont 1980). The hierarchy was based on religious sanctions for him; in *varna* model, the superiority of 'Brahmans' over Kshatriya is due to their monopoly over the knowledge of scriptures and control over offerings during the sacrifices. Brahman and Kshatriya are interdependent, their relationship is regulated through the *jajmani* system. Dumont (1980) also borrowed from Dharmaśāstra, the three goals for individual to lead life: *dharma* (duty), *artha* (profit) and *kama* (pleasure). These notions were used to further corroborate the rationale behind the order of castes.

Dumont insisted on a universalistic encompassing value system of caste that marks the Indian society. Relying much on Indological sources and de facto succumbing to an orientalist perspective Dumont underscored an inherent unequal nature of Indian society and a continuance of the caste system. Dumont was criticized as he failed to recognize the dynamism and social change in the caste system. Berreman (1999) argued that Dumont was heavily influenced by Brahmans and their version of religious texts, idealizing the caste system.

5.2.2.3. Caste System Upside Down

In the late 1960s and early 1970s, Joan Mencher worked among *Harijans* (the ex-untouchables) on the relationship between agriculture and social structure in Chinglepet district of Tamil Nadu and a part comparative study of socio-economic development structure of Madras and Kerala (Mencher 1991). Along with her field data, Mencher used historical materials to show the function of the caste system in preventing the formation of material bases for class contradiction. Such a reading of caste is made possible by altering the point of view of analysing Indian social structure. She looks at it from the point of view of those who are placed at the bottom of the hierarchical system. Like any other system of stratification in the world, caste functions as a very effective system of exploitation, concealing a harsh material reality with an ideational value system. That is why the original title of her paper, published by *Current Anthropology* in 1974 by the University of Chicago Press stands as 'The Caste System Upside Down, or the Not-So-Mysterious East'.

Mencher critiqued the view of the caste system as providing stability and functional 'security' to the Indian society in terms of specialized occupation and division of labour. It is only the higher caste and those who are in the middle ranges who would fit into the specialized occupation as per the traditional *varna* division of labour. They constitute a meagre percentage of the total population. The life of the vast low castes in agricultural labour is left unexplained. Instead, the top–down view of the privileged castes promotes the notion of *dharma* and *karma* (duty and fate). This is imbibed by the vulnerable low castes who succumb to their low ranks and accept the degradation.

The diversity of *jatis* and sub-*jatis* across the country engaged in diverse 'demeaning' labour is sustained by the top–down Brahmanical view of the caste. The field study method of Mencher revealed that the acceptance of the traditional order by the 'untouchables' in most cases is a surface reality. It is an overt compliance on the face of upper castes material dominance in village life, but covertly, they all distaste the degradation and are rebellious. Also, the 'untouchables' are the victims of political manipulations by the dominant castes who not only monopolize the economic and political power but also cleverly divide the poor on caste lines. However, there are signs of social change whenever the 'untouchables' have got exposure and education, having good numerical strength, to challenge the system.

> The caste system has functioned to prevent the formation of social classes with commonality of interests or purpose. In other words, caste derives its viability from its partial masking of extreme socio-economic differences. One of the most serious distortions in understanding the Indian society has been the overriding importance given to the concept of caste. (Mencher 1991, 108)

Dumont had projected a single hierarchy based on purity and pollution, whereas Dipankar Gupta (2000) challenges this; the purity and impurity are social constructions founded on the existing reality of the rural conditions. This is determined by the existing relations of production and property. The disagreements over the hierarchy were due to two reasons. First, the relationships between castes were played out within the confines of the closed natural economy of the village, which left no scope for manoeuvre for the subaltern communities and castes. Second, during pre-colonial times, caste hierarchies were contested and renegotiated intermittently through discourses or major social upheaval. But such instances were rare which created a misconception that castes have never competed and have been politically inactive.

Gupta's (2000) emphasis on the significance of production and property in caste structure ascertains that the *jati* system is dependent on a closed, localized natural economy. In order for a caste to survive as a system, a feudal-like social structure is of utmost importance. The study of caste and politics can be analytically justified only when we accept that castes are essentially discrete entities with ideological legacy. As they are a discrete phenomenon, it is empirically true that there should be multiple hierarchies as each caste always overvalues itself. The element of caste competition is, therefore, a characteristic of the caste order and not a later addition (Gupta 2000). Thus, the caste system could sustain because it was enforced by power and not ideological compliance.

But, according to Jodhka (2015), there have been several changes that have been observed in the institution of caste during the last few decades. These changes are reflective of various efforts, which are as follows:

1. From 'below', through the social movements of those who have been at the receiving end of the traditional hierarchies'
2. From 'above', courtesy constitutional safeguards and other state policies
3. From the 'side', due to the wide-ranging developments of social and economic change, for example, the agrarian transformation or the development of industry and urbanization

Some of these changes have been radical; the traditional understanding of caste as a closed system of stratification cease to exist in many parts of rural India. There is a change in the way the lower castes construct their self-image due to their social and political experiences. Gupta (2004) notes that a lower caste now refuses to accept its own status as polluting and is willing to label other lower castes as polluting. Doing this, a lower caste, unconsciously, end up endorsing the Brahmanical notion of pollution and purity as elemental to caste hierarchy, even when they reject its application to their caste.

Jodhka (2004), through his study, witnessed that the lower castes have started asserting their equal rights over the 'common' village resources, which were earlier contentious on the basis of purity and impurity. These assertions, however, are not entertained by the dominant castes, resulting in a social boycott of the lower castes and often violence. Such occurrences reinforce the point that caste, indeed, works to block those located at the lower strata of the hierarchy (Thorat 2007). The social mobility scenario in India presents a case of 'continuity rather than change' (Kumar et al. 2002). Much of the mobility is horizontal in nature, from the occupational agrarian occupation to insecure informal economic structure. Also, despite the extent of democratic reach, the traditional structures and values continue to be closed in many situations as caste continues to be a critical aspect in which inequalities are created and reproduced.

5.3. STRUCTURAL CHANGES

5.3.1 Changes in the Caste System

Srinivas' works were mostly ideographic, and while examining his work, there should be no confusion between nomothetic and ideographic. The ideographic model describes a variety of factors which affect a phenomenon, whereas the nomothetic model provides a maximum number of explanations with a minimum number of causal variables, and it also aims to uncover the general pattern of cause and effect. Srinivas, as an empiricist, advocated 'field view' of society as compared to 'book view'. Srinivas gives a view of the qualitative changes taking place in Indian society. His concept of Sanskritization which was seminal to the description of caste as a sociocultural phenomenon is discussed, in detail, in the forthcoming chapter.

In rural India, hierarchy is not only associated with caste, but it is also governed by ownership of land. Srinivas's concept of dominant caste is believed to be influenced by dominant lineage. This dominant caste wields economic and political power, has a high rank in the caste hierarchy and possesses a strong numerical strength. Srinivas (1992) argued that caste and other collective identities were sharpening across the country, compounded by the competition for access to limited resources. To acquire access, the numerical strength, wealth, education and political influence are relevant. Castes and other groups in India have been undergoing structural changes over hundreds of years. Constitutional changes of protective discrimination and abolition of untouchability facilitated an inclusive approach in a vertically stratified society. Further, a lower level of protection which is accorded to OBC (other backward classes) comprising a certain socially, educationally and economically backward castes, identified by each state government. The list varies from state to state and is a heterogeneous category. The concessions and other benefits attached to backwardness are valued so much that castes vie with each other to be classified as backward.

Secularization is spreading to new sections; this spread is aided by mass media and by secular processes as the increased popularity of education and greater social and spatial mobility. The unit of endogamy has widened in villages; this widening is, however, around the traditional line. Further, the *jajmani* system which earlier governed the inter-caste ties is becoming weaker due to decline in Brahmanical supremacy because of the aforementioned reasons. Also, with the emerging popularity of egalitarian ideology, the caste system is no more perpetuating values essential to Hinduism.

5.3.2. Caste in Rural and Urban India

Marriott (1976), through his work on Kishan Garhi, explained the ethnic segmentation of caste within the village where there was a tendency among the local caste groups to separate their residential houses spatially from those of other caste groups as far as possible and to consolidate their areas of residence. There was a desire to live in close proximity with their caste members that entailed better information regarding their neighbouring caste mates. Gough (1960) expands that Brahmans show a high degree of internal interaction and external exclusiveness. Kin members invite each other for social and religious ceremonies. Children are socialized within the street and, until the age of five, do not mingle with those of other castes.

Similarly, castes are employed to organize the urban residential patterns and manage segregation on the basis of caste. The macro-level data on population distribution in urban areas in India indicates that scheduled castes (SCs) tend to be concentrated in certain parts of the city (Singh and Vithayathil 2012). Also, Deshpande (2011) in his comprehensive analyses of economic discrimination experienced by Dalits in recent times, highlights that caste discrimination cuts across all levels of employment, from the unskilled labour to graduates from elite institutions.

Singh and Vithayathil (2012), while analysing 2001 census data around residential patterns across cities of Mumbai, Delhi, Kolkata, Chennai, Bangalore, Ahmedabad and Hyderabad, identified prevalent and persisting inequalities which have become individualized continue to be social and cultural. The old system of the hierarchy may have disintegrated, but a new hierarchy of networks based on the institutions of caste and kinship appears to be thriving. Such hierarchies work through control over social and cultural capital and facilitate the reproduction of caste. The discrimination and biases become more profound when old hierarchies collapse and social groups are competing for scarce resources.

5.3.3. Caste and Politics

Caste and politics have been a recurring theme in anthropological studies in India (Srinivas 1962). During the 1980s and 1990s, two significant trends that emerged were increased in Hindu nationalism and political mobilization of lower castes (Yadav 1997). The traditional institution of caste served as a medium of modern function, after Independence, the local 'dominant castes' transformed the *jajmani* (patron–client) relations into a vote bank through 'vertical mobilisation' (Rudolph and Rudolph 1967). This promoted political parties to bring together coalitions of upper and lower castes.

Bailey (1969), while studying Bisipara village, identified three characteristic conflicts: factions, caste-climbing and conflict between castes. Factions in Oriya are called doladoli, in Bisipara; two dolo were formed around two warrior caste to dominate over the limited village resources. Factionalism can be understood as a product of rapid social change and socio-political adjustment of dynamic equilibrium.

In current times, political parties tend to mobilize support from members of their caste/communities. Caste politicization is reflected when the selection of a candidate for a constituency is based on whether he/she will be able to get the support of a particular caste or castes. Gupta (2000) explained the 'limits of caste arithmetic' and what he refers to as 'the presumption of numbers'. He was also against the assumption that political success in India depends on the caste composition of the individual constituencies. Rather, the organizational ability of a caste is more important than their numbers. Ruud (2005) highlighted the importance of the role of a politician as the link between the state and the society. But Brass (1980) and Fuller and Harris (2000), through their respective works in Uttar Pradesh, remark around that how politicians are a link between criminality/corruption, the police and society. Now, certain criminal attributes are considered to be desirable in a political leader; democratic ideas and practices are reinterpreted through vernacular politics.

5.3.4. Caste and Women

In recent years, literature related to gender and feminist discourse in India has brought considerable insight into the problems of women in India. The interface between caste, patriarchy and gender is a theme that needs a thorough theoretical and empirical study for the purpose of understanding the nature and causes of the caste and gender exploitation of women and especially Dalit women. Betielle (1996) argues that the burden of caste may weigh more heavily on the lower than on the upper-caste person. In some parts of rural India, social status, access to education and other basic necessities are regulated by an individual's caste membership.

National Crime Records Bureau reveals that Dalit women face targeted violence by the state actors and other powerful members of the dominant castes. Whereas women from the upper castes do not face as much sexual assault as women from the lower caste do, but male members of the same caste enjoy better living conditions and access to opportunities. Dalit women, due to their structural position, are accorded statuses such as *devadasi* (woman dedicated to God), *dai* (midwife) and *dayan* (witch).

Omvedt (1994), through his work, explored that Dalit girls were dedicated to the goddess Yellamma/Renuka. They were married to the god and were considered accessible to any men but, at the same time, were not polluted by sexual relations. These girls were among *Mahars, Matangi* among the *Madigas* and *Basavi*; this practice led to the institutionalization of sexual accessibility of the Dalit women for higher-caste men, whereas Vijayshree (2004) explains that this prevalence of the *devadasi* custom among Telegu-speaking areas was considered outcaste sacred prostitutes. Bhriggs (1920) also discussed the vulnerable condition of Dalit women among the *Chamars* community of North-India. The landlords often take liberties with the *chamar's* wife in lieu of his payments to *Chamar's* services.

But as Rege (2006) rightly states that the women's movement has often rendered Dalit women's narratives of struggle as not being feminist enough because of what is perceived as prioritization of a community over women's issues. She also pointed out that the writings and manifestoes of various Dalit women's groups had lamented how the feminism in India is influenced by the Brahmanical theory and praxis.

5.4. CLASS

5.4.1. Marxian and Weberian Perspective

According to Marx, wage labourers, capitalists and landowners constitute the three big classes of modern society based upon the capitalist mode of production. However, even physicians and officials constitute two more classes belonging to the two distinct social groups. This conception leads to a perception that there prevail multiple fragmentations of interest and rank into which division of social labour diverges. However, Marx's conceptualization of exploitation endorses a fundamentally polarized conception of class relations in capitalist societies, the bourgeoisie and the proletariat.

Class, in other words, signifies members of a category who share common life chances. Weber (1978) recommends that, empirically, four major categories of social class can be recognized under capitalism, in which social mobility is difficult but within which it is relatively common. These classes are the 'dominant entrepreneurial and propertied groups,' which include the petty bourgeoisie whose only asset is their labour. Also, whether or not, members of a class display 'class consciousness,' which depends on certain contingent factors; it is 'linked to general cultural conditions … and especially linked to the transparency of the connections between the causes and the consequences of the class situation.'

He argued that class situation is ultimately the market situation, the kind of chance in the market is the decisive condition for an individual's fate. Weber also identified the significance of status and party (power). Status for him is the hierarchical system of cultural differentiation that identify particular persons, behaviour and lifestyles as superior or inferior. Weber identified class and social status as different bases for claims to material resources. Many sociologists insist on the analytical separation of the two concepts: class and social status; however, there are difficulties in separating them empirically. See Box 5.2.

BOX 5.2
Problem of Studying Class

Schumpeter (1951) stated that the class structure is the ranking of such individual families by their social value in accordance, with differing aptitudes. Class as per him is more than the mere aggregation of class members; a class is aware of its identity as a whole and redirects itself. The fundamental function of the class phenomenon is that it rests on the individual differences in aptitude. This difference in aptitude is not in the absolute sense but with respect to those functions which environment makes socially necessary. Schumpeter (1951) identifies the following four major sociological problems, which affected the field of class theory:

1. First is the problem of the 'nature of class' (which is different for each individual) and as a part of this problem, the function of class in the vital process of the social whole.
2. The problem of 'class cohesion' that makes every social class to live as an organism and prevent it from scattering.
3. The other problem is of 'class formation', displaying how a social class has never been homogenous and comprises of organic stratification.
4. Finally, the problems that are concerned with the 'concrete causes and conditions of an individual determined, historically given class structure.'

Wright (1979, 2010), while borrowing from Marx, trusts that the category of '"capitalists" is too general.' He suggests that the small business-class owners have their own means of production but have very little in common with large-scale industry owners. He also argues that class in modern capitalism cannot be defined through the Weberian concept based on the level of wealth, power and prestige. Small business-class families consist of people who are self-employed small business owners and craftspeople, who may hire other people as employees but largely look after their work. This category includes jewellers, grocery store owners and retail shop owners; however, a certain group of professionals also falls under this category, for instance, lawyers and doctors. It is important to understand that how people negotiate personal aspirations and claims to urban space, which is one means of deconstructing the urban experience, especially in relation to the rapid developments transforming the city. In order to understand how various social groups claim and are afforded space, it is useful to map socio-spatial exclusion and inclusion.

5.4.2. Agrarian Classes

The nature of land use and land control in Indian society is so diverse that any analysis of PAN-Indian class structure is difficult. Daniel Thorner in the early 1970s forwarded a popular scheme of the class structure of rural India. According to his model, the three fundamental divisions are the *malik*, kisan and *mazdoor*, that is, the proprietors, the working peasants and the labours (Thorner 1991).

The subgroups within the three principal classes are also indicated by Thorner. The following two subgroups constitute the class of maliks:

1. The large absentee landlords, having landholdings in more than one village
2. The smaller proprietor, who resides in the same village where he/she owns land and exercise management and control over cultivation Both groups employ rural labour and receive rural rent.

The kisans are the working peasants, who are small owners or tenants. Their legal and customary rights over land are much inferior to those of maliks. The two subgroups that constitute kisan are:

1. The small landowners whose landholding is just sufficient to support his/her family and one or more members of the family engage with cultivation activity
2. The substantial tenants who have tenurial rights over land whose size is usually above the sufficiency level

The *mazdoor* is agricultural labourers who earn their livelihood by working on other's lands. Some of the *mazdoor* class may have small land. The subgroups that constitute the mazdoor class are:

1. Poor tenants who have small holdings which are too small for family sufficiency
2. The sharecroppers who cultivate the land for others on a sharecropping basis, without any security
3. The huge mass of landless labour

D. N. Dhanagare subsequently qualified Thorner's model of Agrarian classes by elaborating the class divisions (Dhanagare 1991). Dhanagare makes an interesting observation that Thorner has used both the Marxian and the Weberian ideas to develop the *malik–kisan–mazdoor* rural class structure. Based on the relations of production and ownership of the means of production, the three principal classes are identified, but while explicating the subcategories, Thorner employs the Weberian concern of 'the kinds of rights and kinds of services' (i.e., the life opportunities) enjoyed by the members of a group. By taking a note of the internal differentiation within Indian agrarian society, Dhanagare reconfigured the original model of Thorner. He elaborated the threefold divisions into a fivefold one, and their subcategories are as follows:

- **Landlords:** They are the absentee owners/rentiers, having long tracts of land over several villages
- **Rich peasants:** They are the following:
  - Rich landowners, landholding confined to a residential village only
  - Rich tenants who have substantial holdings, have secured rights and pay a nominal rent to their landlords
- **Middle peasants:** They are the following:
  - Landowners of medium-size holdings, self-sufficient
  - Tenants having substantial holdings but pay higher rents to their landlords
- **Poor peasants:** They are the following:
  - Landholdings not sufficient to maintain a family and forced to rent others land
  - Tenants with small holdings but with some tenurial security
  - Tenants at will or sharecroppers
- **Landless labourers:** They are the ones who exclusively rest on selling their labour power agricultural work on other's land

These five categories and the subcategories are regionally specific. The distinction between the rich, middle and poor peasants are more qualitative in character. So a clear-cut class model cannot perfectly capture the agrarian classes in India. It is complicated by the very elements of traditional attributes of caste, religion and ethnic identities. There is a coexistence of agrarian classes and status groups of non-economic nature in a tradition-bound society like India. The non-economic sentiments and identities have created divisions and exploitation in rural India. This has not only hardened the structure of exploitation but also made a clear emergence of class interest more difficult.

5.4.3. The Labour Class and Industrial–Urban Set-up

With the coming of modern technology-based large-scale enterprises in post-colonial India, labour as a class is to be understood as associated primarily with industrial work. The shift from the agrarian–rural order to an industrial–urban one has changed the profile of labour in India though in terms of size the industrial workers constitute a small percentage of the total workforce. Also, of all the labour in the non-agrarian sector, industrial labour constitutes roughly one-fifth of it. According to Jan Breman, irrespective of its size, this industrial labour or labour in the formal sector is politically significant for the future and more advanced stage of Indian society. In the pre-liberalization context of India's planned socialist economy, it was anticipated that industrial employment would hold the key to any understanding of India's class structure as the employers, workers and the state would function in an orchestrated way to further their respective interests (Breman 1991).

Obviously, the industrial–urban complex attracted migration of labour from rural India. Although the agricultural labour growingly started joining industrial employment, the agricultural labour constituted the largest single component of the total labour force. The class of landless labourers in the countryside did not emerge as a breakdown of an earlier tranquil village community of peasants and artisans due to any alien rule. The impoverishment was significantly present in the early colonial times due to degrading labour arrangement fostered by caste inequality. This impoverishment prompted many to shift from agriculture to industrial–urban set-up. So labour was not really 'free' as demanded by classical development of industrial capitalism. 'Free labour' in classical Marxian analysis means free not only from the ownership of the means of production but also to decide and sell their labour power. In effect, always, under-economic duress labour in industrial–urban complex fall prey to a different kind of bondage.

The early generations of the new industrial workforce could never sever their ties with their rural background and value system. In a way, this attachment affected workers' preference for 'self-employment' as against the unknown terrain of regularity, discipline and industrial commitment (Myers 1958). However, Breman poses an opposite argument that such lack of commitment from the side of the labour is more due to a lack of managerial policies and practices. Also, the lack of stable committed labour force is a function of permanency of employment. The numerous small and middle industries engage only seasonal labour. So the economic activity of the industry determines the nature and behaviour of labour, rather than any inbuilt habits of the Indian labour class. The simplistic conclusion about continuance of the traditional value system and institutions as affecting labour as a deterrent for the industrial way of life is quite problematic (Sheth 1968).

5.4.4. Indian Middle Class

Discourse on the middle class is gaining popularity in both public space and academia. It is believed that members of the middle class by merit of their educational and technical knowledge come to occupy positions that give them greater material and cultural advantages over other manual labours. However, D. P. Mukherji (1945) believed that the Indian middle class is unique with its historical antecedents and must be explored through their interaction with both tradition and modernity.

Mishra (1968) formulated the exhaustive categories of rising middle-class people according to the role played by them in the new economy, which are as follows: (a) the commercial middle-class middlemen and brokers, (b) the moneylenders, the brokers, the banias, the agents and the creditors, (c) the industrial middle class and (d) the educated middle class comprised of a class of professionals. He also argues that the primary characteristic of the four groups forming the Indian middle classes was that they acquired prestige not through social status but with education, wealth and power. Correspondingly, Nita Mathur (2007) also argues that though it is accepted that 'the middle class' is not a homogeneous group, in this specific context, the term applies to a consolidated group of people who accentuate their shared distinctiveness in relation to the upper class(es), other middle class and several categories of lower-middle classes, which are all heterogeneous category within. Sociologists denote the term 'petty bourgeoisie' to someone that owns some property and is hierarchically positioned amongst the working class and capitalists, but now, they are categorized as the 'old middle class'. The old middle class is defined in terms of their associations with production; this category also includes traders and professionals who, regardless of having businesses, work in conjunction with their employees. This old middle class is often juxtaposed with the new middle class, which is an educated and often formally well-qualified group of people, usually engaged in professional and other technical forms of employment. Béteille (2003) maintains that this new middle class gives more weightage to the occupation, acquiring quality education and salaried income through employment rather than property ownership. This 'new middle class' is primarily constituted of educated people from all kinds of castes, working in offices, occupying managerial and the so-called white-collar positions.

CONCLUSION

Social structures of caste and class demonstrate persisting inequalities in society. Patterns of relationship do not themselves constitute the social structure, but structure comprises of rules and resources associated with those relationships. The traditional understanding of class divisions is continuously being modified in contemporary situations. Nonetheless, class divisions remain central to the economic inequalities in modern societies. Class and caste continue to exert influence on our lives. The category of youth, where middle-class identities are reinforced through different parameters, is very different from the rigid caste norms. Young people, today, are struggling to live up to their middle-class status. The concept of 'middle class' has illustrious derivations in the discipline of sociology, but still, it continues to remain a baffling and often ambiguous concept to determine. The notion of the middle class is often invoked to highlight the diversity of occupations, class, status situations and life chances that characterize its members.

It is their desire to maintain their status that shapes their consumption patterns and shapes the kind of labour they get engaged in which enables this consumption. Changes in the consumption pattern among the middle class have occurred due to rapidly increasing BPO sector which has given young people from the middle-class background disposable income, generating access to capital; thus, today most middle-class families have all of these TV, stereo, refrigerator, motorbike, scooter and so on. The middle-class youth employed in the BPO sector also have access to the bank loans, credit cards apart from the monthly salary (Nisbett 2007).

Points for Classroom Discussion

- A social structure is institutionalized configurations of normative culture
- The *varna* model is the underlying ideology of the caste hierarchy in India
- Is class an achieved status?
- Purity and pollution are underlying principles of hierarchy in the caste system of India
- Caste as concealing class configuration in India
- Models of agrarian class structure in India
- Class in industrial–urban set-up in India

GLOSSARY

Class: Like caste, it is ascriptive; regulated by religious rituals and observance, a class is the achieved status defined in terms of relations of productions.

Middle class: This class is primarily constituted of educated people from all kinds of castes, working in offices, occupying managerial and the so-called white-collar positions.

Social structure: It refers to the institutionalized patterns of normative culture which are relatively immovable in social relations.

***Varna* model:** It is a system of social stratification of caste structures under four categories Brahmans (priests, teachers, intellectuals), Kshatriyas (warriors, kings, administrators), Vaishyas (agriculturalists, traders, farmers) and Shudras (workers, labourers, artisans).

REFERENCES

Bailey, Frederick G. 1969. *Stratagems and Spoils: A Social Anthropology of Politics*. Oxford: Basil Blackwell.

Beteille, A. 1996. 'Caste in Contemporary India'. In *Caste Today*, edited by C. J. Fuller. New Delhi: Oxford University Press.

Brass, P. R. 1980. The Politicization of the Peasantry in a North Indian State'. *Journal of Peasant Studies,* July-Sept.
Briggs, G. W. 1920. *The Chamars*, republished in 1990. New Delhi: Low Price Publications.
Collins, R. 1981. 'On the Microfoundations of Macrosociology.' *American Journal of Sociology* 86, no. 5 (March): 984–1014.
Deshpande, A. 2011. *The Grammar of Caste: Economic Discrimination in Contemporary India.* New Delhi: Oxford University Press.
Dhanagare, D. N. 1991. 'The Model of Agrarian Classes in India.' In *Social Stratification*, edited by D. Gupta. New Delhi: Oxford University Press.
Dumont, L. 1970. *Homo Hierarchicus: The Caste System and its Implications.* London: Weidenfeld & Nicholson.
——— 1980. *Homo Hierarchicus: The Caste System and Its Implication.* Chicago, IL: University of Chicago Press.
Fuller, C. J., and J. Harriss. 2000. Introduction. In *The Everyday State and Society in India,* edited by C. J. Fuller and V. Bénéï. New Delhi: Social Science Press.
Ghurye, G. S. 1969. *Caste and Race in India.* New Delhi: Popular Prakashan.
Gupta, D., ed. 1991. *Social Stratification.* New Delhi: Oxford University Press.
———. 2000. *Interrogating Caste: Understanding Hierarchy and Difference in Indian Society.* New Delhi: Penguin.
———. 2004. *Caste in Question: Identity or Hierarchy?* New Delhi: SAGE Publications.
Jodhka S. S. 2004. 'Sikhism and the Caste Question: Dalits and Their Politics in Contemporary Punjab'. in Jodhka S.S and P. Louis (2003) 'Caste Tensions in Punjab: Talhan and Beyond' *Economic & Political Weekly,* 38, no. 28: 2923–2926.
——— 2015. *Caste in Contemporary India.* New Delhi: Routledge.
Homans, G. C. 1975. 'What Do We Mean by Social "Structure"?' In *Approaches to the Study of Social Structure,* edited by P. Blau. New York, NY: The Free Press.
Kumar, S., A. Heath, and O. Heath. 2002. 'Changing Patterns of Social Mobility: Some Trends Over Time.' *Economic & Political Weekly* 37, 40: 4091–4096.
Marriott, M. 1976. 'Hindu Transactions: Diversity without Dualism'. In *Transaction and Meaning: Direction In the Anthropology of Exchange and Symbolic Behaviour,* edited by Bruce Kapferer, 109–142. Philadelphia, PA: Institute for the Study of Human Issues.
Mencher, J. 1991. 'The Caste System Upside Down.' In *Social Stratification*, edited by D. Gupta, 93–109. New Delhi: Oxford University Press.
Merton, Robert. K. 1938. 'Social Structure and Anomie.' *American Sociological Review* 3, no. 5 (October): 672–682.
Myers, C. A. 1958. *Labour Problem in the Industrialization of India.* Cambridge, MA: Harvard University Press.
Omvedt, G. 1994. *Dalits and the Democratic Revolution: The Dalit Movement in Colonial India.* New Delhi: SAGE Publications.
Parsons, T. 1961. 'An Outline of the Social System.' In *Theories of Society*, edited by T. Parsons, E. A. Shils, K. D. Naegle, and J. R. Pitts, 30–79. New York, NY: The Free Press.
Porpora, D. 1989. 'Four Concepts of Social Structure.' *Journal for the Theory of Social Behaviour* 19, no. 2 (June): 195–211.
Rege, S. 1998. 'Dalit Women Talk Differently: A Critique of "Difference" and towards a Dalit Feminist Standpoint Position.' *Economic & Political Weekly* 33, no. 44 (October–November): 39–48.
Risley, H. H. 1891. *The Tribes and Castes of Bengal: Anthropometric Data*, (Vols 1 & 2). Calcutta: Bengal Secretariat Press.
Rudolph, L., and S. Rudolph. 1967. *The Modernity of Tradition: Political Development in India,* Chicago, IL: University of Chicago Press.
Ruud, Arild Engelsen. 2001. 'Talking Dirty about Politics: A View from a Bengali Village', in *The Everyday State and Society in Modern India,* edited by C. Fuller and V. Bénéi, 115–136. London: Hurst & Company.

Searle-Chatterjee, M., and Ursula Sharma (eds). 1994. *Contextualising Caste: Post-Dumontian Approaches*, Oxford: Blackwell.
Sheth, N. R. 1968. *The Social Framework of an Indian Factory.* Manchester: Manchester University Press.
Spencer, Herbert. (1873) 1896. *The Study of Sociology.* New York, NY: Appleton.
Singh, G., and T. Vithayathil 2021. 'Residential segregation in Indian cities: Spaces of Discrimination'. *Economic & Political Weekly* 47, no. 37: 60–66.
Srinivas, M. N. 1962. *Caste in Modern India and Other Essays.* New York: Asia Publishing House.
——— 1992. *Social Change in Modern India.* New Delhi: Orient Longman.
Thorat, S., and Attewell, P. 2007. 'The Legacy of Social Exclusion: A Correspondence Study of Job Discrimination In India'. *Economic & Political Weekly* 34, nos 5-6: 4141–4145.
Vijayashree, P. 2004. *Recasting the Devadasi: Patterns of Sacred Prostitution in Colonial South India.* New Delhi: Kanishka.
Weber, M. 1978. 'Economy and Society: An Outline of Interpretive Sociology'. Translated and edited by G. Roth, C. Wittich, E. Fischoff et al. Berkeley: University of California Press.
Yadav, Y. 1997. 'Reconfiguration in Indian Politics: State Assembly Elections 1993–1995'. In *State and Politics in India*, edited by P. Chatteijee. New Delhi: Oxford University Press.

CHAPTER 6

Religion and Tribes in India: Questions of Identity

LEARNING OUTCOMES

- To inquire the relevance of religion in the traditional and the contemporary society, the chapter will acquaint with different theories, approaches and concepts
- To underscore the ways in which different religions construct identity of their followers and highlight the linkages between society and religion
- To explore the tribal categories and their identities in India

Keywords: Hinduism, Islam, Sikhism, Christianity, secularism, tribal identity

A religion is a unified system of beliefs and practices relative to sacred things, that is to say, things set apart and forbidden, beliefs and practices which unite into one single moral community called a church, all those who adhere to them....

—**Emile Durkheim**

Love and the duties it imposes is the real lesion of the forest. Among very poor and exploited people, there was the need to maintain those imponderable values that give dignity to the life of man.... There was the need for reverence, reverence for all life.

—**Verrier Elwin**

INTRODUCTION

Religion has been a subject of study and expression for a very long time. However, the emergence of the sociology of religion as a branch has been a recent phenomenon in the history of the discipline. The oldest branch of study dedicated to religion is theology. Theological approaches have undergone a change in the present times, but theology, still, has major contrast when placed with the sociology of religion. There is a distinction between the normative and the empirical orientation between the theological and the sociological approaches to the study of religion. Theology is different from sociology in its orientation to the plurality of religions. A theologian writes about religion from within, whereas a sociologist approaches religion from the outside even when he/she seeks to understand its inner meaning.

The scheduled tribes (STs) constitute about 8.2 per cent of the total population in India (Census of India 2001). Tribes, though, have been integrated into the larger political and economic system, but complete integration is not achieved, as they inhabit areas of relative geographical and social isolation, and much of their problems are attributed to their isolation. However, there are provisions in the constitution to draw tribal people from their isolation and backwardness and integrate them into the larger society. They have the same rights and status as those conferred upon other members of Indian society through citizenship. A comparison between Census 2001 and 2011 shows that the proportion of cultivators reduced by more than 10 per cent, while the proportion of agricultural labourers increased by 9 per cent among the ST population. It is estimated that, in the last decade, about 3.5 million tribal people have left agriculture and agriculture-related activities to enter the informal labour market. Displacement and enforced migration have also led to an increasing number of indigenous people working as contract labourers in the construction industry and domestic workers in major cities.

The recent time has witnessed growth in the concerns for indigenous people across the world. However, over time, the concept of indigenous people has become synonymous with a sense of powerlessness, marginalization and a kind of social insecurity. This chapter explores the categories of religion and tribes in India and how each of them grapples with the construction of the identity of the individual in particular and society in general.

6.1. RELIGION IN INDIA

6.1.1. Concept of Religion

Durkheim studied primitive societies in order to understand the complexity of religion today. He believed that one cannot understand more advanced religions except by analysing the way they have been progressively constituted throughout history, for only by placing each of the constituent elements of modern religions in the context within which it emerged can we hope to discover the cause which gave rise to it. The simplicity of primitive religions helps us to understand its nature; it also helps us to understand its causes.

According to him, religion is more than the idea of gods or spirits and, consequently, cannot be defined exclusively in relation to these. Durkheim (1957) stated that when approaching the matter of defining religion from the study of its primitive forms, he claimed that the idea of the supernatural and the idea of God were not necessary attributes of religion. He considered the division of all objects into two opposing classes, sanctified by religion profane (i.e., earthly every day, worldly, vulgar and unclean) and sacred, an inherent feature of all religious beliefs without exception. The sacred had a taboo character, separated from the earthly phenomena, and was an object of aspiration, love and respect. The sacred was, thus, simultaneously, a source of constraint (taboo) and respect (authority).

Weber refuses to allow the importance of religion to be reduced to something merely social. He believed that religion provided meaning to individuals who have aspired for it. Religious beliefs are an example of these self-interests. The concept of religion is necessitated by the existence of gods in some societies. He argued that the ineradicable basis of popular religions, particularly in India, is the religious behaviour of not 'worshipping the god' but rather 'coercing the god', and invocation is not prayer but some magical formulae. Weber (1920) argued that 'gods,' too, were originally conceived as 'human-like' beings. To be sure, they came to possess the form of enduring beings, which is essential for them, only after the suppression of the purely naturalistic view still evident in the Vedas (for example, that fire is a god or is at least the body of a concrete god of fire) in favour of the view that a god, forever identical with oneself, possesses all fires, produces or controls them or somehow is incorporated in each of them. This abstract conception becomes actually perceived only through the continuous activity of a 'cult' dedicated to one and the same god-through the god's connection with a continuing band, for which the god has special significance as the enduring being. The increasing significance of typical components and types of action and subjective reflection leads to functional specialization among the gods. This may be of a rather abstract type, or it may lead to specialization according to particular lines of activity, for instance, praying, fishing or ploughing.

6.1.1. Religious Faiths in India

In India, religion is a part of its cultural tradition; it is home to the so-called Indic religions such as Hinduism, Buddhism, Jainism and Sikhism, along with different faiths that arrived here at different junctures such as Christianity, Islam, Judaism and Zoroastrianism. The following section will explore only the major religions Hinduism, Sikhism, Islam and Christianity in India.

6.1.1.1. Hinduism

The discernible feature of Hinduism states belief in many divinities—Brahma, Vishnu, Shiva, the Goddess and many others—as a result of which, from the outside, the tradition is commonly understood to be polytheistic. Simultaneously, however, Hindus also believe in the existence of one supreme God, whom they call *bhagavan* (all opulent one), *paramatma* (supreme self), *parameshwar* (supreme controller), *parampita* (supreme father) and so on. Thus, according to Hindu tradition, God is one but also many. He/she manifests in innumerable forms and shapes and further expands into lesser divinities and even into the entire perceivable world. The Hindu complex of religions teaches that one God can have unlimited forms (*ananta-rupa*) since, by definition, he/she is beyond all limitations. It relates to what we today know as popular Hinduism, with its many gods and goddesses.

There exists a wide range of literature in Hinduism; Srinivas and Shah (1968) state that the doctrines of Hinduism are not represented in one sacred literature and nor does Hinduism have a single historical founder. These works of literature include Vedas, Brahmanas, Upanishads, Vedangas, Dharmashastras, Puranas and so on, and this is only the commencement. Hinduism boasts of an inconceivably large number of individual deities—330 million—according to the ancient Indic texts. Each of these gods and goddesses (while expressions and manifestations of God or *brahman*—the supreme spirit) is considered an individual, with a distinct story or history. For those who choose to worship one of these deities, the scriptures offer a unique set of rituals, tailor-made for that particular form of worship. Some of these deities are male; others are female, while still others are androgynous. Some resemble humans, some animals, and there are even those who are a combination of the two. God also comes to us in certain trees or stones or other aspects of material nature. This aspect of Hinduism keeps it tolerant and open to dissent. Also, there are diverse interactions between the theological or metaphysical and the local levels of Hinduism in practice. In the words of popular author Shashi Tharoor, India is 'a singular land of the plural' and, more, a 'land of maddening paradoxes.' The tolerant aspect of Hinduism was lamented during the revivalist's tendencies which tried to proclaim Vedas, and Indian nationalism was being expressed through Hindu idiom. But the esternized Indian elite group which emerged during the colonial period was committed to independence, democracy, secularism and egalitarianism (Srinivas and Shah 1968, 364).

Hindus believe in an eternal, infinite and all-embracing ultimate force called *brahman* (the universal soul). And the main concern is the relationship between this *brahman* and *atman* (the individual soul). 'The *atman* is considered to be indestructible and passes through series of incarnations—human, animal or superhuman, that is influenced by the net balance of good and bad karma (deeds) in previous births. The goodness or badness is defined with reference to dharma (Srinivas and Shah 1968). The notion of karma and dharma is closely associated with the concept of *moksha* (liberation from the cycle of rebirth). It is the reward of the continuous good deeds (karma) that liberates the individual from the cycle of birth, death and rebirth and ultimately leads them to *brahman*. Hindu theology is engrossed with the issue of attaining *moksha*. The Bhagavad Gita has emphasized the way of works and devotion to attain *moksha* through the performance of karma in accordance with dharma for men, women and the lower castes. The Gita has been reinterpreted by various political leaders to provide for the basis of a life devoted to altruistic actions (Srinivas and Shah 1968, 364).

The goals of Hindu life are achieved by living a life adhering to Hindu social organization. The Hindu society comprises of four divisions in terms of *varnas*: Brahman, Kshatriya, Vaishya and Shudra; every Hindu is born within these *varnas* and has to follow his/her ordained *varnadharma* to achieve *moksha*—the ultimate goal. According to Rigveda, these four *varnas* emerged from the limbs of the primaeval man, who underwent divine sacrifice that produced cosmos. The Brahmans are believed to have emerged from his mouth, thus supposed to engage in the pursuit of knowledge. The Kshatriyas emerged from his arms to be the warriors and ruler. The Vaishya emerged from his thigh and have been ordained to be in the pursuit of trade and commerce. The Shudras emerged from his feet to be in the pursuit of service to the other three *varnas*. It is quite significant that the untouchables do not have any mention in the Vedic hymns (Srinivas and Shah 1968). Further, there are a varied number of castes within each varna with the ascribed occupation, social status and localized concepts of purity and pollution. Every caste performs its *jatidharma* (religion of caste) to achieve the goals of life.

There are also several sects in Hinduism; each believes in and celebrates a particular god/goddess and follows a distinctive text. However, belief in the concepts of *brahman* and *atman, dharma, artha, moksha* is central in all Hinduism sects.

Puja (worship) and *bhakti* (devotion) are important aspects of theistic Hinduism which gradually replaced the Vedic sacrificial cult by devotion and worship to an image of the deity. Hence, based on worship, there exist three important cults in theistic Hinduism: (a) *Vaishnavism*—the worship of Vishnu—emphasizes a personal relationship with a loving and gracious God, (b) *Shaivism*—the worship of Siva—is more ascetically inclined; however, it also often incorporates yogic mystical practices into its worship and (c) *Shaktism*—the cult of goddesses—is an important component of theistic Hinduism in the form of worship of mother goddesses such as Devi, Durga and Kali; it follows the tantric methods of tapping the creating energies (Shaktis) within oneself. *Shaktism* is found within the broad fold of *Vaishnavism* and *Shaivism* whereby Laxmi and Parvati, the divine consorts of Vishnu and Shiva, respectively, are worshipped in many places in India (New Encyclopedia of Britannica 1985, 935). Each of the dominant sects has a distinctive ideology and sacred literature written by its founders and other leaders. While Shiva, Vishnu and Shakti are dominant sects centred around Surya, Ganesha and Dattatreya, there are others that have arisen across the country. Each sect recognizes other minor deities, including the spouse of their main god (Srinivas and Shah 1968). Another problem, while studying sects, is also understanding their relationship with asceticism.

Henotheistic tendency is one when a deity being worshipped and praised above others, which is important in Hindu mythology and ritual. However, pantheism prevails, and all deities, including Shiva and Vishnu to local gods and goddess, are considered to be manifestation of one. Membership to a sect is not ascriptive rather takes place through initiation rites. No sect includes members from all castes. Non-sectarian Hinduism also prevails which is understood as Sanskritic in towns and non-Sanskritic in villages. Non-Sanskritic Hinduism is an ideal type; the deities have non-Sanskritic names and oral myths associated with stone or unhewn images. Their modes of worship are local without following any liturgy (Srinivas and Shah 1968).

6.1.1.2. Islam

The tenets of faith and practice in Islam are explicit and binding. A Muslim must affirm the oneness of *Allah* (God) and decree of *Quran* (holy text to be read and recited) as the words of *Allah*. There is also a prevailing belief in the god's angels and messengers (of whom the last Muhammed was perfect and the last), and at the time of *qayamat* (last day), *Allah* will judge the actions of all and send pious to heaven and sinners to hell. Every Muslim should also recite the *Kalimah* (the word) which affirms the oneness of *Allah* and declaration of Muhammad's prophethood; offer *namaz* (daily prayers) at the assigned times; observe *roza* (yearly month of fasting by the day to clear away sins); give *zakat* (alms), and if circumstances allow, go to Mecca for *haj* (pilgrimage). When Islam reached India, it was already marked by divisions of all kinds; Muhammad himself prophesized that there would be more *firqah* (sects) in Islam. The Sunni (from Sunnah, customary way of life) or traditionalists account for a great majority of Indian Muslims, and their opponents are the Shias (followers), who came into being following Muhammad's death as the adherents of *Ali* (the prophet's cousin and son-in-law) whom they considered the legitimate *khalifah* (successor) and *imam* (leader). And it was not Ali, but Muhammad's father-in-law, Abu Bakr, who was chosen, resulting in the Sunni–Shia split which till today lead to violence in both India and Pakistan.

The Islamic tradition arrived through Muslim settlements in India, an ensuing confluence of two traditions of Islam and Hinduism. It involved processes of indigenization and conversion; Muslims of foreign origin imbibed local traditions and customs, and there were conversions within earlier faiths in India. The process of syncretism and synthesis was promoted by the Sufis. They maintained that Islam should be presented to the Indian people in their own cultural idiom. The Sufis, especially of the Chishti order, were the first among the Muslim intellectual elite to interact closely with the Hindu masses. They had an attitude of tolerance and understanding towards Hindus and Hinduism. The success and popularity of the Chishti saints throughout the country were largely due to the fact that they understood the cultural traditions and religious attitudes of the Indian people. They also adopted many Hindu customs and ceremonies (Nizami 1961).

But this process of syncretism and synthesis, which was invigorated by the Sufis, was not easy as there were reactions against syncretic attempts, especially from the fundamentalist *Ulama*, who wanted to cleanse Islam of all foreign accretions. To a large extent, this was a reflection of the perennial tug of war between the Sufis and the *Ulama*. Whereas the *Ulama* emphasized scholastic formalism and doctrinal teachings, the Sufis underscored service to humanity as the essence of religion (Momin 1977). Hindu influences crept into Muslim society through intermarriages between the Arab traders and soldiers and the local Hindu women. On the other hand, the converts to the new faith brought with them their ancestral beliefs and practices, their occupational hierarchy and their caste consciousness. Moreover, the various immigrant groups which settled in India in the wake of the Muslim conquest imbibed the local mores and traditions. This aspect of cultural adaptation has been neatly characterized as indigenization (Misra 1974).

The Imperial Gazetteer of India (1907) states the division of Muslim communities in India into Ashraf and Ajlaf. The Ashraf included four ethnic groups of foreign extraction: Sayyid, Shaikh, Mughal and Pathan. The Ajlaf, on the other hand, included the artisan and service castes such as weaver, cobbler, butcher, potter, bangle seller and scavenger. These castes are converts from Hinduism and have retained their pre-conversion occupations. The untouchable castes like the scavengers are not allowed to enter mosques or shrines. Other Muslim castes normally do not accept food from them. Both the Ashraf and Ajlaf castes are hierarchically arranged. Momin (1977) pointed out that with changes in the socio-economic structure caused by industrialization, urbanization and certain legislative measures introduced by the government and social mobilization, a number of high-caste groups among the Muslims find it difficult to engage with their traditional occupations. Also, some of the traditionally low-caste groups have become economically and politically dominant. A process of de-Ashrafization is underway in contemporary Muslim social structure which indicates an inclination among the high-caste Muslims to adopt the customs and features of the traditionally low-caste groups which have become economically and politically dominant (Momin 1977). But the Ashraf–Ajlaf dichotomy into which the Indian Muslim population is supposedly divided does not offer a realistic and adequate picture of status gradations and caste distinctions among the Muslims at the regional level. Thus, Imtiaz Ahmad (1966) has observed that this dichotomy is comparable to the *varna* system among the Hindus, but its relevance for understanding the local or regional rank of castes is considerably limited.

6.1.1.3. Sikhism

Sikhism was developed in the early 16th century, following major developments in the history of religions in India with the arrival and growth of Islam. Nanak Dev (1469–1539) was the founder of Sikhism, who developed severe dissatisfaction with the ritualism, idol worship and also rejected caste distinctions. He declared that there are no true Hindus or Muslims to be found anywhere; he called for a third path comprising moral duty (dharma), human effort (karma), spiritual knowledge, truth and divine benevolence.

Uberoi (1991) discuses succinctly five symbols of Sikh identity with a structural method for proper theoretical understanding. He attempted to analyse ceremonial customs and rite by attempting to determine ideological meaning within a particular system or symbolic thought and its social functions within a particular social system of groups or categories. The combination of these two aspects enables to determine all ceremonies and rites are constitutive, expressive and affirmative in character, which means, they communicate and embody meanings and values in concrete shape. Sikh identity comprises the significance of five K's namely *Kesh, Kangha, Kara, Kirpan* and *Kachha*. According to Sikh customs, the unshorn hair (Kesh) is associated with a comb (Kangha), which performs the function of constraining hair and imparting orderly arrangement to it. The meaning of this becomes clear through the customs of the Sikh turban, enclosing both the *Kesh* and *Kangha*. The *Kesh* and *Kangha*, thus, become unitary pair off symbols, each evoking the meaning of the other and the mutual association. The *Kirpan* and the *Kara*, similarly, constitute the other pair of symbols; the *Kirpan* in its conjoining meaning with the *Kara* is a sword ritually constraint to protect the honour of every citizen. And finally, the *Kachha,* the loin and thigh garment, is perceived as a constraining agent for the uncircumcised male members. The aspect of assertion combined with constraints produces a spirit of affirmation which is a characteristic of Sikhism (Uberoi 1991).

As against renunciation, Sikhism espouses the spirit of affirmation which can be explored by considering the wider social context of Sikhism's emergence as a social system. Sikhism emerged as a social movement vis-à-vis the medieval world of Hinduism as well as the Islamic culture. Hinduism is to be comprehensively understood as *varnashrama dharma*. It means that it is not only the institution of caste but the institution of the four stages or roles of individual life (ashramas) which explains the Hindu system as a whole. The caste system, in reality, was always surrounded by a non-caste space which allowed renunciatory religious orders. This space is a negation of the principle of caste and birth, alongside the fourth *ashrama* (sannyas) provided that the stage for an individual to abrogate the world of caste. According to Uberoi, these two contrasting worlds is the essence of Hinduism. The territorial kingship as political institutions was the third structural feature of Hinduism, whose total ideological and social structure was founded upon an interrelated yet tripartite division among the three domains of the king (ruler or the world of rajya), the caste system (varna or grihasta) and finally the orders of renunciation or *sannyas*. Interestingly, a similar underline structure one can detect in the Islamic culture of the same period in the divisions and interrelations between the spheres of (a) state power or *hukumat*, (b) the social order or *shariat* and (c) the Sufi sect as a way of salvation or *tariqat/haqiqat*. Also, there were other sub-orders of Hinduism entailed renouncing caste and its worldly engagements and opened up an escape to *sannyas*, but such protest could later fizzle out, ending up in a return to the world of caste. Overall speaking, alongside the *varnaashram dharma*, the ascetic or protestant drive remain a constant aspect of medieval Hinduism.

Early Sikhism, as a social movement, possessed many features in common with other religious brotherhoods, but it broke free from the convoluted cycle of caste versus non-caste that we find in other order or sub-orders of Hinduism. Asceticism has no recognition in Sikhism. In fact, Sikhism was a social movement aimed at doing away with the division between social and intellectual or the material and the spiritual of the medieval world. It categorically laid to rest the opposition between the householder and the renouncer and of the ruler with the householder and renouncer. The three spheres of political, social and spiritual are not distinct modes of existence, so they are not acknowledged separately. The three spheres of *rajya*, *grihasta* and *sannyas* corresponding to political, social and spiritual respectively are woven into a single body of faith and conduct. The social function of the Sikh initiation right clearly indicates the characteristic rights and responsibilities of the three spheres as equally valid. The neophyte is initiated and invested with the virtues of all the three spheres rolled into one. The new Sikh takes no *Jogi* (renouncer) vow to renounce his/her procreative power and never marry, but he/she wears the *kachha* (cotton undergarment) of continence. Similarly, the new Sikh is entitled to carry weapons or engage in every social occupation open to him/her, be it that of a soldier, householder or political. In this manner, a unique 'renunciation of renunciation' is invoked through the Sikh rites and rituals which can be structurally decoded in an analysis of the five K's or symbols of Sikhism. Since the other religious orders embodied the medievalism of separateness of the different spheres of life, Sikhism abrogated such divisions. Uberoi, through the structural method of analysis, established the connection between the five symbols of Sikhism and its whole nature as a religion. The five symbols of Sikhism 'signify, in their respective pairs, the virtues and roles of *sannyas yoga* (*kes* and *kanga*), *grihasta yoga* (*kachh* and uncircumcised state), and *rajya yoga* (*kirpan* and *kara*)' (Uberoi 1991, 332). The five K's serve as the authenticating sign and seal of Sikhism, and when taken together, they affirm the unity of man as a social being embedded in the material world.

6.1.1.4. Christianity

Among the religions that originated outside India and found a home here, Christianity is the oldest. Christians comprise a significant minority population in India; it is also a majority community in three north-eastern states of Nagaland, Mizoram and Meghalaya. All the non-Hindu religions, such as Islam, Christianity and Sikhism, recognize and promote an egalitarian social order which opposes the ideology of caste. But in India, all these religions have been converted from Hinduism and thus suffer from the malady of caste hierarchy. Despite the efforts of Christian dogmas and missionaries, the status of a Christian in the local community continues to depend on the caste from which he/she has converted. It is believed that St. Thomas, the disciple of Jesus, first introduced the Christian faith to India nearly 2,000 years ago, but the influence of Christianity was observed only with the arrival of Europeans.

The advent of the British in India did not have any impact on the spread of Christianity as East India Company in defiance of the home government did not permit missionary activity. It was only in the 19th century that the British Parliament removed restrictions which were followed by missionaries from Anglicans, Protestants and nonconformists' societies producing a plurality of Churches and an interflow between congregations. The underlying motivation, of course, was their obligation to proclaim the salvation of God through the Christian faith. This period also witnessed the consolidation of British rule and the impact of Western ideas on the social, political and religious life of Indians through the medium of English language. Christian missionaries were pioneers in education.

BOX 6.1
T. N. Madan

Triloki Nath Madan, commonly T. N. Madan (born 12 August 1933 in Kashmir), is an anthropologist, with a PhD from the Australian National University (1960). He is currently a Professor Emeritus of Sociology at the Institute of Economic Growth, Delhi University, and a Distinguished Senior Fellow (Adjunct), Centre for the Study of Developing Societies, New Delhi. His most noted work is *Family and Kinship among the Pandits of Rural Kashmir* (1966, 1989) which presented an account of the social life of Kashmiri Pandits. His more recent publications include *Modern Myths, Locked Minds: Secularism and Fundamentalism in India* (1997, 2009), *Images of the World: Essays on Religion, Secularism, and Culture* (2005) and *Sociological Traditions: Methods and Perspectives in the Sociology of India* (2011).

T. N. Madan (1998), in his essay 'Secularism in Its Place' stated,

> Secularism is the dream of a minority that wishes to shape the majority in its own image, that wishes 'to impose its will upon history but lacks the power to do so under a democratically organized polity. In an open society the state will reflect the character of that society. Secularism is therefore a social myth that draws a cover over the failure of this minority to separate politics from religion in the society in which its members live.' And for the minority to 'stigmatize the majority as primordially oriented' is 'moral arrogance and worse ... political folly.'

6.2. TRIBES IN INDIA

6.2.1. Tribes

The tribe is a colonial concept, defined for the first time in the census of 1901. D. N. Majumdar defines a tribe as a social group with territorial affiliation, endogamous with no specialization of functions ruled by tribal officers hereditary or otherwise, united in language or dialect recognizing social distance with other tribes or castes. W. H. R. Rivers also defined a tribe as 'a social group of simple kind, the members of which speak a common dialect, have a single government, and act together for such common purposes as warfare.' Therefore, it is apt to state that each tribe is distinct from the other and can be identified on the basis of its practices, myths, culture, language and so on.

The British rule in India facilitated tribes and non-tribes under one political and administrative authority. Similarly, they were also subject to rules and regulations in the economic sphere where land, labour, credit and commodity market were brought under single economic order (Xaxa 2011). Earlier, tribes had control and autonomy over land, forest and other resources, including governance as well, but got pushed to the margin of the new political and economic system. There was, thus, the process of integration/inclusion of tribes into the larger system under colonial rule, but this inclusion came to be intertwined with the process of exclusion in the form of loss of access and control over livelihood (economic rights) as well as control over the decision-making process in the determination of their own life. But the tribal in India had to undergo twin colonialism, one from the British rule and the other from the non-tribal population (Xaxa 2011). Verrier Elwin's, one of the leading anthropologists to work in India, helped track the shifting trends in the 20th-century anthropology. He emphasized the need to recognize the tribes as part of the larger Indian civilization while, at the same time, acknowledge their distinct identity. He also expressed his deep agony against the colonial policy and the aggressive Christian and Hindu reformism, which were responsible for the disruption of the tribal society.

Elwin and Ghurye took extreme positions while discussing race and tribe. The former emphasized their uniqueness, and the latter saw them as backward Hindus. Elwin produced the largest corpus of data on Indian ethnography, and indeed, he was one of the most prolific anthropological writers of recent times; his writings were illuminated by personal experience of participant observations. Elwin added the urge to make tribal people known as real people, rather than tiresome savages, and their cultures as worthy of respect. He conducted a series of ethnographic work in the districts of Madhya Pradesh and Orissa. *The Baiga* and *The Muria and Their Ghotul* presented a captivating picture of the amorous life of a tribe in the chiefdom of Bastar. It discussed the dormitory practice or *Ghotul*, where boys and girls first learnt the arts and poetry of sex. Elwin remarked ancient India was rich in such literature, but recent writers have been under the influence of prevailing puritan conventions to treat the subject freely. His monographs are enlivened by the sharp characterization of a novelist, exemplified in evocative life history and the abundance of songs, riddles and poems.

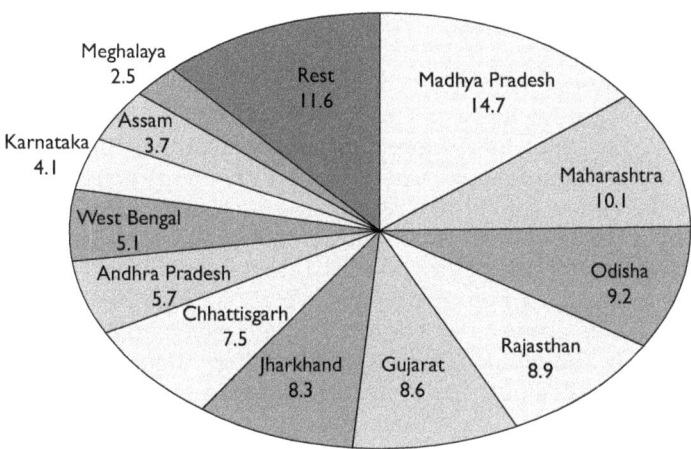

FIGURE 6.1 Distribution of ST Population by States (in %)

Source: Ministry of Tribal Affairs (2013).

Tribes, thus, can also be seen as a dimension of little tradition which cannot be adequately understood unless it is seen in relation to the great tradition (Sinha 1958). As against this, tribes are seen more as remaining outside of state and civilization (Béteille 1986). But even when tribes have been living outside of state and civilization, they were not outside the influence of civilization. For Béteille (1996a, b), citizenship is a status, which entitles an individual's full membership of a community. It confers on individuals an array of rights and obligations. In this sense, the status of an individual, as a citizen, is contrary to the general notion of status which is invariably associated with the notion of hierarchy and inequality.

Broadly, the STs inhabit two distinct geographical area—the central India and the north-eastern area. More than half of the ST population is concentrated in central India, that is, Madhya Pradesh (14.69%), Chhattisgarh (7.5%), Jharkhand (8.29%), Andhra Pradesh (5.7%), Maharashtra (10.08%), Orissa (9.2%), Gujarat (8.55%) and Rajasthan (8.86%). The other distinct area is the Northeast (Assam, Nagaland, Mizoram, Manipur, Meghalaya, Tripura, Sikkim and Arunachal Pradesh. Figure 6.1 shows the states' share of ST population out of India's ST population.

6.2.2. Tribe and Religion

The tribal religions in India are of a distinct kind with some different concepts, terminologies, practices and characteristics. Their religion is distinct from the dominant religions but faces pressure from them due to the pressure imposed through national, economic, social and political integration. One is that some tribe believe in animism, which believes in the sensibility that all material things have spirit. The most important type of animism is the ancestral worship found among Santhals and Oraons. The other feature which is widespread is the faith referred to as animatism. According to animatism, there is some impersonal power behind every material thing besides living things. The weight of belief among most tribes' rests on the idea of spirit, which handles different aspects of the world and must be placated with offerings and prayers to ward of the evil.

Elwin (1955) considered religion to be a heavy item in the Saoras budget and a major cause for their indebtedness. They have a dependency on the Shamans; a lot depends on the type of Shaman you consult—expensive and not so expensive ones. The chief of Sogeda believes that he is constantly under an atmosphere of threat by supernatural beings and spends on expensive Shamans for his protection. Thus, Shamans live a rather free of cost life without paying for their meals, as most of them get invited for feasts more than once a day. Saoras do not have a heretic; there are many who accept their religious duties as a matter of chores. There is no church; rather, it can be said that the tribe itself is the church. Our understanding of sacred and profane is alien to them. There is no religious hierarchy or centralization. However, there are two ideologies that have a paramount influence on the conduct of the Saoras: *Ersi*, which means taboo and *Ukka*, which means customs. *Ukka* is a traditional behaviour and conduct, fidelity to tribal rules, the normal socially approved behaviour. Violation of *Ukka* may earn a fine from offended neighbours but does not bring the wrath of any outraged god. *Ukka* controls the kind of dress you wear, the architecture of your house, the family from which you get your wife and so on. *Ersi*, on the other hand, covers a range of behaviour, which may more often be trivial but yet dangerous. It relates to the individual's conduct as observed by the spirits, whereas *Ukka* is conduct observed by other fellow members. Thus, it may be against *Ukka* to lie, steal or murder, but it is *Ersi* if you lie in the name of god, steal the food offered at sacrifice and kill a dedicated animal. Any breach of *Ukka* often leads to punishment; the culprit may be ostracized or liable to a fine. But the punishment can be modified by discussion, argument, excuses and apology if there is some sense to it. But the danger, the awe-inspiring breach of *Ersi* leads to retribution which reaches out to the offender from the world of spirits against which there is no appeal. The Saora idea of *Ersi* contains a number of elements which combine to produce a complete picture of taboo. It is a particular code of etiquette for dealing with the inhabitants of the other world. According to Elwin (1955), there is a lot of confusion regarding the word taboo, as Freud, Wundt and Frazer all seem to use it in a different sense. Elwin suggested that taboos are prohibitions which, when violated, produce automatically, in the offender, a state of ritual disability taboo stricken only relieved through purification.

Indra Munshi (2004) states that Elwin's work and tribal development state that Elwin's observation of the tribes continues to be relevant; for most of the tribal communities, independence did not bring freedom from poverty and exploitation. They continue to be alienated from the resources on which their survival remains. She also states that the spirit of understanding and appreciation pervaded through all his writings which often led him to question, ridicule and reject the conventional ways of 'the modern and the civilized', and Elwin does not seem to recognize sufficiently the inequalities built into the structures and relations within the tribes.

6.2.3. Tribe and Social Exclusion

Post-Independence, there have been several provisions institutionalized for the welfare and safeguarding the interest of the tribal. In lieu of which, there have been several programmes and policies rolled out in tandem with the provisions. One of the dominant one among them is the affirmative action programmes. However, due to many development projects, the tribal have been impacted adversely: Displacement of tribal and their livelihood has caused the ecological imbalance. Projections of power generation, the extension of irrigation facilities, opportunities for employment, development of infrastructure and so on are some of the things that are invoked in support of such projects. Xaxa (2011) argues that though development contributes to economic growth, the tribal and poor are not the beneficiaries of such development.

In Jharkhand, by 1996, for example, 8 major and 55 medium hydraulic projects along with many more minor projects had come up. This had displaced a large number of households. Yet the area under irrigation in Jharkhand constituted only 7.68 per cent of the net sown area and households electrified was mere 9.04 per cent. As large as 201 large- and medium-scale industries have come up in Jharkhand, displacing a large number of families, on the one hand, and providing employment to lakhs of people, on the other. Yet the benefits of these did not go to displaced tribal people of Jharkhand (Xaxa 2011).

The gap between tribes and the rest of the population is widening. Although there has been increase in the literacy rate, reduction in the size of population below poverty line, the gap remains due to the inability of the state and state apparatus to articulate the problems faced by tribal (Xaxa 2011). The tribal issues have primarily been formulated through economic and social backwardness emanating due to their geographical and social isolation. Xaxa (2011) writes that the whole discourse on tribes has been around the question of their integration by extension of social, political and civil rights, whereas their economic rights to their livelihood have been seized for the aforementioned rights. There has been an unequal exchange between the state and tribal in India; Xaxa (2011) refers to this exchange being steeped in expropriation, domination and discrimination.

The policy pursued by the British was continued in the post-Independence era of development under stricter regulation and enforcement justified in the national public interest. The intensity of the situation gets aggravated due to the increasing number of displaced people. Also, various forest laws have turned them into encroachers; they are living under constant threat of eviction and violence. These displaced tribal were not rehabilitated, leading to serious consequences on their access to basic necessities of life but were dismissed by cash compensation.

6.2.4. Tribe and Issues of Identity

The tribal have been exploited and subjugated; they have been victims of conquest and colonization, as a result of which they lost control over customary territorial resources, faced cultural annihilation and turned powerless (Xaxa 2006). Tribal are a distinct category of people having their own ethnic identity. There are claims that tribal are Hindus which is a distortion of their identity. Tribes are, at times, equated with Dalits which is incorrect as they do not fall within the framework of the caste system of the Hindus. They are the ethnic category as opposed to a caste category. Conversion practices among tribal to other religions, like Christianity, are often misunderstood as a departure from the tribal identity. But in religious conversion, there is the adoption of religion, and the ethnic identity remains unaltered.

In current times, tribe and tribal communities in India are moving towards a paradigm shift with respect to the amplifying exposure due to the internet and changes related to the development, causing a substantial transition in their sociocultural, economic and lifestyle patterns. Youth, being the facilitator of this change, is reproducing images of the changing world in their personal and social relationships. The emergence and development of the new group within the tribal social structure ushered in a new transformation in the erstwhile traditional society. The reservation policy and other developmental schemes doled out by the state empowered a certain population of the STs/SCs setting them apart from the remaining members of their society in terms of disposition and access to sources of power and other metropolitan ways of life. The rise of tribal identity is also related to the emergence of the middle class, particular issues of culture, tradition and livelihood, even control over land and resources as well as the demand for a share in the benefits of the projects of modernity, which have become an integral part of the articulation of identity among the tribes. A new consciousness is coming from the middle class which has been crucial in the articulation of identity among them (Xaxa 2006).

There are nearly 104 million tribal people in India who are largely concentrated in 10 states and the north-east. Almost 90 per cent of the tribal population of the country lives in rural areas. There are 90 districts or 809 blocks with more than 50 per cent tribal population, and they account for nearly 45 per cent of the ST population in the country. In other words, almost 55 per cent of the tribal population lives outside these 809 tribal majority blocks. As per Census 2011, over two-thirds of the tribal population is working in the primary sector (as against 43% of the non-tribal population) and is heavily dependent on agriculture either as cultivators or as agricultural labourers. The tribal communities are increasingly moving from being cultivators to agricultural labourers. Currently, one out of every two tribal households relies on manual labour for survival. This displacement process is aggravated by the mining projects, sanctuaries and construction of dams. Land acquisition has been one of the contentious issues for all such projects, which has led to massive displacement of people. Development displacement population, in turn, is the single largest category among all internally displaced populations. For example, Activist Medha Patkar of the Narmada Bachao Andolan has argued that the construction of dams has led to the dislocation of tribal societies. The official figure indicates that about 42,000 families were displaced due to the Sardar Sarovar dam but non-government organizations, like the Narmada Bachao Andolan, claim the figure is 85,000 families or 200,000 people. Tribes have undergone change not only with relation to land but also their relationship with natural resources such as forests and rivers.

CONCLUSION

The changing reality in India has accentuated concerns about religion's growing role in the geopolitics of the region, and there is a pressing need for religious harmony. Reinforcement of religious identity will intensify conflicts among religious and ethnic communities. In India, most people are socialized into religion since childhood. Religion is reflected in people's identity through their mundane beliefs and practices. Religious authority remains in a secular system but is restricted to governing religious belief and practice. While the term secular relates to the world but is different from religious, whereas secularism is related to discrediting any control of religious organizations over social institutions. That is, secularism does not deny the presence of religion but determines institutions over which religion cannot exercise control.

The whole discourse on tribes has been around the question of integration through the extension of civil, political and social rights. Also, their economic rights have been jeopardized by the state in exchange for the aforementioned rights. Instead, these rights became the legitimizing tool for the expropriation of resources of the tribal people. Thus, this exchange has been rather steeped in subjugation and discrimination. The integration of tribes is often considered to be a panacea for all the tribal population, but their exclusion from the share and the access to development are narratives of neglect and domination.

Points of Classroom Discussion

- Secularization and multiculturalism reflect contemporary aspects of religion
- Beliefs, customs and practices are central to the understanding of every religion
- Tribal identities are noticing the development of a new consciousness

GLOSSARY

Animism: It is the general doctrine of souls and other spiritual beings, a conception that pervades all life forms in nature.

Ashrafization: It is a mechanism of status mobility where people try to acquire the look of the Ashrafs of India and foreign countries.

Identity: It refers to the aspects of qualities, beliefs, personality and expressions that help shape an individual.

Karma and *dharma*: These are the codified practices in Hinduism religion, wherein karma implies an individual's routine action, oriented obligations and their implications which can be either positive or negative. Dharma, on the other hand, is the obligation or the duty to perform those actions according to one's caste, family, age and so on.

Secularism: It can be understood as a social, economic and political tendency that rejects paramountcy of any particular form of religious faith and worship. It separates matters of civil policy from religious interference.

REFERENCES

Ahmad, I. 1966. 'The Ashraf–Ajlaf Dichotomy in Muslim Social Structure in India'. *The Indian Economic & Social History* 3, no. 3 (September): 268–278.

Béteille, A. 1986. 'The Concept of Tribe with Special Reference to India'. *Journal of European Sociology* 27, no. 2: 297–318.

———. 1996a. *Caste, Class and Power: Changing Patterns of Stratification in a Tanjore Village.* 2nd ed. New Delhi: Oxford University Press.

Béteille, A. 1996b. 'Inequality'. In *Encyclopaedia of Social and Cultural Anthropology,* edited by Alan Barnard and Jonathan Spencer. London: Routledge.

Census of India. 2001. Available at https://censusindia.gov.in/2011-common/census_data_2001.html, accessed on 28 February 2021.

Durkheim, É. 1957. *Professional Ethics and Civic Morals.* Glencoe, IL: Free Press.

Elwin, V. 1955. *The Religion of an Indian Tribe.* Mumbai: Oxford University Press.

Madan, T. N. 1998. 'Secularism in Its Place'. *The Journal of Asian Studies* 46, no. 4 (November): 747–759.

Misra, S. C. 1974. 'Indigenization and Islamization in Indian History'. *Secular Democracy* (VII).

Ministry of Tribal Affairs. 2013. *Statistical Profile of Scheduled Tribes in India.* Available at: https://www.brlf.in/wp-content/uploads/2018/05/Statistical-Profile-of-STs_2013.pdf (accessed on 22 February 2021).

Momin, A. R. 1977. 'The Indo Islamic Tradition'. *Sociological Bulletin* 26, no. 2 (September): 242–258.

Munshi, Indra. 2004. 'Verrier Elwin and Tribal Development'. In *Between Ethnography and Fiction: Verrier Elwin and the Tribal Question in India,* edited by T. B. Subba and Sujit Som. New Delhi: Orient Longman.

Nizami, K. A. 1961. *Some Aspects of Religion and Politics in India in the 13th Century.* Aligarh: Publication of the Department of History.

Sinha, Surajit. 1958. 'Tribal Culture of Peninsular India as a Dimension of Little Tradition in the Study of Indian Civilization: A Preliminary Statement'. *Journal of American Folklore* 71, no. 281 (July): 504–518.

Srinivas, M. N., and A. M. Shah. 1968. 'Hinduism'. In *The International Encyclopaedia of Social Sciences* (vol. 6), edited by D. L. Sills, 358–366. New York, NY: Macmillan and Free Press.

Uberoi, J. P. S. 1991. 'Five Symbols of Sikh Identity'. In *Religion in India,* edited by T. N. Madan, 320–332. New Delhi: Oxford University Press.

Xaxa, V. 2011. 'Tribes and Social Exclusion'. Occasional Paper No. 2. Calcutta: CSSSC- UNICEF, 1–18.

———. 2006. 'Culture, Politics and Identity: The Case of Tribes in India'. In *Contested Transformations: Changing Economies and Identities in Contemporary India,* edited by Mary E. John, Praveen Kumar Jha, and Surinder S. Jodhka. New Delhi: Tulika Books.

CHAPTER 7

Family, Marriage and Kinship: Changing Contours

LEARNING OUTCOMES

- To explore different perspectives in the study of institutions of family, marriage and kinship
- Cultivate a methodical perspective on concepts relevant for understanding kinship systems and types of family, marriage
- Acknowledge the shift in kinship and family theories from biological towards cultural understanding

Keywords: Family, household, descent, marriage, alliance

Each house represents a family, elementary or joint.

—**S. C. Dube**

Marriage is 'a relation of one or more men to one or more women which is recognized by customs or law and involves certain rights and duties in case of parties entering into the union and in the case of children born of it'.

—**Westermark**

INTRODUCTION

Family is the basic unit of society. There has been acumulative consideration towards the structure of family as the object of study in the discipline of sociology. Family is one of the important institutions of social life. The American anthropologist George Murdock (1949) examined nearly 250 societies of various kinds. Following his analysis, he explained family as a social group which is a site of common residence, economic cooperation and reproduction where adults of both sexes, at least two of them, shall have socially approved sexual relationship. It is a unit which bears one or more children which can be either procreated or adopted by the sexually cohabiting couple. State uses the concept of family as a group of two or more persons related by marriage, blood, adoption and residing together through census and various governmental policies.

The term 'family', however, is often used to denote different concepts in common understanding, which are as follows: (a) household—the unit of people who cohabit—includes parents, children and servants, (b) set of parents and their children, whether living together or not, (c) in a broader understanding, it may include everyone who is related by blood and affinity, and (d) also those who claim descent from a common ancestor—a lineage, a house and kindred. The above-mentioned situations should be differentiated and need to be sociologically analyzed. The widely accepted meaning of an 'elementary family' comprises a man, his wife and their children. It is usually believed that individuals belonging to the same family are likely to permanently cohabit.

Some believe that the structure of family persists because it is endured through the institution of marriage. Traditionally, marriage is sanctioned social customs where there is a union of a male and female for the purpose of entering into sexual relations to procreate and establish a family to provide care. However, the studies have explored that the concept of marriage varies in nature and composition form community to community and nation to nation.

The system of marriage and kinship is an arrangement which facilitates people to cooperate and live together with one another in an organized manner. They plan an important role in maintaining group cohesion and solidarity. Kinship system refers to a set of persons recognized as relatives by virtue of either a blood or marriage relationship. All kinship systems across the world are the product of social evolution.

7.1. FAMILY

7.1.1. Family in India

In sociology, one of the most remarkable contributions towards the study of the family was by Talcott Parsons. His theory on family socialization and interaction was an important aspect of his structural–functional theory of social change. He was analysing the post-war perceptions regarding the disintegration of family brewing in the USA. Instead of blaming it on the generalized perception of rising divorce rate, declining birth rate and changes in sexual morality, he asserted that changes in

American family were due to the phase of 'transition' and did not project any dysfunction. According to Parsons and Bales (1955), American society was witnessing the culmination of a long-term process of the 'isolation', 'differentiation' and 'specialization' of the nuclear family as a limited subsystem of society. Similarly, Goode (1963) argued that all societies across the world will move towards institutionalization of conjugal family, which essentially comprises husband, wife and their children. He suggested that the process of industrialization is guaranteed to put pressures on traditional family structures due to the increased physical and social mobility which separates individuals from larger kin groups and functions previously performed by the kin groups are taken over by other social agencies.

India exemplifies a unique case study in the comparative sociology to effectively study the institution of a family. In the case of 'joint family', Uberoi (1993) claimed that the concept of Indian joint family was the product of the rendezvous of the British colonial administration with indigenous systems of kinship and marriage, especially with respect to the determination of rights in property and responsibility for revenue payment. The Indological approach to Indian family emphasized the joint family as the typical and the traditional form of family organization in India.

Maine (1861) projected the Indian joint family as the living example of the earliest or 'ancient' form of the human family whose outlines could also be discerned in the legal system of ancient Rome as well as Celtic and Slavic survivals of earlier forms of social organization. According to him, this type of family was patriarchal in nature, as it was constituted by a group of male members related through male descent line and were coparceners in joint property. This common property was divided equally among sons before or after the death of the ascendant; alternatively, the undivided family might expand over several generations to become an organized and self-regulating community. Maine suggested that this joint family organization will evolve through several stages towards a Western-type conjugal unit which will be based on a contract.

The property-holding aspect of the joint family has been the subject of Hindu law throughout Indian history. The law distinguishes between joint family and coparcenary; under *The Mitākṣarā*, a Hindu coparcenary is a narrower group than the joint family. It includes only those males who take by the birth interest in the joint or coparcenary property, that is, a man himself and his sons, son's sons and son's grandsons form for the time being a coparcenary. Also, under *The Dāyabhāga*, there is no coparcenary between a man and his son(s), married or unmarried, during his lifetime, even though they may be living in a single household. The important point here is that the Hindu law is not concerned with the distinction between the elementary family and the joint family or extended family.

According to Shah (1964), 'joint family means "two or more elementary families joined together".' This unit is called patrilineal joint family which is based on patrilineal descent and matrilineal joint family, which is based on the principle of matrilineal descent. Some scholars use the term 'generation' to define the limit of extension of patrilineal descent in the formation of the joint family, for instance, three-generation family, four-generation family and so on. But there is no agreement about the meaning of 'generation' or the way of counting the numbers of generations; a usually accepted joint family, however, comprises a group composed of man, his sons and their sons.

7.1.2. Household and Family

It is important to distinguish between joint family and extended family. The extended family households are classified into two types: (a) 'patrilineal extended' which comprises a man, his wife and unmarried daughters (if any) and an only son, his wife and their children and (b) 'fraternal extended' which comprises a man, his wife, unmarried daughters (if any) and two or three sons, their wives and children. I. P. Desai has taken a view which considers 'a household a nuclear family if it comprises of the husband, wife and unmarried children, not related to their other kin through or by property or income or the rights and obligations pertaining to them and as are expected by those related by kinship' (Desai 1956, 148). But he does not consider a household to be a family necessarily. But Dube (1955) states that each house represents a family, elementary or joint, he used family in the sense of 'household'. Those who take family as a household unit, generally assume that the elementary family is the antithesis of the joint family. But every household may comprise either complete or incomplete elementary family.

S. C. Dube (1955) used the term family, primarily, in the sense of 'household'. He showed how a local term equivalent of 'family' is used to denote three different social units. First, it is 'the elementary family or the "house;" second, it is allied or extended families, and third, it is 'a still larger group comprising the near kin on the paternal side.' Desai (1956) asserted that co-residence and commensality are neither adequate nor reliable criteria for judging the type of family. A household may consist of an elementary family, but it may be a part of a joint family in terms of 'functions'.

Bailey (1960) asserted that there is only one definitive activity of the joint family—common ownership of property and right to maintenance from common ownership (for the whole joint family). And we cannot apply the term 'joint family' or 'coparcenary' to those who have no common property.

7.1.3. Different Types of Family Structures

Each family may represent a kind of arrangement based on either shared norms or personal necessities. The classification of families is primarily done on the basis of their organization, that is, nuclear or joint, followed by the type of marriage. The other sources of this classification are authority (matriarchal or patriarchal) and residence. Please check Table 7.1 for types of family on the basis of residence. The following list encompasses the different types of familial structures:

1. **Nuclear family:** It is a basic unit of a family organization composed of a married couple and their offspring. Kolenda (1987) provided categories of nuclear family structures, which are as follows: (a) it includes a couple with or without children, (b) supplemented nuclear family which comprises nuclear family plus one or more unmarried, separated or widowed relatives of the parents, other than the unmarried children, (c) sub-nuclear family is a fragment of a former nuclear family, for instance, a widower/widow with his/her unmarried children or siblings (unmarried or widower or separated or divorced) living together.

TABLE 7.1 Families Based on the Locality or the Residence: Determined by the Prevailing Authority

When husband resides with wife's kins in their residence post marriage	Matrilocal/uxorilocal
Here, wife resides with husband's kins post marriage (e.g., Jats in Haryana)	Patrilocal/virilocal
When couple moves in independent residence	Neolocal
When couple resides with maternal uncle post marriage (e.g., Nayars from Kerala)	Avunculocal

The above-mentioned types of families focus on the traditional familial structures; however, it becomes imperative to take into considerations the changes in contemporary society. The above-mentioned types of families depict the structural changes in the family system.

2. **Joint family:** This type has been discussed in previous sections. Kolenda listed several types of joint families on the basis of its members. The following enlists two of them:
   a. **Collateral joint family:** It comprises two or more married couples between whom there is a sibling bond, for example, brothers, their wives and their unmarried children.
   b. **Supplemented collateral joint family:** It comprises additional widowed mother or father or an unmarried sibling.
3. **Blended family:** The term blended family or stepfamily is used to refer to families with mixed parents—one or both parents remarried and bringing children from the former family into the new family.
4. **Single parent family:** This type of family consists of one parent raising one or more children on their own.

7.2. SOCIAL INSTITUTION OF MARRIAGE

7.2.1. Types of Marriage

Anthropologists believe that the presence of intricate and extensive systems for arranging and regulating marriages in widely different cultures suggests that marriage often serves to create and maintain alliances and exchanges between groups. Many of these exchanges are made to cultivate strategic relationships. Malinowski believed marriages to be a contract for the production and maintenance of children. In every society, cultural expectations underline prospective marriage partners. There are different types of marriages, which are as follows:

- **Monogamy:** It refers to marriages where there is a union between one man and a woman. These types of families are relatively widespread and stable in comparison to other systems of marriage.

- **Polygamy:** It refers to any marriage which constitutes of multiple partners. There are two types of polygamy: polygyny and polyandry. Polygyny refers to marriages in which there is one husband with many wives. In many societies, sororal polygyny is common where many sisters are married to one man, as it is believed that sisters will get along better as co-wives. Further, in some cases, when a woman dies, the husband marries deceased wife's sister to provide a caregiver to children if any and also to prevent the need to exchange dowry or bride wealth taken at the time of the earlier marriage. This practice is called sororate marriage. Polyandry describes marriages between one woman and several husbands. In some parts of Haryana, fraternal polyandry (marriage between one woman and several brothers) is common due to skewed sex ratio. But in the case of a husband's death, some societies prefer that a woman marry one of her husband's brothers; this practice is called levirate.
- **Same-sex marriage:** It refers to marriage between couples of the same sex, that is, a woman may choose to marry another woman, and a man may choose to marry another man. There has been a considerable increase in the number of same-sex marriages. The Civil Marriage Act (Bill C-38) legalized same-sex marriage in Canada on 20 July 2005. Whereas in 2018, the supreme court had only decriminalized homosexuality, which did not, however, legalize same-sex marriages.

7.2.2. Rules of Marriage

Every society and community exercises certain rules of marriage. These are related to the choice of selecting a potential partner. Box 7.1 states different types of marriages in different religions in India. In marriage and kinship studies, there exists a distinction between two kinds of cousins, parallel and cross—parallel

---

BOX 7.1
Concept of Marriage in Different Religions

The following are the concepts of marriage in different religions:

- In the Hindu tradition, marriage is one of the necessary *samskaras* or religious rites for all Hindus. There are eight types of marriages; these are *brahma, daiva, arsh, prajapatya, gandharva, asura, rakshasa* and *paishacha*.
- In Islamic tradition, marriage is called *niqah*; a legal and social *contract* between two individuals governed by sharia. Marriage is strongly recommended, and polygyny is permitted, whereas polyandry is proscribed.
- The advent of Christianity gave a new form to marriage. The institution of marriage is regarded as a sacrament, and the marital union is considered to be indissoluble.

cousins (children of father's brothers and mother's sisters) and cross cousins (children of father's sister and mother's brother). Marriage between cross cousins is preferred among communities in South India, whereas North Indian communities proscribe them and consider them incestuous.

In endogamy, cultural preferences emphasize the need to marry within the same social group. In several societies, individuals are expected to marry within their respective religious and caste communities. In North India, there is a preferred norm of marrying within a caste group, caste endogamy, whereas marrying outside the caste is considered undesirable. However, among some Hindus *gotra* (clan), *pinda* (common lineage) endogamy is proscribed. Then, there is the rule of exogamy where the expectations are to marry someone outside a particular group/clan. There are several communities among Hindus, which expect an individual to marry outside a particular kin network. The practice of *sapinda* (common ancestor clan) exogamy prohibits marriage with agnatic (relating to common ancestor through either the mother or father) and cognatic (relating to the father's descent line) relations to a certain degree, that is, avoiding blood relationships. Further, in the USA, laws prevent marriage between close relatives like cousins; also, marriage between them is considered a taboo. In India, rules of marriages are further divided into two more categories of hypogamy (pratiloma) and hypergamy (anuloma). When there is a marriage between a man from a higher status with a girl from lower status, this type is referred to as hypergamy or *anuloma* marriage. On the other hand, marriage between a woman of higher status with a man of lower status is called hypogamy or *pratiloma* marriage. The notion of status here encompasses categories of caste, sub-caste, village and clan.

7.2.3. Marriage and Legislations in India

Marriage bestows the right to conjugal relationship denial of which tantamount to cruelty, especially when the parties are young and in good health. There are several family laws in India, also known as personal laws based on religion and legislated by the central government. The Prohibition of Child Marriage Act, 2006, prohibits a man under the age of 21 to get married, and the age limit for women is 18. The Supreme Court in 2017, through the ruling, has termed marital rape is punishable under law. Every religion is governed by certain codes and customary laws of their community. The Hindu Marriage Act is applicable to Hindus, Buddhists, Jains and Sikhs. The Special Marriage Act permits marriage between members of any or no religions; it also regulates their divorces. Hindus living across the country are not governed by the same law, but there has been some synthesis. Muslims are governed by sharia, largely uncodified and subject to plural interpretations. The basic tenets of Muslim marriage are based on a contract which can be terminated or annulled. Marriage can be repudiated by the husband if he pronounces *talaq* three times in written or in oral form. A wife can repudiate marriage only when the husband permits her; also, both of them can initiate divorce through mutual consent through *khula*. Any party can also approach the court for divorce, and Vatuk (2013) states that the courts see their role as dispensing social justice rather than promoting justice for women. Also, there are laws that regulate the essential conditions for a valid marriage in India, the grounds of dissolution, maintenance of spouse and children, adoption, guardianship, inheritance, succession and so on. In addition, there is the presence of some secular laws dealing with matrimonial affairs in the form of Section 125 in the Code Of Criminal Procedure; Sections 498A of the Indian Penal Code; Family Courts Act, 1984, and the Domestic Violence Act, 2005.

7.3. KINSHIP

7.3.1. Approaches to Study Kinship

There are three different approaches to study the kinship system; these are evolutionists, functionalists and structuralist.

Evolutionists believed kinship terminologies to be a means of constructing the past. Morgan (1871) classified the terminology into two types: descriptive (subsumes a relatively small number of kin members who have unique referents) and classificatory (includes a relatively large number of kin members) terms. He explored this typology through his evolutionary framework and stated that 'primitive systems were classificatory whereas civilized systems are descriptive.' Kinship terminology is an important indicator of social relations.

Functionalist believed kinship system deals with a complex set of norms, usages and patterns of behaviour between kindred. During 1930–1940, 'functionalist approach' that tried to explain marriage through descent perspective and stressed exogamy (marriage outside one's own community, clan, tribe) as a negative rule of marriage (as one loses a member which creates disequilibrium).

This approach was succeeded by 'structuralist approach', advocated by Lévi-Strauss, Dumont and Trautman who deliberated 'alliance theory' and proposed exogamy as a positive rule of marriage (as this enables one group to develop and sustain contacts with other groups). Lévi-Strauss arrived at nature–culture distinction, the transition from the natural fact of consanguinity (having the same ancestor) to the cultural fact of the alliance. Structuralist or the alliance theorists classified people as bride givers and takers. Central to this alliance theory is the concept of exchange; primitive societies are marked by the non-economic principle of reciprocity, and this principle largely operates in terms of exchange of scarce goods, that is, food and women. Hence, exogamy is considered to be desirable as it facilitates reciprocity and equitable distribution of women in terms of marriage exchange. Lévi-Strauss borrows from Mauss to understand equitable distribution through reciprocity. Mauss considered gift as a social fact where the return gift is like playing chess where one is not simply playing a move but also evoking the other to make a move as well. Kapadia criticizes structuralists approach, as it marginalizes position of women equating them to commodities in kinship structures.

7.3.2. Kinship Patterns in India

The kinship system of India is associated with the dominant language, Indo–Aryan (a subset of Indo-European in the North), Dravidian (largely in the South) and Munda (central and Eastern affiliated with the larger Austroasiatic family). Karve (1953) travelled across regions of India collecting facts to explore relationships and complex structures of kinship across India. However, her findings are grouped in zones labelled as northern, central, southern and eastern. She documented the distinctions empirically, and to understand kinship in a nuanced manner, she focused on configurations of the linguistic areas, caste institution and organization of the family.

The northern region lies between the Himalayas to the north and the Vindhya Range to the south. It is patrilineal in nature and does not allow cross-cousin marriages. Also, the clans are exogamous in nature; in some caste groups, exogamous clans are stratified in hypergamous rank. All these aspects may not be unanimously present in all the regions of North India. The Northern joint family has unity due to its patriarchal structure, but this unity is impacted as all the brides are from different houses. There is visible rivalry among fathers and sons and collaterals. A man born in the northern zone joint family will have several playmates of his generation. Parents maintain distance from their own child, and the child is often looked after by their aunts (father's brother's wives). The brides are brought from families which are not related by blood.

According to Karve (1953), there is a four-clan rule, and according to this rule, a man must not marry a woman from (a) his father's *gotra*, (b) his mother's *gotra*, (c) his father's mother's *gotra* and (d) his mother's mother's *gotra*. There also prevails local or village exogamy in some parts. The bride givers, in correspondence with their inferior status vis-à-vis bride takers, initiate the process of gift giving during marriage and continue to give gifts on several occasions post marriage. Also, the husband–wife relationship is such, household do not take up primary position in one's life. A woman has to make changes in her life post marriage, whereas a man can continue his earlier life course. Her loyalty to her husband is loyalty to the agnatic joint family of the husband. However, some rules are undergoing change due to unavailability of prospective spouses; for example, there are cases where mother's mother *gotra* is skipped.

The kinship terminology in North India is descriptive in nature because each term describes a relationship from the point of view of the speaker. This is called bifurcate collateral. There is an emphasis on patrilineal descent, and there is a clear-cut distinction between parallel and cross cousins.

The central region includes Rajasthan, Madhya Pradesh, Orissa, Gujarat and Maharashtra. In this system, people predominantly speak languages which are predominantly Sanskritic, though it also includes many tribes speaking Dravidian and Mundari languages. The kinship organization in the central zone, though modelled on the Northern pattern, depicts significant differences which can best be described as being due to culture contact with the other two zones, especially the southern zone of the Dravidian language area.

In the southern region, states of Andhra Pradesh, Karnataka, Tamil Nadu, Kerala and other regions with diverse languages are included. It is a complex system as in some places patrilineal system is widespread, and in some, the matrilineal system is practised. Also referred to as the Dravidian system, it has similar features of caste endogamy. The prevalent joint family in Kerala is called *tharwad*; in relation to the male ego, the members of the family are the mother's mother and her sisters and brothers. Married women live with their mothers. The husbands also live with their mothers and are occasional visitors to their wives and children. In Southern matrilineal family, there is no affinal, that is, relationship by marriage. Sons may be close to their fathers, and the later may wish to secure the property for their sons, but such a practice is debarred in their laws of inheritance. Southern joint families do not have internal stress and strain; the traditional songs do not have themes of rivalries of brothers, sisters-in-law and between daughter-in-law and mother-in-law. In several castes in South India, the first preference is given to the marriage between a man and his elder sister's daughter. Another category of preferred marriage is the marriage of a man with his father's sister's daughter. And finally, the third type of preferential marriage is between man and his mother's brother's daughter. Also, there exists the element of reciprocity, though the bride givers have to pay more gifts than they receive.

The kinship terminology is classificatory in nature, referred to as bifurcate merging. In South India, this terminology clearly separates the two categories of cousins because, in South India, parallel cousins cannot marry each other while cross cousins can. As opposed to the members of a patrilineage, they have the kin group of affinal relatives. They are a person's uterine (from mother's side) and affinal (from wife's side) kin, commonly known as *mama-machchinan.*

The Eastern zone includes the scattered area wherein Austric or Mundari languages are spoken. This zone is not compact, and geographically, it is not contiguous like the other zones. Besides other languages, Mundari and Mon-Khmer languages are also spoken. The main communities are Korku, Annamese, Saka, Semang and Khasi. The other languages are Mon, Khmer and Chain. There is the practice of bride price prevalent. Among Khasi, the husband is considered a stranger. A woman enjoys a greater amount of freedom. Marriages of parallel cousins are not allowed; cross-cousin marriage is also rare.

The Indo-Aryan system is distinct from Dravidian equations which merges affinal and consanguine kin, contrasts cross and parallel cousins and rule of cross-cousin marriage, which acts as an organizing principle. The Indo–Aryan system appears to be structured by the opposition of wife givers and wife takers which differentiates the affine of one side from those of the other side. The procedure of marriage implied by the terminology emphasizes the non-relatedness of the bride and groom and the non-reciprocity of the marriage transaction, which, in principle, flows from the bride's people to the groom's without return. This logic is referred to as *kanyadan.*

Dumont (1968) through his work, *Affinity as a Value*, tried to draw similarities and differences between kinship patterns in North and South India. The South Indian or Dravidian kinship and marriage patterns are bilateral, and there is the preference for cross-cousin marriage. But among Tamilians, the frequently occurring marriage is of unilateral cross cousins (preferably matrilateral cross cousins). In Dravidian kinship or South Indian marriage pattern, the mother's brother has an overriding role at the time of marriage, funeral and puberty ceremonies. Also, they differentiate between kins and affines, that is, who have given daughters, and they are prime gift givers; their parallel and cross relatives are affines. However, there exists a difference between terminological affines and one's own affines, as the former induces marriageability than marriage.

In contrast, in North India, kinship terminology is different. First, there is a distinction between maternal and paternal grandparents and grandchildren. Also, there is different terminology for father's sister husband, father's sister, mother's brother and mother's brother's wife because there are no cross-cousin marriages. However, from the gift-giving aspect, the role of the mother's brother is similar to an affine, that is, wife giver. In South India, consanguinity (the concept of being descended from a common ancestor) is equivalent to affinity, but in North India, affinity is encompassed by consanguinity. Thus, the mother's brother is affine, but ego (individual) cannot marry his children as the relation of affinity is converted into consanguinity. The distinction between North and South Indian marriage forms can be understood synonymously as the distinction between Indo–Aryan and Dravidian marriage pattern and kinship terminology.

The Northern family is strong in the unity of its men. This unity tends to break down because all the brides are from different houses. Also, there is much rivalry among fathers and sons among collaterals. In the Southern matrilineal family, there are no affinal, that is, relations by marriage. *Tharwad* is a system of joint family in South Indian Kerala family consisting of all the descendants in the female line of one common female ancestor. The females are in charge at the functional and ritualistic levels in the hierarchy of the family organization. The kinship vocabulary is the aspect of language and plays an important role in the creation of identity; Morgan anticipated that kinship studies are an instrument for discovering historical relationships. Despite their differences, there are some similarities between North and South Indian patterns: importance of marriage. As caste is a bi-lateral descent group, the group from which the wife comes is critical. Marriage is a point of interaction between caste and kinship; the place of affinity in the system is predominant and valued. The religious texts, in both regions, emphasize *kanyadan* complex (offering of daughter) at the time of marriage. Matriliny in Kerala is withering away as couples set out neo-local households; similarly, in Northeast, it has also become weak.

7.3.3. Women in the Institution of Marriage: Family and Kinship

Gender relations are constructed along the dimensions of caste, class and kinship systems. In several communities in South Asia, a girl's menstruation is marked by a series of rituals which simultaneously celebrate her fecundity and marriageability, also delineating the danger she now poses to her natal kin (Good 1991; Kapadia 1995). Ideologies are exercised to control women's actions, bodies and sexualities. Indian sociocultural marriage system regulates sexuality, and there exists proscription on women's sexuality outside of her marriage, and a woman who engages in premarital sex is considered to bring shame to the family and the community. The stronger the caste identity, the stricter are the regulations against any violations.

It is believed that marriage and motherhood are important cultural indicators that mark the metamorphoses of a girl into a woman. Women are often subjected to unequal access to resources and entitlements in both their natal and affinal families (Sen 1983). As discussed in the previous section, there exist contrasting marriage systems.

Uberoi (1995) feels 'family' is a site of exploitation and violence; however, sociologists seem to neglect its social pathologies. Das (1976), while exploring Punjabi kinship, states that 'pull of the blood' attracts a child to the father. The symbolism of seed and earth helps to emphasize the principle of patrilineal descent and the fact that child derives group identity from the father. Leela Dubey (1996), in her study, equates a woman's body with the field of the earth and semen with the seed; as in patrilineal societies, the process of reproduction is equated with the process of production and rights over the crop. A man's rights over the woman does not only relate to her sexuality and reproductive capacity but also include her productive capacity and labour power. This analogy of seed and earth provides a rationalization for a system in which women are alienated from productive resources and have no rights over their offspring. This leads to gross neglect of women's role in patrilineal kinship.

7.3.4. Changes in Family Marriage and Kinship Patterns

Kinship has been a figment of an anthropologist's imagination and an artefact of bad theory and that comparative studies of kinship had to be situated in 'some other firm ground or abandoned' (Schneider 1980). This statement can be seen as a critique of ethnocentrism suffered from kinship studies. While studying American family, Stacey (1998) described a revolution in domestic life, which was generated by diverse social and economic changes in American society; these changes also impacted the prototypical modern family. The new kinship practices forged by gay men and lesbian women have been attracting scholarly attention across the world. Weston (1991) suggested that gay Americans have contested assumptions that families must not be defined on the basis of genetics and procreative sexuality and have created an alternative kinship paradigm and a distinctive family type, that is, chosen families, which are based on friendship, love and individual choice and a variety of sexual, social and economic relationships. These chosen families provide surrogate kinship ties. Also, there have been ways of challenging the centrality of heterosexual intercourse, and the two opposite sex–gender system of parenthood having babies encompasses a reincorporation of ideas about biological ties and reproduction.

There are some concerns regarding such marriages from socially conservative groups, especially regarding the well-being of children who grow up in same-sex households. However, there are some research reports that claim that same-sex parents are as effective as opposite-sex partners, but same-sex parents express concerns regarding the social devaluation of their relationship and families which may affect the psychological and physical well-being of their children (Wall 2011). But Carrington (1999), while examining the everyday life in households of lesbian, bisexual, and gay families, defined people who engage in a consistent and reciprocal pattern of loving and caring activities.

Intention has been honoured in various recent disputes regarding the custodian rights over children born out of complex reproductive technologies involving gamete donation and surrogacy, with custody being granted to those individuals who put into motion the efforts that created the child (Dolgin 2000). There are rising debates in India against surrogacy; fertile bodies of women have been invaded by invasive techniques to produce children for infertile couples at a cost. Neoliberalism has fostered reproductive markets in India which are thriving in the absence of stringent laws and regulations. With India's billion plus population, poverty and desperate living conditions, women are enticed and coerced into selling their bodies, either whole or in parts. The reproductive industry makes it legitimate for them to sell their reproductive services under the pretext of a 'gift', shrouded in secrecy, due to fear of social stigma. 'Empirical evidence shows the marketability of gametes and wombs, and agents and IVF clinics have come together to respond to the growing demand of infertile couples to have their own biological progeny' (Patel and Reddy 2015).

CONCLUSION

The institutions of the family, kinship and marriage are found in all societies and are part of cultural understandings. And every culture has its own variations in the structure and pattern; individuals and societies have diverse approaches to create a family and form alliance. Every society and community exercises certain rules of marriage. These are related to the choice of selecting a potential partner. Further, marriage is deeply institutionalized and persistent in Indian society. Marriages are typically arranged by parents and other family members since marriage is seemed to affect the status of the family and lineage.

The study of marriage, family and kinship is essential because family and household groups play an indispensable role in defining and maintaining relationships in the society. As cultures change over time, ideas about a family also adapt to new circumstances. There have been changes in the family patterns with increase in the number of cases of single parents and live-in relationships. Migration, mobility and education have weakened the traditional kinship systems and rules of clan organization because members of a caste/sub-caste or a clan do not live in the same household. In India as well, with social, economic and legal changes, there has been a rise in families headed by never-married or divorced mothers, unmarried couples raising children, families with more gender-egalitarian roles and homosexual families.

Also, decisions of not marrying, divorce, remarriage, widespread availability and use of new reproductive technologies present new difficulties for the study of family and kinship. The kinship studies across the world are witnessing a resurgence with allied fields of sexuality, gender studies, demography, social history and evolutionary theory. It is also pertinent to explore the impact of the new reproductive technologies and surrogacy on the cultural structure and regulatory system of family law. The nature of families, as holistic social units imposing on the identities of members, is now paving way for autonomous individuality.

Points for Classroom Discussion

- Types of family structures and their functions
- Marriage is a social institution in India
- The different approaches to study the kinship system
- With a change in culture over time, ideas about family also adapt to new circumstance

GLOSSARY

Bigamy: It is the act of entering into marriage while still married to another person.
Bilateral descent: It is the tracing of kinship through both parents' ancestral lines.
Cohabitation: It is when a couple shares a residence but is not married.

Extended family: It is a household that includes at least one parent and child as well as other relatives such as grandparents, aunts, uncles and cousins.

Family: A family is a socially recognized group of individuals who may be joined by blood, marriage or adoption and who form an emotional connection and an economic unit of society.

Kinship: It is a person's traceable ancestry (by blood, marriage and/or adoption).

Marriage: Marriage is a legally recognized contract between two or more people in a sexual relationship who have an expectation of permanence about their relationship.

Matrilineal descent: It is a type of unilateral descent that follows the mother's side only.

Matrilocal residence: It is a system in which it is customary for a husband to live with his wife's family.

Patrilineal descent: It is a type of unilateral descent that follows the father's line only.

Patrilocal residence: It is a system in which it is customary for the wife to live with (or near) her husband's family.

Unilateral descent: It is the tracing of kinship through one parent only.

REFERENCES

Bailey, F. G. 1960. 'The Joint Family in India: A Framework for discussion'. *The Economic Weekly*, 12, 8: 345-353.

Carrington, C. 1999. *No Place Like Home: Relationships and Family Life Among Lesbians and Gay Men*. Chicago, IL: University of Chicago Press.

Das, V. 1976. 'Masks and Faces: An Essay on Punjabi Kinship'. *Contributions to Indian Sociology* 10, no 1: 1-30.

Desai, I. P. 1956. 'The Joint Family in India—An Analysis.' *Sociological Bulletin* 5, no. 2: 144–156.

Dolgin, J. L. 2000. 'Choice, Tradition, and the New Genetics: The Fragmentation of the Ideology of Family.' *Connecticut Law Review* 32: 523–566.

Dube, L. 1996. 'Caste and Women.' In *Caste: Its Twentieth Century Avatar*, edited by M. N. Srinivas, 1–27. New Delhi: Penguin.

Dube, S. C. 1955. *Indian Village*. London: Routledge.

Dumont, L. 1968. 'Marriage Alliance.' In *International Encyclopedia of the Social Sciences*, edited by D. Shills. New York, NY: Macmillan and Free Press.

Goode, W. J. 1963. *World Revolution and Family Patterns*. New York, NY: The Free Press

Kapadia, K. 1995. *Siva and Her Sisters: Gender, Caste and Class in Rural South India*. Boulder, CO: Westview Press.

Karve, I. 1953. 'The Kinship Map of India.' In *Family, Kinship and Marriage in India*, edited by P. Uberoi, 50–73. New Delhi: Oxford University Press.

Kolenda, P. 1987. *Regional Differences in Family Structure in India*. Jaipur: Rawat Publications.

Maine, H., J. S. 1861. *Ancient Law: Its Connection with the Early History of Society, and Its Relations to Modern Ideas*. (revised edition). New York: Button; London and Toronto: Dent.

Morgan, Louis H. 1871. *Systems of Consanguinity and Affinity of the Human Family* (vol. 17). Washington, DC: Smithsonian Institution.

Murdock, G. 1949. *Social Structure*. New York, NY: Macmillan.

Parsons, T., and R. F. Bales, eds. 1955. *Family, Socialization and Interaction Process*. New York, NY: Free Press.

Patel, T. and S. Reddy. 2015. '"There Are Many Eggs in My Body": Medical Markets and Commodified Bodies in India.' *Global Bioethics* 6, no. 3–4.

Schneider, D. M. 1980. *American Kinship: A Cultural Account*. Englewood Cliffs. Prentice Hall.

Sen, A. 1983. 'Economics and the Family.' *Asian Development Review* 1.

Shah, A. M. 1964. 'Basic Terms and Concepts in the Study of Family in India.' *The Indian Economic & Social History Review* 1, no. 3: 1–36.

Stacey, J. 1998 [1990]. *Brave New Families: Stories of Domestic Upheaval in Late Twentieth Century America.* Berkeley: University of California Press.

Uberoi, P. 1995. *Family, Kinship and Marriage in India.* New Delhi: Oxford University Press, 1–44.

Vatuk, S. 2013. 'The "Women's Court" in India: An Alternative Dispute Resolution Body for Women in Distress.' *The Journal of Legal Pluralism and Unofficial Law* 45, no. 1: 76–103.

Wall, M. 2011. 'Hearing the Voices of Lesbian Women Having Children.' *Journal of GLBT Family Studies* 7, no. 1–2: 93–108.

Weston, K. 1991. *Families We Choose: Lesbians, Gays, Kinship.* New York, NY: Columbia University Press, 261.

SECTION C

RURAL AND URBAN WORLDS

Chapter 8
Panchayat Raj and Rural Development

Chapter 9
Urbanization, Urban Social Transformation and the Right to the City

CHAPTER 8

Panchayat Raj and Rural Development

LEARNING OUTCOMES

- To acquire the understanding of structures of relationships within Indian villages
- To cultivate the ability to engage meaningfully with the village and agrarian communities
- To underscore the initiation and sustenance of the process of rural development in India
- To foster a critical approach and reflective perspective towards unequal power distribution and negotiations around it

Keywords: Rural development, Panchayati Raj, institutional credit system, agrarian structures, rural–urban continuum

The village communities are little Republics, having nearly everything they want within themselves, and almost independent of foreign relations. They seem to last where nothing else lasts. Dynasty after dynasty tumbles down; revolution succeeds revolution; Hindu, Pathan, Mughal, Mahratta, Sikh, English are masters in turn; but the village communities remain the same.

—**Metcalfe (quoted in Cohn 1987, 213)**

INTRODUCTION

Before professional anthropologists and sociologists commenced with village studies, social life in the Indian village was documented by colonial ethnographers. Their understanding emphasized that the village communities were harmonious, isolated and unchanging, which blocked the perceptions of impoverishment caused by colonial policies. Britishers believed that the crucial element of the harmonious relationship among the village communities was due to the absence of private ownership of land; land was thought to be owned by village collectively. This was a rather superficial understanding; the unchanging aspect of the village does not stand up to historical scrutiny since land was in abundance and there was no sale and purchase of land; but not everyone had equal access or rights of cultivation or land produce; they were instead based on land governing rules and customs or grants made by the rulers. Also, during the medieval times, villages were associated to the central authority through the revenue bureaucracy; land revenue served as a dominant medium of surplus appropriation during the medieval times. In India, the study of peasants arrived with the vastly influential assemblage of essays, *Village in India* by Marriott (1955), which introduced and explored concepts and categories of small and large communities. Mahatma Gandhi reinforced the ideology of self-sufficiency, morality upholding and economically integrated community on the conception of villages in India. Villages in India display many elements of structural unity, such as a sentiment of territorial political kinship and economic solidarity. It is observed through several historical and contemporary case studies that the territorial cohesiveness of the villages in India continues to exist. Although the sense of village identity intersects caste loyalties that divides a village, it has been the need and the supremacy of the sentiment of cooperation that maintains cohesiveness among the members of the village. This solidarity was expressed through inter-caste relations not only based on dominance but also on reciprocity. This institution is referred to as the Jajmani system. This system facilitated the economic and ritual mutuality and interdependence of castes. It bonded the members of the castes into solidary relationships. But this system among the *jajmans* is not reciprocal in all villages, because the dominant castes swing the balance of power in their favour in such relationships in many villages across India. Institutional changes introduced through land reforms, CDPs, panchayat elections and national elections have relatively changed the structure of cohesiveness of the village community and its inter-group power relationship. However, these changes have not completely eroded the sense of village identity.

8.1. VILLAGE IN INDIA

8.1.1. Rural Development

In the discipline of sociology, a new sub-discipline of rural sociology emerged within the functionalist paradigm to study the community life of rural people. According to Y. Singh (2007), village is a micro-structure which has not only been recognized but has also become a vital aspect of national development planning and politico-cultural consciousness. Dumont and Pockock (1957) while analysing *Indian villages understood them as a microcosm reflecting the macrocosm of Indian civilization.* Beteille (1974) emphasized that a village in India was characterized by a baffling variety of land relations and a complex hierarchy of land ownership rights. Since Independence, there have been many government-sponsored schemes of development and reforming the village administration.

Rural development is understood as a process of improving the quality of life and facilitating the economic, social and political well-being of people residing in rural areas. As per the reports of 2011 census, 68.4 per cent of the population lives in villages; therefore, any kind of backwardness of the rural sector would impact the economic process in general. Rural development in India holds the key to the overall development of the economy, food security and quality of life. Earlier during the 1970s, rural development was a coterminous with agriculture development to enhance agricultural production. Currently, it has become inclusive to focus on all aspects of rural life.

8.1.1.1. Gandhi's Notion of Rural Development

Gandhi was of the view that the villages must be given their due credit because they are the basic unit of political and economic development. His model of rural development emphasized that independence must originate from grassroots; every village must be self-sustained and capable of managing its affairs and defending it. He aimed to resuscitate the villages through a silent revolution, imparting literacy and intensive learning of local crafts, which would amplify the self-sufficiency of the villagers. He also wanted to emphasize on the revival of the cottage industries as paddy de-husking, oil pressing, handicrafts, handloom weaving, leather work and others. His idea of rural development was multidimensional, with a total focus on human development and with an emphasis on the quality of development. He undertook constructive rural development programmes in Champaran, Sevagram and Wardha, and termed them as an instrument of permanent value. While drafting these constructive programmes, there were consideration towards the economic, political, social and moral aspects of development. His approach could be classified into five segments: economic, educational, social, environmental and political. The constructive programme as revised has nearly 19 items, including communal unity, removal of untouchability, prohibition, khadi, other industries, village sanitation, new basic education, adult education, women empowerment, education health and hygiene, focus on provincial language, national language, economic equality, kisans, labour, Adivasis, lepers, students and improvement of livestock. There was stress on the revival of rural industries, such as handlooms, khadi and handicrafts, to confront the large-scale mass production of industrialization. In India, many industries are concentrated in a few big cities, which creates problem of overpopulation, inequality in income, environmental degradation and monopolistic trends, whereas the development of rural industries can allow for economic decentralization and generate wealth for larger communities. The Gandhian model of self-sufficient village is also relevant in the context of reducing poverty and unemployment in India.

In general, the inclusive aspect of development covers three interrelated dimensions: political, economic and social. Political dimension through the Panchayati Raj

Institutions (PRIs) attempts to improve the opportunities for the marginalized in rural areas to participate effectively and equally in local political processes. The economic aspect of rural development encompasses efforts to provide both capacity and opportunities for poor and low-income households to benefit, in particular, from economic growth. In addition, the social dimension assists to promote gender equality, empowerment and social security to the marginalized section.

8.1.2. Panchayati Raj

In 1992, India ratified 73rd and 74th constitutional amendments establishing a new system of local government, the Panchayati Raj system, to decentralize administration at the local village level. The Indian scenario necessitates regional solutions for regional problems. This amendment reserved seats in local-level panchayats for historically disadvantaged groups: 'Scheduled' castes and tribes and women. Simply in terms of numbers, the results were impressive. In 2014, nearly 3 million Indians were elected to almost 250,000 panchayats, of whom 19 per cent were SCs, 12 per cent were STs and 46 per cent were women.

Panchayats are expected to play an important role in rural development in India. In India, rural development is of the utmost concern as nearly 72.22 per cent (Census 2001) of its population continues to live in rural areas. The Five-Year Plan, especially the 2nd Five-Year Plan, envisaged panchayat's responsibility for rural development and the social and economic transformation of communities residing within the area of the village. It is thus essential to conceptualize the system of Panchayati Raj to understand its nature and scope.

Panchayati Raj is associated with two broad conceptions: (a) it is a government in itself and (b) it is an agency of state government. The current three-tier representative structure, where the administrators, elected leaders and the local population participate and coordinate towards social economic development. Refer to Box 8.1 for the salient features of the 73rd and 74th amendment act. Here, the role of elected leaders is crucial in decision-making. The emphasis of rural development policies is to involve people in development programmes, which is possible only through elected or chosen leaders. Therefore, in India, Panchayati Raj is often a coterminous with rural development.

BOX 8.1

Salient Features of the 73rd and 74th Constitution Amendment Acts

Panchayats and municipalities will be 'institutions of self-government'.

1. Basic units of the democratic system—gram sabhas (villages) and ward committees (municipalities)—comprising all adult members registered as voters.
2. Three-tier system of panchayats at the village, intermediate block/taluk/mandal and district levels, except in states with a population below 20 lakh (Article 243B).

3. Seats at all levels to be filled by direct elections (Article 243C [2]).
4. Seats shall be reserved for SCs and STs, and posts of chairpersons of panchayats at all levels shall also be reserved for SCs and STs in proportion to their population.
5. One-third of the total number of seats to be reserved for women. One-third of the seats reserved for SCs and STs also to be reserved for women. One-third offices of chairpersons at all levels to be reserved for women (Article 243D).
6. Uniform five-year term and elections to constitute new bodies to be completed before the expiry of the term. In the event of dissolution, elections must be held compulsorily within six months (Article 243E).
7. Independent Election Commission in each state for the superintendence, direction and control of the electoral rolls (Article 243K).
8. Panchayats to prepare plans for economic development and social justice in respect of subjects as devolved by law to the various levels of panchayats, including subjects as illustrated in the Eleventh Schedule (Article 243G).
9. The 74th amendment provides for a District Planning Committee to consolidate the plans prepared by panchayats and municipalities (Article 243ZD).
10. Budgetary allocation from state governments, share of revenue of certain taxes, collection and retention of revenue it raises, central government programmes and grants, and Union Finance Commission grants (Article 243H).
11. Establish a Finance Commission in each state to determine principles on the basis of which adequate financial resources would be ensured for panchayats and municipalities (Article 243I).

Along with the panchayat at the grassroot level, there are taluk boards or panchayat samitis whose territorial limit overlaps with the revenue taluk and the community development blocks, and finally the District Development Council.

8.1.2.1 Structure of Panchayati Raj

The organizational set-up of the PRIs added a new dimension to the administration. The basic structure of the PRI is similar across states in India, but it is described under different nomenclatures in different states. In every state, it has its own characteristics and election procedures. A district panchayat or Zila Parishad is coterminous with the district, each district has one Zila Parishad. Similarly, block panchayats or panchayat samitis are coterminous with blocks of the same district. Further, a block may have several villages within it, but a gram panchayat may not always be coterminous with each village. The size of the population (number of voters) in a village (gram) is defined under the law with a specific geographical area which may comprise a single village or a cluster of adjoining villages.

Members of Panchayats

1. **Zila panchayat:** Each block panchayat under a Zila Parishad elects one/two/three members directly, depending on the number of voters within it its

area. The presidents of all the block panchayats are also ex-officio members of the Zila Parishad. In some states, the Member of Legislative Assembly (MLA) and the Member of Parliament (MP) of the district/constituency are also ex-officio members.
2. **Block panchayat or panchayat samiti:** Every gram panchayat under a block panchayat elects one/two/three members directly to the block panchayat. Gram panchayat pradhans are ex-officio members of the block panchayats.
3. **Gram panchayat:** They are at the lowest level of the PRI; a gram as defined under the Act (refers to a village or a cluster of villages) is divided into a minimum of five constituencies (which depend on the number of voters the village is having). From each of these constituencies, one member is elected. The body of these elected members is called the gram panchayat. The size of these gram panchayats varies widely across states in India. In Haryana, there are 6,197 gram panchayats, whereas a bigger state like Rajasthan has 723 gram panchayats.

    Panchayats, as per constitutional provisions, shall prepare economic development and social justice plans for their respective areas and shall work towards their execution. States are required to facilitate this by devolving 29 subjects as mandated to panchayats and also to generate funds for the same as per the recommendations of the State Finance Commission. The functions of the panchayats are divided among the different committees, such as Standing Committees, Sthayee Samitis and Upa Samitis. One of the members remains in charge of such committees, while the overall charge rests with the chairperson of the panchayat. Panchayats are supported by a host of other officials, the numbers of which vary from state to state. Apart from the grants received from the government under the recommendation of the Finance Commission, panchayats receive schematic funds for the implementation of schemes (Mahatma Gandhi National Rural Employment Guarantee Scheme [MGNREGS], Backward Regions Grant Fund [BRGF], Indira Awas Yojana [IAY] and so on). They can also raise revenue by imposing taxes, fees, penalties and so on as per the rule of the state.
4. **Gram sabha:** Each constituency of the members of the gram panchayat is called gram sabha, and all voters of the same constituency are members of this body. However, in some states, this is referred to as ward sabha/palli sabha. In West Bengal, it is called gram sansad and, here too, the voters of the gram panchayat as a whole constitute the gram sabha.

As per the constitutional provisions, there can only be three tiers of panchayat. Gram sabha is not a tier of the Panchayati Raj system, it functions as a recommending body only. It holds meetings twice or four times a year but can meet whenever necessary. The issue to be discussed in the meetings can be wide ranging, but the essential agenda includes annual action plan and budget, annual accounts and annual report of the gram panchayat, along with the selection of beneficiaries (for different social service programmes [IAY], pension schemes and so on), the identification of schemes for the preparation of annual plan for development programmes (e.g., MGNREGS) and analysing audit reports and gram panchayats performance.

8.1.3. Change in the Power Structure

An important change is visible in the realm of power structure in the villages. Although the abolition of privileges and economic rights of intermediaries, such as zamindars and feudal, has not been completely successful in creating an egalitarian class structure in villages, it has made a great social psychological impact on previously disadvantaged groups and stimulated them for competing with traditional powerful groups for access to positions of power and social status. This process has been augmented due to the emergence of Panchayati Raj, which has transformed the structure of village leadership. The village leadership is changing to become a logical peace-making agency in several villages. The traditional power structures of older elite groups have paved a way for reconciling with factions and opposite interest groups to stay in power. The leaders in villages now have to be reasonable; and they must exercise control through informal relationships and bureaucratic innovations to improvise and sustain their positions. Studies have shown that informal leadership is more effective than formal leadership to mitigate faction-emerged crisis. In the village of Morsalli in Bangalore, the growth of factions in village is associated with the introduction of government-sponsored reforms and with interference in village affairs by the government; new factional leaders have acquired additional economic autonomy through cash-crop farming and hired labourers from outside, as opposed to traditional free cooperative labour. This has given the factional leaders the edge over the traditional leaders whose only sanction was to manipulate the free cooperative supply of labour. These new changes in economic and administrative structures introduced a new dynamic element in the leadership of Morsalli (McCormack 1960). Similarly, in Andhra Pradesh village of Padu, the leadership is with economically dominant families within each caste and wealth along with high-caste status. Families that are more outward looking, rich and follow traditional patterns hold leadership positions. Oscar Lewis' study on the Jats of Rampura village in North India delineates four characteristic features of Jat leadership: (a) the tendency to minimize the status difference between the leader and the led within the caste; (b) resistance to delegate authority to leaders permanently without consultation with the appropriate faction; (c) complete absence of youth leadership and (d) lack of direct role of women in leadership. This pattern may not be completely relevant; however, it continues to be prevalent in some parts. Another important study by Bailey on Bisipara village discusses the upward economic and political mobility of traditional Ganjam and Boad distillers. These two lower castes, by trading in liquor, could earn enough money to purchase land in the village which formerly was the sole monopoly of the Warrior caste, the dominant group in Bisipara. This reflects a change in the traditional system of social stratification.

The examples discussed above reflect a wider perspective on leadership and power structure of villages in India. Its structure still seems to be dominated by rich and upper caste groups, but there is a tendency towards recruiting literate young members to leadership roles. An important aspect to gain leadership in a village and have dominance over its affairs is landed property. Leadership is an indirect manifestation of the system of social stratification, and the process of change reveals a tendency towards redefinition and readaptation of roles among traditionally powerful groups in order to maintain their position in the power structure. New democratic rights and constitutional safeguards have motivated the disadvantaged to aspire for power, but their economic conditions act as a deterrent. The emergent tensions for power of this type ultimately end up in a reconciliation by which the traditionally dominant castes and classes remain in power by a series of accommodations and manipulations (Singh 1986).

8.1.3.1. Unequal Distribution of Power

Status mobility and rising motivation towards education is impacting the local, regional and national share of power structures. This change has also been a result of the politicization of villages in India through contemporary political reforms. It has also been motivated by community development schemes, which now cover almost all of the villages in India. Dube (1958) lamented that the benefits of this development and progress have generally gone to the upper castes and classes in the village. However, there have been visible changes in the standard of living, conditions of housing, health and sanitation of most of the villages in the country.

The existential structure has not kept pace with the aspiration, as the social stratification and power structure of the villages shows only marginal changes of adaptive nature rather than structural changes, the rate of economic and social progress has also not been of a revolutionary character (Singh 1986). According to Lewis (1965), the process of change and its tensions continue, and the hopeful aspect of the process is that the village micro-structure has now ceased to be 'inward-looking' and is poised for more dynamic internal adjustments as the external pressure for change gains strength. Uncertainty and tension are a natural by-product of this process in the interim period.

Changes in rural micro-structure are more adjustive than structural in significance. Traditionally influential groups still continue to wield influence and power. Caste privileges still continue to coincide with the privileged class status. The upper castes now hold on to power not by traditional legitimation of their authority but through consensus, which is often manipulated, but democratic ethos is maintained. Nonetheless, change is happening. Singh (1986) states that power is held by a traditional privileged class, but it is no longer institutionalized by tradition.

8.2. POLITICAL IDENTITY IN VILLAGES

8.2.1. Struggle for Political Identity

As discussed in the previous section, 73rd and 74th amendments have caused changes in the traditional power structure. An important radical measure underlying this legislation is regarding the reservation for women, SCs and STs not only in membership to the PRI but also in positions of office such as sarpanch. This has allowed for enhanced participation and share in power at the local level of communities which were previously marginalized. Ahlawat (2015) explored the extent to which the new provisions have enabled the above-mentioned categories in the state of Haryana. It was noted in the study that during the 2010 panchayat elections, 1,978 women were elected as sarpanches, of which 397 were SCs, since there are no tribes in Haryana, this special category was not included for the panchayat elections. Total 17,918 women were elected as members of the panchayats, 3,851 belonged to the SCs; 37 women were elected as chairpersons of panchayat samitis, 7 of whom belonged to the SC category. The figures reveal that the PRI has given identity and dignity to the Dalits and women who were earlier invisible from the power structure of village.

8.2.1.1. Dalits

For the Dalits to be able to get elected as sarpanches or members of panchayat, the members have been forced to renegotiate their relationships with them. Also, in many villages, dominant castes rekindle their networks to make SCs their allies for winning the panchayat elections. The increased influence of politics at the PRI stage has also created caste-based political mobilization among the Dalits. Medha (2001) argued that though *caste has lost its 'moral basis' ideologically, the subjugation of the Dalits was seen to be due to their dependence on landowners*. The caste-related structures of domination have not disappeared in the day-to-day functioning of the panchayats. Dalits' domination is limited. The dominant castes resist the sharing of power with the Dalits, and their opinions in the gram sabha meetings do not carry as much weightage as those of the sarpanch of the dominant caste (Ahlawat 2015). It was also observed that when a woman is elected from a non-dominant or Dalit caste, the members of the panchayat create a crisis of legitimacy for the gram panchayat (Ahlawat 2015).

8.2.1.2. Women

PRIs have allowed for democratic percolation to the grassroots level and have created women empowerment through granting them 33 per cent reservation. This decentralization is a blend of realism and tokenism. PRIs have challenged patriarchal stereotypes by providing opportunities to women of all castes to play an effective role in bringing change in the society. With the help of women, PRIs facilitated the development and promotion of self-help groups, cooperatives and micro, small and medium enterprises for better employment and livelihood options in rural areas. This political empowerment has also enabled many women to gain confidence in their private space. However, though women get political representation, the real power is usurped by their husbands, referred to as sarpanch pati. This situation is further complicated due to widespread illiteracy, which restricts their ability to perform or speak without hesitation. Recent criteria to participate in PRI election requires an education qualification up to 10th standard, which has been observed as another setback to women empowerment, as many women in rural areas are deprived of education due to gender bias and inequality. Illiteracy acts as an impediment towards their general and political awareness.

8.3. ECONOMIC DEVELOPMENT

8.3.1. Changes in the Agrarian Structure

The colonial regime initiated the task of reorganizing local society within a framework that would make governance easy and manageable with the introduction of new property rights in land. The most controversial was the Permanent Settlement introduced in Bengal in 1793. Under this intermediary, zamindars were granted ownership rights over lands on which they earlier had only revenue collection rights. It had political and strategic implications, as in the landlords Britishers saw a possible support base in local society. But, contrary to expectations, it had accelerated 'parasitic landlordism'. After this experience in Bengal, Britishers introduced a new system called the Ryotwari system in the regions of Madras, Bombay and Berar. Here, the *ryot* was a tenant of the state. Another arrangement was the Mahalwari or Malguzari system introduced in the United Provinces, Punjab and the Central Provinces. Here, the ownership of the cultivated land was with the cultivator and the revenue was collectively paid by the village as a unit. The different arrangement introduced similar patterns of change across parts of British India. Although these settlements changed the formal structure of authority, these also revitalized the older quasi-feudal order where peasants faced extensive exploitation.

In India, a major economic change that has had an impact on the village structure was the introduction of land reforms. According to Y. Singh (2007), post-Independence land reforms were introduced through (a) the abolition of intermediaries, (b) tenancy reforms, (c) ceiling on landholdings and redistribution of land, (d) the consolidation of holdings and the prevention of holdings from deteriorating to uneconomic size, (e) the emphasis on and development of cooperative farming and (f) the religio-economic movement for the gift of surplus land by rich to the poor as *bhoodan*. These measures have been implemented differently in different states, but they have created some uniform sociological consequences towards rural development.

8.3.2. Institutional Credit System and CDP

The former hold of moneylenders over the peasantry had to be weakened by providing credit through institutional sources, initially by credit societies and later by nationalized commercial banks. The Indian state planned to expand the network of cooperative credit societies to dismantle informal sources of credit. Through the imposition of social control and later their nationalization, commercial banks were also asked to lend to the agriculture sector on a priority basis. This resulted in a subsequent and sharp decline in the dependence of rural households on informal sources for credit. However, the assessment of cooperative credit societies revealed that a significant portion of their credit went to relatively better-off sections of rural society, and the poor continued to rely on more expensive informal sources (Oommen 1985). The state intervention was through the bureaucratization of cooperative societies. In some regions this helped in releasing credit societies from the hold of big landowners, but it also led to rampant corruption and increasing apathy among those whom they were supposed to serve (Jodhka 1995). Although banks were never controlled directly by the rural rich, the benefit of their credit has largely gone to those who had substantial landholdings (Jodhka 1995). Nonetheless, the credit system played a significant role in marginalizing the role of moneylenders in the rural power structure.

CDP was launched in 1952 in a few blocks and later extended to the entire country. It was a strategy different from land reforms and the institutional credit system. It emanated from a protectionist approach to rural development, whereas earlier programmes reflected an institutionalist perspective. Its objective was to provide a substantial increase in agricultural production and improvement in basic services, which would ultimately lead to a transformation in the social and economic life of the village (Dube 1958). However, this programme benefitted the already powerful rural elites.

8.3.3. Green Revolution

It is considered to be the most successful programmes launched after Independence; however, its negative consequences are surfacing now in many regions of Punjab. The Green Revolution conceptualized agrarian change in technological terms and was based on the trickle-down theory of economic growth. It refers to the effects of higher yielding variety of seeds of wheat and rice in lower-middle income countries. It also included other measures such as chemical fertilizers, controlled irrigation conditions and pesticides, cheap institutional credit, price incentives and marketing facilities. However, this revolution provided different results for smaller farmers as compared to big landed farmers. The latter had enough surplus to invest in new capital-intensive farming; for smaller farmers, it meant greater dependence on borrowing, generally from informal sources. *The category of new rich farmers mobilized a 'new farmers' movements to strike a better deal for the agriculture sector. Although initiated in the 1970s, it gained momentum in the 1980s by using the language of neo-populism* (Dhanagare 1991). The leaders argued that there was a growing division between the city and the village; the agrarian sector was exploited by the city for the industrial sector through a mechanism of 'unequal exchange'.

8.3.4. Post-1991 Change

The rural economy is represented as an agrarian economy, with farming and agriculture as primary activities. However, since the time of economic liberalization and globalization, there were policies that have been argued to be adversarial to the environment and have impacted agriculture growth. Nearly 61.5 per cent (2011 Census) is dependent on agriculture, and technical advancements in the field have widened the gap between the rich and the poor, as only the rich and large farm holding farmers could adopt modern technology. This issue has been a critical aspect as it can disrupt the process of developing the rural economy. Most of the labour force in India depends on agriculture, not because it is remunerative but because there is a lack of alternative opportunities that creates backwardness in the agriculture sector.

There has been a constant decline in the share allotted to agriculture, which has affected productivity. Moreover, public investment declined since 1991, coupled with a lack of adequate infrastructure, credit, transport, employment and so on; therefore, the agriculture output has grown at only 3.2 per cent during 2007–2011. Crisis farmers' suicide in various regions across the country due to the unavailability of adequate resources, reducing output and mounting debts is becoming a matter of concern for the government at both the central and the state levels. Available studies on rural India also provide a detailed description on the composition of rural output and patterns of employment and unemployment, along with income inequalities across sectors and between rural and urban sectors. During 2001–2011, India's urban population increased 31.8 per cent compared to 12.8 per cent increase in the rural population. Nearly 50 per cent increase in urban population during this period was attributed to rural–urban migration and the re-classification of rural settlements into urban (Pradhan 2013). Population projections indicate that India will continue to be predominantly rural till 2050, after which the urban population will take over the rural population (UN-Habitat 2013).

8.4. RURAL–URBAN CONTINUUM

The rural–urban continuum is a process of socio-economic and cultural interaction between cities and villages. Redfield (1930) introduced the concept of *rural–urban continuum* during his study of the Mexican peasant community. He observed that the community moves from the folk to the urban end of the continuum; with people, there are movements of ideas, practices and environmental impact. This movement also leads to a mutual impact on the lifestyle, culture and economy of both rural and urban areas. This migration from rural to urban is often unplanned, particularly in the search for better economic opportunities, which places severe pressure on urban amenities and compels a large number of low-wage migrants from rural areas to live in unhygienic and deprived conditions. Thus, to check unplanned migration from rural to urban areas and to improve the socio-economic conditions of the vast majority of population in the country, there is a need to revive rural economy and make it stronger and create employment opportunities in the rural economy. The improvement in economic conditions of rural households will effectively reduce the disparity between rural and urban per capita income. However, this would require significantly higher investments in rural economy.

Another important aspect of the rural–urban continuum in India is that we cannot establish or demarcate between the urban and rural boundaries in a few areas. For instance, the capital city of Delhi is surrounded by several villages such as Narela, Rajokri and many exist in the heartland of the city itself, such as Munirka and Hauz Khas. This makes the spatial distinction between rural and urban perplexing.

8.4.1. Social Development

In the efforts to provide gainful employment, to alleviate poverty, to provide dignity of work and life to a large population, there has to be some planned intervention. Refer to the Box 8.2 for the list of development programmes. Cooperatives have been an alternative and a meaningful form of development activity in the Indian context. The cooperative movement has been important in the socio-economic transformation of rural society. These cooperatives were launched mainly to take care of the financial needs of farmers at critical times like harvesting and so on. These cooperatives were also involved in the procurement and distribution of inputs required for agriculture purpose, ensuring the availability of quality inputs at optimum prices to the farmers. They also provided gainful employment and dignity to many households in rural areas. The success of cooperatives—the Amul experiment, sugar cooperatives and so on—could be seen in states such as Gujarat, Maharashtra, Karnataka and Andhra Pradesh. They have also been instrumental in developing rural areas with facilities such as education centres, hospitals, entertainment centres and cooperative stores. They have become models of emulation and are a classic example of how cooperative movements could be contributing to the socio-economic development of the rural sector. Similar adaptation has been attempted in many other sectors, such as oilseeds, spinning, fisheries and handlooms. There is also scope for cooperatives to promote tourism and to harness opportunities to create foreign exchange. Also, the schemes such as Integrated Rural Development Program launched in 1980 helped in providing employment opportunities by developing skills. From the 1990s, the literacy campaign missions have attempted to rectify the gap in terms of adult literacy, with varying degree of success in different states.

BOX 8.2
Rural Social Development Programmes

In India, since Independence, various programmes have been launched to secure the social structure in rural India. The following are a few of the active programmes:

1. The government assured to provide electricity and clean cooking facility to all willing rural families by 2022 under the **Ujjwala Yojana and the Saubhagya Yojana.**
2. **Pradhan Mantri Awas Yojana-Gramin :** This will provide 1.95 crore houses to eligible beneficiaries during its second phase (2019–2020 to 2021–2022) along with amenities such as toilets, electricity and LPG connections.
3. **Deen Dayal Upadhyaya Grameen Kaushalya Yojana (DDUGKY):** This is a placement-linked skill development scheme for rural poor youth. It was launched on 25 September 2014 and aims to target young people aged between 15 and 35 years. A total of 52,000 candidates have been skilled under this programme till 2014–2015.
4. **Roshni (a skill development scheme for tribals):** The Ministry of Rural Development on 7 June 2013 launched a new skill development scheme designed to offer employment to tribal youth in 24 Naxal-affected districts. The scheme, which is named Roshni, is supposed to provide training and employment to an anticipated 50,000 young people in the 10–35 years age group for a period of three years.
5. Swachh Bharat Mission was launched in 2014 to provide every person with access to sanitation facilities, including toilets, solid and liquid waste disposal systems, village cleanliness, and safe and adequate drinking water supply. The programme is to be implemented by the Ministry of Drinking Water and Sanitation.
6. **Sansad Adarsh Gram Yojana (SAGY):** This programme was launched by Prime Minister Narendra Modi on the birth anniversary of Lok Nayak Jai Prakash Narayan on 11 October 2014. The Ministry of Rural Development will be the supervising authority for this programme. Under this programme, each MP will

take the responsibility for developing physical and institutional infrastructure in three villages by 2019.

7. **MGNREGS:** It was launched as the National Rural Employment Guarantee Act, 2005, in February 2006. Now the new name of this scheme is 'Mahatma Gandhi National Rural Employment Guarantee Act'. This scheme is an Indian labour law and social security measure that aims to provide the 'right to work' to people falling below the poverty line (BPL). It guarantees 100 days of employment in a year to the village people. Fifty per cent workers should be women. Its 90 per cent funding is borne by the central government and 10 per cent by the state government.

8. **National Rural Livelihoods Mission:** This scheme was restructured from the Swarna Jayanti Gram Swarozgar Yojana in 2011. The National Rural Livelihoods Mission (Aajeevika) aims to empower the women's self-help group model across the country. Under this scheme, the government provides loan up to ₹3 lakh at the rate of 7 per cent, which could be lowered to 4 per cent on timely repayment.

9. **Pradhan Mantri Gram Sadak Yojana:** This scheme is launched by the Ministry of Rural Development. Initially, it was 100 per cent centrally funded scheme, launched on 25 December 2000. After the recommendation of the 14th Finance Commission's report, expenditure will now be shared between the centre and the state in the ratio of 60:40. The main aim of this scheme is to provide all-weather road connectivity to rural areas with a population more than 500 persons and in terms of hilly areas it is 250 persons.

10. **Antyodaya Anna Yojana:** Launched in 2000, it provides food grains to around 2 crore BPL families at a very subsidized rate. Total 35 kg of food grains is provided to a family. Rice is provided at the rate of ₹3/kg and wheat at ₹2/kg.

11. **National Rural Health Mission:** The National Rural Health Mission, now under the National Health Mission, was initiated on 12 April 2005. The main aim of this plan is to provide accessible, affordable and accountable quality health services even to the poorest households in the remotest rural regions.

Source: googleimages.com.

12. **Aam Aadmi Bima Yojana:** Launched in 2007, it aims to provide social security for rural households. Under this scheme, one member of the family is covered; the premium of ₹200 per person per annum is shared by the state and central government. The insured person need not to pay any premium if his/her *age is between 18 and 59* years.
13. **Sarva Shiksha Abhiyan** has been operational since 2000–2001. Its main aim is to make free and compulsory education to children between the ages of 6 and 14 (a fundamental right). Currently, its expenditure is shared by the centre and state in a ratio of 50:50.

CONCLUSION

The rural sector in India has been neglected and remains underdeveloped; basic amenities such as drinking water, electricity, healthcare, educational transport, communication and other facilities continue to be unevenly distributed. The processes of political, economic and social development have empowered rural people. The increasing interaction of villages in the market and the increasing availability of alternative sources of employment opportunities outside agriculture, coupled with a changing political framework, had weakened the control of landowners over labourers. New agrarian technologies have impacted the position of women in the household and on the farm. Dube (1985) pointed out 'gender blindness' of development theory and surveys on issues such as poverty and land rights of women. Female wage labour in agriculture is marginalized in terms of work and earnings. Also, the questions of ecology and displacement with new social movements against the construction of power projects are also critical of India's development model.

It is essential to understand that while social policy is desirable and a necessary concomitant of the development process, its existence and form in each social context cannot be taken for granted. Policies also depend upon the political and economic configurations which influence both its extent and its evolution. This is clearly evident from the Indian experience, which depicts both the need for an effective social policy and the relative inadequacy of what has been provided by the state in terms of meeting the basic objectives of the nationalist developmental project.

Points for Classroom Discussion

- Rural development has impacted the process of village transformation in India
- Rural–urban continuum redefines the division and interaction between cities and villages
- The agrarian economy is indispensable for overall country's development
- The role of Dalit and women is crucial to rural development

GLOSSARY

Agrarian economy: It is calculated on the basis of rural growth and is centred around the production, consumption, trade and sale of agricultural commodities, including grains, livestock and so on.

Institutional credit system: It is a means where agriculture credits are provided by government institutions, such as RRBs, commercial banks, cooperative banks and microfinance institutions.

Rural development: It is the process of improving the quality of life and economic well-being of people living in rural areas. This initiative traditionally focuses around land-intensive natural resources.

Rural–urban continuum: It refers to a process on which the peripheries of town and the villages merge. This also recognizes that there is no clear physical or social division between urban and rural populations.

REFERENCES

Ahlawat, S. R. 2015. 'Inclusion of Excluded Communities: A Study of Local Governance Crises of Social Transformation in India'. In *Crises of Social Transformation in India*, edited by S. R. Ahlawat and Neerja Ahlawat. New Delhi: Rawat Publications.

Beteille, A. 1974. *India: Studies in Agrarian Social Structure*. New Delhi: Oxford University Press.

Cohn, B. S. 1987. *An Anthropologist Among Historians and Other Essays.* New Delhi: Oxford University Press.

Dhanagare, D. N. 1991. 'The Model of Agrarian Classes in India'. In *Social Stratification*, edited by D. Gupta, 358–366. New Delhi: Oxford University Press.

Dube, S. C. 1958. *India's Changing Villages*. London: Routledge and Kegan Paul.

Dumont, L. and D. F. Pockock. 1957. 'Village Studies'. *Contributions to Indian Sociology*, 1: 23-41.

Jodhka, S. S. 1995. 'Who Borrows? Who Lends?: Changing Structure of Informal Credit in Rural Haryana'. *Economic & Political Weekly* 30, no. 39: A123–A132.

Lewis, O. 1965. *Village Life in Northern India: Studies in a Delhi Village*. Champaign, IL: University of Illinois Press.

Marriott, M. 1955. *Village India: Studies in the Little Community* (Comparative Studies of Cultures and Civilizations [No. 6]). Chicago, IL: University of Chicago Press.

McCormack, W. 1960. 'Factionalism in a Mysore Village'. In *Leadership and Political Institutions in India*, edited by R. L. Park and I. Tinker, 349. London: Oxford University Press.

Medha, K. L. 2001. 'Local Governments: Conflict of Interests and Issues of Legitimization'. *Economic & Political Weekly* 42, no. 41: 4121–4124.

Oommen, T. K. 1985. *From Mobilization to Institutionalization: The Dynamics of Agrarian Movement in 20 Century Kerala*. Bombay: Popular Prakashan.

Pradhan, K. C. 2013. 'Unacknowledged Urbanisation: The New Census Towns in India.' *Economic & Political Weekly* XLVIII, no 36: 43–51.

Redfield, R. 1930. *Tepoztlán, a Mexican Village: A Study of Folk Life*. Chicago, IL: University of Chicago Press.

Singh, Y. 1986. *Modernization of Indian Tradition*. New Delhi: Rawat Publications.

———. 2007. 'Composite Culture, Community and Identity: Interface with Social Change in India'. In *Composite Culture in Multicultural Society* edited by Bipin Chandra and Sucheta Mahajan. 195–218. New Delhi: Pearson Longman.

UN-Habitat. 2013. *State of the World's Cities Report 2012/2013: Prosperity of Cities*. London: Routledge.

CHAPTER 9

Urbanization, Urban Social Transformation and the Right to the City

LEARNING OUTCOMES

- To comprehend the significance of the city and the process of urbanization and its consequences
- To identify the historical and modern context of the process of urbanism and development of urban space
- To expose students to critical theoretical debates around urban space and its intersection with institutions and identities
- To facilitate a better understanding of city life, urban environment and their access

Keywords: Urbanization, urbanism, slum, poverty, urban space, professionals

A city is an administratively defined unit of territory containing 'a relatively large, dense and permanent settlement of socially heterogeneous individuals.'

—**Wirth (1938)**

INTRODUCTION

Urban refers to a set of specialized, non-agricultural activities that are characteristic of, but not exclusive to, city dwellers. The perception around the word city is, often, associated with an urban settlement with extensive systems of housing, civic utilities, communications permeated with modern conveniences. There exists a predominantly rural and agricultural aspect to India which often fails to give adequate attention to its historical urbanism. Also, many sociologists believe that the distinction between rural and urban sociology cannot be meaningful in the Indian context since nearly 80 per cent of people live in the villages. Unlike Europe, where nearly 150 years of economic change brought a revolution, India never experienced anything similar. However, the number of city dwellers has continued to increase through government reports. Sociologists overlook the size of the population in the definition of a city because the minimum population standards vary greatly.

Cities and towns are also the sites of protest by citizens who are against the government. For instance, the university spaces across the country allow for critical protest against suppressing government policies which affect millions. The incidences of protests, marches and dharna have become a symbol of resistance to express intolerance towards brutalities, corruption and weak government. In India, Western capitalist patterns of land use coexist with rigid and persistent older patterns. One notices that urban dwellers change from Redfield's little communities to Karl Manheim's 'mass society' where kinship groups dissolve into nuclear families. Also, many individuals, here, will patronize a temple and club equally.

The combination of industry, trade and transportation was the significant occupational grouping for a city population. Economic development, almost consistently, results in an accentuation of the process of urbanization and implies a change in the occupational structure of the workforce in favour of non-agricultural activities. Urbanization, as a structural process of change, is generally related to industrialization, but it is not always the result of industrialization. Urbanization results due to the concentration of large- and small-scale industrial and commercial, financial and administrative set-up in the cities, technological development in transport and communication and cultural and recreational activities. In India, a peculiar phenomenon is seen: Industrial growth is seen without a significant shift of population from agriculture to industries and growth of urban population is observed without a significant rise in the ratio of the urban to the total population. While, in terms of ratio, there may not be a great shift from rural to urban activities, there is still a large migration of population from rural areas to urban areas.

9.1. URBANIZATION

9.1.1. The City

The model of a city is multidimensional; the city is a relatively closed settlement and not simply a collection of a number of separate dwellings. Sociologically speaking, it is a settlement of closely spaced dwellings which form a colony so extensive that the reciprocal personal acquaintance of the inhabitants, elsewhere characteristic of the neighbourhood, is lacking (Weber 1922, 1212). But this definition is dysfunctional as, by this, only large localities would qualify as cities, and size alone cannot be decisive. He rejects Simmel's concept of a city in terms of size in unequivocal terms. Instead, he argues, 'size alone, certainly, cannot be decisive' (Weber 1922, 1213). Weber gives a cumulative definition of the city in his ideal-type construct; his ideal city is the medieval guild city, which combined economic enterprise and religious activity as well as private and public life, and he argued that community life progressively deteriorates with the development of capitalism. Weber constructs an ideal type of city, which exhibits the following features:

- Where authority had rested on a rational rather than on a charismatic or traditional basis
- Where the law was enforced on a universalistic basis rather than on a personal basis
- Where grouping existed on the basis of class rather than family and clan
- Where citizens were governed by trade groups rather than by religious groups
- Where city's strength derived from an economic base rather than a military base

For the emergence of a truly urban space, a ruling class with a capacity for taxation and capital accumulation and writing and its application to predictive sciences, artistic expression and trade for vital materials are the kinds of specialized activities that are necessary (Childe 1950). A city is also a place in which cultural change takes place. The roles differ as to the character of the change. When the city has an orthogenetic role, it is not to maintain culture as it was; the orthogenetic city is not static; it is the place where religious, philosophical and literary specialists reflect, synthesize and create, out of the traditional material, new arrangements and developments which are felt by the people to be outgrowths of the old. What is changed is a further statement of what was there before. And when the city has a heterogenetic role, it is a place of the conflict of differing traditions, a centre of heresy, heterodoxy and dissent, interruption and destruction of ancient tradition and anomie (Redfield 1953).

9.1.2. Process of Urbanization

The preceding account of different types of cities is perhaps satisfactory as a preliminary, but their cultural roles in the civilizations which they represent cannot be fully understood except in relation to the entire pattern of urbanization within that civilization, that is, the number, size, composition, distribution, duration, sequence, morphology, function, rates of growth and decline and the relation to the countryside and each other of the cities within a civilization. Such information is rare for any civilization. In the present state of our knowledge, it may be useful to guide further inquiry by assuming two hypothetical patterns of urbanization: primary and secondary.

1. **Primary pattern:** In the primary phase, a pre-civilized folk society is transformed by urbanization into a peasant society and correlated urban centre. It is primary in the sense that the people making up the pre-civilized

folk, more or less, share a common culture which remains as the matrix also for the peasant and urban cultures which develop from it in the course of urbanization. Such a development, occurring slowly in communities not radically disturbed, tends to produce a 'sacred culture' which is gradually transmuted by the literati of the cities into a 'great tradition'. Primary urbanization, thus, takes place almost entirely within the framework of a core culture which develops, as the local cultures become urbanized and transformed, into an indigenous civilization. This core culture dominates the civilization despite occasional intrusions of foreign people and cultures. When the encounter with other people and civilization is too rapid and intense, an indigenous civilization may be destroyed.

2. **Secondary pattern:** The secondary pattern of urbanization—the case in which a folk society, pre-civilized, peasant or partly urbanized is further urbanized by contact with people of widely different cultures from that of its own members. This comes about through the expansion of local culture, now partly urbanized, to regions inhabited by people of different cultures or by the invasion of a culture civilization by alien colonists or conquerors. This secondary pattern produces not only a new form of urban life in some part in conflict with local folk cultures but also new social types in both city and country. 'In the city appear "marginal" and "cosmopolitan" men and an "intelligentsia"; in the country various types of marginal folk: enclaved, minority-, imperialized, transplanted-, remade-, quasi-folk, etc., depending on the kind of relation to the urban center' (Redfield 1930).

Redfield's concept of rural–urban continuum, based on his study of Mexican peasants of Tepoztlán, underline the rapid process of urbanization through the establishment of industries, urban traits and facilities which have decreased the differences between villages and cities. The urban occupational structure is as closely related to manufacturing and service as the rural function is to cultivation.

9.1.3. The Course of Urbanization and Its Implications

Urbanization implies a cultural and social psychological process whereby people acquire the material and non-material culture, including behavioural patterns, forms of organization and ideas that originated in or are distinctive of the city. Although the flow of cultural influences is in both directions—both towards and away from the city—there is substantial agreement that the cultural influences exerted by the city on non-urban people are probably more pervasive than the reverse. Urbanization, as seen in this light, has also resulted in what Toynbee has called the 'Westernization' of the world.

The idea of urbanization may be made more precise and meaningful when interpreted as aspects of diffusion and acculturation. Urbanization may be manifested either as intra-society or intersociety diffusion, that is, urban culture may spread to various parts of the same society, or it may cross cultural or national boundaries and spread to other societies. It involves both borrowing and lending. On the other side of the diffusion coin, there is acculturation, the process whereby individuals acquire the material possessions, behavioural patterns, social organization, bodies of knowledge and meanings of groups whose culture differs in certain respects from their own. Urbanization, as seen in this light, is a complex process (Gist and Fava 1933).

The history of urbanization in India reveals, broadly, four processes of urbanization at work throughout the historical period. These are as follows:

1. The emergence of new social relationships among people in cities and between people in cities and those in villages through a process of social change
2. The rise and fall of cities with changes in the political order
3. The growth of cities based on new productive processes, which alter the economic base of the city
4. The physical spread of cities with the inflow of migrants, who come in search of a means of livelihood as well as a new way of life

For M. S. A Rao, urbanization is a complex multifaceted process comprising ideological, cultural, historical, demographic, comparative, traditional and sociological elements. Rao defines a city as a centre of urbanization and urban way of life. For him, urbanism is a heterogeneous process, and hence, there can be many forms of urbanisms giving rise to many types of urbanization. Rao states that the dichotomy between cities and villages is incorrect as both have the same structural features of caste and kinship and are parts of the same civilization. Urbanization in India is not a uniform process but occurs along different axes—administrative, political, commercial, religious and educational axes—giving rise to several types of urbanisms. These different axes give rise to different types of contact which the city has with the villagers leading to distinct patterns of urbanization (Rao 1970).

9.1.3. Modernization and Education

The substantial economic development and swift urbanization of several cities have brought conspicuous modernization. Industrialization leads to major processes of change, which is bringing bureaucratization, hierarchy, centralization of authority, secularization and a shift from traditional to secular–rational values. But the post-industrial phase of modernization brings an increasing emphasis on individual autonomy and self-expression of values, which erode the legitimacy of authoritarian regimes and make the features of democracy increasingly likely to emerge. Moreover, modernization's changes are not irreversible. The traditional desire structure of the people has become more diverse, and as a result, villagers have become more dependent on the external market than they were about 40 years ago. The manner in which new items find their way into the want structure is by no means involuntary as it involves changes in the traditional values, and the new items, which are accepted, tend to become symbols of status differentiation. There is an identifiable pattern of urban lifestyle based on different components of consumption such as possession of modern urban looking house and furniture, cars and membership to clubs. The new style of life, which is more concretized by the new customer households, forms the basis of the modern status group. It has given a common ground for interaction among many castes and indicates a changing trend from the traditional system to a modem status group involving several castes.

Education has also played a vital role in inserting a new perspective in Indian society. The role of education as an agent or instrument of social change and social development is widely recognized today. According to MacIver, social change takes place as a response to many types of changes that take place in the social and non-social environment. Education can initiate social changes by bringing about a change in outlook and attitude of an individual. In the course of child-centred learning, students are able to see their own role in transformation. Societal change comes from the collective transformation of the individuals within that society. It can bring about a change in the pattern of social relationships, and thereby, it may cause social changes. The literacy rate shows a positive correlation to urban development; high literacy rate strongly correlates with a high degree of modernization. The general level of literacy is higher among the urban population than among the rural dwellers, but in both subgroups, literacy among females is considerably below the level for males.

9.1.4. Urban Spaces and Middle Class

The 'restructuring of urban space' in cities occurs through the 'spatial practices' that, Mathur (2007) says, are 'technologies for the production of a vision of a liberalizing India that centers on the visibility of the new Indian middle class'. These spatial practices, she says, include making the 'public spaces' accessible to only the middle class by cleaning 'such spaces of the poor and working classes', and the middle class actively participates in such exclusionary practices by claiming exclusive rights over the public spaces. She contends that the state plays an important role in this entire process of 'spatial purification and the production of a new middle-class-based vision of the Indian nation' (Fernandes 2004, 2417). New Indian middle class is also characterized by a considerable increase in consumption practices and aspirations for privileged lifestyles, establishing and continuously reviving its social and class identity through conspicuous consumer culture, unseen in the country earlier (Conroy 1998). Precipitous and conspicuous rise of consumerism in India is clearly being fuelled by the increasing accessibility of reusable income with the escalating middle class. Entertainment and leisure business observed momentous progress in the 1990s; the advent of enterprises catering to new lifestyle demands of liberalizing middle class with restaurants, movie theatres, malls and so on highlighted the proliferation of entertainment and other related service industries. This contributed to increasing public and social focus on questions of lifestyle. The social significance of 'lifestyle', as an autonomous sociocultural sphere of activity, must be understood in terms of the broader processes of socio-economic reorganization. Such discursive processes, primarily, characterize the new middle class. This social group is marked by the political and shifting nature of its boundaries that define it. At one end of the spectrum, there is a romanticized representation of this class by the media, and at the other, the public discourses depict them as urban English-speaking professionals, who are profiting from new employment opportunities and growing salaries in private companies. Additionally, the foundation of such understanding of this class is founded on the assumption that other segments of the middle classes and upwardly mobile working classes can aspire to this idealized representation (Mankekar 1999).

In order to understand the production of complex and dynamic relationships between class and urban space in India today, one must also take the real-estate industry into account (Searle 2013). Real-estate developers, investors, marketers, interior designers, industry consultants and even high-rise residents themselves consistently used the word 'professional' to designate the suggested inhabitants of the National Capital Region's new high-rises and gated communities. 'Professionals', they told me, are people who earn high salaries working in white-collar jobs with private sector companies, live in a nuclear family with a spouse who works and have Western consumerist tastes.

> Professionals speak English, enjoy travelling and shun flashy displays of wealth.' In relaying this narrative, my informants contrasted the 'professional' with other types not suited for new buildings: the old-moneyed elites of central Delhi, 'middle-class' civil servants and the poor. In particular, the participants contrasted post-liberalisation 'professionals', who earn 'white' or taxed salaries, with what they called, using the English term, 'businessmen', dubious dealers associated with the old economy who operate in cash or untaxed 'black' money. (Searle 2013, 273)

The category of consumer that developers describe as an indicator of demand—what Searle calls the 'professional'—resembles the 'new middle class' of marketing discourse (the scholarly literature as well): The 'English-speaking, urban white-collar segments of the middle class who are benefiting from new employment opportunities' available since liberalization (Deshpande 2003; Fernandes 2006, 18). International marketing agencies, consultancies and the Indian government have found the term 'middle class' useful in selling India as an investment destination to foreign companies looking for new consumers because the term suggests an internationally familiar way of life and a degree of wealth.

9.1.5. Consumption and Urban Identities

Consumption refers to the behaviour that unfolds itself through the cultural symbols, approaches and meanings created over a period of time. Goods and experiences that are objects of consumption are, as if, wrenched from a number of different contexts which are then effaced through the contemporary acts of consuming them. Surplus consumption is the 'strategy of engaging with the intensity of social and cultural changes introduced by (a number) of global forces' (Srivastava 2007, 185). Consumption discloses various ways of creating modern urban identities. The activities of this class that sees itself as 'truly' Indian because it is not defined by foreign modernity, but is capable of explaining its own account. This middle class can both participate in the process of modernity when required and retract to its realms of tradition. Srivastava (2009) maintains that such situations are a product as well as a process in themselves which recounts to the state mechanisms, the schemes of the market and the negotiations of a family with the urban life apprehensions. It is believed a successful female consumer takes consumption in her stride of being a housewife and not as its substitute. Meanwhile, the eccentricity of consumerism and its associated values ensure assured spaces of self-fulfilment but not at the cost of household maintenance.

The contemporary ethos of consumption is marked by ephemerality, which reflects the overriding intention of contemporary societies (Appadurai 1997; Bauman 2000). Appadurai argues that consumption creates time, but modern consumption replaces appeal of time with ephemerality. He believes, 'mediascapes' play a significant role in influencing the global reality with regards to the progression of cultures. Media exerts influence on local cultures with its selection of images and narratives which establishes a representation (see Box 9.1 for Veblen's concept of conspicuous consumption). The meanings involved with products and their subsequent consumption is symbolically constituted (Sahlins 1976). At the micro level, religion, well-being and development are tightly intertwined in people's aspirations and their framing. When enquired regarding what is important to live well, people offer a range of responses: Enough money, education, a decent place to live, respect in the community, good health and a happy home. While such lists tend to focus on material and social goods, the importance of religion to the poor is widely noted (Narayan 2000). But this is not restricted to any sacred or transcendental space of religious practice. Appadurai, reflecting on people's struggles for housing in Bombay's slums, identifies a transcendental frame of reference for even apparently mundane desires; '... aspirations form parts aspirations form parts of wider ethical and metaphysical ides which derive from larger cultural norms' (2004, 67–68).

BOX 9.1
Thorstein Veblen (1857–1929)

Veblen maintains that as people become more nomadic, communities become less interdependent. In a more mobile society, people may be less aware of the leisure activities in which other people participate, and so the demonstration of wealth through consumption of goods becomes more significant than the display of leisure (Veblen 1994). Veblen brands this type of behaviour as 'conspicuous consumption'; people spend money on objects of consumption in order to give a hint of their wealth to other members of society. Veblen views conspicuous consumption as the most important factor in determining consumer behaviour not only among the rich but also other social classes. 'The result is that the members of each stratum accept as their ideal of decency the scheme of life in vogue in the next higher stratum, and bend their energies to live up to that ideal' (Veblen 1994, 84). Each social class tries to emulate the consumption behaviour of the class above it, to such an extent that even the poorest people are subject to pressures to engage in conspicuous consumption.

9.2. CITY AND URBANISM

9.2.1. Urbanism

According to Mehrotra (2002), the disintegration in the locations of service and production sector has resulted in new bazaar-like urbanism which has made its presence felt in an entirely urban landscape. This kind of urbanism is created by those outside the elite domains of the formal modern state; Mehrotra calls it 'pirate' modernity which simply glides over the city laws in order to survive without making a conscious attempt towards constructing a counterculture. Such a phenomenon is often critical to the modern economy of the city; thus, spaces created by such phenomenon are excluded from elite cultural discourses on globalization. Kinetic space is a space where such formal and informal models are not binaries but are viewed as singular entities where the meanings are fluid and rather imprecise.

This is a hybrid form of urbanism where the 'images' of the formal (represented in permanent structure and infrastructure) coalesce in the same space with the temporal landscapes of the informal. But critically, these do not define mutually exclusive economic classes. The rich, poor and middle class all use both of these landscapes, simultaneously, to live, celebrate and most importantly for economic exchange. The theoretical category of the kinetic city offers a fascinating idea which helps to comprehend the fuzzy boundaries of present urbanism and transform the roles of spaces in urban society and people residing there. Furthermore, the concentration of global market currents has amplified the inequalities and spatial divisions of social classes.

Conversion of space by middle-class residents has been legitimized by both legal structures and state policies. The transformation of Delhi, identified as one of 'bourgeois environmentalism converging with the disciplining zeal of the state', has strong implications for the future of Delhi and inclusion of the poor in the urban fabric (Baviskar 2003, 93). It is important to understand how people negotiate personal aspirations and claims to urban space which is a means of deconstructing the urban experience, especially in relation to the rapid developments transforming the city. In order to understand how various social groups claim and are afforded space, it is useful to map socio-spatial exclusion and inclusion. The market of an area speaks volume of the class of people residing in the area, and the absence of not so modern markets or malls clearly depicts the consumer habits of the residents.

9.2.1.1. Contesting Spaces

The occupants of many residential areas in Indian cities maintain a distinction from the other localities. More than just separation, Baviskar documents an emotional response to the 'other', which refers to deep-seated 'bourgeois anxieties' of being in close proximity to the poor for fear of contamination, criminality, aesthetic appeal and so on. Emergent cultural visibility of the new Indian middle class marks the emergence of a wider national political culture in liberalizing India. This visibility represents a shift from older ideologies of state socialism to a political culture that is centred on a middle-class-based culture of consumption (Fernandes 2004). Middle-class consumers are characterized as the cultural representation of a country which has endorsed travelling of consumer goods through its boundaries that were unavailable during earlier decades of state-controlled markets. For instance, both Gurugram and Delhi epitomizes the popular perception of global, developed and capital city with a high standard of living. But on the other hand, the unchecked growth is leading to an expansion of slum areas along with increasing pollution, and mindless encroachments of nature distress the residents and their ambitions. Similarly, ceaseless loss of agricultural land and continuum of rural and urban cosmos may disturb development trends. Amidst such capricious conditions, there prevails perpetual anxiety about the future among the people. These cities in India have become a critical site for negotiation between elite and subaltern cultures.

Wright (1979, 2010), while borrowing from Marx, trusts that the category of 'capitalists' is also general. He suggests that the small business-class owners have their own means of production but have very little in common with large-scale industry owners. He also argues that a class in modern capitalism cannot be defined through the Weberian concept based on the level of wealth, power and prestige. Small business-class families consist of people who are self-employed small business owners and craftspeople, who may hire other people as employees but largely look after their work. This category includes jewellers, grocery store owners and retail shop owners; however, a certain group of professionals also falls under this category, for instance, lawyers and doctors. In order to understand how various social groups claim and are afforded space, it is useful to map socio-spatial exclusion and inclusion. The term 'professional', therefore, has been found to be useful to attract both potential investors and 'the consuming upper middle class' as it 'suggests global familiarity and prestige'. This term is employed to hide the poverty suffered by a large number of Indians from the investors as such a reality would discourage investment in the Indian real-estate market due to the gap that exists between the cost of the new constructions and affordability of most Indians. Thus, the production of a certain class and a certain kind of people has been felt to be necessary to increase the consumption of the Indian real estate, and the individuals of this class are often described by the developers as 'high net-worth individuals', 'professionals who are doing well', 'a certain income class plus', 'a very affording class' and 'consuming upper middle class'. New consumption pattern in India is centred on a middle-class-based culture of consumption, and citizenship is, thus, exclusionary in nature. They are exclusionary because certain (marginalized) sections of the population have been forgotten in the wake of economic liberalization which has exclusively catered to the rich. But this class of poor people has never let the state and the middle class standardize this exclusion by periodically contesting and fighting back all forms of exclusion.

9.2.1.2. Urban Conflict

There are studies which highlight that different urban groups did not always exist peacefully. Roche (1975) explored that in Madras, the left-hand castes tried to keep out of the right-hand castes. Similarly, Weber (1978) argued that upper-caste Christians would challenge the pariahs in Pondicherry. Rival groups would dispute over the control of a temple in Madras (Appadurai 1981), Shias and Sunnis would clash during Muharram in Lucknow and Mumbai (Hassan 1997). The conflicts which exist in urban spaces are ostensibly over symbols and observed infringements of status. When immigrants move to cities, they also try to carry along the potential to become a proletariat from being unskilled labour. Also, they prefer to inhabit close to their own kin and *jati* groups due to their conscious affinity, which is reinforced through urban media discourse. They also develop loyalties to a particular political party or leader linking towns and cities into the chain of larger political associations created for common behaviour prototype.

Buildings are often abused in ways that indicate a pent-up rage that might otherwise be unleashed in a frenzy of social destruction (Evenson 1989). There are reports in public discourse that increasing violence against women is an expression of alienation and mounting frustration due to inaccessible aspirations. As discussed above, with high rises and plush localities as the features of modern urbanism, there is still a prevalence of mohallas. But a town or city is considered better than a village; there is a sense of superiority that urban culture exerts which negates even its material discomforts.

9.2.1.3. Displacement

Often, there are incidents across the world, which compels a certain population to migrate from the area of residence due to war, violence, environmental hazards and so on. Migrant communities have been subjected to interest and contestations. The notion of 'home' becomes a critical aspect as it is expected to create and shape the identity of individuals. Datta (2016) explores the issue of displacement through experiences of place and migration of Kashmiri Pundits. While writing about experiences of uncertainty among Kashmiri Pundits in the city of Jammu, their memories of past lives in Kashmir and experiences in forging a new relationship with the local inhabitants. Lives of the displaced are filled with nostalgic recollections of 'home' from the past in Kashmir and challenges of rebuilding life and settlement in Jammu.

> Many Kashmiri Pandits have settled in Jammu and other areas leading to emergence of new suburbs. While these suburbs were poor in the early 1990s, they became thriving with Pandit families. There are shops in the area which sell specialised Kashmiri items, there are temples which look alike Kashmiri Pandit shrines which have become a part of urbanscape of Jammu. (Datta 2016)

The communities of Pundits, like other displaced communities, have reshaped their lives due to forced migration. There is a continuous feeling of lack of security in the new place; although there are efforts to mediate socio-economic differences, the political context and overriding desire to attain a secure place are associated with it.

9.2.1.4. Slums

A slum can be defined as 'a heavily populated urban area characterized by standard housing and squalor' (UN-Habitat 2007). In India, according to the Census reports of 2011, there are nearly 13.8 million households located in city slums nationwide with 64 million people residing in them, which roughly accounts for nearly one-third of India's 1.2 billion people. A. R. Desai and S. D. Pillai (1972) argued that Indian cities are growing in a haphazard manner with not enough provision to accommodate the increasing number of migrants. The increase in employment opportunities have caused migration to cities and towns. Rapid rural–urban migration becomes a major reason for substandard living spaces; both pull and push factors operate here. Cities require migrant workforce but cannot accommodate them along with the other city dwellers. Thus, slums become a place where migrants find shelter to retain and

TABLE 9.1 National Poverty Estimates (% BPL) from 1993–1994 to 2011–2012

Year	Urban (%)	Rural (%)	Total
1993–1994	31.8	50.1	45.3
2004–2005	25.7	41.8	37.2
2009–2010	20.9	33.8	29.8
2011–2012	13.7	25.7	21.9

Source: PRS (2013).

reimpose their rural symbols through decorations and observing festivals. But in the slums, there exists the absence of exclusive lavatories or regular water supply for each household, and the number of users per lavatory creates poor sanitation due to overcrowding. This overcrowding is not merely a question of low per capita living space; it signifies health hazards, increase crime against women, petty crimes and so on. Such areas are usually distant or cleared distinguished in urban space and are referred to as *chawl, bastee or jhuggis*.

9.2.1.5. Urban Poor

According to UN-Habitat report 2007, the cyclical nature of capitalism, increased demand for skilled over unskilled labour and the negative effect of globalization—in particular economic booms and busts which ratchet up inequality and distribute new wealthy—contribute towards the growth of the slum. Among urban poor, it can be difficult to emerge out of exclusion as they have weak social networks and circulation of available employment, community events or political activities may be less. High level of unemployment and no or low-income level strains family life; crime and juvenile delinquency undermine the overall quality of life in the neighbourhood. Homelessness is another form of exclusion among urban poor; the government and social sector facilitate shelter homes but to allow their inclusion in wider social life through employment continues to be a challenge. See Table 9.1. to know about the national poverty estimates (% below poverty line) during 1993–94 to 2011–12 in India. Although there has been a considerable increase in opportunities in the service sector, many of these available positions are low paid and have very less scope of advancement.

9.3. CITY AND SPACE

9.3.1. Public Spaces

In cities, public and private spaces coexist. Public spaces include roads, streets, gardens, riverbanks, places of worship and market. There have been many studies which focus on the built style, but there have been fewer studies on how the city dwellers perceived and used these public spaces. Evenson (1989) stated that the secular public architecture is relatively new in India and is associated with government; it often engenders a sense of alienation as town dwellers do not have a sense of pride or affinity with space. Markets commonly referred to as bazaars in the Indian context are usually busy with frequent transactions. Markets with sprawling shops and malls have also become a place of leisure activity called 'window shopping' where commodities are displayed for preview. There are others who want to seize these consumers like hawkers and other small temporary assemblies outside big shops. Some markets also intersect neighbourhoods, increasing the accessibility. Beyond markets, roads are the connecting veins of the city—often understood in terms of connectivity, traffic, road rage and accidents. Parks are common spaces and do not restrict entry; they are open 24 hours though have maximum public exodus during morning and evening hours. However, many localities restrict outsider entry to their parks claiming that they cause problems of safety and infringement.

9.3.2. Gender and Public Spaces

Public areas are generally considered to be male-dominated domains. Women are generally guarded and 'escorted' to many public places which are beyond their private territory. Narayani Gupta (2000), in her works, has argued that this degree of protection is proportionate with social status. She further argued that till the 20th century, most women did not know much about their town beyond the mohalla, and even today, many know very less about the town they live in. In Kolkata, for example, even shopping for the household is the prerogative of men. Markets are spaces where women can exercise their choices and agency. A woman's agency is boosted when she has the ability to make economic decisions.

The recent reports across the country highlight increasing violence against women, which has received considerable attention from law agency, citizens and media. But much of the agitation is restricted to certain public incidents of physical and sexual violence, which neglects the day-to-day discomfort on the streets faced by several women. Such incidences of everyday harassment often become excuses used by families and communities to forbid women from complete access to public spaces. Their concern often gets manifested through policing; women and girls' timings in public spaces are regulated. Women are suggested to dress appropriately, behave decently and avoid late working hours. Such policing curtails women's freedom to access public spaces. Studies have revealed that in many cities and towns, public space design is driven by the impulse to exclude rather than include.

CONCLUSION

The agents of urbanization, modernization and education have been successful in uplifting the face of a rural district, but they are oriented towards promoting values of an urban, competitive consumer society. Modernization, instead of rupturing the established structures, was assimilated with tradition, leading to the emergence of renovated social and economic structures. There is a noticeable higher cash income resulting from commercialization and urban employment which has affected the traditional status system, and the changes in the latter are largely articulated through consumption behaviour. The culture of the city is going through the liminal stage due to pandemonium between global and local. Many cities in India recount a colourful allegory of descent, association, migration and survival of diverse groups of people. A city becomes a sprawling space with several localities inhabiting people from a wide range of economic, social, political status, and with the increase in population and continual influx of immigrants, it also faces problems of traffic congestion, accommodation, electricity and water. And when a city fails to sustain the increasing demands of its growing population for more commercial as well as residential space, it becomes imperative to reconfigure urban spaces by developing adjoining regions.

Slums and squatter settlements are increasingly emerging as the main feature of many third world cities. Their emergence is linked to the economic processes; recent trends associate it with unequal distribution of national income and irregular economic development policies. Slums and squatter settlements are not an economic phenomenon; rather, they are social and political circumstance. It is important to understand that how people negotiate personal aspirations and claim urban space, which is one means of deconstructing the urban experience, especially in relation to the rapid developments transforming the city. Open public spaces are perceived as threatful from undesirable anti-social beings. But even the high-walled spaces and structures are less safe for women and children. There are initiatives being taken by urban authorities to install more lights and CCTV cameras to ensure better security and make spaces more gender inclusive.

Points for Classroom Discussion

- Urbanization is an indispensable aspect of modern society
- Theoretical perspectives effectively inform understanding of urban phenomena through historical and contemporary contexts
- Slums, poverty, displacement and others reflect vital concerns of urban living while describing the subjective experiences of urban communities
- Discuss how urbanism is a way of urban life

GLOSSARY

Displacement: It refers to incidents across the world, which compels a certain population to migrate from their area of residence due to war, violence, environmental hazards and so on.

Urbanization: It is a process where the population shifts from rural areas to cities, primarily motivated by prevalent economic factors.

Urbanism: It is the characteristic way of life of cities and towns which is manifested through development and planning.

Urban poverty: It is usually defined in two ways—first, as an absolute standard based on a minimum amount of income needed to sustain a healthy and minimally comfortable life and second as a relative standard that is set based on average the standard of living in a nation.

REFERENCES

Appadurai, A. 1981. *Worship and Conflict under Colonial Rule: A South Indian Case.* New York, London: Cambridge University Press.
———.1997. *Modernity at Large: Cultural Dimensions of Globalization.* New Delhi: Oxford University Press.
Bauman, Z. 2000. *Liquid Modernity.* Cambridge: Cambridge University Press.
Baviskar, A. 2003. 'Between Violence and Desire: Space, Power, and Identity in the Making of Metropolitan Delhi.' *International Social Science Journal* 55: 89–98.
Childe, G. 1950. 'The Urban Revolution.' *The Town Planning Review* 21, no. 1 (April): 3–17.
Conroy, M. 1998. 'Discount Dreams: Factory Outlet, Malls, Consumption, and the Performance of Middle Class Identity.' *Social Text* 54, no. 1: 63–83.
Desai, A. R., and S. D. Pillai. 1972. *A Profile of an Indian Slum.* Mumbai: University of Mumbai.
Deshpande, S. 2003. *Contemporary India: A Sociological View.* New Delhi: Penguin Books.
Datta, A. 2016. Dealing with Dislocation: Migration, Place and Home among Displaced Kashmiri Pandits in Jammu and Kashmir. *Contributions to Indian Sociology* 50, no 1:52-79.
Evenson, N. 1989. *The Indian Metropolis: A View toward the West.* New Delhi: Oxford University Press.
Fernandes, L. 2004. 'The Politics of Forgetting: Class Politics, State Power, and the Restructuring of Urban Space in India.' *Urban Studies* 41, no. 12 (November): 2415–2430.
———. 2006. *India's New Middle Class: Democratic Politics in an Era of Economic Reform.* New Delhi: Oxford University Press.
Gist, N. P., and S. F. Fava. 1974. *Urban Society.* New York, NY: Crowell Company.
Gupta, N. 2000. 'Concern, Indifference, Controversy: Reflections on Fifty Years of "Conservation" in Delhi.' In *Delhi: Urban Space and Human Destinies,* edited by V. Dupont, E. Tarlo & D. Vidal, 157–172. New Delhi: Manohar.
Hasan, M. 1997, *Legacy of a Divided Nation: India's Muslims since Independence.* London: Hurst.
Mankekar, P. 1999. *Screening Culture, Viewing Politics: An Ethnography of Television, Womanhood, and Nation in Postcolonial India.* Durham, NC: Duke University Press.
Mathur, N. 2007 'Consumerism'. In *Alternative Economic Survey: India,* edited by In Alternative Survey Group, 197–204. New Delhi: Daanish Books.
Mehrotra, R. 2002. 'Bazaar City: A Metaphor for South Asian Urbanism.' In *Kapital & Karma,* edited by Gerald Matt, Angelika Fitz, and Michael Wörgötter. Berlin: Hatje Cantz.
PRS. 2013. *Poverty Estimation in India.* Available at: https://www.prsindia.org/theprsblog/poverty-estimation-india (accessed on 16 February 2021).
Rao, M. S. A. 1970. *Urbanization and Social Change: A Study of a Rural Community on a Metropolitan Fringe.* Poona. Orient Longman.
Redfield, R. 1930. *Tepoztlán, a Mexican Village: A Study of Folk Life.* Chicago, IL: University of Chicago Press.
———. 1953. *The Primitive World and Its Transformations.* Ithaca, NY: Cornell University Press.
Roche, P. A 1975. 'Caste and the British Merchant Government in Madras'. *The Indian Economic & Social History Review* 12, no. 4: 381–407.
Sahlins, M. D. 1976. *Culture and Practical Reason.* Chicago, IL: The University of Chicago Press.
Searle, Llerena G. 2013. 'Constructing Prestige and Elaborating the "Professional": Elite Residential Complexes in the National Capital Region, India.' *Contributions to Indian Sociology* 47, no. 2: 271–302.
Srivastava, S. 2007. *Passionate Modernity, Sexuality, Consumption, and Class in India.* New Delhi: Routledge.
———. 2009. 'Urban Spaces, Disney-divinity and Moral Middle Classes in Delhi.' *Economic & Political Weekly* 27, no. 26–27.

UN-Habitat. 2007. *Enhancing Urban Safety and Security Global Report on Human Settlements. 2007*. United Nations Human Settlements Programme.
Veblen, T. 1994. *The Theory of the Leisure Class*. New York, NY: Dover Publications.
Weber, M. 1922. *The City*. New York, NY: Free Press.
———. 1978. *Economy and Society*. Berkeley, CA: University of California Press.
Wirth, L. 1938. 'Urbanism as a Way of Life.' *The American Journal of Sociology* 44, no. 1: 1–24.
Wright, E. O. 1979. *Class Structure and Income Determination*. New York, NY: Academic Press.

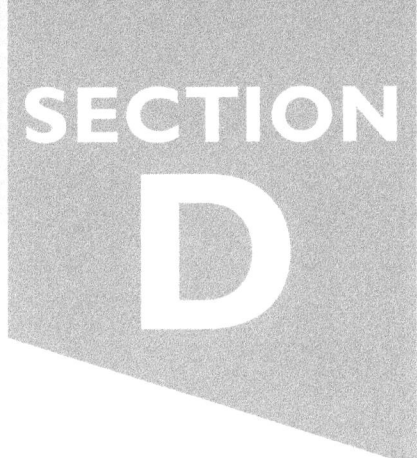

SECTION D

SOCIAL CHANGE

Chapter 10
Sanskritization, Westernization and Modernization

Chapter 11
Industrialism to Globalization and the Role of the Media

CHAPTER 10

Sanskritization, Westernization and Modernization

LEARNING OUTCOMES

- To comprehend the idea of social change and identify the context of social change in India
- To familiarize with the conceptual categories of Sanskritization, Westernization and modernization
- To appreciate the structural as well as ideological, value and belief aspects of social change
- To understand the process of social change with specific reference to indigenous case studies

Keywords: Social change, heterogenetic change, orthogenetic change, tradition, Sanskritization, Westernization, modernity, modernization

A change from a relatively indefinite, incoherent, homogeneity to a state of relatively definite, coherent, heterogeneity.

—Coser (1979)

INTRODUCTION

Social change is a procedural way that modifies the structure of society; it can affect social institutions, the relationship between individuals, their behaviour and the value system. This concept of social change in the discipline of sociology has been influenced from various other fields. There have been different schools of thought, each emphasizing the different aspects of social change in a unique manner. It began with the law of three stages propounded by Auguste Comte, in which society progresses in three stages from theological, which is dominated by religion, to metaphysical, where speculative thinking originates and, finally, to positivist, which is the stage of scientific and empirical reasoning. Herbert Spencer's evolutionary approach is crucial, as he associated social change with biological evolution. According to him, societies grow and become complex. He stated that society is ordered in the same manner as an individual, and though social change is different from other evolutionary phenomena, the evolution of the societies is also a case of the coherent universal natural law (Spencer 1896).

Social change can be caused by several factors, such as **cultural** (through the process of diffusion, there might be change in the social composition of an area), **environmental** (any kind of natural calamity changes the nature of social relationships), **demographic** (fluctuations in birth and death rates and deviation in sex ratio have an immediate impact on the institution of marriage, family and kinship and also economic institutions) and, finally, **technological** (the development in the modes of communication and transportation significantly alter the nature of social relationships). Moreover, it is pertinent that there are changes made in the structures of society because of the change in ideologies due to economic, political and religious movements.

Before exploring the concept of social change, let us look at the different approaches—structural, dialectic, historical and integrated—to study social change. It is imperative to distinguish structural analysis of change from cultural change in terms of the particularities of customs, values and ideational phenomena, their integration, interaction and change. Structural analysis will focus on the network of social relationships, such as caste, kinship, class and occupational groups, emerging from the existential conditions of individuals and their needs. Structural analysis presupposes the formulation of abstract concepts over research findings. The second approach to study social change is the dialectic approach, D. P. Mukherji being its major proponent in India. Mukherji believes it to be a process of synthesis emerging from the interplay and conflict between contradictory systems of values and class interests. Third approach is the historical approach, which was postulated by Louis Dumont; Indian society is conceived not in terms of system of relationship but as a system of ideational or value patterns. Dumont argued that the focus in the study of social change should be on the reaction of Indian minds to the revelation of the Western cultures.

Finally, an integrated approach was suggested by Yogendra Singh (1986), who argued that the causation of social change is to be sought both from within and without the social system or traditions (Table 10.1), for which he employed concepts by Redfield and Singer: heterogenetic or exogenous and orthogenetic or endogenous sources of change. Simultaneously, a distinction between the cultural structure and

TABLE 10.1 Paradigm of an Integrated Approach

Sources of Change	Modernization			
	Cultural Structure		Social Structure	
Heterogenetic changes	Little tradition	Great tradition	Micro-structure	Macro-structure
	Islamization	Second Islamic impact	Role differentiations	Political innovations
	Primary Westernization	Secondary Westernization (or modernization)	New legitimization	New structures of elite, bureaucracy, industry and so on
Orthogenetic changes	Sanskritization or traditionalization	Cultural Renaissance	Pattern, recurrence, compulsive migration or population shift	Elite circulation, succession of kings, rise and fall of cities and trade centres

Source: Singh (1986).

the social structure is also sought to perceive changes at the level of above-mentioned independent categories. The cultural structure was further subdivided into categories of little tradition and great tradition; and the social structure was divided into micro-structure and macro-structure. These distinctions were created to focus on the contexts through which the processes of change could be evaluated. But it is not easy to distinguish between the primary (orthogenetic) and secondary (heterogenetic) stages of growth in the Indian context on the basis of historical data. The direction of change was also represented in a linear fashion from traditionalization to modernization (the course of social change is studied primarily with two types of theories: cyclical theories, emphasizing the notion that human society passes through prescribed cycle, and linear theories, which believe that a society gradually moves towards higher state of civilization). Social change in India can well be understood under the aforementioned factors, where it becomes a reasonable case study.

10.1. SANSKRITIZATION

Srinivas inscribes, 'Sanskritization is a process by which a lower caste or tribe or any other group changes its customs, rituals, ideology and way of life in the direction of a higher or more often twice-born caste.' Srinivas' description of the process of Sanskritization vacillates from cultural, social, religious, economic and political point of view. Sanskritization as an empirical process of cultural change has contextual significance; it has a particularistic origin and thus belongs to the little tradition. The concept of Sanskritization was presented by M. N. Srinivas in his work titled *Religion and Society among the Coorgs of South India*. The book explained the social mobility in the traditional caste structures of the Indian Society, taking the reference of Coorgs from Mysore, emphasizing how individuals from lower castes attempted to elevate their ranking in the social hierarchy by emulating the practices cultural ideals of the Brahmans. In this process of emulation, there was a concurrent act of abandoning of some of their ideals, which were considered to be impure by the Brahmans. At the advent of the study, Srinivas used the term 'Brahamanization' to explain this act of mobility, but eventually decided to employ the term 'Sanskritization', as there were other terms related to emulation existing in the other studies, such as Kshatriyaization (J. G. A. Pockock) and tribalization (S. L. Kalia).

His work has attracted several criticisms and suggestions, and major suggestions were made during a conference in Madras to rename the process of Sanskritization to Hinduization, Brahamanization or Acculturation. But Srinivas rejected them on the relevant grounds, stating that the label of Hinduization would exclude some communities and castes in India which are not within the purview of Hinduism. It is important to mention a particular type of local acculturation that exists in the Indian society.

Srinivas argued that it is not possible to understand the process of Sanskritization without reference to the structural understanding of caste in Indian society. See Box 10.1 to know more about Srinivas. Understanding of caste system was borrowed from Dumont's (1972) Varna Model, and the castes were assigned a respective status of high or low as per their characteristics, based on their ranking in the Varna Model. In the Varna system, the highest ranking was accorded to the Brahmans, followed by Kshatriya, Vaishya, Shudra and, lastly, Antyaj, which were the untouchables. According to Srinivas, there appears to be acts of pursuing the Varna above, where the lower caste copes with the ideals and lifestyles of the superior castes. The wearing of the sacred thread by the twice born, while also abstaining from meat and liquor, the observance of endogamy, the prohibition of inter-caste marriage and strict compliance to the rituals of purity and pollution mark the status and honour of the upper castes. Further, strict adherence to the modes of worship and the reception and perpetuation of Sanskritic textual knowledge through religious practices have provided the sacredness to the traditional cultural mechanics of the caste system.

BOX 10.1
M. N. Srinivas

M. N. Srinivas (1916–1999) is one of the founding members of the discipline of sociology in India. He is known for his work on stratification, caste system and villages in India. He coined words such as 'Sanskritization', 'dominant caste' and 'vote banks'. Srinivas rejected what he referred to as 'book view' to understand society and instead pioneered 'field view' through intensive fieldwork in local village communities to identify the process of social change in the Indian society.

The above-mentioned parameters are considered to be the assessing measures of sacredness and purity according to religious parameters. There are studies that highlight how, like Brahmans, lower caste people go to the temple regularly and perform bhajans and artis. They also have given up on prohibited non-vegetarian food. Acceptance and emulation of these standards confers upon honour and superiority on the observant caste, which is understood as a form of Sanskritization. The act of Sanskritization is performed to elevate the social status and to acquire a higher ranking in the social order. The social aspect here is hegemonic, as the individual is seen as merely a fraction of the totality. Sanskritization is the amalgamation of the dual understanding of the term 'Sanskrit' as a language and as a culture (Shah 2005).

Sanskritization is also visible in the economic sphere, where lower caste people are giving up their unclean considered occupation for other petty jobs. This is primarily done to elevate not only their economic status for betterment but also to enable them to acquire better social standing. Lower caste people in villages are also building cement houses, and they aspire to keep their houses and dresses clean like higher castes, reflecting the perceived notions of cleanliness of higher castes.

10.1.1. Structural Functional Perspective

The structure functional perspective asserts that structures contribute towards stabilizing the existing social order in a society. Following the structure functional perspective, Sanskritization can be understood to have two major functions.

First, since the process was common to all the castes, the Brahmanical way of life spread among all the Hindus, and this led to the emergence of one common dominant culture and the prevalence of completely Sanskritized worship of natural existence such as trees, rivers and mountains through mythologies and folklores; such uniformity assisted in the easier assimilation of rituals between lower castes and communities that were earlier outside of Hinduism.

The second function was to allow for social mobility within the otherwise rigid social structures of the caste system. The process of Sanskritization gave way to vertical social mobility and reflected the dynamic nature of the Hindu society.

There have been several studies in the discipline and interdisciplinary research on the legitimacy of this process. The instances from across India share a commensality of several decades of struggle to consciously elevate their status in the hierarchy of the caste ladder. Practices of outlawing beef eating by the chamars of Madhopur, replacing the bride price with dowry and changes in death rituals are propagated through strict conformism (Cohn 1954). It is pertinent to mention here the role of traditionally educated Brahmans, who were able to impel sufficient members of society towards increasing acceptance towards Sanskritic values and aspirations.

Srinivas' work, however, failed to provide important explanations on contemporary times and caste mobilization. Shah (2005) stated that the caste hierarchy is getting dissociated from the process of Sanskritization, and that several non-caste structures and institutions have become powerful agents, leading to a deeper Sanskritization of society. The appropriation of the *Harijans* and the lower caste individuals in the Hindutva ideology can be seen as a new strategy in the political and nationalist agendas. The political rise of backward castes and Dalits, along with state provisions to protect lower castes, welfare measures and affirmative actions, has reduced dependence on higher castes, which was traditionally perpetuated through the Jajmani system. Rudolph and Rudolph (1967) argued that this is causing vertical hierarchy to be reorganized as horizontal blocks and caste groups are competing for jobs and other social advantages. As per Spencer (2007), the democratization of Indian politics and society has opened up opportunities, which were inconceivable earlier, for communities like Ahir to fraternize with high-caste people.

Upadhyay (2013) argues that there are several modalities of inter-caste developing in contemporary India that affect the process of Sanskritization. First, the aversion towards 'low castes' and Dalits and Bahujans in the Hindu social system and its direct challenge to the ideologies of the upper castes, second, the willingness of caste communities to retain their names in the state list for certain material benefits and, finally, as discussed above, the inclusion of low castes by Hindutva groups confirm their positional change.

Srinivas' description of the process does not focus on the structural changes much, but emphasizes on the positional changes, which is merely the recognition of certain rights, or the sharing of some spaces, and permitting collective seating in groups. Acquired independence in the economic and political space has led to the assertion by the lower castes in society. Such emerging caste dynamics are undermining the process of Sanskritization as a process of upper caste cultural emulation. In contemporary times, there are changes in the very culture of the upper castes due to several factors, and Srinivas can be critiqued for his presumption of understanding the upper caste to remain Sanskritized throughout and the lower caste to always look up to them. The category of 'dominant castes' is prevalent across rural belts in the states of the northern region, where dominance is not only decided by the acquired knowledge of religious scriptures but also by the economic standing through landholdings along with the conspicuous political presence. This leads to the emergence of certain practices where numerical strength governs the dominant (accepted) culture of the region.

10.1.2. De-Sanskritization

It is important to acknowledge that the coherence in the Hindu system is diffused and variable, and there are diversities in practices across regions and communities. Marriott (1992) discussed multiple forms of Hinduism. Dalits are questioning Brahmanical hegemony through the political emancipation, they are also contesting it through conversion to other religions such as Buddhism and Christianity. This act of conversion reflects the rupture in low-caste religious affiliations with Hinduism. Singh (1986) notes that the process of Sanskritization has a much broader connotation and should not restrict itself to Brahmans as a reference point. Singh also argues that Srinivas' idea of Sanskritization is a fluid one, where there is not only imitation of habits and culture but also of ideas.

In the recent past, there has been a proclivity among various social groups to manifest themselves as 'backward', or to belong to a low-status caste group, primarily to accrue the benefits of the state policies of reservation. The agitation of the Gujjars and Meenas in Rajasthan to claim the status of ST and the claims of the Jats (the otherwise dominant caste in Haryana) exemplify this trend, which we understood as a paradox in the process of Sanskritization. This development is referred to as de-Sanskritization, where reservation and political mobilization correlated with caste identities have reversed the trend/aspiration of upward mobility. Another process in Sanskritization, which is becoming prevalent along with de-Sanskritization, is the process of re-Sanskritization, where the previously modernized or Westernized group is discarding many Western/modern cultural symbols, such as language, food, clothing and living standards, and reverting to traditional symbols and beliefs. Singer has mentioned that Sanskritization and de-Sanskritization are cyclical processes. But Y. Singh (1986) emphasized that while we should expect that modernizing changes would be de-Sanskritizing and traditional change would be Sanskritizing, this may not always be the norm.

Finally, it is pertinent to mention that the process of Sanskritization received a major threat from the influence of Westernization, which enabled individuals to believe that it was a rather cogent mechanism of catching up with the upper castes. A complete understanding of social change in India can be achieved only if there is focus on Westernization and its interaction with Sanskritization (Srinivas 1956).

10.2. WESTERNIZATION

Westernization primarily is 'the changes brought about in Indian society and culture as a result of over 150 years of British rule, the term subsuming changes occurring at different levels...technology, institutions, ideology and values' (Srinivas 1966, 55).

Nonetheless, the earliest contact of any Western tradition was with the Portuguese, with premodern values and prejudices. They were followed by the Dutch and the French, and both of these cultures had different intentions; the former was interested in commerce and the latter had political motivations. Thus, their influence was marginal and the primary Western influence can be traced back to the advent of the British in India. Cultural tradition was different from the major traditions and cultural patterns in both Hinduism and Islam; they differed in their ethos and structure. This Western tradition was based on a certain kind of rational legal framework; it relied on the values of equality, equity achieved through bureaucratic structures, achievement through education in contrast to communal and caste-based status allocation. Cumulatively, these new traditions posed a severe threat to the cardinal principles of Indian traditions, namely hierarchy and holism.

10.2.1. Phases of Westernization

The changes introduced by Westernization can be understood in two phases. The first phase was the emergence of a Westernized subcultural pattern through a minority section of Indians who first came into contact with the Western culture. The impact of this subculture was localized, and Y. Singh (1986) treated this as the primary stage of Westernization.

The second phase can be understood with reference to the general diffusion of the Western cultural traits. There were attempts to accept and imitate their ways across different regions in India. This act of trying to be like them varied from one section of the population to the other, with few relying on the use of new technology to copy their dress patterns, eating habits, language and mannerisms in order to be Westernized, and the other section acquired the Western literature, knowledge and their scientific temperament. This process of Westernization was easily accessible to the upper castes, such as Brahmans, Kshatriyas and Vaishyas, because of their hierarchical dominance and literary awareness. Any act of Western imitation by the lower caste was, however, subject to ridicule.

Westernization was in sync with the acculturation process in India, where there was selection and adaptation. The position of the Brahmans was very crucial in this new developing hierarchy: they became the filters through which Westernization reached the rest of the Indian society (Srinivas 1956). There were some aspects that were initially approached with reluctance. But the change in the choice of occupation and food habits had a far-reaching impact, whereby certain professions, such as that of doctor, were welcomed and opinions pertaining to individual defilement due to the touching of corpse were done away with. For instance, the Brahmans of Mysore were divided into two categories of Vaidikas (priests) and Laukikas (laities). It is only the Vaidikas who practised a priestly vocation, whereas the Laukikas pursued other secular occupations. Although the priests enjoyed higher status ritually, it was the Laukikas who enjoyed economic and political power in the secular context.

10.2.2 Changes in the Cultural Structures

There were changes in the cultural structures such as science, education, technology, law, industrialization, urbanization and new forms of politicization, facilitated by enhanced communicative medium of transportation and the press. These cultural innovations bring us to the perennial dilemma of the coexistence of tradition and modernity in the Indian context. At the time of contact with the Western forces, the Hindu tradition was troubled with stagnancy, and the former had just achieved success through the Industrial Revolution. The Western culture was, thus, steeped in the positivism of rationalism and universal progress. The Hindu tradition, however, continued its aversion, but the emergence of the early middle class in the regions of Madras and Calcutta emulated the Western customs without much hesitation. This particular class also played a significant role in the cultural breakthrough and in the promotion of foreign Western cultural traits among the traditional society. This new achieved status was due to their acquired education and training in their respective skillset. It also facilitated the interjection of the Western values and ideologies as well as the rise of cultural and social reform movements. The localized and elitist composition of these movements created an anticipated impact on the policies promoted by the British government to implement radical social reforms. These reforms were directed towards the social practices generated by the little tradition of Hindu culture, like sati; these changes in the social customs of Hindu society were signs of fundamental cultural readaptations to be followed later. The underlying ethos of these reformations emanated from humanism, universal equality, human dignity and human freedom.

Historical factors, like the revolt of 1857, brought about a radical change in the response patterns of educated Indians towards the phenomenon of Westernization, which gradually began to be associated with secularism and nationalism. Another reason for this could be attributed to the new policies pursued by the British in the fields of education, commerce, law and so on, which created a new consciousness. These movements of primary Westernization were led by men who aspired to assimilate the Western culture and thought in the name of progress but were nonetheless grounded in the Hindu tradition. Ghosh (1941) argued that the young followers (college youth) of such movements had a contradictory orientation. According to him, they were denationalized and hyper-Westernized, being completely dissociated from their indigenous tradition. The impact of such subcultures of Westernization was short-lived and limited. But despite its value and significance, such subcultural movements did not have an institutional basis for wider mobilization, as their organizational structure was weak and restricted to the urban-dwelling middle class, student population.

However, the Western civilization provided Indian society with important drivers for progress: railways and postal services. Development in these fields laid the foundation for elaborating the networks of communication and institutions of modernization. Y. Singh (1986) discusses some of the institutional developments that have been helpful in the creation of a great tradition of modernization in India: (a) the growth of a universalistic legal superstructure; (b) the expansion of education; (c) urbanization and industrialization; (d) an enhanced network of communication and (e) the growth of nationalism and the politicization of society. Each of these factors had a ubiquitous reach, unlike the subcultural processes of primary Westernization.

10.3. MODERNIZATION

Modernization presupposes rationality of goals which, in the ultimate analysis, could not be taken for granted since human ends are based on value preferences and rationality could only be predicted of the means and not of the ends of social action.

—M. N. Srinivas

Modernization, as a form of cultural response, includes characteristics that are universalistic and evolutionary. It symbolizes a rational attitude to the perception of issues, not from a non-particularistic, but rather a universalistic approach. As a transitional process of moving from a traditional or primitive state of being, it is associated with the state of modernity, which originated in the West and acquired new meanings only after the period of Enlightenment. It began in the post-feudal Western European society, gradually influencing other civilizations. It was in the late 18th century that the world realized the course of social change introduced by modernity. It is inseparable from science and reason; it requires a dynamic capitalist and bureaucratic order for its sustenance and perpetuation. Sociology as a discipline developed as a response to modernity. Saint Simon and Comte were trying to grapple with the notions of modernity that appeared in their society through the French Revolution.

It is essential to acknowledge that modernization is treated as historical rather than universal evolutionary reality (Bendix 1964, 9–13). This means that the process of modernization in India is not identical to any other part of the world. Modernization might take different forms in different cultural traditions, it may have distinctive features. Nonetheless, modernization as a system of values and cognitive structures continues to share common recurrent characteristics. Marx stated that 'modernity is revolutionizing of production, uninterrupted disturbance of every social relations, everlasting uncertainty and agitation.... All fixed fast-frozen relationship and with their train of venerable ideas and opinions, are swept away, all new formed one become obsolete before they can ossify. All that is solid will melt into the air' (Marx and Engles 1970, 70). Thus, the process of modernization incessantly impacts the societies with constant, rapid and often permanent change. This can be understood as a principal difference between tradition and modernity. According to Giddens, tradition attempts to preserve and honour the past and value symbols as they contain and perpetuate experiences of generations. Tradition is a means of handling time and space so as to insert the notions of continuity into recurrent social practices. The practices of acculturation that lead to modernization do not function independently, instead with other syncretic processes.

The British colonial rule did not only foster rational thought through modern values and innovation but also introduced the propagation of Christianity and other cultural ways that did not resonate with modernity. Singh (1986) believed that the first heterogenetic cultural encounter began with Islamic culture, later followed by the imposition of British rule in India. He first analysed the consequences of both the Islamic and Western modes of cultural impacts to examine the force of modernization. Both Hinduism and Islam had a different traditional perception of society, and the cultural syncretism between the two religions also had a discernible bearing on the culture in Indian society. But the little tradition of Islam in India has one distinctive historical characteristic: it mainly consists of the converts from Hinduism and might also include the descendants of the immigrant Muslim elites who, due to loss of fortune, slipped into the lower status of the masses (Singh 1986). Modernization, in a certain sense, implied a policy of liberalism and rationality that allowed people to create their own present and future instead of relying on the belief that destiny is preordained. However, it continued to face resistance to any social and cultural change through caste-like principles of hierarchy, religious revivalism and conservatism.

Modernization studies were introduced in the 1950s as part of a vast multidisciplinary project launched by the USA with the primary objective to win the Cold War comprising both negative and positive implications. Modernization theories focused on the progress of social change as a multidimensional development. At microcosmic evaluations, it focused on the processes of urbanization, gender inequality, the role of media and politics; whereas at the macrocosmic level, it focused on the empirical trajectories of nations, their societies, economies and political systems. Modernity, now, has come to be accepted as a goal rather than merely a foreign imposition across the world.

10.3.1. Agents of Modernization

Let us now revisit the institutions that contributed towards modernization; the first is the growth of a universalistic legal structure that challenges the traditional value system of hierarchy and holism through new norms and the establishment of the rule of law. It also facilitated egalitarianism by promoting social justice. But it can be argued that though the lower castes have become increasingly aware of their legal rights and try to enforce them through the courts of law, the success rate needs evaluation. Weber, however, points out that legal innovation is essential for the growth of a rational economic structure that ultimately leads to modernization.

Second is the expansion of education; contemporary education was fundamentally different from the traditional education system. Its content, ways of dissemination and equal access questioned the hierarchical, hereditary and rather restricted admission to education. Science and technology intervened as powerful tools in progressive education. It allowed for the mobilization of people's aspirations for nationalism, liberalism and freedom. It is also responsible for the growth of an intelligentsia group that carried out the movement of freedom struggle as well as social and cultural reforms. This generation incidentally was the one that followed Macaulay's assertion of the Western literature and, simultaneously, there was an introspection of traditional literature that was going on in the Indian society. Symbols were drawn from the empiricism of the Vedas, the metaphysics of the Upanishads and the philosophies mentioned in the Gita. Leaders such as Tilak, Gandhi and Aurobindo established this tradition. Modernization, according to Y. Singh (1986), in all cultures goes through the process of creating a new identity consciousness. This identity is based on the traditional structure but assimilates the modern attributes of the requisite advancement.

Third, the processes of urbanization and industrialization assumed a way of logical necessity. Both the processes of urbanization and industrialization are essentially to be modernized, and their extent and patterns may vary. Urban culture in India is ancient; it has led to the growth of commercialism, the monetization of economic relationships, and factory and workshop employment. Urbanization acquires underpinning from industrialization, rather they share a reciprocal relationship with each other. This symbiotic relationship has also witnessed advancement in technology that has enabled better transport and communication, leading to better health facilities through modern medicine, a rational and modern system of education and a secure banking infrastructure for better economic transactions; all these are indicators of modernization. Modernization is a relative phenomenon and is not a closed but rather an open-ended process.

Fourth, the expansion of communication has augmented the growth of modernization. As discussed earlier, the invention of railways and postal services allowed accessibility of otherwise distant areas. This simplified communication and allowed the formation of associations and other traditional group activities through cerebral mobility. It also allowed for a medium of restoration and preservation of traditional characteristics in times of dominant assimilation by the dominant Western modernity.

Finally, the development of nationalism and politicization provided an essential modern ethos towards the modernization of the Indian society. Both these processes are of exogenous nature and pose severe challenges to the primordial normative structure of traditional society. Nationalism can be understood as a collective conscience emerging from a political agreement of one nation state and its associated political identity. In India, the process of nationalism contributed to politicization; its role can be understood through the issues of secularism and communalism. Also, the Constitution acknowledges the diversity and attempts smooth governance through the practice of federalism and decentralization. These political concepts may seem to be borrowed from the ideas of Western democracy, but they embody attributes proclaimed by Gandhi of welfare state, humanism and tolerance. The modernization of politics in India aspires for a change towards more universalistic group identities, questioning the particularistic identities of caste, ethnicity and others. It can be assumed that modernization in traditional societies progresses through a transitional stage, where tradition and modernity are often syncretized.

Thus, it can be argued that both the concepts of tradition and modernity are heuristic. Modernization is a rather flexible concept that continues to reinvent itself under the aegis of continuous falsification and review of its value system. Also, tradition does not always delay the process of modernization; also, the old traditions are not displaced by modernity. The character of the Indian state provides for a reasonable case where modernity has been assimilated with tradition instead of replacing it. Studies confirm that traditional structures of family and marriage continue to coexist along the modern value systems.

10.4. CURRENT COMPLEX

Every sociologist in each of their analysis referred to modernity uniquely; Giddens explained it as a 'double-edged' phenomenon. Modernity reflects on the experience of social practices being continuously reinvented through new technology and information (Giddens 1990, 38). He employs the concept of 'disembedding of the social system', that is, lifting out of social relations from the local context of interaction and their restructuring to explain the transformation of time and space. Modernization caused certain institutions such as family, kinship, education and politics to undergo change due to the prevalence of mechanisms of token system; economic transactions of currencies have modified traditional transactions across time and space; second, the expert system further modifies the earlier traditional rules of a community by replacing them with expert knowledge of doctors, engineers, lawyers and so on. Modernity is multidimensional and Giddens (1990) further analysed four different indicators of modernity—capitalism, industrialism, administrative power through surveillance and military power—to explore its scope in society.

Modern science and technology have been instrumental in alleviating human standards of living with respect to health and poverty; they have also contributed to the strengthening of human relations across the world. However, they have also led to a crisis of alienation, the decaying of local culture and the unconscious embracing of hyper-consumerism. Pathak (1998) reflected on how even traditional intellectual perspectives were critical of modernity, citing Gandhian agenda reflected in *Hind Swaraj*. Nonetheless, he insisted that modernity should be rescued from its Eurocentric and colonial ambitions. Critical modernization, according to Pathak, can resist liberalization and its excessive dependence on technology, rather than commit itself to foster symbiotic human relationships. Pathak (1998) discusses how Indian culture is continuously evolving, developing and changing because of the presence of diversities in language, tradition, cultural practices and ethnic identities. Indian culture has the creativity and ability to accommodate and synthesize multiple currents and traditions. Presently, modernity transpires from different domains, such as law, media film, academic disciplines and institutions of the state.

10.4.1. Perplexing Indian Reality

Gupta (2011) in his work explored the false indicators of modernity in the Indian context and argued that people in India failed to commit themselves to the major prerequisites to the modernity of individualism and universalism. He brings out several illustrations from a wide spectrum of political, social and economic activities to describe a noticeable lack of modernity. He states, 'thus while we are not modern, we are not quite traditional either. It is in this sense that India is between worlds' (Gupta 2011, 217). In Indian context, the poor rural migrants migrate to cities not only for employment but also to escape the caste and status atrocities in village. Urbanization brings anonymity; however, primordial ties are retained through family and kin to sustain family farms to augment their urban income. The lack of provisions for any social insurance and urban life being full of vicissitudes requires traditions to be kept alive. Further, Gupta (2011) criticizes the modern Indian elite to be merely superficially modern, and the members are more 'Westoxicated' than Westernized. Modernity should not be mistaken merely with the acquisition of certain materials, but rather by adhering to the modern approach of living. Even today, the loyalties bred through interpersonal associations resemble the political factions of traditional societies. And Indians, instead of relying on modern institutions, rely on personal relations and, more than often, elect patrons and not leaders. A major reason for the failure of institutions in their public responsibility, according to Gupta, is that influential Indians can successfully divert the resources of these institutions for their private ends. For instance, politicians generally invoke their caste identity to garner support on the basis of affinities. Caste is employed aggressively in electoral politics, competing against each other. It is likely believed by a certain section of elites that the relevance of the caste system is slowly declining. Nonetheless, paradoxically, caste identities continue to thrive across the country.

Deshpande (2003) also inspects the system of caste through the process of modernization. He insists that the relationship between modernity and caste differs according to different caste identities across the country. The upper caste has been in a better position to exploit the advantages of modernity due to its traditional privilege, whereas the lower caste's interaction with modernity is often problematic. That is to say that the upper caste's flair with modernity is a result of its traditionally sustained caste benefits. And, on the other hand, the lower caste is embroiled in modernity by installing a peculiar caste identity that is inconsistent with the ideals of modernity (refer to Box 10.2). One of the promises of modernity is to liberate citizens from the shackles of the caste system; however, the issue is that the regulation of modernity in society is controlled by the upper castes. The complexity of the contemporary caste problem is situated in identifying two separate relationships that both upper and lower castes have with caste in modernity. It is important to point out that the transformation of the social and economic landscape in contemporary India reveals a concoction of anxiety and ambivalence towards modernity. The role of the middle class is critical in fuelling the former, which insists on the invisibility of caste

> **BOX 10.2**
> **Critique of Modernity**
>
> Nandy's critique of modernity is associated directly to the idea of the future, to utopia, which is an extremely problematic theme in violent-inflicted contemporary time. Recognizing this implies that both the idea of the future and the utopia must be founded in a perception of violence that several 'faiths' can unleash. Utopias must be screened bearing in mind their capacity of self-evaluation and responsibility for their 'legitimate and illegitimate brain children', let alone the fact that imperfect societies produce imperfect medicines. Utopians must be prone to engage in dialogue, and this cannot work if 'heretics' and outsiders are treated as inferior. In any society, including Indian society, it is necessary to embrace the elements of its culture as well as to reject many of its other features.
>
> **Source:** Nandy ([1984]1992, 6–9, 22).

despite its public prominence during the political and social process, where one witnesses the development of nation amid the ideologies of Hindutva along with the progress envisioned under the of modernity.

10.4.2. Nationalism and Modernity

In 'mapping a distinctive modernity', Deshpande (2003) reverberated Yogendra Singh's understanding of tradition and modernity; as Indians, we blend both tradition and modernity to achieve 'distinct' and better results. For Singh (1986), modernization began with the Independence movement, and its normative and structural ideals were to reconstruct India, making it economically independent and socially an egalitarian republic. It has been repeatedly pointed out in the following text that European modernity is established on the premise of universality, but a complete dissociation from local influences is not possible. It can only be addressed at the higher level of abstraction. The arrival of modernity in no manner completely replaced traditional or cultural society, but it, of course, influenced it immensely. The unique case like that of India observes that both the old and the new powers are working simultaneously to create a structure of influence for the development of a new social functional order.

Deshpande (2003) also pointed out the social dominance of nationalism and the existence of modern institutions for intellectual expression, which cumulatively allowed for an unusual way of modernization in India. Colonization has also been majorly responsible for bringing about massive change and reshaping the way Indians think and function. It has changed the ideological frameworks and intellectual tools for scrutiny of any particular or general event. These movements are responsible for creating the popular image that the country currently holds. Previously, scholarly interests in India did not focus on the process of social change; however, post-Independence, it became an important element on the schematic interpretations of social anthropologists. Indian nationalism also reiterates the impact of modernization on its unifying thought. But Deshpande mentions, 'that Indians want to be "modern", but not "too modern" or "only modern"'. This highlights the ever-perplexing and challenging presence of modernity in the Indian context, which has been previously discussed in detail with the assistance of various scholars in the chapter. He argues that the trend of beauty queens is repeatedly informing that the true essence of Indian womanhood lies in the blending of tradition and modernity. We are constantly being fed, through popular mass media, with notions of what comprises a perfect blend of tradition and modernity. It does not need to claimed vociferously that the ideas and institutions of modernity have yielded enormous material and moral power. Also, there is a prevalence of dualism with regard to tradition and modernity in India, both of which are located with a mutual articulation, often within the same personality. Modern ways are often restricted to the spheres of professional life and, once back home, the traditional self seeks prominence. Srinivas (1972) tries to understand this ambivalence as an act of 'cultural schizophrenia' but observes caution and dispels the readiness to treat it as pathological. Instead, the theme of coexistence is reflected in the routine narratives of society.

Similarly, Dube (1974) stated that contemporary India, like other developing countries, can be described by blurred images and goals. The dominant discourse is influenced by few modernizing elites. However, the forces of tradition and conservatism are by no means becoming insignificant, because when the aspirations of progress fail, 'the appeal of obscurantism becomes attractive'. Despite the act of assuaging traditional ideals, the goals of modernization continue to be hegemonic. There is, however, a general consensus on the preservation of traditional elements in society. Finally, Madan (1994) discusses D. P. Mukherji's ideas about modernity, which are allegedly founded on the understanding that Indian modernity is rooted in its culture and history. Therefore, Western modernity has to be modified along the lines of genuine Indian culture.

CONCLUSION

It is pertinent to distinguish social changes of Sanskritization and Westernization from Modernization, especially to evaluate changes in the traditional society of India. The traditional cultural structure comprising the little and great traditions in India came into contact with many agents of social change prior to experiencing Westernization. Buddhism and Jainism emerged as protest movements against the oppressive Hindu caste hierarchy. Emergence of Sikhism, along with Bhakti movements, Arya Samaj and Brahmo Samaj, was orthogenetic. And the changes that occurred were restricted to distinction within the framework of traditional social structure. The Islamic tradition in India came from a heterogenetic source. There were structural dissimilarities between the great traditions of Hinduism and Islam, but each of them also had its own cultural beliefs and traditions that contributed towards their little traditions. The two important processes of traditional change have been Sanskritization and Islamization, where the former refers to change from within the Hindu tradition and the latter refers to change introduced with response to external tradition.

The impact of the Western tradition was fundamentally different from Islamization, primarily because it had already undergone transformation, through the Industrial Revolution, before coming into contact with Indian tradition. The contact initially led to the development of a subculture of Westernization, where groups of urban middle-class entrepreneurs and traders began to assimilate the British ways of living, finally leading to the modernization of the legal system, communication, education and so on. There was one important feature of modernization in traditional society: the growth was selective and segmental.

Another most noticeable change in the Indian academic arena is the presence of Indian social theory, which is no longer subjugated by European or Western notions. The presence of scholars of great intellect and discernibility has not only allowed for the realization of being modern but also distinctly modern. D. P. Mukherji stated that 'the study of the thing that is changing becomes more important than the change per se'. Deshpande (2003) believed that modern and traditional should not be treated as descriptive entities, but instead as models of perceptions that require to be adopted towards analysing an object or an event in the Indian context. Pathak (1998) raised pertinent questions around the efficacy of modernity, where he argued that though modernity has come to dominate our cognitive maps and has become a central part of our respective routine practices, it also poses a serious threat through its sheer arrogance towards the superiority of science and technology, which also causes mass destruction and violence. The idea of emancipation is related to modernity, as modernity provides emancipation from the tyranny of tradition. However, there is a contradiction here: modernity is gradually becoming a trap for an individual's autonomy owing to its hyper-technology and bureaucratization.

Points for Classroom Discussion

- The significance of the concept of Sanskritization in explaining social change in India
- The structural–functional approach to explain social change in India
- A critical evaluation of the process of Westernization and modernization in the Indian society
- The dimensions of social change in contemporary India

GLOSSARY

Heterogenetic change: It refers to exogenous change that transforms little tradition, such as Islamization and primary Westernization.

Modernization: It indicates a process of adopting modern ways of life and values. It is a process of comprehensive transformation of a traditional society and has both good and bad implications.

Orthogenetic change: It refers to endogenous changes, where cultural transformations are introduced through the primordial traditional structure itself. Hinduism constitutes the basis of an orthogenetic cultural tradition in India.

Sanskritization: The process that describes social mobility where lower caste individuals emulate practices and beliefs to acquire a higher social status. It is a process of cultural change that promotes a rather religious and sacred outlook.

Westernization: It is a way through which non-Western countries alter their ways of living by adopting practices of the Western countries. It primarily characterizes the changes brought about by the 150 years of British rule in India.

REFERENCES

Bendix, R. 1964. *Nation Building and Citizenship*. New York, NY: John Wiley & Sons.

Cohn, B. 1954. 'Chamars of Senapur' (Unpublished PhD thesis). Ithaca, NY: Cornell University.

Coser, L. A. 1979. Masters of Sociological Thought. New York, NY. Harcourt. Brace.

Deshpande, S. 2003. *Contemporary India: A Sociological View*. London: Penguin Books.

Dube, S. C. 1974. *Contemporary India and Its Modernization*. New Delhi: Vikas Publishing House.

Ghosh, J. C. 1941. 'Literature and Drama: Bengali'. In *Modern India and the West*, edited by L. S. S. O'Malley, 46. London: Macmillan.

Giddens, A. 1990. *The Consequences of Modernity*. Stanford: Stanford University Press.

Gupta, D. 2011. *Mistaken Modernity: In between Worlds*. New York, NY: HarperCollins.

Madan, T. N. 1994. *Pathways: Approaches to the Study of Society in India*. New Delhi: Oxford University Press.

Marx, K. and F. Engels, 1970. *The German Ideology,* New York, NY: International Publishers Co.

Marriott, M. 1992. 'Multiple References in Indian Caste System'. In *Social Stratification*, edited by Dipankar Gupta, 49–59. New Delhi: Oxford University Press.

Nandy, A. ([1984]1992). 'Evaluating Utopias: Considerations for a Dialogue of Cultures and Faiths'. In *Traditions, Tyranny, and Utopias. Essays in the Politics of Awareness*. New Delhi: Oxford University Press.

Pathak, A. 1998. *Indian Modernity: Contradictions, Paradoxes and Possibilities*. New Delhi: Gyan Publishing House.

Rudolph, L. and S. Rudolph. 1967. *The Modernity of Tradition: Political Development in India*. Chicago, IL: University of Chicago Press.

Shah. A. M. 2005. 'Sanskritization Revisited'. *Sociological Bulletin* 54, no 2: 238–249.

Singh, Y. 1986. *Modernization of Indian Tradition*. New Delhi: Rawat Publications.

———. 2012. 'Modernization and Its Contradictions: Contemporary Social Changes in India'. *Polish Sociological Review* 178, no. 2: 151–166.

Spencer, H. 1896. *The Principles of Sociology*, Vol. 3,. London: Williams and Norgate.

Spencer, J. 2007. Anthropology, Politics and the State: Democracy and Violence in South Asia. Cambridge. Cambridge University Press.

Srinivas, M. N. 1956. 'A Note on Sanskritization and Westernization'. *The Far Eastern Quarterly* 15, no. 4: 481–496.

———. 1966. *Social Change in Modern India*. Los Angeles, CA: Orient BlackSwan.

———. 1972. *Social Change in Modern India* (revised edition). New Delhi: Orient Longman.

Upadhyay, S. P. 2013. 'Sanskritization at Large: Cultural Changes in Contemporary India'. *Indian Anthropologist* 43, no. 2: 1–24.

Singh, Y. 1986. *Modernization of Indian Tradition*. New Delhi: Rawat Publications.

CHAPTER 11

Industrialism to Globalization and the Role of the Media

LEARNING OUTCOMES

- To understand the changes in social structure introduced by industrialization.
- To explore the historical development of processes of industrialization and globalization.
- To identify the impact of globalization on the process of industrialization and vice versa.
- To highlight the global significance of media.

Keywords: Industrialization, industrialism, globalization, developing federalism, post-industrial society, role of media

Industrialization is the systemic exploitation of wasting assets. In all too many cases, the thing we call progress is merely an acceleration in the rate of that exploitation.

—**Aldous Huxley**

'Globalization' is itself globalized.

—**Dator**

INTRODUCTION

Sociology as a discipline attempts to explore changes in social structure, social consciousness and the interrelationship between them. Concepts are instrumental in establishing and maintaining the actuality of the world we inhabit. They are the abstractions which represent ways of thinking, and according to Raymond Williams, 'these abstractions are necessary to establish the reality of social life. In order to explain the concepts of industrialism and globalization, it is imperative to explain simultaneously the structural relationships within industrial society and its manifestation in the structures of the relationship between industrial society and the Third World. The inquiry of any society is commonly facilitated by recognizing major epochs; the societies can be categorized on the basis of their social and economic structure. We begin by discussing the different kinds of societies:

1. **Tribal society:** In a tribal society, hunting and gathering constitute the major occupational work in which the members of the society engage. There prevails a simple division of labour on the basis of sex and age. There is the absence of any private ownership of the product, and instead, there is a prevalence of exchange marking simple and undifferentiated economic structure. The social structure is unified and integrated with patterns of interaction similar to that of a primary group. Social control is exercised through folkways.
2. **Agrarian society:** This type has agriculture as their dominant occupation along with the presence of other economic activities such as potters, weavers and artisans. Family is an important institution in an agrarian society which caters to various needs. There is also animal domestication; both have allowed setting stable communities. There are different types of ownership that exist within an agrarian society. The government has tried to away with exploitative ownership of land through policies and acts, for example, the Zamindari Abolition and Land Reforms Act, 1956, which conferred the land rights to tenants. However, there has been gradual change and shift of agrarian society members towards the industrial society due to lack of interest and policies to alleviate the economic crisis faced by the agrarian societies in contemporary times.
3. **Industrial society:** Another important epoch in world history is that of the Industrial Revolution. The phenomenon of the Industrial Revolution meant a transition from a pre-industrial society to an industrial society characterized by modern growth. Revolution, in no way, remarked sudden and drastic change; rather, it had deep and pervasive ramifications. To begin with, first, in an industrial society, the enterprise is completely separated from the family; however, it may not be universal. Second, an industrial society initiates new forms of division of labour based on the technological division of labour within the firm. Third, industrial enterprise emphasizes the accumulation of wealth in terms of profit to achieve the state of a progressive economy. Fourth, there exists a concentration of labours in the workplace. It is, therefore, essential to look at the industrial society through characteristics of an economic system.

An economic system can be defined as the administration of scarce resources with the relation between means and ends where means are scarce and have alternate uses. In developed and developing societies, individuals have many clearly stated goals. With continuous increasing needs, there are numerous means to satisfy them which have alternative uses. Here, the use of money as a generally accepted valuation of goods introduces choice through alternative ways of spending. Money has become a universal way of acquiring the above-discussed set goals. Unlike the earlier type of societies, there exists higher physical mobility among the members of industrial society that also leads to greater social mobility in terms of their status. The first modern industries in India were cotton, jute, coal mines and railways.

In the above-mentioned societies where economic activity is not discrete, there are often attempts to identify it with the satisfaction of basic needs.

11.1. INDUSTRIALIZATION

11.1.1. Historical Development of Industrialization

The world is entering a new era characterized by complete industrialization where there are some countries far ahead on this path, and many are at the beginning. Industrialization means the course of transition from the preceding agrarian society towards the industrial society. It all began from the Industrial Revolution in England; the process of industrialization spread from Britain, as its centre, to Western countries and Japan. According to Kerr et al. (1973), the international commodity, capital and labour markets were decisive instruments in the dissemination of economic development to the USA, Canada, Australia and parts of South America. Industrialization largely spread through diffusion. The Soviet Union boarded on rapid industrialization supported by its socialist agrarian structure. Post Second World War, ambitious industrializing plans were adopted by nations in Asia, Africa and the Middle East. In the beginning, there was only one model of industrialization; however, now, a range of economic and political procedures are available along with the experienced industrialization (refer to Box 11.1). Although industrialization adopts different patterns in different countries, some characteristics are common to all. These are intrinsic to the process of the Industrial Revolution. In many parts of the

---

BOX 11.1
Phases of Industrial Revolution

According to Klaus Schwab (2017), the process of industrialization can be implied through four phases of the Industrial Revolution. He described the Industrial Revolution as a process where 'new technologies and novel ways of perceiving the world (that) trigger a profound change in economic and social structures.' The four phases are as follows:

1. **First Industrial Revolution:** In 1760, the advent of the steam engine began to provide power across agriculture and manufacturing. The process of urbanization was accelerated; people relied on steam power to commute, and factories which became the centre of community life used it to power machine tools. Advancing industrialization created a new middle class comprising skilled labour.
2. **Second Industrial Revolution:** The second phase occurred between the end of the 19th century and the first two decades of the 20th century. It was marked as the age of science and mass production. It brought major innovations in electricity distribution, both wireless and wired communication. The assembly line effectively powered mass production. Inventions of gasoline engines, aeroplanes, chemical fertilizers and so on facilitated migration.
3. **Third Industrial Revolution:** This phase, which somewhere began in the 1950s, is remarked with the Digital Revolution, computer, internet and World Wide Web, which have become handy to access information. The earlier analogue technologies moved to digital technologies, like old television which required tuning with the antenna was replaced by tablets which used function through the internet. This transition drastically affected the industries, especially global communications and energy. Information and electronics technology began to automate production and supply chains.
4. **Fourth Industrial Revolution:** This current period can be understood as the commencement of the fourth Industrial Revolution. As a society, we are ushering into 'cyber-physical systems' comprising novel capacities for both humans and machines. These capacities are instituted and reliant on the infrastructure and technologies of the third revolution. But the fourth Industrial Revolution manifests innovative ways in which technology becomes embedded within societies and even human bodies. Examples will include genome editing, artificial intelligence and approaches to governance, which rely on cryptographic methods like the blockchain.

world, the effects of the third Industrial Revolution are yet to be experienced. This process of the Industrial Revolution has, nonetheless, been unevenly distributed. United Nations in 2013 stated that more people have access to mobile phones than basic sanitation.

11.1.2. Industrialization in India

In India, the first few decades were committed to the process of industrialization to alleviate poverty. Industrialization facilitated self-sufficiency and also created technical progress in the new sovereign state. Considering the ability of agriculture and exports to be inadequate, the Indian government gave priority to the heavy industry. The centralized planned economy was thought to be essential to industrialize country rapidly. This was actualized with the Industries (Development and Regulation) Act in 1951.

Indian state intervention in industrial development has been extensive. Unlike many East-Asian countries, which employed state intervention to create a strong private sector, India chose state control over key industries. At different times, nationalized industries included chemicals, electric power, steel, transportation, life insurance, coal, textile and banking. The government levied high tariffs, imposed import restrictions and also subsidized the nationalized firms to promote these industries.

During the period of 1966–1977, there were two substantial changes in the role of the state. First was the revival of agriculture through subsidizing new seeds and fertilizers, providing agricultural credit and rural electrification, which fostered the Green Revolution to achieve self-sufficiency in grain production. The second change was further stringency over every aspect of the economy. This was reflected through nationalization of banks, price control on a wide range of products, restriction trade and foreign investments. However, the restrictive framework and planning were criticized as several targets remained unachieved.

At the beginning of the early 1980s, a mild trend towards deregulation was initiated through policies to liberalize trade and provide tax concessions, and the improved rate of Indian currency incentivized exports. But it was in July 1991 when major economic reforms were introduced—liberalization, privatization and globalization. There were measures to reduce government's influence on corporate investment decisions. Privatization was introduced in industries such as electricity, oil industry, heavy industry and air transport. Foreign investments were then welcomed, and India became an open economy. These measures accelerated the growth of the gross domestic product.

Foreign direct investment (FDI) of up to 51 per cent in foreign equity was permitted in high-priority industries. The government also provided automatic approval for technological agreements in high-priority industries to promote dynamism in Indian industry. In order to enhance technological dynamism, the government provided automatic approval for technological agreements pertaining to high priority industries and eased procedures for hiring foreign technical expertise.

In 2004, FDI limits were raised in the private banking sector (up to 74%), oil exploration (up to 100%), petroleum product marketing and pipeline (up to 100%), natural gas and liquefied natural gas pipeline (100%) and printing of scientific and technical magazines and journals (up to 100%). Similarly, there was an increase in the percentage of FDI in telecom and other sectors influencing the society directly.

11.1.2.1. Current Scenario: Developing Federalism

Ten years ago, several multinational investors and consumers perceived India as a single homogenous market. However, in the last seven years, the federal structure has come into a sharper focus, which highlighted India as an agglomeration of 29 states. It happened due to policymaking powers and funds being decentralized to the states. The measure of cooperative federalism is promoted by the central government. In cooperative federalism, the centre and the state share a horizontal relationship where they 'cooperate' in the larger public interest. It enables states' participation in the formulation and implementation of national policies.

However, the process of cooperative federalism also transforms into competitive federalism in which states compete with each other for investment. The investors prefer more developed states for investing money. Investors now need to evaluate the political and regulatory settings at both the federal and the state level and take into consideration the state-wise ease-of-doing-business rankings published annually. Even the union government devolves funds to the states on the basis of the usage of previously allocated funds.

In the middle of 2017, India implemented goods and services tax (GST); it replaced dozens of state and federal taxes. The idea was to create a more unified national market, and despite its early glitches, the tax is intended to lead to greater efficiencies and a more attractive business environment. The tax is also supposed to reduce the cost of production in manufacturing industries. The manufacturing sector in India is a major economic driver. The GST plans to dole out a transformational shift in the manufacturing industry, from a complex multi-layered tax structure to one consistent tax. But there are other factors such as lack of adequate infrastructure, misalignment with global supply chains, inadequate innovation and a quagmire of legal and bureaucratic delays which affect the Indian manufacturing sector.

11.1.3. Industrialization and Industrialism

The process of industrialization can be understood as the course of the shift from the traditional society towards industrialism. Haddon (1971) stated that there exists a distinction between industrialization and industrialism; the transitional period of industrialization lacks fundamental structural congruence between the institutions of traditional society and an emerging industrial economy. Industrialism, on the other hand, is a concept that envisages much wider participation of all sectors of society in the industrial economy; it implies not a static social order, but at least a coherent principle of social organization whereby social institutions and structures maintain a much greater degree of structural consistency with a technologically advanced economy.

Haddon (1971) further explains the concept of industrialism as an abstraction, a limit approached through historical industrialization. Industrialism is a concept of a completely industrialized society, which is created by the process of industrialization. This concept of industrialism serves to enable transcending of any historical time. Industrialism can be similar to Weberian ideal type, that is, it can become a template against which different societies can be measured.

Kerr et al. (1973) believed that industrial systems, irrespective of their respective cultural backgrounds, tend to become more alike with time. These systems may be under middle-class or communist or dynastic leadership move towards 'pluralistic industrialism' where the state, the association or an enterprise or even an individual share a substantial degree of power and influence over productive activities. This process of convergence may wary in its speed and degree and be reversed but has a significant indicator of change. Pluralistic industrialism emphasizes mixed sovereignty. Kerr et al. (1973) suggested four generalized models of pluralistic industrialism, which are as follows:

1. The state has a capital investment plan and determines the general direction of economic growth. Where the state permits substantial independence to enterprises to determine products, set prices and wages in response to consumer demand and market conditions.

2. Private ownership has the fundamental sovereignty, with the state more in the role of support. The state maintains law and order and protect property rights and takes complete responsibility for price stabilization, employment, growth and security.
3. The interest of organized workers and consumers is paramount. Here, the workers and consumers through their own organizations and their considerable political influence in the state are protected through legislative efforts and agreements from exploitation by the industrial enterprises and the state.
4. Finally, the self-governing groups of workers and consumers regulate agriculture, handicrafts and services through their productive efforts. The state provides central services of defence, welfare and so on.

In all the above-mentioned situations, the state, private enterprises and the individuals all have considerable influence; however, the influence will vary. In the first, the state is more dominant; in the second, the enterprise; in the third, the associated workers and consumers, and in fourth, the workers and consumers as owners. The pluralism of the state, the enterprise and the individual are matched by the industrial relations systems of the state, the manager of the enterprise and the worker associations.

Goldthorpe argues that political considerations will have more impact on the 'life chances' of individuals in a strongly statist pluralism, and the class situation will have more impact on the 'life chances' in market-oriented pluralism. But Kerr et al. (1973) rejected Goldthorpe's interpretation of a one-way total convergence; rather, they believed in two-way partial convergence between market capitalism and state socialism.

It is pertinent to highlight that the advancing educational system stimulated not only individualism but also a scientific approach in the long run. There are claims that the Industrial Revolution marks the most fundamental transformation of human life in the history of the world (Hobsbawm 1968, 7). With passing centuries, the world economy began to emerge as a single unit in which advanced regions were linked to the colonies with a certain division of economic activity. These interactions were described as a system of economic flows, trade, international payments, migration and capital transfer (Wallerstein 1974).

11.2. POST-INDUSTRIALISM

11.2.1. Post-Industrial society

Bell (1973) initiated formulating the concept of post-industrial society in 1959–1962. Although the concept of post-industrial society has developed earlier, Bell developed it to give a modern understanding. In his work, *The Coming of Post-Industrial Society*, he discusses the idea of post-industrial society as a 'social forecast about a change in the social framework of western society'. The predicted change is a transition from industrial to a post-industrial society, which would be achieved by the year 2000. Post-industrial society will be fully realized by the year 2020.

Bell stated that the USA, at the beginning of 1970, was in the first stage of a post-industrial society. He outlined the following five dimensions of the concept of the post-industrial society, each of which refers to changes in the organization of Western society:

1. First, the economic sector shifts from goods production, with its reliance on energy and machinery, to services.
2. Second, occupations related to the distribution of information and a variety of services grow at a relatively high rate.
3. Third, he pointed out the rapid growth of scientists and engineers in the 1960s. He had suggested that the expansion of science-based industries would necessitate an increase in the numbers of engineers, mathematicians and chemists.
4. Fourth, he projected snowballing in societal planning of and control over technological change, a principal objective of which would be the protection of the environment.
5. Fifth, societal decision-making would also necessitate a new intellectual technology, which will allow for the ordering of mass society.

Further, regarding the fate of the standard of living in the post-industrial society, Bell stated that the expansion of the service sector will become a constraint on economic growth and also a constant source of inflation, and overall productivity of the economy may decline as productivity will grow more slowly in the expanding service sector. On the other hand, he implies that the production of goods will not be displaced in the post-industrial society, and output will continue to rise. In conclusion, he suggested that the standard of living would continue to improve for the next 100 years. And he also rejected the Kahn's optimistic vision of the super-abundant society and its polar opposite, the pessimistic predictions of depleted resources and zero economic growth.

It is believed that the Industrial Revolution has been the most prominent impetus of globalization process, as it created its own structures across the world on the capitalist mode of production, whose main components are production, consumption, international trade, rivalry and wars among competition states. Polyani (1957) aptly puts that the logic of industrial production has transformed the economic life of people.

11.3. GLOBALIZATION

11.3.1. Exploring the Concept of Globalization

The term globalization has its origin in the English language; the word 'globalization' refers to the emergence of a universal network, pertaining to an economic and social system. An analogous term 'giant corporation' was used in 1897 by Charles Russell Tazel to describe the big national trusts and other large enterprises of the time. And from 1960 to mid-1980, both terms began to use interchangeably by social scientists and economists. Post-Cold War, the term began to be used to describe the world becoming increasingly interdependent in the dimensions of information and economy. Robertson (1992) was the first sociologist to define globalization as 'the understanding of the world and the increased perception of the world as a whole.' Further, Giddens (1991) stated that globalization can be defined as 'the intensification of social relations throughout the world, linking distant localities in such a way that local happenings are formed as a result of events that occur many miles away and vice versa.'

The term globalization is often visible in a different context and diverse spheres of political, academic and economic discourse. The concept of globalization is legitimized under the neoliberal paradigm of capitalism. This paradigm of neoliberalism gets endorsement and validation through state economic and political policies. The aspects of globalization include not only supertankers, jets and container ships, migratory labour, electronic and genetic communication technologies but also global anthropogenic climate change, pollution, diseases, religions, criminal and terrorist activities and counter-state police and military forces, popular culture, mass media and sports (Dator 2006). Globalization is not a new phenomenon and is well explained by Joseph Nye (Keohane and Nye 2000).

> The oldest form of globalization is environmental: climate change has affected the ebb and flow of human populations for millions of years. Migration is a long-standing global phenomenon. The human species began to leave its place of origins, Africa, about 1.25 million years ago and reached the Americas sometime between 30,000 and 13,000 years ago. One of the most important forms of globalization is biological. The first smallpox epidemic is recorded in Egypt in 1350 BC. It reached China in 49 AD, Europe after 700, the Americas in 1520, and Australia in 1789. The plague or Black Death originated in Asia, but its spread killed a quarter to a third of the population of Europe between 1346 and 1352. When Europeans journeyed to the New World in the fifteenth and sixteenth centuries they carried pathogens that destroyed up to 95 percent of the indigenous population.

People in the past have travelled and enabled cultural diffusion. However, with the invention of the press, telegraph, phone, radio, television, satellites, mobile and the internet, there has been an increase in the pace and extent of communication, increasing the prospects of hassle-free exchange by reducing the restrictions of previous technologies. Globalization may refer to both spatial and temporal processes, which establishes the rubric of human transformation across regions. In the absence of any mention of expansion in the space of the connections, there can be no clear and coherent formulation of the concept of globalization. A coherent definition of globalization, thus, should focus on extension, intensity, celebrity and impact. Often, 'globalization' is inferred with respect to the attempts of the International Monetary Fund, World Bank and the institutions towards establishing a free global market for goods and services. Such attempts are designed to develop and exploit more complex processes; whereby through increased economic interconnectedness, the political changes have intensified leading to higher dependence of the underdeveloped and developing nations on the central economies of the world like the USA.

The process of globalization encompasses dissemination of ideas, practices and technologies and moves beyond universalization. It also cannot be understood in terms of modernization or Westernization and cannot be restricted to merely market liberalization. Thus, it can be argued that it is not a single process but involves the following four distinct types of change, according to Held et al. (1999):

1. It stretches social, political and economic activities across political frontiers, regions and continents.
2. It intensifies our dependence on each other, as flows of trade, investment, finance, migration and culture increase.
3. It speeds up the world. New systems of transport and communication mean that ideas, goods, information, capital and people move more quickly.
4. It means that distant events have a deeper impact on our lives. Even most local developments may come to have enormous global consequences. The boundaries between domestic matters and global affairs can become increasingly blurred.

Finally, globalization is about the associations between different regions of the world from cultural to criminal, to environmental and to financial and the ways in which they expand and diminish with time.

The globalization has proceeded through five trajectories that impact human society and trajectories, which influence the development of human society. These trajectories through which globalization interacts with society locally, regionally and internationally are: the economic, the military, the political, the religious and the cultural.

11.3.2. Agents of Globalization

When globalization is perceived as an effect of modernity, which originated in Western Europe, it is extensively criticized about its Eurocentrism, which is only Western kind of modernity. It arises because it implies the 'Westernization' approach to globalization. As mentioned earlier, globalization started very early with human voyages, but with the end of the Cold War and the reunification of Eastern and Western Germany in 1990, physical and symbolic walls became supportive and accelerated our globalizing and apparently borderless world (Ohmae 1992). There are the following three forces that are accelerating globalization:

1. Increased connectivity
2. Improved technology
3. Perceived convergence

People across the world have previously survived on traditional knowledge and ways of life. But now, the new discoveries and every information in the world are available at the touch of the mobile technology which is connecting the world.

These forces cumulatively lead to three innovations of growing interdependence, growing numbers of multi-directional migrations and the slow erosion of national politics. Further, these forces and innovations also trigger global exchange in the context of economic, cultural and media. Appadurai (1996, 33) identified five types of transnational flows in a global context, which are as follows:

1. **Ethnoscapes:** It refers to the shifting landscape of people across culture and borders through tourism, migration, exile, refugees and so on. For instance, Singapore's diverse ethnoscape reflect the blending of different styles of

scientific work and the interconnected flow of intellectual capital of people from varied backgrounds.
2. **Technoscapes:** It is the transmission of culture through technology. Innovative processing of cultural interaction and exchange are fostered through the internet. This globally integrated information network has become an influential source to determine the flow of culture and communication across the world.
3. **Financescapes:** It refers to the global movement of money, including currency, trade and commodity, especially when goods are exchanged freely in global markets. However, this leads to higher competitions among corporations.
4. **Mediascapes:** It refers to the electronic proficiencies of production and dissemination of information through media. Mediascapes and ideoscapes have a close relationship and usually work upon the support of other scapes.
5. **Ideoscapes:** It refers to the global flow and exchange of ideologies. These are very sensitive to local conditions. This is often used with respect to the political ideologies employed by governments or counter-government groups to claim power. Examples of ideoscapes include notions and images behind democracy, welfare, human rights and so on.

These five-dimensional scapes are fluid and often fluctuate, like culture. However, within each of these scapes remains some disjuncture, but 'sheer speed, scale and volume of each of these flows are now so great that disjunctures have become central to the politics of global culture' (Appadurai 1996).

11.3.3. Local–Global Dialect

This section will briefly introduce the different forces and effects that accelerate global flows and connectedness, along with the cultural meaning of globalization.

Anthony Giddens (1990) introduces the concept of local–global dialect, which emphasizes that individual actions on a local level have a global impact. For instance, in the clothing industry, buying a T-shirt has an effect on a Bangladeshi worker thousand miles away from the place of purchase. Similarly, the news is spread around the world in an instant; the awareness of such interconnectedness shifts the attention to the so-called butterfly effect or chaos theory (Keil et al. 1996, 58) in which local events can trigger global actions, problems, disputes or even catastrophes. Therefore, in a global context, 'the world has become one network of social relationships' (Hannerz 1990, 237) in which the different cultural flows interconnect the different localities. Castells (2004) calls this effect a 'network society', and global network society is characterized by both its common features and diversity. It is conceived as a system of different network societies communicating with each other, forming a global network of information.

These effects of globalization become influential forces themselves, improving a circular process of forces and effects. Hannerz (1990) stated that globalization, as a process, constantly drives connectivity that leads to increased networking around the globe. Increased connectivity translates into a fast and an instant exchange of information with regard to politics, media and security. As discussed earlier, technological advances are accompanied by an increase in connectivity and experienced convergence. The entire globe seems to be connected by new or better means of infrastructure, transportation, information or digital devices. While the global encompassing phenomenon of Twitter, Instagram and Facebook have rapidly changed information technology and the entertainment industry, these social networking websites have also had an increasing impact on the youth across the world, creating transnational and translingual 'imagined communities.' Technology, thus, evolves as a capitalist vehicle of a culture where different cultural elements are transported via different carrying systems, the mass media or other electronic devices.

11.3.3.1. Homogenization and Hybridization

The following sections discuss the effects and repercussions of globalization. It also provides an analysis of cultural diversity in an urban global context. Globalization can be observed as the universalization with regard to consumerism or variation as cultural disintegration. This act of universalization can also be seen as an act of homogenization, which has been achieved through (a) Westernization and (b) standardization.

Americanization can be interpreted as neocolonialism due to its focus on consumerism, commercials, mass media, mass production and sales. Everything essentially revolves around money. Colonizing is no longer achieved in a physical manner but rather via the transference of trends, values and legends like the 'American dream'. The USA is teaching the values of self-determination, self-development and self-worth through TV shows and Hollywood. In accordance with cultural homogenization, globalization, like standardization, is a process of 'synchronization to the demands of standardized consumer culture, making everywhere seem more or less same' (Tomlinson 2001, 6). This is further established through 'commodification of culture' (Tomlinson 2001, 85f), which can be interpreted as uniform ways of global shopping, consuming fast food, television, the internet and travel. According to Tomlinson (2001), such acts raises controversial questions such as whether the world is becoming a single cultural setting or whether cultural convergence leads to unity or uniformity of cultures. The global homogenization theory is doubted and feared; rather, hybridization is preferred over cultural imposition. Standardization and Westernization (Americanization) are questioned because there is always conversion, adaptation or 'indigenization' of the receiving culture (Appadurai 1990).

Further, globalization is not entirely about being 'Westernized', as the process is not organized but haphazardly induced an influenced by multiple forces. Cultural hybridization during globalization can be regarded as a positive outcome of colonization because 'population movement and settlement established during colonialism and its aftermath, combined with more recent acceleration of globalization, particularly of electronic communications, have enabled increased cultural juxta positioning, meeting and mixing' (Barker 1989). Therefore, the present culture is extremely influenced by the hybridization process. Globalization is a process of blurring boundaries; nonetheless, the boundaries remain. It is that engine which accelerates the process of hybridization, capturing the spirit of current times of celebrating cultural differences. With the mass migration happening across the globe, there is the emerging usage of words such as melange and hotchpotch, which is rendering new identity.

11.3.4. Impact of Globalization

11.3.4.1. Environment

Environmental change has been an issue for many states locally. However, in the current scenario, it poses a severe global threat, which necessitates a global measure to combat. The concerns around global environment came to rise when it was established that ecological processes do not always respect national boundaries, and environmental problems often have effects beyond borders. Monitoring and evaluating environmental issues regularly pushes the need for synchronized global governance. Essentially, the environment is inherently linked to economic development, as natural resources fuel the growth and development. Although it has been established that there are strong links between globalization and environmental change, the available literature is vague and partial, focusing only on the impact of globalization on the environment and not vice versa.

The history validates how environmental changes have occurred primarily through anthropogenic activities. The Industrial Revolution and colonization affected the indigenous population and eventually disturbed their ecosystems, landscapes and agricultural systems. The forests were destroyed to meet the demands of Europe and the USA. Earlier, maximum environmental degradation was largely local until the middle of this century; however, globalization has accelerated degradation. Basu (2005) argued that for 'winners' of the process, globalization becomes an integrating phenomenon—one that brings together markets, ideas, individuals, goods, services and communications. But for the 'losers' in the process, it can be a marginalizing phenomenon. Just as the winners come closer to each other, they become 'distant' from the losers. Environmental pressure has a similar impact on the vulnerable and the weak; although climate change will eventually impact everyone, it will impact the poorest communities first and harshest. Several decades of resource-intensive and high pollution in the Organisation for Economic Co-operation and Development countries and even dishonest industrialization of Russia and Eastern Europe have taken a toll on their environment.

Oil, timber, metals which are extracted for economic growth exist only in finite numbers. There has been a quantum increase in the consumption of such resources degrading ecological processes. And fragile ecosystems could impede the current rate of globalization. Environmental degradation also affects productivity through damages to health. Several international agencies have listed the numbers of deaths (2.5 million people die every year) that occur in Asia-Pacific region due to poor environmental issues comprising air pollution, unhealthy water and poor sanitation (Nierenberg and Starke 2006). People across the globe are increasingly aware of the array of global and regional environmental problems. There are reactions to global warming, ozone depletion, destruction of global rainforests and loss of biodiversity, toxic waste, pollution of rivers and oceans and nuclear risks with the outbreak of global and regional initiatives, institutions, regimes, networks and treaties. There is also proliferation in transnational environmental movements, which are more politically visible. To manage the threats posed by globalization and garner benefits through it, the state and policymakers have to be informed, prepared and have the capacity to introduce investments, particularly in developing countries, for immediate and sustainable benefits. The role of international assistance in enhancing such capacity is critical.

11.3.4.2. Political Structure

Globalization signifies the onset of a new period in establishing human associations. It is changing societies and the world order, creating a significant impact. This transformation is occurring in complex and diverse ways. Although, as discussed in the previous section, globalization can be identified as having a historical presence, its present scale and form are completely different. Globalization is lamented to widen the gaps between the richest and poorest countries and has increased divisions across and within societies. It is becoming increasingly contested and politicized, wherein states are being crammed between global forces and local demands. By confirming the transnational and multilateral agreements, a state adopts major changes in its domestic policy. For example, the various environment and climate treaties are coercing the Third-World countries to reduce their carbon footprints.

Held (1990) explained that under such circumstances, states power and political authority are shifting, and states now deploy their sovereignty and autonomy as bargaining pieces in multilateral and transnational negotiations, as they collaborate and coordinate actions in fluctuating regional and global networks. Held further argued that the right of most states to rule within restricted territories does not ruin their sovereignty, although its capacity to rule is changing. The developing shape of governance means that we need to stop thinking of state power as something indivisible and territorially exclusive. Rather, it is pertinent to acknowledge the transformation of state power; the array of government policies motivated by globalization is creating more of an activist state. Globalization has disturbed ordered communication between national territory, sovereignty, political space and the democratic political community. It allows power to flow across, around and over territorial boundaries. Globalization allows for rethinking politics where, according to Held (1990), we need to take our existing ideas about political, equality, social justice and liberty and modify these into coherent a robust political project where power is exercised on a transnational scale and where risks are shared by people across the world.

11.4. MEDIA

11.4.1. Role of the Media

'Mass media' is a term which encompasses all forms of information communicated to large groups of people from a handmade signage to an international news network. The term is wide and vague and can be used to refer a group of corporate media houses, publishers, journalists and others who constitute the communication industry and profession. It collectively represents all media technologies that are intended to reach a large audience via mass communication platforms. Refer to Box 11.2 for understanding various models of communication and media By the 20th

> **BOX 11.2**
> **Media Theories Overview**
>
> The following are some media theories:
>
> 1. Magic bullet theory is also referred to as the hypodermic needle model. Lasswell conceived that the magic bullet approach intended that the originator of the message could directly influence and manipulate the recipients' perception. It believes that the public is gullible, making it easier for the source to influence its audience. For instance, WhatsApp is being lamented as a platform that often allows unchecked circulation of fake news and agonizing messages against communities, leading to the prevalence of mistrust.
> 2. The authoritarian theory explains how media and communication are subject to the liking of the ruling regime, and any expression which undermines the customary political order can be prohibited. This theory breaches freedom of expression but can be invoked in certain conditions.
> 3. Social responsibility theory is prevalent in European countries and is a modified version of free press theory. Nonetheless, it emphasizes the accountability of the broadcasting media to society. It is either self-regulated or is administered by public intervention.
> 4. Development media theory assumes various forms, but it highlights subjugation of the media by the requirements of economic, social and political development.
> 5. Alternative media theory promotes critical perspective; it favours the grassroots of society, small-scale, participatory and non-commercial approach.

century, mass media could be classified into books, newspapers, magazines, recordings, radio, movies, television and the internet. Lasswell (1948) mentions that the prominent function of mass communication is surveillance of the environment, whereas Mcquail (1987) stated that mass media enables mobilization. In today's time, media, more than often, promotes certain desirable values towards national interest and campaigns for welfare of the majority and minority. There exist several theories discussing the relevance and pervasiveness of media in society. Media theory implies complex social–political–philosophical principles which establish ideas about the relationship between media and society. One such theory subscribing to this understanding is 'normative theory', which focuses on what the obligatory aspect of the media—what it ought to do in a society. However, there exists uncertainty in the normative theory, because of the changes in the media and rise of new forms of media (Nerone 1995).

11.4.2. Global Media Debate

The global debate around media was launched during the 1973 General Conference of the United Nations Educational, Scientific and Cultural Organization (UNESCO) in Nairobi, Kenya. The debates from Western industrialized nations insisted on 'free flow of information', advocating 'free trade' in information and media programs without any restrictions. Whereas another block accused western countries of invoking the free flow of information ideology to justify their economic and cultural domination. The gap between the two groups was one of the major reasons for the withdrawal of the USA and the United Kingdom from UNESCO, which eventually resulted in the de facto fall of the global media debate.

Cultural imperialism has its weaknesses; it raises concerns in several countries where people fear that their culture gets diluted. Nevertheless, the term cultural imperialism is replaced by the concept of globalization, which thrives on international communication flows and processes. Media has maximum potential, here, for spreading information to places where earlier, it was absent. However, it has the ability to promote dominant interest; nonetheless, it has the capabilities to contribute towards democratic processes, especially in countries and regimes which are not democratic. Cultural globalization is perhaps the most familiar form of globalization for people. As discussed in the previous section, the process or act of Americanization and Westernization can be even understood as cultural imperialism, and the driving force behind them is the mass media. Technological developments are accompanied by an increase in connectivity and experienced convergence. The entire world seems to be connected by new or better means of infrastructure, transportation and information through digital devices. According to Alfonso de Toro (2006), on the one hand, the new internet technology is transforming the world into an ever-growing virtual space and expands the world in an almost infinite way and on the other hand, compresses it radically so that we live in a permanent implosion.

While taking into consideration the spectrum of communication in modern society, there are noticeable barriers: monopolistic controls, technical disparities, restrictive media practice and exclusion of disadvantaged groups. Nonetheless, a tendency towards democratization seems to be increasing with cultivating the role of public opinion. The governments across the world are becoming increasingly aware that they must take into consideration not only national opinion but 'world public opinion' because today's media is capable of diffusing 'information on international issues throughout the world' (Mac Bride and Roach 2000). And at times, opinion crystallizes on some issue to force action. And the social networking platforms such as Facebook and Instagram have had an increasing impact on the youth of the world, creating transnational and translingual 'imagined communities' (Anderson 1983). Thus, technology becomes the capitalist vehicle of culture in which varied cultural elements are transferred via different carrier systems of mass media.

CONCLUSION

The chapter succinctly reckoned the processes of change through industrialization and globalization. Every economy, even in primitive society, comprises the processes of production, exchange and consumption. It will be unfair to assume that there could be no further changes in industrial society. There will be interventions to modify, accelerate and impede the pace of industrial development. Currently, social expectations of industrial organization and corporations are changing, as public concerns are growing about climate change, automation, corporate ownership of private data, inequality and many others. In the fourth Industrial Revolution, governance along with corporate policies are under immense pressure to modernize the societies further through technological intervention. There is an increased momentum around developing industrial corridors and smart cities, which are believed to further assist in integrating and developing a conducive environment for industrial development.

Due to globalization, places such as New York, Los Angeles, London, Paris, Mumbai and New Delhi have emerged as global cities and function as cultural nodes in a network of the world, encompassing movements. At such time, we need to assess the efficacy of the existing economic and political structures and shape the established ideas of equality, social justice and liberty. Transformation in international communication has not only created increased interconnectedness and developed the idea of a shrinking world, but it has also increased competition in world economics and affected national and transnational political dynamics. A good environment is needed to realize the complete potential of globalization, and the absence of the former can significantly undermine the promise of economic prosperity through globalization. New technologies lead to quicker information services and growing global networks of individuals, ideologies and capitalism. The global encompassing instant messaging platform like Twitter has rapidly transformed information technology and the entertainment industry. Globalization has distressed controlled communication between national territory, sovereignty, political space and the democratic political community. It has allowed power to flow across, around and over territorial boundaries.

Points for Classroom Discussion

- Industrialization can be understood through the Industrial Revolution
- New technologies and media play a central role in the process of globalization
- The logic of industrial production has transformed the economic life of people

GLOSSARY

Globalization: It is a process of increased movement and exchange of human beings, goods, services, technologies, capital and cultural practices across the world.
Industrialization: It refers to the process of wide-scale development of industries for economic development around an area.
Industrialism: It is a system that represents a prevalence of manufacturing industries.
Post-industrial society: It is a stage of society's development when the service sector[1] generates more wealth than the manufacturing sector[2] of the economy.

---

[1] https://en.wikipedia.org/wiki/Tertiary_sector_of_the_economy
[2] https://en.wikipedia.org/wiki/Secondary_sector_of_the_economy

REFERENCES

Anderson, B. 1983. Imagined Communities: Reflections on the spread of Nationalism. London: Verso.

Appadurai, A. 1990. 'Disjuncture and Difference in the Global Cultural Economy'. *Theory, Culture & Society* 7, no. 2: 295–310.

Appadurai, A. 1996. *Modernity at Large: Cultural Dimensions of Globalization*. Minneapolis, MN: University of Minnesota Press.

Barker M. 1989. *Comics: Ideology, Power and Critics*. Manchester: Manchester University Press.

Basu, K. 2005. 'Globalization, Poverty and Inequality: What Is the Relationship? What Can Be Done?' Research Paper No. 2005/32, Helsinki, Finland, UNU-WIDER. Available at: https://www.econstor.eu/bitstream/10419/63487/1/500809232.pdf (accessed on 17 February 2021).

Bell, D. 1973. *The Coming of Post-Industrial Society*. London: Heineman.

Castells, M. 2004. *The Information Age: Economy Society and Culture. Volume II: The Power of Identity*. 2nd ed. Oxford: Blackwell.

Giddens, A. 1990. *The Consequences of Modernity*. Cambridge: Polity Press.

———. 1991. *The Consequences of Modernity*. Cambridge: Polity Press.

Haddon, R. 1971. 'Foreword.' In *Industrialism and Industrial Man*, edited by Clark Kerr. New York, NY: Oxford University Press.

Hannerz, U. 1990. 'Cosmopolitans and Locals in World Culture.' *Theory, Culture and Society* 7, no. 2–3: 237–251.

Held, D. 1995. Democracy and the Global Order: From the Modern State to Cosmopolitan Governance. Cambridge: Polity Press.

Held, D., A. McGrew, D. Goldblatt, and J. Perraton. 1999. 'Globalization.' *Global Governance* 5, no. 4 (October–December): 483–496.

Hobsbawm, E. C. 1968. *Industry and Empire*. New York, NY: Pantheon Books.

Keohane, R. O., and J. S. Nye, Jr. 2000. 'Introduction.' In *Governance in a Globalizing World*, edited by Joseph S. Nye and John D. Donahue. Washington, DC, WA: Brookings Institution Press.

Kerr, C., J. Dunlop, F. Harbison, and C. A. Myers. 1973. *Industrialism and Industrial Man: The Problems of Labour and Management in Economic Growth*. Harmondsworth: Penguin.

Kiel, L. Douglas, and E. Elliott, eds. 1996. *Chaos Theory in the Social Sciences: Foundations and Applications*. Ann Arbor, MI: University of Michigan Press.

Lasswell, H. D. 1948. 'The Structure and Function of Communication in Society'. In *The Communication of Ideas*, edited by Bryson, L. New York: Harper and Brothers.

Mac Bride, S., and C. Roach. 2000. 'The New International Information Order'. In *The Globalization Reader*, edited by Frank Lechner and John Boli. Malden, MA: Blackwell Publishers.

McQuail, D. 1987. *Mass Communication Theory: An Introduction*. London: SAGE Publications.

Nerone, J., ed. 1995. *Last Rights: Revisiting Four Theories of the Press*. Urbana, IL: University of Illinois Press.

Nierenberg, D., and L. Starke. 2006. *State of the World 2006: A Worldwatch Institute Report on Progress Toward a Sustainable Society*. New York, London: W.W. Norton.

Ohmae, K. 1992. *The Borderless World: Power and Strategy in the Interlinked Economy*. New York: Harper Collins.

Polanyi, K. 1957. 'The Economy as Instituted Process. In *Trade and Market in the Early Empires: Economies in History and Theory*, edited by K. Polanyi, C. M. Arensberg, and H. W. Pearson. New York: The Free Press.

Robertson, R. 1992. *Globalization: Social Theory and Global Culture*. London: SAGE Publications.
Schwab, K. 2017. 'The Fourth Industrial Revolution'. *Quality Management Journal* 25, no 2: 108–109.
Tomlinson, J. 2001. *Cultural Imperialism: A Critical Introduction*. London: Continuum.
Toro, A. 2006. Globalization - New Hybridities - Transidentities- Transnations: Recognition – Difference'. In *New Hybridities: Societies and Cultures in Transition*, edited by Frank Heidemann and Alfonso de Toro, Hildesheim: Olms, 19-37.
Wallerstein, I. 1974. *The Modern World System I: Capitalist Agriculture and the Origins of the European World-Economy in the Sixteenth Century*. New York, NY: Academic Press.

SECTION E

SOCIAL MOVEMENTS, RESISTANCE AND NATION BUILDING

Chapter 12
Peasant Movement and Middle-class Phenomenon

Chapter 13
Dalit Movement

Chapter 14
Women's Movement

Chapter 15
Ethnic Movements

CHAPTER 12

Peasant Movement and Middle-class Phenomenon

LEARNING OUTCOMES

- To conceptualize peasantry and Peasant movement in India
- To examine the analytical strengths of the concept dominant peasantry vis-à-vis middle peasantry
- To historicize the growth and role of the middle class in India
- To understand the middle class in the contemporary context of liberalization and globalization

Keywords: Peasant society, middle peasant, dominant peasantry, class collaboration, middle class, intermediate class, hegemony, cultural capital, developmental state, globalization

The bourgeoisie, in truth, is bound to fear the stupidity of the masses so long as they remain conservative, and the insight of the masses as soon as they become revolutionary.

—**Karl Marx**[1]

---

[1] https://www.goodreads.com/work/quotes/819841-der-18te-brumaire-des-louis-napoleon

INTRODUCTION

For ages, agriculture has been the primary life-giving and life-sustaining activity of the Indian people. Agricultural revenue was important for the ancient and medieval states, yet as such, till the medieval time, no significant peasant movement is documented. It is difficult to comment on whether the agricultural relation and revenue collection was non-oppressive or not, given the absence of the peasant movement. It is quite possible that the system was encompassed within a wider structure of domination and power.

The arrival of the British East India Company in India altered the agricultural relation. The introduction of new agricultural revenue systems from time to time prepared the ground for collective resistance from the people attached to agriculture. It was not only economic or political appropriation of the Indian people that the colonial regime ensured, but it also destabilized the sociocultural–religious aspects of the peasantry. The arrival of the peasant movement needs to be seen in this specific historical context. The same is true for understanding the peasant movement in Independent India too.

Various scholarly research works have been done on Indian peasantry and the peasant movement. They indicate a meaningful debate on the correct conceptualization of the term 'peasantry'. In the Indian context, due to religion, caste and ethnic factors, the peasantry as a concept and social category is quite a differentiated social group. The peasantry in India is constituted of not only a vast majority of landless agricultural labourers, tenants, sharecroppers, small cultivators and rural artisans but also a dominant section who are economically as well socially quite powerful. The stratified agrarian society and the identity as well as the interests of the various sections govern the trajectory of the peasant movement in India.

Similarly, the middle class has been a contentious concept in Marxist scholarship as handed down to us from the classicist. In classical Marxist texts, classes are understood as social groups who share similar positions in a social relation of production. Marx understood classes as a product of historical development and as such was interested to identify classes that would be the motive forces of historical development.

Analytically examining the march of society from the primitive stage, Marx arrived at the era of industrial capitalism to identify the two protagonist classes—the bourgeoisie and the proletariat. The identification of a bipolar contradiction between capital and labour was primary for Marx. He theorized that labour being the mover of history, the proletariat will score a victory over the capitalist class to initiate the socialist stage of society. Subsequently in Marxist literature, primarily from Italian theorist Antonio Gramsci, we find useful insights on the question of intermediate classes.

Subsequently, it is being realized that an orthodox theory of class would fall short of capturing the empirical reality of advanced capitalist societies or post-colonial societies which are witnessing not a singular capital versus labour contestation. Instead, in between, a host of intermediary classes have come to play significant roles in the respective social formations. In this context, the role, nature and significance of the middle class demand a sociological understanding. Especially in the changing global scenario impacted by overwhelming forces of liberalization in post-colonial societies like India, the middle-class as a phenomenon invites innovative sociological commentaries.

12.1. THE PEASANT MOVEMENT IN INDIA

12.1.1. Conceptualizing Peasantry and the Peasant Movement

Different disciplines and different scholars have theorized the concept of peasant with different contents by emphasizing various aspects of it at variance. Earlier, in Anthropology, cultural and social aspects were given prominence, whereas of late, the interest has turned to the economic dimensions. Anthropological definitions of peasants have emerged in the context of contextualizing peasants against tribes as a social category. Most of the sociological literature on peasantry has taken generic attributes (either cultural or economic) of the peasantry, abstracting it from the historical and social framework of its existence. A general definition of a peasant is bound to be ahistorical and, at best, has only a descriptive utility. Instead, the peasantry should also be examined contextually, that is, within the particular sociocultural milieu in which it is embedded and which gives it a particular character.

Daniel Thorner has pointed out that the term 'peasant' may be used in a broad as well as a narrow sense. In the narrow sense, peasants are small landholders who live by cultivating land which they own or control. In the broader sense, peasants are all those who live by working on the land including sharecroppers and agricultural workers. In the real world, there is frequent and considerable overlapping between the two categories as noted by Thorner (Thorner 1968). On the other hand, the anthropological concept of peasant does not take into account fully that the peasantry and peasant societies have taken a new shape in the developing countries. Also, if we go by the classic definition of the peasantry, we have to exclude landless labourers and the farmers from our analysis. Hence, while discussing the peasant movement, we need to study peasants, farmers and landless labourers and their interrelationships (Bernstein 1979). Conceptualizing the Indian peasantry is more problematic. The criteria of landownership and family labour become meaningless due to the wide variety of land tenures and cultural sanctions against manual work in India.

Can every protest movement with participation of rural people be termed as the peasant movement? It is pertinent to ask this as, nothing specifically peasant, one can trace in every protest movement attributed to the peasants. The role of peasants keeps changing as they are placed in different contexts of colonialism, authoritarianism, nationalism or class struggle.

T. K. Oommen has studied the relationship between peasant protest and its relationship with national movement (Oommen 1985). He demarcates the characteristics of the two contexts—the colonial and the national. In the colonial situation, the primary enemy is external and political, whereas in the post-colonial situation, the enemy is internal and economic. According to Oommen, the character of the collective action of peasantry differs under conditions of colonialism as compared with the situation in a nation state. Based on the Indian experience, it can also be pointed out that one has to acknowledge the contextualization of the identity of participants in a social movement. In the colonial context, peasants were fighting as not only peasants but also subjects against colonial masters. The identity that was contextually crucial was not that of an occupation/class identity but that of being an Indian. Hence, instead of class identity, we need to accept multiple identities of a peasant. So for a comprehensive understanding of the peasant movement in Indian society, we take into consideration the historicity, the elements of the social structure, the nature of state and its development strategy where a particular peasant movement originates and operates.

12.1.2. Peasant Movement in India

In order to examine the class character of the peasant movements since the First World War, one has to explore the social composition of those movements. Eight such peasant movements are listed by Jacques Pouchepadass (1980) in his 'Peasant Classes in Twentieth Century Agrarian Movements in India'. Chronologically they are as follows:

1. **The Champaran movement in Bihar (1917):** The rural agitation was propelled by the Gandhian principle of *Satyagraha*. The villagers agitated against the British indigo planters. The movement was led by the rich and well-to-do family, who were at the same time from high-caste groups. The rich and well-to-do peasants successfully obtained the participation of the rest of the peasantry, including the agricultural workers.
2. **The movement in Kheda district (Gujarat; 1918):** On the question of exploitative land revenue, a showdown resulted in which the Kheda ryots withheld the payment against the British government. It was also guided by the Gandhian *Satyagraha* principle and an anti-imperial approach. Similar to the Champaran movement, Kheda also was driven by rich and middle peasants' action. The participation of the poor peasantry and the agricultural workers was lacking. This movement was studied in detail by David Hardiman (1976). The *Satyagraha* was able to attract the poor peasantry only because of the degradation suffered due to the First World War.
3. **1920–1922, a series of rural agitations in the United Province:** At the initiative of the peasant associations (Kisan Sabha) of the Indian National Congress, the rural population agitated sporadically throughout these years. The agitations took place in the backdrop of the non-cooperation movement led by Gandhi. The Kisan Sabhas of Congress were essentially made up of prosperous peasants and the nationalist sections of the party.

    Majid Hayat Siddiqi's historical research on the rural unrest in the United Provinces concludes that the rise in the prices of staple food grains and their poor quality essentially affected the tenants and agricultural labourers. This, along with the oppression of the landlords, prompted the tenant farmers to agitate (Siddique 1978). Overall speaking, the middle and the poor peasants dominated the movement. In different districts, the character and composition of the movement kept changing over time. Landless peasants came to the forefront gradually. Interestingly, the poor tenant farmers and the landless peasants, as the driving force, made the agitation violent and disorderly.
4. **The Bardoli agitation (Gujarat; 1928):** The Bardoli agitation in the Surat district of Gujarat is studied by Ghanashyam Shah (1974). He shows how caste, traditional social obligations, religious beliefs and symbols, rituals, coercion, ridicule and so on were all used in political mobilization. As far as the composition of the movement is concerned, the dominant well-to-do

patidar peasant caste played a vital role. It largely followed the Gandhian *Satyagraha* style where the rich peasants were joined by the tenant farmers and the landless peasants at a later point. The leaders, who had wider contacts with the outside world, used their local rootedness to mobilize the hitherto apolitical masses for the *Satyagraha* against the British government.

5. **The 1920s movements in the Andhra Delta:** J. Pouchepadass (1980) cites the study on the Andhra delta by farmer leader N. G. Ranga's *Revolutionary Peasants* (1949) to explore the class character of the movements. Ranga decried any class character of the movements and observed them as representing an undifferentiated entire peasantry. Pouchepadass, however, considers such a stance as symptomatic of higher strata dominated the peasant movement. The powerful castes of the Kamma and Reddy dominated the issues as they constituted the middle and rich peasantry. Although the movements were shaped in the initial years by the Congress ideology of the Kisan Sabhas, from the late 1930s, the movement came to be influenced by the Communist Party. This did not alter the class character of the movement as the rich Kamma peasant caste dominated the Communist Party as well.

6. **Peasant movements in Oudh (1930–1932):** D. N. Dhanagare studied the 12 districts of Oudh in the United Provinces (now, Uttar Pradesh) as they emerged from the nation-wide Civil Disobedience Movement (Dhanagare 1975). Primarily, these agitations were known as the 'No Rent Campaign'. The movement was also a fall out of the great world economic depression of 1929–1930. The movement could not sustain itself as the peasants were restrained by the limits set up by the Congress ideology. The Kisan Sabha impressed upon the local leaders who were prone to explore the political potential of violent methods. The rich and the middle peasants remained as the leading force, as they were directly affected by the crisis of rent. The poorer sections were less involved as they were wage labourers and not affected by a rent increase.

7. **The Tebhaga movement in Bengal (1946):** Post-Bengal famine and the Second World War, the entire countryside of Bengal was seething with rebellious activities. The provincial Kisan Sabha was led by the Communist Party. The popular movement Tebhaga was named as such to signify the nature of the demand of the sharecroppers. It demanded two-thirds of the harvest from the *jotedars* (tenants of absentee landlords) as against one-half they used to get before. As a participant of the movement, Sunil Sen (1972) showed that the sharecroppers were joined by the small and poor peasants as they got radicalized due to the repressive governmental measure.

   The movement was spontaneous and massive with the growing participation of poor peasants, who widened the scope of the movement to demand the revolutionary idea of 'land to the tiller'. The movement hoped to strike a final blow to landlordism. The majority of rich peasants were close to the *jotedars* and withdrew from the agitation logically. The brutal state action repressed the movement, but it resulted in an exalted political consciousness among the tribal sharecroppers and the poor peasants (Dhanagare 1976).

8. **The Telangana movement in the princely state of Hyderabad (1946):** Like Tebhaga, the Telangana movement was also led by the Communists. A very wide mix of social classes formed the social base of the struggle as the

demands were also very broad. Rich peasants of high-caste status secured the support of the middle peasants, tenants, sharecroppers and landless labourers to challenge the big absentee landlords. The absentee landlords were the lackeys of the princely order of Hyderabad.

Dhanagare, working with the Marxian frame of analysis, found the objective of the agrarian struggle quite conflicting as the movement was constituted by divergent class interests. The broad alliance of divergent classes failed as the poor peasants took over the movement and started seizing the land of the landlords. The rich peasants who initiated the mobilization got alarmed and left the movement. More so, as the agitators took up arms to wage the agrarian struggle, the Indian army was deployed to crush it in 1948. The movement took the form of guerrilla warfare by the poor peasants, agricultural labourers who belonged to tribes or 'untouchable' castes (Dhanagare 1983).

The eight peasant movements were picked up by Jacques Pouchepadass to understand the nature and basis of class collaboration within the Indian peasantry. Beyond the 1950s, however, peasant movements took different configurations in terms of class composition as well as objective goals. Mostly, rural agitations are led by Communist ideologies. Also, there have been farmers movements of rich peasants as well as 'new' agrarian movements dominated by Dalit ideologies in post-Independent India. One can notice the organizing principle of such movements exhibits less of class identity but more of caste, gender and other socio-economic identities (Ray and Katzenstein 2005).

12.1.3. Middle Peasantry and Marxist Theory

Neo-Marxist analyses of the peasantry have placed the middle peasant as the vital force of the rural agrarian movement. The historical failure of the rural proletariat to emerge as the principal driving force of the agrarian revolution prompted neo-Marxist scholars such as Eric Wolf and Hamza Alavi to theorize the potentiality of the middle peasants to take the lead as they are relatively better placed to challenge the higher strata of rural society. They have the material security and stability to risk a rebellion. Surveying different cases of peasant involvement in revolutionary movements in Mexico, Russia, China, Vietnam, Algeria and Cuba, Eric Wolf concluded that the middle peasantry is the most vital force of revolutionary activities. The middle peasantry as the owner of family-based smallholdings is materially well-placed to challenge the rich peasants and landlords. The material conditions of poor peasants as well as landless agricultural workers are not conducive to go against the rich landlords and risk revolutionary action. They need to be secured or protected adequately for taking such a plunge in leading the rebellious movement (Wolf 1969).

Hamza Alavi, in his *Peasants and Revolutions* (1973), also arrived at the conclusion that the middle peasant plays a pivotal role in the peasant uprising. As a Marxist scholar, Alavi questioned the revolutionary potential of the peasantry as a homogenous undifferentiated mass. He looked at the constellation of peasant forces as they participate differentially in the revolutionary movement, depending upon the different stage and aims of such movements. He studied the roles which different components of the peasantry had played in Russian and Chinese revolutions and peasant struggles in India. He concluded that it is the middle peasants who play the initial militant role to free the poor peasants from their age-old bondage and inhibitions and bring them to the centre of any revolutionary movement.

> The middle peasants ... are initially the most militant element of the peasantry, and they can be a powerful ally of the proletarian movement in the countryside, especially in generating the initial impetus of the peasant revolution. But their social perspective is limited by their class position. When the movement in the countryside advances to a revolutionary stage they may move away from the revolutionary movement. (Alavi 1973, 275)

To understand the objective and character of agrarian movements, the classical Marxist theories on the peasantry are abundantly used by social scientists. More than Marx's writings on the peasantry, it is the theory and applications of Vladimir Lenin and Mao Tse-tung which pass as Marxist analysis on the peasantry. In fact, Marx's scattered analysis of peasantry has given rise to multiple interpretations about their relation to the capitalist mode of production. Generally, Marx assigned the peasantry to a separate 'petty' mode of production as flourishing when the labourer is the private owner of his/her means of production. In the context of the 18th century, the peasantry in France, Marx observed that peasants do not form a class for themselves, and thus, they are incapable of enforcing class interest in their own name (Marx 1974). Under the impact of capitalism, this 'petty' mode would disintegrate automatically, and proletarianization of peasantry was expected.

The writings of Lenin, Engels and Mao do not offer a very precise definition of the middle peasantry. The two polar opposite classes at the two ends of a class that divided rural society are the rural proletariat at one end and the rich peasants and landlords at the other. Between these two well-defined categories, Marxists have not been consistent in delineating the nature and composition of the intermediate peasant classes. Jacques Pouchepadass critically examines the conceptualization of the middle-peasantry as done by Lenin, Engels and Mao Tse-tung (Pouchepadass 1980).

Lenin identified three classes between the rich peasants and the rural proletariat. They are the semi-proletariats, the small peasants and the middle peasants. In his characterization, the middle peasants are small farmers who can produce a surplus and often employ labourer (Lenin 1964). Engels, on the other hand, puts only two classes above the proletariat—a class of self-sufficient peasants (less in numbers) and a large agglomerate of 'bigger' peasants. A subsidiary division between middle and big peasants he introduces later on. Still, a precise characterization is lacking about middle peasants. It was the Chinese revolutionary and theoretician Mao Tse-tung who talks about two intermediate classes between the proletariat and the rich peasants, the poor and the middle peasants. Mao is quite clear in his understanding that the middle peasants are surplus, producing self-sufficient cultivators and employ wage labour only during peak season. Subsequently, he introduces another subsidiary division in the middle peasantry, a 'well-to-do middle peasants'.

Pouchepadass observes that in the Marxist formulation the characterization of the middle-peasants has been nebulous. This class is understood loosely with ill-defined economic boundaries. Therefore, such a heterogeneous social category cannot have a specific class interest or position in the social relation of production. So no revolutionary potential could be accorded to them. It is the most ambivalent class that has historically shown political vacillations (Mao 1945). The thesis of Eric Wolf and Hamza Alavi on the vitality of the middle peasants is refuted by Pouchepadass and many other scholars who have historicized the traditional structure of the Indian rural society. The complexity of the peasant movements in India between 1920 and 1950 clearly shows the inappropriateness of the concept of the middle peasant to understand the peasant movement in Indian social reality.

12.1.4. The Concept of Dominant Peasantry in Indian Rural Society

Indian countryside is marked with varying structural arrangements; from region to region, the social differentiation varies. From the examples of the prominent peasant movements from the 1920s to the 1950s, it is difficult to suggest a clear bounded middle-peasant category as the motive force behind peasant struggles. This is because of the complicated and layered relations of production as well as land rights prevalent across India. To indicate, who would take up the vanguard role in the peasant movement in India is difficult. The Indian case is unique in contrast to other countries because the inequalities are not only reflections of existential realities but also of values that are institutionalized by religion (Beteille 1979).

Assessing the peasant movements, Pouchepadass (1980) has concluded that the movements exhibited class collaborations but in different combinations and contexts. The chief features are as follows:

1. In the majority of the cases, the upper strata of the peasantry played the vanguard role.
2. In a minority of cases, the poor lower strata formed the principal actors of the movement.
3. A clear-cut antagonism between the poor landless peasantry and the rich peasantry (at times, even a part of middle peasants) was the unique feature of the Tebhaga and Telangana agitation.

The redundancy of the middle peasantry is observed as,

> In none of the three types of peasant mobilization did the middle peasantry play a separate role. In most of the movements, it acted in conjunction with the rich peasantry, but there were also cases in which at least some of its member followed the poor peasants when it was they who took the lead. In other cases, the middle peasantry played no distinctive role. On no occasion did the middle category alone take the initiative in a movement. (Puchepadass 1980, 142)

The vacuity of the concept and potential of the middle peasants brings us to the concept of the *dominant peasantry*. David Hardiman in a special article in *Economic and Political Weekly*, 1976, first floated the idea of the dominant peasantry. As an operational term, the dominant peasantry was adopted by Hardiman to account for the history of the rural social organization of different areas and as a vital determining factor of peasant mobilization in India.

> During the first half of the twentieth century, a widespread 'political awakening' took place in rural India amongst the dominant peasantry. By this it is meant that the peasant groups which had political power within their villages became directly linked to political parties found at district and provincial, and even national levels. (Hardiman 1976, 365)

> **BOX 12.1**
> **The Dominant Peasantry**
>
> By dominant peasantry, we refer to the oligarchy of rich and well-off peasants belonging to respectable castes who hold the bulk of the land rights in each village either as owners or tenants ... a category which includes the whole group of peasants of a respectable caste who hold enough land so that they can supply the needs of their families without having to go out for work for anyone else.
>
> **Source:** Pouchepadass (1980).

It is not just on the basis of land and economic strength that one becomes powerful or plays a decisive role in the agrarian society. The cultural–ritual aspects embedded in the traditional rural structure are also determinants of the dominant peasantry. Using the concept of the dominant peasantry, Pouchepadass analyses the peasant movements of Champaran, Kheda, Bardoli and alike as results of not only class collaborations but also a multi-caste affair where the primordial loyalties were abundantly used. It is the large category of the dominant peasantry who had led the movements. Castes locally dominant by the virtue of land rights constituted the dominant peasantry, which even characterized the initial phase of both the Tebhaga and the Telengana movements. Interestingly enough, these movements led by the dominant peasantry were all expressions of the traditional pattern of power and authority operating at the local level.

The same pattern could be observed everywhere, including the initial phases of the Communist-led Tebhaga and Telangana peasant uprisings. It was only in the later phases that the campaigns were taken over by poor peasants and landless labourers. Such radicalization of the Kisan Sabhas was not endorsed by the leadership. The Communist leadership, which dominated the All India Kisan Sabha after 1936, took care not to attack small zamindar or rich peasants in their moderate agrarian line. Such a political campaign allowed the dominant peasantry to play an important role even in the Communist-led peasant agitations. However, the 'closure' of both the movements gave rise to a political awakening of the poor peasants and the agricultural labourers. The leadership was defied, the government crushed the agitation, but a clear break of the rural masses with the rich peasants signalled a new phase of peasant mobilization in India (Sen 1972).

12.1.5. Critical Assessment of Dominant Peasantry

The concept of the dominant peasantry has been subjected to critical scrutiny by many. T. K. Oommen is of the opinion that even if the description of dominant peasantry appears to be accurate, this category can never act as the driving force in a peasant movement (Oommen 1990). The reasons given by him are as follows:

1. Those who have power, status and resources are less likely to question the status quo.

2. Only some specific enlightened ones from the large group of the dominant peasantry may come forward to defy the status quo.
3. In the local rural context, the dominant peasantry could be the logical target of any peasant uprising, as they are the bearers of power and prestige in an uneven society.

It is only because of the time period, the historical juncture of the society fighting a liberation struggle against a colonial power that made the dominant peasantry in India to play a lead role. It has nothing to do with the social attributes of this category to act as such. The critical variable then is the time at which the movements were located. This also explains why the Communists took up a strong anti-colonial and pro-national political tone immediately after the Independence. The leadership dithered on the question of direct armed rebellion in order to give the independent Indian state a scope to resolve the peasants' demands through constitutional means (Oommen 1990).

In Independent India, according to Oommen, peasant movements are exhibiting a clearer class basis. The poor peasants and landless labourers are the active vanguard component of most of the movements. This is so, as the goal of the movements is no longer directed at any external energy; now, the enemy is within the system. It is important to note that since the 1960s, non-farm economic activities have expanded and altered the face of rural India steadily. The penetration of capitalist market forces has accelerated the proletarianization of agricultural labourers. As a result of uneven capitalist development in Indian agricultural society, the term 'farmer' is preferable over the use of the term 'peasant', which is found to be less useful to examine the agrarian relationship. The term 'farmer' is marked by their market involvement as community producers and also as purchasers of inputs (Shah 2004). Any class analysis of the Indian rural society is fraught with the problem of a lack of a unified agrarian structure throughout the country.

Against the popular contention that Indian peasants are incapable of any revolutionary potential, studies of Kathleen Gough and D. N. Dhanagare stand as substantive counterpoints. In a sweeping historical review of certain tribal belts of Bengal, Bihar, Andhra Pradesh and Kerala, Gough clearly identifies the combination of the poor peasants and agricultural labourers as a potent force to organize revolutionary movement (Gough 1974). The same observation is drawn by D. H. Dhanagare. According to him, a combination of poor peasants and agricultural labourers constitute the major section of the rural population, and they have exhibited transformative potential historically. Organized movements of the poor peasantry, tenants and landless labourers, led by radical left groups, have intermittently risen in parts of Bengal, Bihar and Andhra Pradesh since the late 1960s and have spilt over to some other states subsequently.

On the other hand, scholars like Gail Omvedt contests the possibility of class action cutting across caste and other boundaries of primordial identities. She prefers to theorize contemporary farmers' movements as 'new' and non-class movements. Beyond the narrow application of the Marxist class analysis as confined within capital versus labour struggle, she then brings a wider arena of capital accumulation. Factors other than economic exploitation would lead us to acknowledge the coincidence of the farmers' movement with the growing environmental movement (Omvedt 2005).

Dipankar Gupta's study of the farmers' movement in Western Uttar Pradesh in the 1990s shows the significance of clan and caste honour as reflected in the wider mobilization for political action. Such factors, at times, facilitate and, in some other context, may create obstacles for collective action. Gupta feels that rural mobilizations understood as revolving around the peasantry need not assume the peasants to be indifferent to political or ideological commitment. He identifies two types of agrarian mobilization. First, movements of peasants, agricultural labourers and marginal farmers with a clear-cut class angle to improve their livelihood. Second, there are movements by better off owner–cultivators who produce a marketable surplus (Gupta 1997). Against the orthodox Marxian theories of mobilization, the subaltern school holds that peasants are the makers of their own fate and action. They have their own political agency irrespective of being led by 'outsiders'. The indigenous peasants own a domain of autonomous politics in opposition to the domain of the elite, drawing their consciousness from native structures of knowledge and tradition (Guha 1983). Such understanding has been indicted by Dipankar Gupta, as it shuts off the whole field of external structural interaction and determination. This way the scope of any movement and its limits are understood in terms of what culture allows and not in terms of what the structure forecloses (Gupta 1985).

To analyse peasant movements in India, we need to situate them in their ecosystem. There is a palpable uneasiness to work with a definition of peasant formulated primarily on the basis of European experience. Indian agrarian society is unique in contrast to other societies because inequalities are reflections of not only existential realities but also values that are institutionalized by religion (Beteille 1979). The peasant movement in India is a very extensive and complex subject. The critical variables in understanding such movement are not the attributes of the social category which initiated the action but the situation, the nature of the enemy and the purpose behind mobilization.

12.2. MIDDLE CLASS PHENOMENON

12.2.1. Middle Class and Marxist Theory of Class

Simply put, the Marxist concept of class is understood as a social group that shares a similar position in a social relation of production. Marx examined classes as a product of historical development and as such was interested to identify classes that would be the motive force of historical development. By analysing the march of human society from a primitive stage, he arrived at the era of industrial capitalism to identify the two protagonist classes as the bourgeoisie and the proletariat. The bipolar contradiction between capital and labour was primary for him to theorize his revolutionary theory of emancipation.

> Our epoch, the epoch of the bourgeoisie, possesses, however, this distinctive feature: it has simplified the class antagonisms. Society as a whole is more and more splitting up into two great hostile camps, into two great classes directly facing each other: Bourgeoisie and Proletariat. (Marx and Engels 1952, 41)

The classical theory of class fell short of capturing the empirical reality of advanced capitalist societies or post-colonial societies which have witnessed not a simple capital versus labour contradiction. Instead, in between, a host of intermediary classes have come to play a significant role. The advanced capitalist societies have been experiencing a divergence of the spheres of power—the economic, the social and the political. The clear opposition between the two historic classes has been muddled with the emergence of new middle classes (intermediate classes) with complex differentiation of occupational status. Also, the setbacks of the socialist blocks have put the Marxist theory of class contradiction and class struggle on a trial. The 'new' social movements along different axes (gender, race and ethnicity) other than capital–labour contradiction and with unique participation of intermediate classes and class collaboration have prompted a fresh look at Marx's theory.

In all fairness, much later to his avowed political manual, *The Communist Manifesto* (1848), Marx did notice the multiplicity of society and the multitude of 'middle and intermediate strata'. *The Communist Manifesto* gives us only a very compressed understanding of the development of classes under modern capitalism. One can trace a much profound understanding in Marx's ([1852] 1974) brilliant text *The Eighteenth Brumaire of Louis Bonaparte*. Here, he discusses the dynamics of the 'middle and intermediate strata'. Also, we need to note that the manuscript of Marx's Chapter 52 of *Capital* titled 'Classes' (Marx [1863–1883] 1894) breaks off after a short beginning. So practically, we are left with inadequate treatment of a very crucial Marxian concept of class.

Satish Deshpande (2003) very lucidly commented that 'what we are decides what we experience, which in turn shapes what we do'. Theoretically, the core concept of class tells us that the three spheres of the economy, society and polity are interpenetrating and hierarchically ordered. While the economic sphere is the base, on which thrives the socio-cultural world of ideas. And these cultural ideas shape the political consciousness necessary for any political action. The causal primacy of the economy is well spelt out although the three spheres are well integrated. The point is that material existence limits our agency, although we enjoy creative autonomy to change the given society (Deshpande 2003).

If we stick to the orthodox explanation, we must expect that all the three spheres—economic, sociocultural and political—would exactly coincide if they are superimposed on each other. That is, all those who constitute the same economic class would exactly be sharing the same sociocultural world with the same political interests. One cannot expect such a world except the model bipolar two-class image of capitalist society. The contemporary world has seen the growing importance of the intermediate strata as falsification of the growing polarization of the two confronting classes of the bourgeoisie and the proletariat. The middle classes have emerged as a vital social segment in post-colonial societies like India as well.

12.2.2. Middle Class as a Signifier

In popular parlance, the middle class is the class that stands for the whole society. However, loosely defined and having frayed edges, the middle class stands for the stability of a given social structure. By default, it serves as an active agent of the ideology that contains the social structure. As per the classical Marxist theory, such an intermediate class can never play a decisive role in social transformation. A qualified understanding of the intermediate class one can find in the works of Italian Marxist Antonio Gramsci. Gramsci's analysis of class is deeper and subtler. Without assuming an abstract universal proposition of an 'economic man', he worked on Marx's analysis of the class structure. Incisively, he commented on the Italian society where the proletariat was numerically very less and disparate with a weak development of the capitalist state. He found a 'continuous process of disintegration and reintegration, decomposition and recomposition' of strata and classes in the Italian population (Gramsci [1971] 1999, 144).

A profound idea that we gain from Gramsci is that class is a relation and classes shape each other. He indicates a 'broad stratum of intermediate classes', which includes wealthy and middle peasants in the countryside and a middle bourgeoisie and small and medium industrialists in the cities. Along with them, there are numerous petty bourgeoisies spread across both rural and urban society. They share the ideas of the other intermediate classes. Gramsci theorizes that these intermediate classes and the petty bourgeoisie substantiate the structure of society by providing the consensus and generating the commonsense.

> The petty bourgeoisie and the intellectuals, through the position which they enjoy in society and through their way of life, are naturally led to deny the class struggle and are thus condemned to understand nothing of the development of either world history or the national history which forms a part of the world system. (Gramsci [1977] 1991 492)

The middle class as a phenomenon has been explored by Satish Deshpande in the Indian context. The middle class is a coveted position as it represents society as its average face. Avoiding the possible distortion due to the presence of extreme values, this average in statistical parlance is more like a median value, not the frequently used 'mean'. It is also not like the 'mode'; the actual value that occurs most frequently is a distribution series. The notion of representation by virtue of the 'middleness' of being the middle class is best captured through the attributes of a median. That is, the middle class signifies the stable centre of the social structure. It plays the much sought after role of modulation, being neither the progressive nor the conservative as a class. Interestingly, this middleness may become the most popular one in a society that has stabilized itself ideologically over a period of time (Deshpande 2003).

The question is why the middle class enjoy the popular location in an advanced stratified society. The immediate reference that comes to the Indian mind is that of the 'common man', the iconic creation of cartoonist R. K. Laxman. The middle class is that 'common man' as widely imagined in Indian society. Such is the middle-class identity and its resultant legitimacy as an upholder of moral values. It represents the society on account of such moral legitimacy. So it is popular. In fact, in Western societies, post Second World War prosperity and emergence of a welfare state, the middle classes have formed the largest plurality of the population.

Defining the middle class in India, theoretically with sound empirical references, is still quite elusive. To define a social group in terms of 'sameness' with respect to the three components of class attribute—economic, sociocultural and political continues to be difficult. Neither data collected on income tax-payers nor consumption expenditure could be used meaningfully to demarcate classes. Income tax-payers in India leave out the majority of the population. If we use consumption expenditure as a proxy, the problem still persists. The consumption pattern is not an exact function of one's income. As the poor tend to consume almost the last pie of their income, while the rich save the maximum for asset creation. Deshpande makes an intelligent input on this vexing problem of defining the middle class. Accordingly, we define a concept for heuristic purpose and the consideration should not be to capture an already existing empirical reality accurately. Heuristic in the sense that it will help understand society better.

As a vibrant segment of consumers, the middle class has been understood in purely economic terms. As such, after the liberalization of the 1990s, it was felt by the market researchers that a huge growth of the consumer segment would take place. Technically, excluding all the non-rich and non-poor, the middle class could emerge as the ever expansive 'consumer class'. However, all market surveys indicated that the size expected or assumed to be was an inflated reality. Factually in India, the middle class is hardly a huge category; its widespread acceptance is just because of its symbolic value. The extravagant projection is an ideological ploy to present the middle class as a large plurality representing everyone.

12.2.3. Middle Class in Post-Colonial Societies

The role of the middle class in post-colonial societies like India can be examined in terms of three crucial aspects of *hegemony, cultural capital and ideology.* They are hypothesized by Satish Deshpande as providing clues to arrive at theoretical definitions of the middle class.

1. **Hegemony:** In post-colonial India, as political scientists such as Sudipta Kaviraj and many others have concluded, no single class rule is possible in India. Instead, it requires a ruling bloc of a coalition of classes. The developmental state relies on the hegemony of a ruling bloc, and the middle class plays a pivotal role to legitimize this hegemony. The middle class enjoys the unique role of articulating this hegemony by (a) expressing this hegemony, the relations of domination are legitimated by it and (b) mediating the relationship between the classes of the ruling bloc, namely the relation between the industrial finance and agrarian capital.

    Overall, in the Nehruvian model, the middle class acted as the leading protagonist of the dominant ideology of development. The techno-rational model pampered the professional class and the technocrats who overwhelmingly constituted the middle class. The Nehruvian development model provided the middle class with the legitimacy to act as a representation of the whole nation.

2. **Cultural capital:** The middle class could be defined by its ownership and control of the cultural capital. French sociologist Pierre Bourdieu coined the term, cultural capital, to refer to the repertoire of knowledge, behaviours and skills that a person can claim access to demonstrate one's cultural competence and social status. Both in terms of identities, like caste, community or region, or competencies such as educational, social and language skill, the middle class is endowed with cultural capital. Cultural capital, though non-material, is empowering in many ways. They can be owned exclusively to provide and boost psychological confidence and can be transmitted across generation. The access to such symbolic cultural capital is restricted to a select group, and so is its consumption pattern and reproduction. The consumption of abstract ideologies, beliefs and stereotypes is obviously invisible, and thereby, it creates a misconception that the middle class possesses this as something innate to them. Accordingly, the middle class rests on a self-image of being an achiever through merits.

3. **Ideologies:** The hegemony of social order is possible only when it is backed up by a legitimate ideology. It is not enough for an ideology to be legitimate;

it needs to be consumed or sincerely believed in. As a differentiated class, the middle class performs the role of producing, transmitting and legitimizing the dominant ideology of a society. The elite section of the middle class produces the ideologies of domination to which the mass of the middle class commits loyalty. Thereby, the ideologies take a firm grip over the social order.

These three aspects could serve as valuable inputs to develop a tentative and hypothetical definition of the Indian middle class, according to Deshpande. One can study the history and characteristics of the middle classes to examine the applicability of the alternative theoretical dispositions. The historical character is shaped by three considerations, which are as follows:

1. Due to the lack of development of capital, the industrial bourgeoisie did not develop in India. The intermediate classes consisting of professionals, technical and managerial personnel and the intelligentsia gained prominence in the colonial context, as a result.
2. The intermediate classes continue as the middle class to dominate the process of development after Independence.
3. The middle classes played the leading role in the freedom movement, especially the lawyers who constituted the leadership of the Indian National Congress. This helped them to achieve political legitimacy after Independence and emerge as a dominant class.

The above observations are in league with studies by political–cultural essayist Perry Anderson and sociologist A. Ahmad. Anderson concluded that it was the middle class who took advantage of the English education and ideas to constitute the ranks of the bureaucracy and such other crucial organs of the colonial rule. At some point, the colonial power put a stop to their expansive role; as a rebound, the elites confronted the British with the idea of nation and nationalism (Anderson 2012).

The middle class continued to enjoy privileged position in the post-colonial period, not just as an adage to the ruling bloc but as an active part of it. After all, Indian nationalism took shape in their hands only.

> Far from being mere 'agents' of the ruling classes or a mere 'vacillating mass' ... the intermediate and auxiliary classes of the periphery occupy a strategic field in the economy and politics of their countries, thus obtaining power and initiatives which make it possible for them to struggle for political dominance over other classes including the bourgeoisie. (Ahmad 1985, p 44)

In the specific Indian scenario, the middle class has been understood as a part of the dominant coalition governing India, by political economist Pranab Bardhan too. More importantly, it is being conceptualized as a class building hegemony for the socio-political order of the post-independent developmental state. 'The members of the emergent Indian middle class- urban professionals, white-collar workers in government and industry, and the intelligentsia- self-consciously invoked this model based on a moral privileging of the middle class' (Deshpande 2003, 143).

The unique aspect of the moral privileges commanded by the middle class comes as a mix of the Western model or values in the material sphere, while retaining or revitalizing the Indian classical tradition in the inner spiritual sphere. The cultural leadership of the indigenous people, thereby, depended on the middle class only (Chatterjee 1992).

> **BOX 12.2**
> **The Shallow Middle Class**
>
> In India, it is really the better off who call themselves middle class. But in the West, it practically includes the entire population. The Western middle class has such a wide social base that it leaves little room for the politics of patronage and privilege to flourish. There, the middle class is seen not in consumption terms but in how it relates to and interacts with others in society. This stands to reason, as it is the middle class in Europe that formed up institutions of democracy, eroded feudal privileges and ushered in the era of individualism. The Indian middle class scores negatively on all these counts.
>
> **Source:** Gupta (2000).

12.2.4. Contemporary Middle Classes and Globalization

In India, the emergence of the middle class was tied up with the implant of Western education and ideas that allowed job opportunities in administration, commerce and so on offered by the colonial government. In the post-Independence scenario, the middle class emerged as a more crystallized category. It is the category that practised professional life and jobs based on education and cultural capital. They are not the typical property-owning class. One can consider this middle class as the Nehruvian civil service-oriented salaried class. At the ideological and institutional levels, they are the pillars of the developmental state. It enjoyed the prestige and honour as skilled professionals and technical workforce. The top–down development model left out popular participation of the masses and rode on its shoulder. The high demand for such a class was matched by a vast expanse of techno-scientific and higher-learning centres that ensured a flow of such personnel.

Deshpande makes a convincing point that the moral high-ground enjoyed by the middle class, the protagonist of the nation-building process, concealed much of the inequalities and uneven benefits with respect to caste, region, language and classes. The avowed secular–socialist narrative could not be actualized in reality. Subtle policies of exclusion and selection allowed the middle class to enjoy pre-modern privileges. Caste privileges and discrimination overshadowed the other discriminating variables of gender, community and region.

Beyond the synchrony between the nation, the developmental state and its protagonist, the middle class was bound to face the crisis after an initial period of euphoria. The simplistic creation of scientific and technical manpower was also instrumental to sustain the top–down developmental model. The dissonance was complete by the 1970s, as the middle class also wished to exercise its own agency in a much different manner. It no longer has remained small and homogenous like the initial years of its formation. The continuous differentiation of the middle class corresponded to the end of the Nehruvian model, and after a decade in the 1980s, it signalled a stage for a liberalized model of development.

Otherwise, the homogeneity of the erstwhile middle class still had a fundamental fissure—the centre and the regional middle-class groups. The fractions could be understood as one that produces the legitimizing ideologies, that is, the elite fraction and the 'mass' fraction that consumes it. In other words, one can observe a clear split between the intelligentsia on one side and the lower, middle class on the other. Each of the fractions can be characterized on the basis of the nature and type of cultural capital as commanded by a coherent group. There is a wide range of professional, technical, administrative, white-collar jobs and so on that could mark a group. Another important criterion of fraction could be based on the skill and competence of the English language. The division is marked by a class's ability to speak and write English. A variable combination of English with other Indian language is also possible to designate a class.

Finally, one can notice the broad-based division between the metropolitan and regional middle-class fractions. The metropolitan one is globalized, while the region-specific success of the agricultural green revolution has given rise to a rural-based fraction. The growing differentiation and the resultant fractions of the middle class have a consequence. They all drifted away from the nation-state based ideology of development. On one side, there was the emergence of sub-national sentiments, caused by excessive centralization of the Nehruvian developmental model, but on the other, there was the lure of transnational identity promoted by a globalized world.

According to Deshpande, if the promise of globalization succeeded in offering the possibility of a 'new publics' or new identities, it perfectly matched the aspirations and desires of the new middle class created due to the inevitable differentiation of the old one. The flexible, liberal model fits in with the post-patriotic identities, often thought to be emancipatory than the older rigid model. The 'new' middle class could be understood as the active social group negotiating with the global economy and transnational cultural identities. It is implicated with both economic and cultural dimensions. As beneficiaries of the material benefits of jobs and business in India's new liberalized economy, this new middle class is the show boy of the socio-symbolic practices of commodity consumption.

In contemporary India, if one is keen to find out who actually benefits from the multicultural existence in a globalized world, it is the small upper segment (managerial-professional) of the middle class. The charm and benefits of globalization accrue to them; in the same manner, the erstwhile developmental model propped them up. One witnesses a seamless transition of this group as the new middle class; it no longer just represents the nation as its 'average', but itself becomes the nation, as a portrait of it.

The Indian middle class, as a phenomenon, is shaped by a melange of critical historical conjectures. From the colonial times to the contemporary globalized era, through the early years of Independence, the middle class has evolved. It evolved as a key actor of the society. It depicts an interesting trajectory of adopting a variety of worldviews and self-perpetuating itself as the most decisive arbiter of society.

CONCLUSION

Indian rural society has its own historic specificity. The divisions and relations within the rural agrarian society are marked by many socio-economic and sociocultural signifier. Agrarian mobilization and agitations have been commonly termed as the peasant movement, although peasantry in India constitutes a wide range of people engaged differentially with the rural society. The very concept of the peasant has been a contentious issue in classical Marxist literature on class structure and class struggle.

After studying the various peasant movements in India, one can gain insights into the actual differentiation of the rural society and the relative positions of the different sections of the rural society to organize for social change. The colonial and post-colonial contexts have altered the nature of collective mobilization as well as the goal for such collective action. The Marxist classical analysis could not comprehensively assign middle peasantry or intermediate agrarian classes any leading role in social transformation. Examining the Marxist framework of analysis, anthropologist Eric Wolf and sociologist Hamza Alavi argued in favour of the middle peasantry as a potential actor of rural transformation.

The contention of Eric Wolf and Hamza Alavi was put to test by many scholars engaged in peasant and agrarian studies of colonial and post-colonial societies. One important study is by Jacques Pouchepadass, who made a careful analysis of the peasant classes in various agrarian movements of the first half of the 20th century in India. It is being argued that in most cases, the movements were premised on class collaboration. The middle peasantry did not play any significant exclusive role as a protagonist. The revolutionary potentiality of the middle peasant is a misplaced one. Many other sociologists also arrived at the same conclusion that the 'middle peasant thesis' cannot be sustained.

Instead, the concept of the dominant peasantry has been advanced by Pouchepadass to identify the driving force of the Indian peasant movement. Apart from the economic strengths of landholdings and so on, the sources of power of the dominant peasantry can be traced to entrenched cultural–ritual values of traditional India. The introduction of the concept of the dominant peasantry and its precise characterizations is a useful contribution to the studies of the peasant movement in India. Subsequently, the growing penetration of market forces into the agriculture sector, radicalization of the poor peasantry and interlocking of the peasant society with the wider society makes peasants movement in India a challenging sociological subject matter. The real nature of the rural rebellions, unrest and movement requires a non-dogmatic approach to appreciate the changing ideological and structural conditioning of the agrarian society.

As noticed in studies of rural society, the middle class, as an intermediate position in a class structure, lacks a precise definition and characterization in the Marxist orthodox theory. Only the Italian communist theoretician Antonio Gramsci has given it a serious thought and examined the broad intermediate stratum as providing the consensus so necessary for the continuance of any social order.

Commenting on the centrality of the middle class in India, Satish Deshpande examined its historical trajectory. The middle class enjoys a coveted position. By virtue of being the leading component of the nationalist movement, it has attained a moral pedestal to represent the nation and its future course in post-colonial times. It prospered as the chief protagonist of the development state, but the paradigm of the Nehruvian model was not all that inclusive as claimed. The disillusionment was bound to set in after the initial decades of Independence. Simultaneously, the fractions or differentiations of the middle class also showed up.

As a class that commands hegemony over the ideologies that hold a society together and also in possession of cultural capital, the middle class could exhibit its agency beyond the exhaustion of the Nehruvian developmental stage in Indian polity. The growing differentiation of the middle class along various axes also prepared a fertile ground for a different model of 'development'. That is, the globalized model of liberalization could find its purchase amongst the middle class only. As a receptive actor, the middle class now reaped the benefits of the globalized liberal economy. They legitimated the charm of transnational cultural identities in the changed scenario that leaves out a vast majority of the society, the public, out of contention.

Points for Classroom Discussion

- Nature of the peasant movement in the first half of the 20th century in India
- Critique of a middle peasant as an initiator of rural transformation
- The dominant peasantry as a protagonist in the Indian peasant movement
- The middle class in the Marxian classical theory of class
- Evolution of the middle class in Indian society
- The salience of middle class in post-Independent India and challenges of globalization

GLOSSARY

Cultural capital: It is a term coined by French sociologist Pierre Bourdieu. It refers to the collection of symbolic elements such as skills, tastes, posture, clothing, mannerisms, material belongings and credentials that one is endowed with, by virtue of belonging to a particular social class.

Dominant peasantry: It is a particular agrarian social group that enjoys power in rural society by virtue of economic as well as non-economic resources of domination.

Globalization: It is an interlocking of all nations resulting in the spread of products, technology, information and jobs across national borders and cultures.

Hegemony: It is a political, ideological or cultural dominance of any group over others.

Liberalization: It is the removal of barriers and restrictions for free exchange and movement of goods and services across national economies.

Middle peasant: Simply put, it is the intermediate position between the labouring or poor and the rich peasant class in an agrarian structure.

Modernist: Modernist is the one who is inspired by the vision of modernism that marked the 19th- and early 20th-century philosophical break from conservative tradition in Europe. It believes in progress through reason and science.

Neo-Marxist: It is a 20th-century Marxist school that attempts to qualify the orthodox analysis by incorporating elements from other intellectual traditions like critical theory, psychoanalysis or existentialism.

Petty bourgeoisie: It is the 'small' class located between these two fundamental classes of the bourgeoisie and the proletariat in terms of its interests as well as its social situation, as examined in the Marxist literature.

Satyagraha: It is the Gandhian method of non-violent resistance, focusing on the power of truth.

Sharecropper: In an agrarian economy, a sharecropper is a tenant farmer who gives a part of each crop as rent to the landowner.

Tenant: In rural society, a tenant is the one who occupies land or property rented from a landlord.

REFERENCES

Ahmad, A. 1985. 'Class, Nation and State: Intermediate Classes in the Peripheral Societies.' In *Middle Classes in Dependent Countries*, edited by D. L. Johnson. London: SAGE Publications.

Alavi, H. 1973. 'Peasants and Revolutions.' In *Imperialism and Revolution in South Asia*, edited by K. Gough and H. P. Sharma. New York, NY: Monthly Review Press.

Anderson, P. 2012. *The Indian Ideology*. New Delhi: Three Essays Collective.

Bernstein, H. 1979. 'African Peasantry: A Theoretical Framewor.' *Journal of Peasant Studies* 6, no. 4: 421–443.

Beteille, A. 1979. *Studies in Agrarian Social Structure*. New Delhi: Oxford University Press.

Bourdieu, P. 1986. 'The Forms of Capital.' In *Handbook of Theory and Research for the Sociology of Education*, edited by J. Richardson, 241–258. New York, NY: Greenwood.

Chatterjee, P. 1992. *Subaltern Studies VII (with Gyanendra Pandey)*. New Delhi: Oxford University Press, Delhi.

Deshpande, S. 2003. *Contemporary India: A Sociological View*. New Delhi: Viking.

Dhanagare, D. N. 1975. 'Congress and Agrarian Agitation in Oudh, 1920–22 and 1930–32.' *South Asia: Journal of South Asian Studies* 5, no. 1: 67–77.

———. 1976. Peasant Protest and Politics—The Tebhaga Movement in Bengal (India), 1946–47.' *The Journal of Peasant Studies* 3, no. 3: 360–378.

———. 1983. *Peasant Movement in India, 1920–1950*. New Delhi: Oxford University Press.

Gough, K. 1974. 'Indian Peasant Uprisings.' *Economic & Political Weekly* 9, no. 32/34: 1391–1412.

Gramsci, A. (1971) 1999. *Selections From Prison Notebooks,* (1910–1920), edited by Q. Hoare and G. N. Smith. London: Elec Books.

Gramsci, A. 1977/1999. Selections from Political Writings (1910-1920), edited by Q. Hoare and translated by John Mathews. London: ElecBook, transcribed from the edition published by Lawrence and Wishart, London, 1977. [SPW 1910-1920].

Guha, R. 1983. *Elementary Aspects of Peasant Insurgency in Colonial India*. New Delhi: Oxford University Press.

Gupta, D., 1997. *Rivalry and Brother hood: Politics in the Life of Farmers in Northern India*. New Delhi, Oxford University Press.

———. 1985. 'On Altering the Ego in Peasant History.' *Journal of Peasant Studies* 13, no. 1: 5–24.

———. 2000. *Mistaken Modernity: India between Worlds*. New Delhi: HarperCollins.

Hardiman, D. 1976. 'Politicization and Agitation among Dominant Peasants in Early Twentieth Century India.' *Economic & Political Weekly* 11, no. 9.

Lenin, V. I., ed. 1964. 'The Development of Capitalism in Russia.' In *Collected Works* (vol. 3). Moscow: Progress Publishers.

Mao, Tse Tung. 1965 [1945]. *Selected Works Vol I.* Beijing: Foreign Languages Press.

Marx, K., and F. Engels. 1952. *Manifesto of the Communist Party*. Moscow: Progress Publishers.

Marx, K. (1852) 1974. 'The Eighteenth Brumaire of Louis Bonaparte.' In *Selected Works* (vol. 1), edited by K. Marx and F. Engels. London: Lawrence and Wishart.

———. (1852) 1974. 'The Class Struggle in France 1848–1850.' In *Selected Works* (vol. 1), edited by K. Marx and F. Engels. London: Lawrence and Wishart.

———. (1863–1883) 1894. 'Classes.' In *Capital* (vol. 3), edited by F. Engels. New York, NY: International Publishers. Available at: https://www.marxists.org/archive/marx/works/download/pdf/Capital-Volume-III.pdf (accessed on 17 February 2021).

Oommen, T. K. 1985. *From Mobilization to Institutionalization: The Dynamics of Agrarian Movements in Twentieth Century Kerala*. Mumbai: Popular Prakashan.

———. 1990. Protest and Change: Studies in Social Movements. New Delhi: SAGE Publications.

Pouchepadass, J. 1974. 'Local Leaders and the Intelligentsia in the Champaran (1917).' *Contribution to Indian Sociology* 8, no. 1: 67–87.

———. 1980. 'Peasant Classes in Twentieth Century Agrarian Movements in India.' In *Peasants in History*, edited by L. Hobsbawm, 136–155. New Delhi: Oxford University Press.

Ray, R., and M. F. Katzenstein, eds. 2005. *Social Movements in India*. New Delhi: Oxford University Press.

Sen, S. 1972. *Agrarian Struggle in Bengal, 1946–47*. New Delhi: People's Publishing House.

Shah, G. 1974. 'Traditional Society and Political Mobilization: The Experience of Bardoli Satyagraha (1920–1928).' *Contribution to India Sociology* 8, no. 1: 89–107.

———. 2004. *Social Movements in India: A Review of Literature*. New Delhi: SAGE Publications.

Siddiqui, M. H. 1978. *Agrarian Unrest in North India: The United Province, 1918–1922*. New Delhi: Vikas Publishing House.

Thorner, D. 1968. 'Peasant.' In *International Encyclopedia of the Social Sciences*, edited by David L. Sills, 503–511. New York, NY: Macmillan and Free Press.

Wolf, E. 1969. Peasant Wars of the Twentieth Century. Oklahoma City, OK: University of Oklahoma Press.

CHAPTER 13

Dalit Movement

LEARNING OUTCOMES

- To explore the question of Dalit identity and ideology
- To trace the historical trajectory of the Dalit movement
- To get sensitized with the Dalit issues in India
- To assess the new phase in the Dalit movement and its success

Keywords: Caste, Dalit identity, untouchability, *Harijan*, Dalit, emancipation

The sun of self-respect has burst into flame-
let it burn up these castes!
Smash, break, destroy
these walls of hatred ...

—A Maratha song from the 1990s Dalit Panthers' Movement

INTRODUCTION

In October 2009, a conference titled 'Caste and Contemporary India' was held at Columbia University, USA, in honour of its alumnus B. R. Ambedkar. Interestingly, mainstream sociology in India has hardly given any academic space to this alumnus's research paper, 'Castes in India: Their Mechanisms, Genesis and Development', which he read out for the anthropology seminar in the same university way back in 1916. Symptomatically, we can sense the changing world of Dalit research and studies from the above scenario.

From the colonial to the post-colonial period, the privileged Hindu caste elite not only dominated the political—cultural agenda of India but also defined the politics of Indian society. However, since the last few decades, the assertion of the depressed Dalit castes, their entry into the academic and political canvas of India has challenged the invisibility of Dalits from the mainstream. In a significant fashion, Dalit activists, thinkers and intellectuals have been able to alter the higher-caste order at the level of discourse as well as in collective political action. No longer Ambedkar's writings are considered as 'text from the margin' but as an alternative text about Indian caste society.

Although, post 1990s, political and intellectual developments in India have transformed the very face of polity, the Dalit movement in India has a deeper history of a varied stream of ideology. The struggle for dignity and against caste inequality had to negotiate the fundamental question of identity assertion. It is not simply a political project but an historico-cultural project for the Dalits.

Dalits movements in India are constituted of competing ideologies. Also, the forms and objectives of Dalit struggles keep changing with respect to historical context. A major aspect of the struggles has been the contestation over cultural symbols and idioms. Culture has been an integral arena of struggle for Dalits. The existential economic upliftment is intrinsically linked with cultural ritual assertions of the Dalits.

Dalit movements have emerged in India with differing ideologies. However, one thing is clear that the low-caste status and poverty have always been recognized as having strong collinearity in all Dalit movements. Academic, intellectual as well as political response to this socio-economic reality has been varied. Babasaheb Ambedkar's writings, speeches and political activism have actually galvanized much of Dalit activism in modern India. On the other hand, Gandhi inspired Dalit movements by organizing campaigns against the practice of untouchability while remaining within the Hindu fold. Modernist thinker Jawaharlal Nehru viewed the Dalit deprivation mainly as a matter of poverty. He expected that the modernizing forces of Independent India would nullify caste degradations.

Surveys at the national and regional level, both by the government and independent agencies, have shown that Dalit suffers from cumulative disabilities that are apart from the major source of humiliation due to caste position; the Dalits experience backwardness on many other grounds. Dalit struggles in Independent India have followed more than one trajectory and have emerged under different banners. In every sense, irrespective of varied orientations and goals of collective action, the Dalit movement in India has gained substantial success. It constitutes a major area of study in Indian sociology today.

13.1. DALIT POLITICS: IDENTITY AND ASSERTIONS

13.1.1. Dalits in India

As a generic term, 'Dalit' signifies the poor or downtrodden in Indian vernacular languages. The word 'Dalit' would include the three categories of scheduled castes, scheduled tribes and other backward classes in usual administrative purposes. However, in the popular political discourse, it means the scheduled castes only (Shah 2001). In legal terms, the ex-untouchables are called scheduled castes. It is through the Government of India Act, 1935, by the British that the term scheduled caste was used to do away with the derogatory signifying terms used for them. It is important to note that not all the castes included in the schedule suffer from the same degree of social humiliation.

The SCs traditionally were placed at the lowest rung of the Hindu caste hierarchy. The commonly used term for them was 'achhut' (untouchable). Placed outside the *chaturvarna* system, they were considered as 'polluting' the purity of caste Hindus. The stigma continues although legally the very concept of 'untouchability' has been struck down as a criminal offence. The SCs constitute roughly 16 per cent of the Indian population.

As a matter of self-esteem, inspired by Ambedkerite thoughts, the neo-Buddhist activists first used the term 'Dalit'. They tried to make a new cultural connotation as being the downtrodden who are struggling off the cloak of age-old caste practices. Therefore, as a relational term, it stands for 'those who have been broken, ground down by those above them in a deliberate and active way. There is in the word itself an inherent denial of pollution, Karma that justified caste hierarchy' (Zelliot 1978, 77).

As Babasaheb Ambedkar theorized, it is the Hindu *shastra* that gives this uneven arrangement a religious sanctity. Thereby, this degrading system has attained moral and spiritual backup. The caste hierarchy over the years has produced a socio-economic hierarchy where the Dalits occupy the lowest position. Discrimination is ramified in every sphere of economic activity.

S. K. Thorat and R. S. Deshpande (2001) in 'Caste System and Economic Inequality: Economic Theory and Evidence' with the help of available data have reaffirmed Ambedkar's contention that in all economic spheres, caste-based economic disparities thrive in contemporary India. The most glaring being the fact that the Dalits constitute the major chunk of bonded labourers, although the practice was legally abolished in 1976 through the Bonded Labour System (Abolition) Act. The Dalits are discriminated against in terms of access to land, capital, market and employment and are mainly placed in low-paid jobs.

However, it is to be admitted that the democratic politics of India has opened up new opportunities for the Dalits by delegitimizing caste-based discrimination. Certain capitalist development, as well as land reforms, including land redistribution, have also created a better situation for the Dalits. Yet there is a good section of Dalits who are engaged in traditional caste occupations such as scavengers, leather workers, weavers and basket makers (Shah 2001). Visible caste atrocities have come down in the public sphere, but atrocities against Dalits in varied forms go unchecked. Dalits are at the receiving end in rural India mainly because of the upper-caste and middle-caste combinations, who control the landholdings and deny the state welfare measures to the Dalits. Overall speaking, the stigma and humiliations for the Dalits go unabated in modern India. For the urban-middle upper caste and upper class, the caste system has become 'invisible'. Paradoxically, the Dalits, in many layered ways, have been experiencing caste humiliation even in urban set-ups in their day to day lives.

13.1.2. Dalit Identity and Ideology

Identity, essentially, is a relational concept. Be it real or imagined, identity is a matter of self-esteem and self-image of a community vis-à-vis others. The identity issue takes immense significance as the Dalit as a community, historically, has suffered from deprivations and humiliations essentially in the symbolic order of human existence, that is, discriminations at the cultural–ritual realm of life over and above inequality at the material level of existence.

The very coinage of the term *Harijan* (children of God) adopted and popularized by Mahatma Gandhi stands as the foremost normative attempt to do away with the degrading and humiliating tag of *achhuta or antyaja* (untouchable) with a particular social group. By invoking the condescending term *Harijan*, Gandhi tried to resist the Ambedkarite proposition to place them as separate and outside the Hindu religious fold. Gandhi campaigned for a new identity for the 'untouchables' in the context of the nationalist movement in order to retain a perfect unified picture of Hindu society. By using the nomenclature of *Harijan*, he appealed to the caste Hindus for a change of heart and rise spiritually to repent for the age-old inhuman treatment meted out to the 'untouchable' castes.

The *Harijan* perspective dominated Indian historiography as far as documenting Dalit struggles is concerned. Caste studies and struggles against untouchability have mostly revolved around the role of Gandhi-led campaigns where 'untouchables' were represented as objects of reform, for example, largely considered as scavengers (Guru 1993).

The Dalit perspective considers the *Harijan* perspective self-defeating and problematic.

> It represents Dalits through the powerful stereotype of the bhangi (scavenger) figure and stigmatized victim in need of reform from above. Removing other more prominent forms of Dalit lives from discussion, the scavenger figure became the dominant trope through which questions related to Dalits were discussed and debated in the nationalist discourse. (Rawat and Satyanarayana 2016, 9)

The Gandhian model, *Harijan* perspective, denies Dalits active political consciousness and agency. Ambedkar struck at the very premise of this identity by arguing that the very religious sanction of the caste system needs to be dismantled. He was very precise to point out the inegalitarian character of the Hindu religion, while he fought for an egalitarian society. An egalitarian society based on fraternity needs to contest the divine authority of the Hindu Shastras (Ambedkar [1945] 2014). In his essay, 'What Congress and Gandhi Have Done to the Untouchables', Ambedkar put forward a scathing critic of the *Harijan* perspective, replacing the approach of a charitable exercise, he spoke in favour of an organized and educated struggle for self-respect.

Ambedkar's approach and ideology impacted Dalit assertions in Independent India in a big way. Beyond the connotation of just an identity, the term Dalit captured the imagination of a wider exploited and oppressed sections of society. The term 'Dalit' gained entry into public discourse through Marathi literary activist writers. The cultural and literary world offered a new way to reconstruct the world of the exploited and depressed 'untouchable' castes. The Dalit Panthers party used the term to denote their struggle for dignity and self-respect in the 1970s. On the one hand, the term Dalit stands for an emancipatory ideology for a revolutionary change of a caste-ridden society, and on the other hand, it denotes the emergence of a significant political category (Shah 2001).

Kancha Ilaiah takes Dalitism to the highest acme of ideological conflict with Brahmanism, 'The Dalitist School is an ideology of socio-political change, and the Brahmanical school represents a kind of modernized Hindu fundamentalist social base' (Ilaiah 2001). Ilaiah brings out the fundamental dichotomy between the two world views—the Dalit and the Brahmanical—as opposed to each other. The

> **BOX 13.1**
> **Self-image of a Dalit**
>
> Dalit is not a caste. Dalit is a symbol of change and revolution. The Dalit believes in humanism. He rejects the existence of God, rebirth, soul and sacred books that teach discrimination, faith and heaven because these have made him a slave. He represents the exploited man in his country.
>
> **Source:** Gangadhar Pantawane, a Dalit literary activist, as cited by Shah (2001).

Brahmanical world view is a by-product of Aryan epistemology. He maintains that the Aryans as an invader brought Brahmanism into this land by subjugating the original inhabitants. The Brahmanical epistemology rests on metaphysical ideas and abstract ideals. Against such a delusional supernatural explanation of the world, one finds the Dalit epistemology drawn upon the materialist philosophy of the *Lokayats* or *Charvakas*. Also, the Buddhist philosophy shaped the Dalit's self-image as it ran counter to the metaphysical ideals of karma (duty), purity, *punarjanma* (rebirth) and *moksha* (salvation). The majority of the Dalits were actually bound by Ambedkar's campaign for a rationalist-materialist ideology.

At the existential level, the Dalit identity is all about self-recognition. Over a period of time, the term widened its scope to include all oppressed sections. The Hindu Dalits might be reading the Hindu epics or worshipping the Hindu gods and goddesses but were focused on the material world of struggle for equality. The term got popular currency; as with any other social groups, Dalits could also muster multiple identities. Every identity is contextual. While retaining one's specific caste, linguistic group, religious community and so on, the term Dalit is used as a suffix (Shah 2001).

There is no doubt that the Dalit, as a community, is not homogenous across society; they are socially and economically stratified. So a new community identity is fraught with a certain amount of 'ifs and buts', more so, when a new identity, at times, is used by a section to dominate the majority of the same social group. Due to state welfare measures, benefits are made available, but they are not in abundance. Therefore, the possibility of material gains, be it political or economic, are being cornered by some at the expense of the more disadvantaged points to divisions between the elite and masses within the Dalits. Thus, Dalit identity and unity cannot be taken for granted in examining the Dalit movement.

13.1.3. Cultural Consensus or Counter Ideology

Can the Brahmanical caste order be unitedly challenged by OBCs and the Dalits jointly? Although there have been political attempts at forging such a unity, achieving an alternative common culture on an everyday basis is still a far cry. This is all due to differentiated material positions enjoyed by OBCs vis-à-vis the Dalit and their attitudes towards the Dalit. Political adjustments and coming together is one thing, and contesting the Brahmanical ideology is something else.

In fact, there are more than 400 *jatis* being notified as SCs, which make Dalit a broad category. This leads to a hierarchical structure within the Dalits, to the extent of even practising untouchability (Shah 2001). Social scientists impacted by Indological texts have suggested that Hindu hierarchy is an all-encompassing ideology shared even by those at the bottom. It is being theorized that those at the top (Brahmans) and those at the lowest ranks (*atisudras*, i.e., the untouchables) share the same value, a common world view. A 'cultural consensus' could be seen from top to bottom. Although different from the caste Hindus, the lowest castes with their different deities practice their own model of purity and pollution. Anthropologist of Rutgers University, Michael Moffatt, studied the ex-untouchables to arrive at the observation:

> Untouchables do not necessarily possess distinctively different social and cultural forms as a result of their position in the system. They do not possess a separate sub-culture ... the cultural system of Indian untouchables does not distinctively question or revalue the dominant social order. Rather, it continuously recreates among untouchables a microcosm of the larger system. (Moffatt 1979, 3)

The 'cultural consensus' theory has been contested by many social anthropological pieces of research. Joan Mencher and Kathleen Gough have indicated that the implication of hierarchy among the low caste is unlike that of high caste values of karma, *punarjanmma* and *moksha*. That is, they are not at all other-worldly like the caste Hindus. On the contrary, they are more oriented towards the materiality of their existence.

> The notions of dharma and karma (or duty and fate) are more useful as rationalizations of the system from the viewpoint of high caste people. Untouchables may accept these notions to some extent, but it is important to distinguish between the overt acceptance of such values and the holding of other value usually unexpressed to outsiders. (Mencher 1975, 846)

The most interesting and ironical takeaway from the debate on 'cultural consensus' is that a Dalit without losing roots and traditional identity can engage in demanding justice and equality in the social sphere in his worships of Hindu deities.

> A dalit who sings Rama and Krishna bhajans in the morning, reads Ramayana or Mahabharata in the evening, observes fast on ekadashi (11th day of a month), goes to pilgrimage and worships god from a distance no longer subscribes to the karma theory. Whenever possible, he asserts his rights and equal status with others. (Shah 1995, 32)

Finally, conversion to non-Hindu religious faiths was also thought of as another avenue to escape the humiliation of being lowly placed in the Hindu fold. If the root cause of untouchability is the inegalitarian Hindu religion, then the best way is to quit and embrace other religion which is premised on equality. Buddhism, Islam and Christianity were the religious faiths that attracted many Dalits to convert into. However, there were instances where Dalits converted into other religions in order to escape from the exploitations of the local dominant classes. Only a large-scale conversion to Buddhism by the Mahar caste under the leadership of Ambedkar stands out as a major counter ideology in the Dalit movement.

To signify and discuss the ex-untouchables of India, the term Dalit has been most successful and has retained its potentiality. It represents a very active, self-conscious and assertive social category. In the discursive politics of caste, the uses of the term and its growing acceptance since the 1970s has foregrounded identity politics in a big way. Although he did not invoke the term Dalit, Ambedkar has remained as the iconic figure, the central symbol of the Dalit movement in India in contemporary times. His inspiration is reflected not only in agitations and assertions of Dalits but also in radical Dalit literature.

13.2. DALIT MOVEMENT IN INDIA

13.2.1. Pre-Colonial and Colonial Times

Historically, organized or otherwise oppressed group of people have always raised their voices against subjugations. Caste oppression has been contested through different means and strategies. The contexts of struggle always have shaped the texture of such struggles. As the nature of the subjugation in a major way damages the honour and dignity of the specific category (ex-untouchables), much of the struggles have been to 'occupy' the cultural world through competing idioms and symbols.

Another historical attempt was to Sanskritize ways of life on the part of the lower castes to claim higher status. It was a 'purifying' exercise to bring about changes in the styles of life to leave behind the 'polluting' aspects of their sociocultural lives. As noted by T. K. Oommen, such Sankritizing movements were resorted to by the Dalits often 'in a spirit of recalcitrance and the upper castes invariably opposed such attempts' (Oommen 1990, 260).

By the turn of the 19th century, the Dalit movement in India acquired a character of its own. The pre-colonial protests and assertions were mainly adaptive in character. Be it the Buddhist revolt of the 6th century BCE, the Bhakti movement and the Neo-Vedantic interventions, all essentially were premised on critiquing the Brahmanic ideology of the concept of 'purity and pollution'. Apart from such attempts to cleanse the doctrines of Hinduism, the other movement was to disengage from Hinduism. Rejecting Hinduism, conversion to other religions was thought to be emancipatory. But most often, religious sects and cults get implicated by dominant socio-economic power relations. Without a transformative agenda of socio-economic upliftment of the entire community, all these attempts were reformist in nature. Most importantly, they were all (except conversion to Buddhism) led by upper-caste Hindu reformers or non-Dalit missionaries. The arrival of 'insiders', that is, from the same section of the depressed population, we could see only during the colonial period. The three iconic ideological warriors from the rank of the depressed castes are Jyotiba Phule (1826–1890) from Maharashtra, B. R. Ambedkar (1891–1956) also from Maharashtra and E. V. Ramaswamy Naicker (1879–1973) from Tamil Nadu. As direct bearers of humiliation and scorn of the caste system, they all inspired the 'untouchables' to challenge the Brahmanic knowledge and rituals. The assertions of the depressed sections took a new form in the context of new socio–politico–legal order implanted by the British colonial power in India.

The politico–legal system implanted by the British rulers was products of the Western liberal ideology so necessary for the capitalist development in 19th-century Europe. It was a sort of a welcome change from the rigid pre-British order as the spheres of power became separated and autonomous to an extent. The depressed and the hitherto subjugated castes could see an opening and opportunity to secure basic civil rights, for example, using the same public roads, entering the temples, dressing like caste Hindus, admission rights in educational institutions and so on. The depressed castes growingly sensed their rights, as they sought justice and protection from the colonial state. Their participation in the political arena also became conspicuous (Shah 2001).

During the colonial rule, two iconic figures of the freedom movement, Gandhi and Ambedkar, presented two contrasting vision for the upliftment of the depressed classes (the colonial administration used the term to refer to the 'untouchable' low castes). The Poona Pact of 1935 is seen as a watershed of the movement for a separate electorate for the depressed classes. Ambedkar had to yield before Gandhi's indefinite fast against the creation of separate electorate for the depressed classes; instead, he accepted the reservation of seats for them. Gandhi was consistent in his opposition to the Communal Award, the offer for a separate electorate to Muslims, Sikhs and Christians. Initially, the British offer was not meant for the depressed classes. They were offered a double vote. So that, those qualified to vote would be entitled to vote as a caste Hindu in the general constituencies and in addition can vote as a depressed caste in special depressed classes' category.

Ambedkar, through his consistent participation in all legislative bodies and commissions, be it the Simon Commission of 1928 or the Round Table Conferences in the 1930s, argued for a separate electorate. He always questioned the Indian National Congress's reformist approach towards the depressed castes and especially on the issue of untouchability. Since the last two decades of the 19th century, some social reformers impressed upon the Congress leadership to raise the issue of untouchability, which the Congress ignored till the concrete demand for protection and separate representation started taking shape. Some leaders of the depressed classes even opposed the very concept of Home Rule of the Indian National Congress; as they apprehended that with the passing of power to Congress, they would be at the mercy of the higher castes (Shah 2001). Only in 1917, Congress realized and acknowledged formally the issue of untouchability.

Instead of a dependency framework for upliftment of the depressed sections, Ambedkar worked to empower them through direct political participation. He himself deliberated in various legislative forums and institutions to further the legal aspects of equality. He realized that the social ostracizing of the depressed classes had to be contested at the ground level too. As a member of the Bombay Legislative Council, he took up the fight from the streets to the corridors of power. In 1927, he led the Mahar *Satyagraha* to claim the right of the 'untouchables' to use water of a public tank *Chavdar* in Mahad, Maharashtra. The 'protest ideology' advanced by him has shaped much of Dalit politics of the post-Independent period (Ambedkar 2018).

13.2.2. Post-Independent Dalit Struggle

It is clear that depressed classes christened as scheduled castes by the British administration suffer from multiple deprivations. The term Dalit got popular currency to signify this subjugated section in Independent India, courtesy of the neo-Buddhist activists and political activism of the Dalit Panther party in Maharashtra. Overall speaking, the Dalits first agitated to secure social prestige against stigmatization and the practice of untouchability. The importance of securing political power was the next step. So mobilization towards political empowerment among the Dalits emerged. Lastly, to sustain such struggles economic strength and resources of the participants was felt to be imperative. Movements for economic equality and against economic exploitation at varied spheres are the culmination of the Dalit protest movement in India. However, these sequence of protest movements aimed at different spheres is a function of the hierarchy of deprivations as experienced by the participants (Oommen 1990).

Ambedkar realized both removing the cultural stigma and securing economic equality as the pivot for Dalit emancipation. To achieve that goal, he unequivocally campaigned for increasing the participation of the victims in the political sphere. Political representation was crucial for him. His Independent Labour Party during the colonial period survived from 1936 to 1942. He envisaged a broad alliance of peasants, workers and SCs but without much fruition. The Republican Party of India, formed in 1957 by one of his associates, hoped to carry forward the goals of Ambedkar. The Republican Party of India failed as an electoral proposition, but it needs to be credited with the success of pressurizing the Government of India to replace the Untouchability (Offences) Act, 1955, with a more stringent Protection of Civil Rights Act, 1976.

In the 1970s only, the Dalit literary and art movement gained ground in Maharashtra. Along with the Dalit Panther group emerged with a distinct cultural-political ideology. Dalit Panthers were essentially based in Bombay and Poona. The backdrop of both the Dalit literary movement and the Dalit Panther movement was the conversion movement to Buddhism. The collective act did not actually result in a large number of conversions, but it had a great symbolic effect. As an act of defiance, it attracted the attention of the nation and enthused the Dalits across the country.

The Dalit Panther was a result of disillusionment amongst the Dalits youths with the conversion movement as well as the parliamentary expectation of the Republican Party of India. They opted for a creative mix of both Ambedkar and Karl Marx in their understanding of Indian society. Without the Marxian insistence of privileging economic factors over others, they observed that the Dalits were subjected to cumulative domination. The multiple socio-economic deprivations and political oppression could not be fought with 'tokenism' in the form of economic concessions or political reservation. Their objective of capturing political power through collective mobilization could not make much headway. However, they could identify not only SCs, STs and neo-Buddhists as Dalits but also all the toiling section of the industry and agriculture irrespective of their caste status. A wider notion of Dalit evolved largely due to the efforts of the Panthers Party.

13.2.3. State Action and Dalit Politics

Apart from the movements of the people and by the people of the affected social group, one needs to acknowledge the 'movement' in the form of state action of the independent Government of India. The state action of protective discrimination is a case in point. The policy of 'reservation' for the SCs roughly in proportion to their population in the various legislative bodies of the government is the foremost state action in India to secure the political empowerment of the Dalits. Also, 'reservation' is put in practice for Dalits in public educational institutions and government employment to secure the life and expectations of the historically exploited social group. Major political parties have also admitted to such representations given their electoral compulsion. Due to competitive politics, Dalits have found cabinet positions also in various governments.

The gain of the 'reservation 'policy for a holistic betterment of Dalit lives has been disputed by most sociologists. First, the co-option of Dalits into the political order is divisive as they get divided into party lines. The party interest often takes precedence over their avowed task of serving the cause of the Dalits. Second, Dalit leaders of the same party compete with each other to further personal ambitions. Eventually, it leads to factions and fissions among the Dalits only (Oommen 1990).

Ghanashyam Shah in his introduction to *Dalit Identity and Politics* (2001) has indicted the shortcomings of the 'reservation' policy in legislative bodies. Citing various research studies on this subject, he observes that, only the 'advanced' section from Dalits (either intellectually or materially) secure the political positions through 'reservation' policy. The real cause is lost out as they fail to play autonomous roles but capitulate to the party higher commands. Any Dalit initiatives trying to break the unstated codes of mainstream politics were either co-opted or discarded forthwith by the party bosses. So effective political representation for the Dalit cause could not be fulfilled by such a policy. Studies of legislative behaviour of the elected scheduled caste members as well as scheduled tribes have shown their lackadaisical performances in the lawmaking houses. They seem to utilize their numbers as a block to bargain in whichever ruling party they belong to, to secure plum positions in various statutory bodies, cabinet and ministerial positions and so on.

This is not to suggest that absolutely no progress for the Dalits has been achieved through state action. The 'reservation policy' and the role of the elected MP or MLAs have, to an extent, checked upper-caste domination in all state policies and ensured the continuance of developmental programmes for the Dalits. It has also created a sense of political empowerment and inspired greater participation of Dalits in electoral politics. In actuality, the participation of Dalits has increased over time, for which the emergence and role of the Bahujan Samaj Party (BSP) stand as the best example. A strong electorally motivated Dalit movement one can see with the successes of BSP in Indian polity for a while.

BSP was formed by Kanshi Ram, a Sikh Dalit from Punjab. As a professional in bureaucracy and having exposure to caste politics in Maharashtra, he took a serious plunge in mobilizing Dalits for electoral politics. Prior to the formation of the formal political party BSP in 1984, Kanshi Ram tried his mobilizing skill by organizing the All India Backward and Minority Employees Federation in 1973. Amongst the West and North Indian Dalit government employees, this federation tried to spread the ideas of Ambedkar. Subsequently, he organized the Dalit Shosit Samaj Sangharsh Samiti in 1982. It worked in rural North India to mobilize the Dalits for political ends. Finally, BSP was formed with a political strategy of invoking the strength of a *bahujan* community. It aimed at securing a numerical majority by consolidating all the toiling masses that would include the Dalits along with the poor and subjugated sections from the STs, OBC and also the poorer Muslims. It was constituted as a Dalit-based political party aimed at capturing political power. By the 1990s, BSP could successfully forge the unity of a *bahujan samaj* and play a crucial role as a national-level party. It tasted electoral success intermittently and even enjoyed government power through coalitions with other parties in Uttar Pradesh.

> The BSP is the vehicle through which a certain class of dalits has aimed, through electoral victory, to capture Sate power and control public policy. It represents the efforts of a generation of dalits who have benefitted from the State's development programs and affirmative action in education, employment, and politics. (Guru and Chakravarty 2005, 149)

Sudha Pai, in her study of the BSP's electoral performances in Uttar Pradesh, has observed that the party under the leadership of Kanshi Ram and Mayavati has used political power to instil a sense of confidence amongst the Dalits. It subverted an entrenched high caste politics of the state. However, BSP never attempted any substantive transformation of the socio-economic system. The radical posture of BSP got compromised in its hunger for power, as time to time, it entered into opportunistic alliances with upper-caste parties, especially after 1995 (Pai 2001).

Gail Omvedt also has incisively pointed at the failure of such Dalit movements. Dalit politics has failed short of acting as a transformative agent. Dalit politics has engaged itself in electoral politics which has its own purchase. Post-Ambedkar, the Dalit movement has lost the original vision of Ambedkar, a vision for a total transformation of the social order. Instead, it has got entangled in reformist and opportunist politics. Although caste has been used for mobilization purpose, the performance is much ideologically distracted. Hardly, these movements addressed the majority of the Dalits in their everyday toil and misery at the hands of upper castes (Omvedt 2001).

12.2.4. The New Phase

Faced with the failure of the Dalit movements to substantiate people's aspirations and sensing their lack of transformative potentiality, many non-governmental organizations came up in the 1990s to contest the state. International networks for Dalit solidarity were forged to engage the state in fulfilling its highly valued programmes of social justice and equality. They rely on advocacy campaigns, information dissemination strategies, trail network building and pressure tactics (Guru and Chakravarty 2005). Realizing that accelerated globalization has aggravated the misery instead of the promised benefits, non-governmental organizations seek to bring together broad-based coalitions of toiling masses from every sector. Nevertheless, non-governmental organizations cannot be expected to address the Dalit aspirations by galvanizing an all India movement.

The growing irrelevance of various grassroot movements and the fuzzy ideological framework of political bodies created a possibility of autonomous Dalit politics in the 1990s. The context of post-1990 in terms of political and intellectual developments facilitated the rise of the independent and autonomous Dalit intelligentsia from the younger generation. The implementation of the Mandal Commission recommendation (reservation for OBC) by the Government of India demystified the caste neutrality of the urban class and pointed to the deep roots of casteist values. The bitter debate over the extension of statutory reservation policies from Dalits to OBCs revealed the dominance of caste Hindu intelligentsia in academia. Seemingly, they are a homogenous group sharing the same socio-economic and educational background (Rawat and Satyanarayana 2016).

Caste became a legitimate political category as one could growingly realize the exclusion of Dalits from leading academic institutions, media and private sectors. The growing discontent among the younger generation led to an upsurge of critical Dalit assertions across the public sphere. The Dalit youths who previously identified with the class framework of classical Marxist schools started questioning the high-caste dominance in all the leading progressive political parties. The idea of caste as the form and means of discrimination has been placed in the centre stage of Indian polity.

A new wave of Ambedkarite students and youth forums sprang up across many leading university campuses (Omvedt 1990).

The post-liberalization phase ushering in a globalized world is a double-faced one. We have seen that it belied its promise of ensuring development with a human face. On the other side, the new liberalized institutional and formal public spaces created new opportunities for those who were struggling to access restricted resources. The Dalit writers, activists, intelligentsia could breathe fresh air with the arrival of the internet and networking society. The splurge in the vernacular media and availability of forums and spaces outside the state framework has been enabling the marginal to connect with global resources, indulge and initiate new dialogues in their own terms. A new possibility is still being explored in Dalit politics and movement despite its setbacks.

It might be a crossroad for the future Dalit movement, as the contemporary Indian state is embedded in the neo-liberal feat of withdrawing from its social responsibilities, while the Dalits pin hopes on state action to salvage them from disgrace and exploitation. Also, it is true that from time to time, a large number of them, mainly sharing similar class positions (being the impoverished category) has agitated militantly against the system. Landless agricultural labourers, small and marginal farmers, workers in informal sectors could be mobilized as they share the same life opportunities, whereas a section of Dalits has definitely drifted away, having benefitted from the affirmative action of the state and otherwise.

It is clear that since Independence, there have been some changes in the lives of Dalits. First, a Dalit middle class has come up via the governmental policy of protective discrimination. Reservation in government jobs and admission to educational institutions has helped the section to build confidence to move up the social ladder. Again, the situation is a double-faced one. While there has been a sense of Dalit consciousness developing among the oppressed section as a unifying bond, occupational diversification has stratified the Dalits much more than before (Shah 2001).

The following two decisive changes have been identified by Ghanashyam Shah, which have impacted Dalit lives over the years:

1. Crude and blatant forms of social humiliation have minimized, at least in the public sphere.
2. An assertive Dalit has evolved.

He cites the following four reasons for such a development:

1. There is an overall acceptance of the values of social dignity and equality. The liberal ideas of Phule and Ambedkar have found social acceptance. This is helped by the modern development of communication, technology and so on which have outdated older models of society,
2. The traditional occupational structure as determined by caste has been altered by the market-oriented capitalist development. Occupational diversification has created a better economic space for the Dalits,
3. The reservation policy created a Dalit middle class. This class now plays an important role as an articulate section of the community,
4. Political consciousness has risen amongst the Dalits due to competitive politics. This is facilitated by the provision of reserved seats for the Dalits in the political set-up.

For sure, there have been changes in the lives of Dalits. More than the betterment in the material spheres of life, the transformation at the discursive level of the very term caste is most remarkable. In his review of Ghanashyam Shah's edited book, *Dalit Identity and Politics* (2001), Surinder S. Jodhka has noted that caste has been retrieved from the clutches of the high-caste narratives. Instead, it has been placed as a vital social reality, as a definite political category by those who bear the brunt of the historical hierarchical structure of inequality and exploitation. The political ramification of the disengagement of the newer generation of Dalit activists and intelligentsia from the political structure of patronage and co-optation is bound to impact Indian democracy (Jodhka 2002).

CONCLUSION

There is increasing visibility of Dalits in contemporary Indian socio-political map. This is accompanied by a rise of not only a distinct Dalit middle class but also a Dalit intelligentsia. To understand the Dalit movement and Dalit politics, one has to acknowledge that it is inextricably linked to the question of Dalit identity. Here we are dealing with a social category of the Indian population who has been historically subjugated by Power. The subjugation is based on an assigned low-ritual status. The existential Dalit reality is a historical product of cumulative deprivations.

Around competing ideologies, the Dalit movement in India has emerged. The different historical contexts have shaped up the strategies, objectives and nature of the Dalit movement in India. The constant thing about the Dalit movement is that all such struggles have foregrounded cultural contestations as an integral part of the economic and political upliftment of their degraded lives.

The struggle for equality in the Dalit movement has to be built around identity assertion. It is the Dalit Panther movement of the 1970s which popularized the Dalit identity as a strategic one to explore a wider social and radical political mobilization. The vibrant cultural and literary movement tried to forge a unity of all toiling masses, whom the Dalit Panthers wanted to mobilize and represent. The historical trajectory of Dalit assertion for an identity for dignity and economic upliftment has shown that from a phase of patronizing, philanthropic gestures from upper-caste Hindu social reformers, gradually voices from their own ranks have come to occupy the arena of resistance. The agitations of the 'insiders' brought about a qualitative change in the sociocultural identity and self-definition of the Dalits. The colonial rule, to an extent, provided a socio-legal space for the low-castes to claim justice and equality.

Ambedkar as a statesman and a leading figure in the cause of the ex-untouchables led a frontal attack on the Hindu normative order that naturalizes the caste divisions. Gandhi, however, mobilized and fought against 'untouchability' on a different premise, upholding the harmonious tradition of *Sanatan dharma*. Ambedkar staged a two-pronged approach to mobilize the depressed classes. First, he utilized his stature as a constitutional–legal expert to campaign vigorously in the corridors of power for the cause of the subjugated. Second, he led from the front on ground level agitation programmes. Ambedkar's thoughts continued to inspire all Dalit assertions in the post-Independence years. Electoral performances of political formations exclusively aimed at Dalit cause could not prosper beyond a limited success. The role of the Dalit

Panthers in the 1970s with militant and vibrant cultural overtones is remarkable for a fresh understanding of Dalit lives and politics. On the electoral platform, only BSP could achieve some intermittent success, though not a big headway could be made as opportunism and caste coalition defeated the very ideological thrust of Dalit emancipation.

The state action of affirmative action did not hugely help to improve the lives of the Dalits. It has a limited scope, and it only created an assertive middle class amongst the Dalits. The policy of reservation even in lawmaking bodies could not really serve the avowed purpose, as the Dalit representatives often got assimilated and co-opted into the ruling class politics, leaving behind the causes of the wider society to which they belong. Due to much disillusionment, along with a new phase of the liberalized economy, one could perceive a fresh wave of Dalit assertion in the post-1990s Indian polity. The emergence of autonomous movements gave rise to new leadership from the ranks of the Dalits. It is logical that due to the reality of the interface of low-caste status and economic misery as well as the state acknowledgement of caste consideration in policy matters, the Dalit, as a social category, has emerged as a significant subject matter of emergent Indian society. Dalit politics squarely lies on the Dalit mobilization with a renewed attempt to synchronize the gains from Ambedkerite ideas, Gandhian values and the class framework of Marxist understanding.

Points for Classroom Discussion

- Importance of Dalit identity for analysing the Dalit movement
- History of the Dalit movement in pre-Independence times
- The post-Independence phase in the Dalit assertion in India
- The role of Ambedkar in Dalit politics in India
- The changing nature of Dalit politics in India
- The success and failures of the Dalit movement in India

GLOSSARY

Affirmative action: Set of actions and policies taken up by the state addressing particular social groups to uplift them from historically inflicted disadvantages.

Chaturvarna: The four *varna*s as depicted in Vedic literature of *varna* system—the Brahmans, Kshatriya, Vaishya and Shudra.

Neo-Buddhist: B. R. Ambedkar attempted a re-interpretation of Buddhism, calling it *navayana*, a 'new vehicle' to come out of the stranglehold of Hinduism. The Dalits who defied this 'new vehicle' are known as neo-Buddhist in Dalit history.

Post-liberalization: The phase of society after the introduction of a liberal economy (post-1991), which opened up not only the economy from state control but also marked by many associated changes in the social set-up.

Varnashramic: Pertaining to the principle of varnashram, that provides a structure of *Vedic* society as divided into four major varnas and four ashramas. It provides a stable system of cooperation between different varnas while prescribing appropriate task of each varna and duties in different stages of life.

REFERENCES

Ambedkar, B. R. (1945) 2014. 'What Congress and Gandhi Have Done to the Untouchables.' In *Babasaheb Ambedkar Writings and Speeches* (vol. 9). Mumbai: The Education Department of Maharashtra.

———. 2018. *Ambedkar: An Overview*. New Delhi: Rupa Publications.

Guru, G. 1993. 'Dalit Movements in Mainstream Sociology.' *Economic & Political Weekly* 28, no. 14 (April): 570–573.

Guru, G., and A. Chakravarty. 2005. 'Who Are the Country's Poor? Social Movement, Politics and Dalit Poverty.' In *Social Movements in India: Poverty, Power, and Politics*, edited by Raka Ray and Mary Fainsod Katzenstein. New Delhi: Oxford University Press.

Jodhka, Surinder S. 2002. 'Meanings of Dalit Identity.' *Economic & Political Weekly* 37, no. 13: 1255–1257.

llaiah, K. 2001.'Dalitism vs Brahmanism: The Epistemological Conflict in History.' In *Dalit Identity and Politics*, edited by G. Shah. New Delhi: SAGE Publications.

Mencher, J. 1975. 'The Caste System Upside Down or the Not-So-Mysterious East.' *Current Anthropology* 15, no. 4: 469–493.

Moffat, M. 1979. *An Untouchable Community in South India: Structure and Consensus*. Princeton, NJ: Princeton University Press.

Omvedt, G. 1990. 'Twice Born Riot against Democracy.' *Economic & Political Weekly* 25, no. 39: 2195–2201.

———. 2001. 'Ambedkar and after: The Dalit Movement in India.' In *Dalit Identity and Politics*, edited by G. Shah. New Delhi: SAGE Publications.

Oommen, T. K. 1990. *Protest and Change: Studies in Social Movements*. New Delhi: SAGE Publications.

Pai, S. 2001. 'From Harijans to Dalits: Identity Formation, Political Consciousness and Electoral Mobilisation of the Scheduled Castes in Uttar Pradesh.' In *Dalit Identity and Politics*, edited by G. Shah. New Delhi: SAGE Publications.

Rawat, R. S., and K. Satyanarayana, eds. 2016. *Dalit Studies: New Perspectives on Indian History and Society*. Durham, NC: Duke University Press.

Shah, G., ed. 2001. 'Introduction.' In *Dalit Identity and Politics*. New Delhi: SAGE Publications.

———. 1995. 'Dalit Movements and the Search for Identity.' In *Contradictions in Indian Society*, edited by M. Savur and Indra Munshi. New Delhi: Rawat Publications.

Thorat, S. K., and R. S. Deshpande. 2001. 'Caste System and Economic Inequality.' In *Dalit Identity and Politics*, edited by G. Shah. New Delhi: SAGE Publications.

Zelliot, E. 1978. 'Dalit: New Cultural Context for an Old Marathi World.' *Journal of Developing Societies* 11: 77.

CHAPTER 14

Women's Movement

LEARNING OUTCOMES

- To probe the ideals of womanhood in traditional texts
- To understand gender as a social construct
- To explore the changing themes of woman's movement in India
- To study some major woman's movement in contemporary India

Keywords: Gender, patrilineal, social construction, ideal womanhood, social reformism, feminist assertion, women's studies, women's mobilization

It is time now to look at the world and interpret the world through the eyes of women and have a balanced view; get not half-truths but the truth.

—**Kamla Bhasin**

INTRODUCTION

Women's movement is intimately connected to the life experiences of women in any society. The social organization and the institutional structures within which women live their lives are the essential subject area to understand women's movement. In India, the academic concern about the women's movement is largely a product of woman's studies that took shape in the 1970s. The decade of the 1970s is special as a systematic study of women's lives and movements were taken up by many special centres and university departments. The United Nations declaration of 1975 as the International Women's Year propelled a new scope of study in sociology and other social sciences.

In the Indian context, the confrontation with the colonial system of knowledge during the 19th century gave rise to awareness with respect to women's status in society. Understood as an oppressed social category, women became the pivotal focus for all socio-religious thinking. The rethinking prompted social reforms, which were all in reaction to the anticipated impact of Western ideas on women's lives. Ancient Indian history was the favourite area of study of historians interested to figure out women in history. Such studies definitely informed the women's movement in India in its march towards empowerment and contesting the patriarchal order.

The roots of the women's movement in India run deep into history. For more than a century, the movement has grown and matured with different objectives, compositions and outreach. The form and style also have undergone changes as the nature of the conditions of women's subjugation has changed over all these long years. Interestingly, the nature of participation steadily changed. The initial years of the movement were conceptualized and led by benevolent male members of society. Gradually, the women's movement found its own leaders, which altered the very consciousness of the rank and file.

With leading women activists and thinkers taking over the leadership of the movement, the older paradigm of the betterment of women within the same cultural order came under scrutiny. Beyond the upper class and caste concern of women's lives, more and more the ordinariness of the movement came to the fore. The women's movement in India revolved around diverse issues and ideologies. Feminist thinking has also evolved through contending theories of the oppression and subjugated conditions of women. At times, the movements were exclusive to women's lives only, and at some other moments, the movement tried to be inclusive to acknowledge the need for intersubjectivity of egalitarian social living. We need to note the multiple texture and content of the women's movement in India as expressed through a variety of popular campaigns. Finally, we need to conceptualize all such agitations, as congregating into a network, that work towards transforming the world of women.

14.1. WOMEN IN INDIA

14.1.1. The Cultural Ideal of Indian Womanhood

In India, the very awareness and realization of the inferior status of women is a result of the cultural confrontation with colonial Western culture. The ideals of modernity that the colonial west floated in India created cultural anxiety and inferiority amongst the India literati class. The germination of the women's movement is located at this historical juncture. It is interesting to observe that whenever socio-religious thinkers and reformers examine the traditional Hindu religion and custom, they were inevitably led to the ways women's lives were implicated in such traditional order. So the symbolic order of religion and custom automatically demanded a fresh look at it—a reevaluation of the normative order with respect to the daily lives of women.

The 'women's question' was central to the 19th-century social reform movement. The anti-colonial nationalist feelings in the early stages were to rebuff the Western challenge of a superior culture. The two aspects of Hindu society, the caste system and the low status of women were most glaring before the eyes of the socio-religious reformers. All the major reform movements tried to retrieve a cultural model of the ideal woman by going back to the ancient Vedic texts. Be it the question of sati, child marriage, widow remarriage or enforced widowhood the dominant model for a cleansed Hindu order was the upper caste Sanskritic one (Chakravarti 1999).

The traditional woman was imagined in a way that run counter to the egalitarian principles of modern times. A dualism between tradition and modernity was invoked and for women's emancipation; the classical tradition was upheld as the chief barrier. As against this, many scholars were interested to emphasize the uniqueness of Indian tradition and counter the popular conception. Asha Jayant and Indira Rothermund have quoted noted sociologist Radhakamal Mukerjee to substantiate their favourable disposition towards classical view of Indian womanhood.

> There is a widespread ignorance about the original sanskrit literature, both the vedic and classical and of the Dharmashastra (law books) in which are to be found the laws, customs and traditions which define the true status of women in early times. It is pointed out that in the vedic period highest place was accorded to women in India. (Jayant and Rothermund 1989, 1722)

The contention is that in the Vedic society, the status of women was not at all degraded as claimed by the modernist. However, the Vedic ideals lost their edge in post-Vedic times. The downgrading of women is best exemplified in *Manusmriti*. On the other hand, Marxist historian Uma Chakravarti identifies these 'ideals' as the work of nationalist historians. The nationalist historians had to face up to the fierce criticism levelled against Hindu social institutions by idealizing an image of a traditional Hindu woman. Not only that the sources used by the nationalist historians were problematic, but also if such upper-caste Brahmanic sources were used, counter propositions are abundant in ancient India (Chakravarti 1999).

The best-known nationalist work on the position of women from the earliest times right up to the 1950s is by A. S. Altekar (1987). Despite the detailed research by him into the vast body of opinion of the lawmakers pertaining to various aspects of women's rights and privileges, Altekar could perceive a woman vis-à-vis her role in the family and marriage only. In Altekar's study, 'A Vindication of Hindu Civilization One Can Find', Uma Chakravarti finds that such an attempt ignores the specific social organization and patriarchal structure that actually downgrade women. She extensively quotes Altekar to argue that he has reflected a problematic perspective of biological determinism and the physical inferiority of women. 'Landed property could be owned only by one who had the power to defend it against actual or potential rivals and enemies. Women were obviously unable to do this and so could hold no property' (Altekar 1987, 339).

Altekar is completely insensitive to explanations other than the classical Brahmanical ones and in league with the nationalist historiography of India. His exclusive attention and examination of high-caste women do not allow him to study the Shudra women, who toiled hard in the making of ancient society. The possibility of Shudra women, as a more active subject in the shaping of Indian womanhood, could also be explained in contrast to the Altekarian paradigm. Upper-caste consciousness, even in modern India, is dominantly impacted by such a truncated perspective.

> **BOX 14.1**
> **Gender and Nation**
>
> The Committee on the Status of Women in India 1974, in its report submitted at the start of the United Nations Decade for Women, drew direct links between the dismal condition of women's lives and increasing social disparities. Women's problems reflected in more concentrated form the canvass of macro-politics which denied land, employment, education health, security and legal rights to the vast mass of Indians. The daily trauma most women battle with was integral to their existence as Adivasis and Dalits, the rural landless or urban poor.
>
> **Source:** Agnihotri and Palriwala (2001).

14.1.2. Hindu Girls in Patrilineal India

Sociologist Leela Dube has shown how the Hindu rituals and practices have contributed majorly in the structuring of women as gendered subjects. The imprint of patrilineal society and the subjugation of women are located by Dube in those essentialized Hindu idioms and values, which to a large extent have ensured a reproduction of the system of subordination. Through the rituals, certain familial roles are inculcated among women and the very socialization process ensured a limited role and dispositions of women in traditional Hindu society (Dube 1988).

Patrilineality naturalizes gender differences that are actually culturally produced. As a 'natural order of things', patrilineal Hindu society designs the roles of father and mother in procreation in such a way; as a man provides the seed, a woman receives the seed as the field. A child carries the blood of the father to signify descent and lineage. The natal family assigns transferability or non-functional as far as the continuity of the family is concerned. The husband's family considers a wife as a mere vehicle for the perpetuation of the family. A woman is considered a receptacle. So in the family and kinship structure itself, men and women have unequal rights, roles and statuses.

To understand the subordinate position of women, it is important to study the way family structure is embedded in the wider context of kinship. Kinship provides the organizing principle to designate individuals in social groups. The obligations as well as the rights of an individual are all governed by the kinship rules, which in turn, are closely linked with religious practices and values. Thereby, the socialization process is a function of the kinship rules. The institution of caste is eventually implicated in the family and kinship structure. Belongingness to a caste is protected by a strict maintenance of its boundary. This is accomplished by the regulation of marriage and sexual relations. Since women have a role in biological reproduction, they are crucial in maintaining the 'purity' of the caste boundary. Thereby, Dube (1988) explained how a woman's subordination is impacted by caste too.

Popular ceremonies, rituals and narratives establish the preference of a male child over a girl child. The change of a grown-up daughter's relationship with her natal home post-marriage is narrated through many grand festivals, customized to regional variations and practices. In popular culture, Dube traces the threads of differential treatment and perception of women in Hindu India, often dramatized through wedding or puberty rituals. Femininity is socially constructed in a manner that denies a woman an autonomous independent agency. The very idea of 'fortunate' or 'auspicious' is implicated with a gendered notion of marital status or of begetting a male heir. A clear dichotomy of masculinity and femininity is culturally constructed whereby femininity is mirrored as something which is not masculine, that is, an identity premised on a 'lack'.

Ideal femininity subscribes to loyalty, obedience and submission. Through the constructed ideals of wifehood and motherhood, resting on the ideal feminine virtues, women are conferred with appropriate social roles. Their status of personhood is limited by such a process of socialization. Her 'purity' is always under the scanner, whereby the control over her body and sexuality is transferred to male control. The domestic space and world are so gendered that a girl grows up with the feeling of being not equal to a boy. The question remains, how would a woman within such limitations imposed express their resentment or adopt strategies to overcome them. Women's movement in contemporary India has to take a clue from such projected idyllic images of women of traditional India and move ahead (Chakravarti 1999).

14.1.3. The Colonial Experience

The trope of modernity always marked the British colonial power to legitimize their colonial rule in India. The civilizing mission of the colonial power was justified by pointing out the abject degradation of women in India. Against the brutal atrocities inflicted on the Indian women—sati, female infanticide, enforcement of celibate and ascetic widowhood, child marriage practice and so on—the colonial state claimed the role of a protector. Taking advantage of the politico-legal structure of the British rule the elite enlightened class, all men initiated the social reforms movements. Most of the movements were directed at legislative cures for abolishing the pernicious practices that affected the position of women. The success of the legislation such as the abolition of sati (1829) and the Hindu Widows' Remarriage Act (1856) could inspire women to join the men in social reforms movements.

The campaign for women's education subsequently picked up. Nevertheless, women's participation in such movements was only from educated and enlightened families. It was a project to explore the 'new woman' who would come out of the seclusion and join their male counterparts in the public domain. Education was understood as a vital tool for women's emancipation. Patronized by fathers and husbands, a select group of women, all from elite upper-caste background could make their presence felt in the public domain (Sen 2000).

Such accomplishment by a limited class of women needs to be acknowledged and not be dismissed as being elite. Such women had to tread the unchartered path to taste 'freedom' at the cost of being ridiculed, ostracized or socially harassed. Not all of them could enjoy the support of their male members of their families. Many had to face severe familial non-cooperation (Karlekar 1991). It is interesting to note that the liberal agenda was to seek redressal from the colonial politico-legal set-up to cleanse the tradition of its inegalitarian prescriptions. On the other hand, the conservatives were in favour of protecting the traditional social relations from any colonial intervention. Gradually, it was the domestic space that became the idealized space for Indianness. The liberals also recasted the domestic space in terms of their reinvention of tradition (Chatterjee 1989).

The decisive break with social reformism with respect to women's lives became very conspicuous towards the end of the 19th century as more and more women joined in movements for the betterment of their own lives. By the turn of the 20th century, women's own autonomous organizations began to be formed. The 1920s is being considered a significant decade for the women's movement in India, as women came out to form their associations and becoming active in politics. Sarala Devi Chaudhurani was one of the first women to realize the need for an independent association for women. She was critical of the ways that women's question remained as an appendage of the concern of the male leaders of the Indian National Congress. As quoted by Samita Sen, Sarala Devi thought of the men as 'who advertise themselves as champions of the weaker sex, equal opportunities for women, female education and female emancipation ... their pet subjects of oratory at the annual show, but who actually lived in the shade of Manu' (Sen 2000).

Inspired by Sarala Devi, women formed autonomous organizations for themselves. The associations were called Mahila Samitis which were mainly neighbourhood based having an urban character. Although they were small in their sizes, their scope of activities was quite wide. It ranged from imparting elementary education to teaching women on health, hygiene, nutrition and childcare to training women in basic social skill for livelihood purposes (Forbes 1996). Subsequently, a number of women's body emerged in the national scene. First, it was the Women's Indian Association in 1917 in Madras presidency. The National Council of Indian Women was the next to be founded in 1925, affiliated with the International Council of Women. Both the bodies were limited in class and caste composition and were removed from the masses of women.

The most significant women organization, the All India Women's Conference, came up in 1927 out of a conference held in Pune. It was conceived as a platform to build women's movement to demand adult franchise and equal rights for women in health, education, property rights, marriage laws and so on. Ideologically speaking, the initial phase of the reform movement idealized the domestic space by rationalizing the family. The subsequent nationalist discourse of the first half of the 20th century created the archetypal mother figure as a symbolic rallying device for women's assertions. The feminist assertion of maternal power, as propounded by Madame Cama or Sarojini Naidu, conveyed an active intervention of women's agency in transforming all that bad and evil.

Gandhi invoked different imagery of motherhood. Gandhi's politics was to lay emphasis on the nurturing and creative qualities of motherhood as against the aggressive aspects of femininity. As noted by Radha Kumar (1993), Gandhi's feminization of politics was favourably responded to by many feminists. It also drew a large number of women to come out of their private spaces and join Gandhi in mass movements. However, it had its ambivalences.

> His view of the relationship between the sexes was neither fully nor widely accepted by the feminists: while to him the sexes were different but complementary, there was a considerable ambivalence among the feminists on this question ... pre-independence feminists clung with one hand to gender based definitions of themselves while reaching with the other for an existence based on equality and sameness rather than complementarity and difference. (Kumar 1993, 2)

It is true that the Gandhian strategy of invoking India's sacred Hindu legends appealed to a wide section of Hindu women across class and caste, but it excluded the other communities who could not find resonance with the political idiom of mother image. Geraldine Forbes credited the success of Gandhi's idiom to its reliance on traditional gender ideology, which assuaged both men and women of their insecurities (Forbes 1996). Only a few exceptional women influenced by Communist Party of India could take up a radical position to question the stereotyped gender roles. They also questioned the social segregation and discriminatory gender roles. They were revolutionary in the scope by advocating intercommunal and intercaste marriages.

In the 1940s, as the national freedom movement reached its climax, much of the gender issues and women's movements were subsumed by the nationalist movement (Chatterjee 1989). The 1940s was a tumultuous decade with divergences emerging in the women's movement. Even within the radical section, although small in number, there were questions raised about the patriarchal biases of political parties. So a ground was ready for autonomous women's organization to prosper in the next phase of the women's movement.

14.2. CONTEMPORARY FEMINIST IDEAS

14.2.1. The Background

From the 1970s onwards, the women's movement in India became more articulate, visible and focused. But the groundwork for the efflorescence of the women struggles was laid down in the post-Independence years. There was a definite break from the earlier scope of women's issues.

> In post-independence India the contemporary feminist movement began by basing itself firmly on principles of equality and asserting that gender based structures, such as the sexual division of labor oppressed and subordinated women. The difference between men and women was held largely (and by implication 'merely') to be a biological one, which should not affect women's right to equality with men in both public and private spheres. (Kumar 1993, 2)

The initial two decades of the nation-building phase almost put the women's movement into non-existence. It revived in the 1970s with a sharp break from the earlier framework where the women's lives were conceived only in relation to men. According to Radha Kumar, gradually, the earlier feminist assertion receded to the back. Instead of understanding woman as a daughter, the image of working woman was invoked to claim the woman as a subject and maker of the society. There was a change in forms from the wife–mother–power image to that of a working woman who is economically independent. Hence, women at the workplace were conceived as a locus of women's movement.

Post-Independence, the government made attempts through constitution to safeguard women's rights. A number of steps were taken to create opportunities for women, but these were only partial. Only in the 1970s due to the input of left politics in India of various hues, a radical shift to a 'new' understanding of women's oppression emerged along with the emergence of a number of women's organization. The focus of the organizations shifted to the existential material condition of women's exploitation. Radha Kumar listed a number of such organizations which were mostly from Western India and Hyderabad. The declaration of the year 1975 as the International Women's Year by the United Nations gave rise to a number of militant women's organization in Maharashtra. The participants in such organizations were varied from rural and urban poor woman to tribal groups, folk activists to middle-class woman, labourers to students or from radical leftist to Gandhian socialists. The scope of their agitation also ranged from resistance to physical violence to demanding government measures to fix price rise and unscrupulous hoardings. Their modes of agitation also varied from door-to-door campaigning in villages to physically accosting offending husbands, collective bargaining to providing training and technical help to women, militant mass demonstration or hunger strikes to gheraoing government officers and elected representatives.

The salient feature of women's organization and the movement of the late 1970s and the early 1980s was that almost all the organizations were autonomous bodies, not affiliated with political parties. Political parties, even the Left, were considered to be hierarchical, male-dominated and competitive structures. Interestingly, the new women's groups were formed by members drawn from various Left groups only. The urban-educated middle class dominated these new women's movement, and questions about the viability of the autonomous feminist movement were also debated across the country. The question was whether such feminist groups could appropriately represent the mass of women. The generally accepted vision was that these organizations could build up feminist issues and spread them, coordinating with other mass organizations. The city-based feminist campaigns raised not only feminist consciousness but often allied with rural agricultural labourers agitations.

The influence of the leftist ideology and initiatives affected the new awareness among the activist. A class-conscious understanding made the women's groups to see multiple inequalities between not only men and women but also among women. These inequalities were understood as embedded and operationalized by power structures that were historically constituted along the axes of class, caste, tribe, language, religion and region. The biggest women's association in India since the independence All India Democratic Women's Association (AIDWA) was founded in 1981. Out of the experiences of the previous decades, it was constituted with an understanding that without the participation of women in the general democratic movement no real emancipation of women or the emancipation of working people could be achieved (Ranadive 1990).

14.2.2. Campaigns by Women and the State

Post-emergency (1975–1977), a realization dawned onto women activist that the issues of women in India cannot be separated from the wider political struggle for the restoration of civil rights and social transformation. A triadic relationship between the state, women's movement and the tradition brought to the fore a sociological understanding of women's politics and movement. Family was understood as the greatest repository of tradition. The wider state policies that failed to satisfy the just demands for land, employment, health, education and legal rights had their direct bearing on low standards of women's lives. In light of this understanding, certain issue-specific women's campaigns were examined from the post-1977 period by feminist scholars. The major issues that confronted the women's movement in India are (a) anti-dowry campaign, (b) anti-rape campaign, (c) anti-Muslim women's bill campaign and (d) anti-sati campaign (Agnihotri and Palriwala 2001; Kumar 1999).

Although the anti-dowry and anti-rape campaigns were essentially city based, all the four agitations had a nationwide spread and participation of women. All four campaigns brought out the essence of the political trends, which could help us to identify the possible directions as well as hurdles of the women's movement in India.

1. **Anti-dowry campaign:** Although in 1975, the progressive organization of women in Hyderabad for the first time protested against dowry, it fizzled out with the imposition of Emergency. In 1978 and 1979, anti-dowry protest emerged as an important issue across the country. Delhi became the most prominent site of protests against violence inflicted on women for dowries, which led to murders or abetment to suicide.

    In most cases, the dowry harassment led to the death of the woman by fire (being doused and set on fire by husband or in-laws) so that they could be passed off as suicides or accidents. The issue of dowry was taken up first by Mahila Dakshata Samiti; then, it was spread more widely by Stri Sangharsh founded in 1979. One single case of dowry death of Tarvinder Kaur in the same year led to the formation of Nari Raksha Samiti, which led to a massive demonstration and awareness in the city of Delhi.

    A decisive change was brought about by such women agitation as the state and its police were forced to take cognizance and link death by the fire with dowry harassment. It pointed out that many official suicides were actually murder. Reversing the trend of scare, ignominy, helplessness and loneliness, the activists encouraged family, friends and neighbourhood to come up with evidence. They recorded the dying statements of any victim, as well as that of family testimony, to fix the perpetrators as well as push the police into action.

    In their agitations, the women's group unmasked the trauma hidden in the idealized domestic space of the family. The Dahej Virodhi Chetna Manch expanded the scope of the agitation by claiming that dowry is linked with the overall structure of female subordination. The sustained agitation by the Dahej Virodhi Chetna Manch demanding comprehensive reform of women related laws and stringent measures forced the Law Commission to recommend amendments to the Criminal Procedure Code and Indian Evidence Act in 1983. All these made cruelty to a wife a cognizable and non-bailable offence; it redefined cruelty to include mental as well as physical harassment and so on. Overall, the burden of proof was shifted to the accused from the complainant.

    Radha Kumar finds that even with the amendment, the conviction is still hard to come by through Indian courts, as in the course of evidence, most of the cases fall through. The stranglehold of the tradition, the lack of support system deter affected women and their family to depose properly before the court. Also, as most of the dowry deaths are the result of burns, the post-mortem reports find it difficult to conclude that the deaths were from murder. Rajni Palriwala and Indu Agnihotri, on the other hand, find that the moral outcry and public awareness were the definite successes of the movement. The movement really could build up a strong public response and impacted the lawmaking bodies. It also realized the difficulty to get the laws to deliver as expected.

2. **Anti-rape campaign:** Rape is the ultimate exercise of male domination of female, which is used as intimidation as well as a patriarchal tool to dehumanize female and strip them from control of their body. One can obtain the yearly figures of reported cases of rape in India, from the reports published by the Bureau of Police, New Delhi, or the National Crime Record. Over the years, it shows that the incidence of the largest number of rapes occurs inside the home, and they are committed by persons known to the victim. However, women's campaign against the state tends to focus on custodial rapes or cases in public spaces. Although the figures are alarming, incidents of mass rape by the police (mostly as repressive measures inflicted on subaltern uprisings) are not usually covered.

In 1978–1979, two specific incidents which caught the attention of the media and women activists were galvanized into a coordinated national campaign. The two incidents are noted by Radha Kumar (1999) and the further developments on anti-rape agitations showed that even small groups of activists could attain the attention of the large public. While on the one hand, they could secure support from both women and men, on the other, they also ran the risk of political exploitation. Of the two incidents, one is known as the Mathura rape case (Maharashtra) and the other is the Rameeza Bai case (Hyderabad).

In 1972, Mathura, a 16-year old Adivasi girl, was gang-raped by policemen in a police station in Gadchiroli, Maharashtra. The case came to be known as the 'Mathura case'. The Supreme Court of India acquitted the accused in 1978. The court accepted the defence agreement that Mathura had a boyfriend; hence, she is a girl of loose morals. Such a judgement was openly challenged by four leading professors and a legal expert in 1979. In an open letter, Upendra Baxi, Lotika Sarkar, Raghunath Kelkar and Vasudha Dhagamwar challenged the violation of human rights and constitutional provisions. The women's groups agitated by building networks across cities to demand that the state be accounted for the crimes committed by its agents.

In 1979, a 25-year-old woman, Rameeza Bai was gang-raped in a police station, and her husband was murdered in Hyderabad. A popular violent agitation followed as a result. It led to the dismissal of the state government, and a commission was constituted to probe the incident. In 1980, a nationwide demonstration against rape on the women's day, 8 March, led to the formation of the Forum Against Rape in Bombay, which later expanded its scope to be renamed as the Forum Against Oppression of Women.

Protests against police atrocities on women, including rape, attracted wider participation beyond neighbourhood protests. Trade unions and even political parties invested themselves, which often took the shape of using it as a political lever against the rivals. Given the gravity of the crime and the situation, the government promptly introduced radical legislations. However, the more the law changes, the more the things remain the same. In 1988, in the Suman Rani custodial rape case, the Supreme Court judgement fell short of the expectation of the feminists. The purpose of the law got defeated as again the issue of the victim having a lover was hailed as a denominator to reduce the quantum of punishment of the convicted. This infuriated the activists, and the government responded in the face of stiff women's movement by amending the laws. The feminists also debated the definition of rape to widen the understanding of 'sexual assault'.

The agitations faced problems not only because the women's issues were conveniently used by competitive political parties, but the very nature of the issue, social sanction associated with it and the problem of acquiring technically sound pieces of evidence in places away from the coveted urban centres also posed obstacles to such campaigns against rape.

3. **Anti-Muslim women's bill:** In the very decade of the 1970s, known as the women's decade, women's organization got activated on issues affecting women's lives, but the most important ones are governed by various personal laws. For example, issues relating to divorce, maintenance, adoption, custody of child and property are contentious ones as religion-based personal laws are all in favour of men. The path-breaking Shah Bano case brought to the fore the entanglement of the state, fundamentalist forces and women's movement in India.

Trying to save women from the tyranny of the personal laws which are governed by religious precepts, the demand for the Uniform Civil Code was the unanimous campaign by the Committee on the Status of Women in India in 1975. Coincidentally, around the time, the specifics for the Uniform Civil Code were supposed to be worked out in 1985, the Supreme Court's historic decision on Shan Bano case was delivered.

A woman married under Muslim or Hindu law is not entitled to maintenance or seek divorce under secular law. She is bound by the religious laws by which she was married. Sections 125 and 127 of the Code of Criminal Procedure, 1973, ensure entitlement of destitute divorced women to maintenance by their husbands. Abandoned by her husband, Shah Bano, a 75-year-old woman, sought a redressal through Section 125 in the Code of Criminal Procedure, Indian Penal Code. She secured a historic decision in her favour from the Supreme Court.

> It asserted that sec 125 transcended personal law. The court was critical of the way women had traditionally being subjected to unjust treatment, citing statements by Manu, the Hindu lawmaker, and the Prophet as examples of traditional injustice. (Kumar 1999, 361–362)

Under the direction of the court, the government was to frame and realize the constitutional promise of a common or uniform civil code. When the women's organizations were about to celebrate the decisive victory for women, the terms of discourse were altered by fundamentalist forces. Communal passions were ignited to deflect the very cause of women's demand for equality. Fundamentalist forces within different religious communities in collusion with political forces made the issue into a tussle between traditions and Westernized modernists, synonymously called cultural colonialists.

The Shah Bano judgement led to the political reformulation and mobilization under the spectre of communalism. While the judgement directly angered the Muslim fundamentalists, the Hindu fundamentalists already whipped up (prior to the judgement, 1984–1985) across the country a Hindu sentiment over the Babri Masjid in Ayodhya, Uttar Pradesh. Already the 1984 killings of Sikh (the aftermath of the assassination of Indira Gandhi) left its scar with signals of Hindu communalism raising its head. The ruling Congress (I) wavered as it sensed that competing communal sentiments would harm its electoral prospect. The government made a volte-face on extending Section 125 to Muslim women. The bill, which was brought by a Muslim League MP in 1985, was recommended by the President and Muslim Women Bill was enacted. And, as a balance, the government allowed the unlocking of the disputed shrine in Ayodhya for the Hindus in the same year (Agnihotri and Palriwala 2001).

The women's issue of rights was soon subsumed by the discourse of 'community', that is, the fundamentalists were successful in projecting the popular idiom of 'community in danger' to distract the issue away from the feminist assertion. Under duress, Shah Bano surrendered the rights she had 'won' through the Supreme Court. A real woman image was construed as the one who follows faithfully her religious precepts. The problematic for subsequent women's movement was substantively impacted by such communal–fundamentalist discourse (Kumar 1999). Realizing that the Indian State makes compromises with both Hindu and Muslim reactionary elements, a joint petition was made by social reformers, feminists and left-political groups. They argued that all religious-personal laws are tools to deny and subjugate women. So religion should not be allowed to govern man to man or man to woman social relationships. The government made a mockery of the secular credential by asserting that everyone has the right to make their own laws.

The campaign against the government's back tracking galvanized women's activist across the length and breadth of India. All leading women's bodies, including Muslim groups from Maharashtra, Kerala and research institutions built up the movements. In a highly surcharged atmosphere, in Delhi, Janwadi Mahila Samiti carried out the agitation in association with AIDWA to elicit support for the cause, while facing the wrath of the fundamentalist (Mustafa 1986).

4. **Anti-sati campaign:** Immediately, after the controversy over the Muslim women's bill, the 1987 sati incident put the women's question and women's movement under a serious challenge of confronting the 'tradition' and the state. The incident happened in the Deorala village, Rajasthan. Belonging to a Rajput family, Roop Kanwar was dragged out from her hiding, drugged and dressed in bridal attire and put on the funeral pyre of her deceased husband. The Rajput clan of the family celebrated it as an honour for their past tradition. Roop Kanwar projected as a sati was used as a symbol of identity politics (Vaid and Sangari, 1991).

The horrific incident infuriated the progressive canvas of the country. It was not just a stray incident but a meticulously carried out act. It was orchestrated to glorify as well as justify the Rajput identity. Impromptu around the site of the immolation, a Hindu religious ambience of a pilgrimage sprang up. Influential men from the Rajput village formed a trust in the name of Sati Dharam Raksha Samiti and started collecting a huge sum to build a sati temple. The local and state administration was virtually accomplice to the Rajput identity assertion in the glorification of sati. Pro-sati campaigns gathered momentum as head priest of Puri and Banaras argued that practices like sati came under the Hindu personal law. One sees a striking similarity of position with the Muslim clerics who opposed the Shah Bano verdict of the Supreme Court.

Widespread protests and demonstrations against sati worship followed at old temples and in the proposed new sites. AIDWA concentrated more on door-to-door direct campaigns, covering the working-class areas. Among students and teachers, the campaign was overwhelming while the theatre performances of Janwadi Natya Manch in the nook and corner of Delhi city attracted women, especially the widows (Agnihotri and Palriwala 2001). Opposition to sati came from the anti-caste movement as well as Gandhians. The Hindu reformist tradition argued against it. Swami Agnivesh of Arya Samaj openly challenged the head priests to re-examine and debate tradition (Kumar 1999).

Agnihotri and Palriwala observed that the new bill of the Commission of Sati (Prevention) Act, 1987, was a half-hearted effort as it did not categorically dismiss the ideology of sati. The Sati Virodhi Sangharsh Manch criticized the bill as contradictory which failed to take cognizance of sati as a murder. The experience of the women's movement against sati was bitter enough. And women's fight for their rights in India entered a complicated stage thereon. The pro-sati campaign phrased it as 'Hinduism in danger' to depict the feminists as unrepresentative of the 'real' true Hindu women. As studied by Radha Kumar, growing opposition to feminism gathered momentum through pro- Sati campaigns.

14.2.3. Challenges of Women's movement

The campaigns for women's rights in contemporary times have shown that the question for women's lives has to confront different power structures which feed into each other. The important lesson for women's organizations has been to interrogate the male definitions of community. It demands a discursive engagement in laying claims on the familial spaces and re-inventing public cultures (Das 1999). The bedrock of tradition and the vulnerability of the modern state of India make women's mobilization a daunting task for the activists.

Historically, the women's movement has been divided on ideological ground. However, the different organizations and groups came together in joint struggles with a shared notion of a welfare state to address their demands. Instead of being a homogenous group, the contemporary women's movement is a network that includes organized party-based as well as autonomous groups from a wide political spectrum from centrist to the far left.

And assessment of the women's movement inevitably leads one to study its methods and tactics vis-à-vis the state. Radha Kumar has indicated the performance and possibilities of the movement by contextualizing it in the wider political development of the country (Kumar 1999). The points raised are as follows:

1. **About the efficacy of campaigns aimed at the state to enact favourable laws:** One stream insisted on taking up each individual case of violation of women's rights and following them up through all the legal hurdles and intricacies. On a substantive level, Nivedita Menon puts forward the argument that the emancipatory agenda of the women's movement is much lost, the more the rights movement are directed at the state for a legal redressal. The emphasis has to be more on political activism rather than legislation (Mazumdar 2000; Menon 1999).
2. **About rejecting the conventional methods of agitation and demonstrations:** This stream focused on setting up alternate support structures for distressed women. From the early 1980s, women's centres were formed to provide legal and health aid as well as counselling for employment. Subsequently, the scope of the centres was widened to cover all interrelated issues of woman's place in society. The ideological motivation was no longer social welfare but a feminist worldview. Also, the traditionally coded roles of women were re-iterated to make friendship by highlighting the concept of sisterhood.
3. **Use of traditional idioms and images to reclaim women's history and strength:** Since the women's movement had to face the biggest challenge from the fundamentalist forces, who communalized the tradition, the women's movement tried to reclaim the same tradition. Women's power and strength have been sought in myth, folklore, epics that constitute living tradition. Beyond the stereotypical images of suffering, images of women as survivors and warriors are emphasized.
4. **About re-organizing the domestic space:** The domestic and the familial space was re-organized to the advantage of women. This is done by appropriating religious practices, at times, simulating (faking) possession by the goddess to negotiate and rectify erring husbands.
5. **About getting energized by eco-feminism:** Beyond the framework of the conventional feminist movement, the role of women in broader social transformative project served as a source of woman empowerment. Eco-feminism has a paradigm that recognizes that the domination of women and nature are interlinked so much so that women have to lead the movement to arrest the degradation of nature. The connection between the subjugation of women and that of nature is ideological, whereby the ideas, values, beliefs and their representations place women and the non-human world subjugated by men. The commercial developmental policies that led to the depreciation in the hills impacted women's life. It found expression in the environmental movement for forest protection and regeneration in the Garhwal Hills, for example, the Chipko Movement (Agarwal 1992).
6. **About branching out the feminist movement from issue-based groups to distinct organizations:** Efforts were made to build women's unions at workplaces especially in the unorganized sectors. A wide range of activities saw feminist interventions, mainly in the field of art, literature and culture.

In journalism, academia and medicine a better representation of feminist voices ensured a wider audience for women's causes.

7. **About proliferation of women's study centre:** Across the country, special research centres for woman's studies were opened by the University Grants Commission in many universities, post-1980s. The research centres produced not only fresh studies from empirical data on woman's lives in India, but also retrieved woman's writings, autobiography, memoirs and so on from the past. Regular conferences and seminars are organized by the Centre for Women's Development Studies (Delhi), SNDT Women's University (Mumbai) and many others to popularize the subject.
8. **About the realization of the important link between feminism and medical practices:** Against harmful or unaware practices pertaining to pregnancy and reproductive behaviour, many medical organizations worked in tandem with women's organizations. They raised women's health issues to a feminist understanding of caring for women's bodies. Campaigns were effective in checking the abuse of medicines, amniocentesis (test for detecting sex of the foetuses) and so on.
9. **About facing the communal counter-movements:** Women's movement had to face the divisive design of a number of Hindu chauvinist groups who used their women's wings to further the communal agenda. Since almost all the women's issues are inextricably linked to religious tradition, the women activists had to face the anger of the fundamentalists. Rumours, slander campaign along communal and sexual abuses are regularly used in all such counter-movements. Especially during the sati incident, militant counter-demonstrations and processions usurped the language of rights. The arrival of the new consciousness amongst women altered women's attitudes, and as a reaction, the traditionalist increasingly resorted to communal idioms in a hostile manner.

The convergence of the nation, religion, violence and women's rights has emerged as the complicated theoretical challenge before the women's movement. The success of the progressive women's movement has been tentative to resist or anticipate communal violence. At the very formation of the nation, the gendered nature of communal violence has been researched by historians (Sarkar and Butalia 1995). The history of Partition has shown the use of rape and mass-scale abduction of women as the political weapon to establish domination. Communal images of the Partition are often resorted to by the Rightist forces to mobilize popular participation against the women's movement.

In present times, the violence against women and its correlation with politics, religion and ethnicity have presented a stark reality. The victims face both societal and judicial prejudices due to multiple disabilities—religion, caste, economic status and so on (Murthy and Dasgupta 2013). The 'nude' protests by middle-aged women of Manipur in 2004 against the infamous Manorama case brings home the fertile undertaking of women's awareness and protest methods. Manorama, a 35-year-old woman, was raped and murdered by paramilitary personnel of Northeast India. Through trials and tribulations, the women's movement in India has given expression to a multitude of issues that confront women's life—from the equity in domestic space to the assertion of civil rights in public spheres.

CONCLUSION

The women's movement in India has evolved over a long period of time. In terms of form and content, too, the women's movement has matured to encompass the widest range of issues that variously and independently impact the lives of women in contemporary India. It exhibits a horizontal spread of women's assertions through a combination of autonomous groups or professional groups to women's wings of political parties. Vertically, it reaches from the grassroots rural activism to representation in the higher echelons of power and lawmaking bodies.

In earlier times, women's issues and rights were represented by male social reformers and subsequently by upper-class male nationalist leaders. Gradually, by the end of the 19th century and beyond, women came out of their domestic confinement. First, it was the upper caste/class women, but mass participation started taking place in the first half of the 20th century. Women found their autonomous voices and representation with the formation of women's organizations. The demands for equality and honour metamorphosed to rights for self-determination as the women's movement progressed. The nationalist discourse and the freedom movement subsumed the women's question for a while, but post-Independence years saw a revival of the women's movement. The belief and reliance on State policies gradually faded, as the decade of the 1970s witnessed a flurry of radical women activism. The report on women's condition, *Towards Equality* (1974–1975), commissioned by the United Nation, brought out the gross discriminatory conditions of women's lives in India.

Various women's groups of different ideological orientation emerged, but first, it was the city-based feminist groups who took to the streets. The urban-based movements addressed the glaring issues of rape and dowry. The movement could stir the government to enact protective laws and also energize a wide cross-section of women to activism. The movement encountered the hold of tradition and religion as implicated in women's lives in India.

The women's movement looked beyond the repressive years of 1975–1977 (Emergency) to revive itself and had to engage with the Shah Bano case (Muslim women's bill) and the anti-sati agitation (Roop Kanwar case). These two agitations were more complex as they brought to the fore the intricate relation between religion, tradition and the state. The women's movement had to weather the bedrock of tradition, the stranglehold of religion and the vulnerability of the state to mobilize women. While seeking relief and justice from the Indian state, the women's group had to parallelly build an autonomous movement to carry forward their emancipatory mission. The spectre of growing communalism has made things difficult for the women's movement, but it has been successful to explore new avenues to expand its scope. The new networks of women's groups across the globe and the enriched understanding of women's issues are the visible gains of the movement.

A distinct new phase in the women's movement is its flexible character to accommodate all shades of democratic and progressive forces. The realization of the multiple power structures as responsible for the subjugation of women across caste, class, religion or regions made the women's movement to synchronize with many parallel trade union, peasants or workers movement. A feminist intervention in orthodox mass movements is visible in contemporary India. The gains are incremental for women's movement across India. The women's movement can be best understood as one significant burgeoning task to claim citizen's rights to participate in every form of public affairs, especially as equals in the development process.

> **Points for Classroom Discussion**
>
> - The classical idea of womanhood in India
> - The patrilineal construction of woman in India
> - The women's question in colonial times
> - Challenges of the women's movement in India
> - A brief history of some contemporary women's movement
> - The gains and failures of the women's movement

GLOSSARY

Dowry: A system that makes it mandatory for a bride's family to give cash or kind to the groom's family as a pre-condition for marriage.

Eco-feminism: An approach in feminism that sees the degradation of women and nature as an entangled one.

Feminist: One who believes in social movement and ideology that fights for the political, economic and social rights of women.

Patrilineal: Relationship when traced through the father or male descent line.

Sati: Originally meant a woman who performed the act of immolating herself after her husband's death, claimed to be an ancient Hindu tradition.

Symbolic order: Essentially used in psychoanalytic theories that signify a universal order encompassing all human existence which shapes our identities and our destinies.

REFERENCES

Agarwal, B. 1992. 'The Gender and Environment Debate: Lessons from India.' *Feminist Studies* 18, no. 1: 119–158.

Agnihotri, I., and Rajni P. 2001. 'Tradition, The Family, and The State: Politics of Women's Movement in the Eighties.' In *Gender and Nation*, edited by Nira Yuval-Davis. New Delhi: Nehru Memorial Museum and Library.

Altekar, A. S. 1987. *The Position of Women in Hindu Civilization*. New Delhi: Motilal Banarsidass.

Chakravarti, U. 1999. 'Beyond the Altekerian Paradigm: Towards a New Understanding of Gender Relations in Early Indian History.' In *Readings in Early Indian History*, edited by Kumkum Roy. New Delhi: Manohar.

Chatterjee, P. 1989. 'The Nationalist Resolution of The Women's Question.' In *Recasting Women: Essays in Colonial History*, edited by Kumkum Sangari and Sudesh Vaid. New Delhi: Kali for Women.

Das, V. 1999. 'Communities as Political Actors: The Question of Cultural Rights'. In *Gender and Politics in India*, edited by N. Menon. New Delhi: Oxford University Press.

Dube, L. 1988. 'On the Construction of Gender: Hindu Girls in Patrilineal India.' In *Socialisation, Education and Women: Explorations in Gender Identity*, edited by K. Chanana. New Delhi: Orient Longman.

Forbes, G. 1996. *Women in Modern India, New Cambridge History of India.* Cambridge: Cambridge University Press.

Jayant, A., and I. Rothermund. 1989. 'Women, Emancipation and Equality.' *Economic & Political Weekly* 24, no. 30 (July).

Karlekar, M. 1991. *Voices from Within: Early Personal Narratives of Bengali Women.* New Delhi: Oxford University Press.

Kumar, R. 1993. *A History of Doing: An Illustrated Account of Movements for Women's Rights and Feminism in India 1800–1990.* London: Verso.

———. 1999. 'From Chipko to Sati: The Contemporary Indian Women's Movement.' In *Gender and Politics in India*, edited by N. Menon. New Delhi: Oxford University Press.

Mazumdar, V. 2000. 'Political Ideology of the Women's Movement's Engagement with Law.' CWDS Occasional Papers no 34. New Delhi. Available at: https://www.cwds.ac.in/wp-content/uploads/2016/09/PoliticalIdeology.pdf (accessed on 18 February 2021).

Menon, N., ed. 1999. 'Introduction.' *Gender Politics in India.* New Delhi: Oxford University Press.

Murthy, L., and R. Dasgupta. 2013. *Our Pictures, Our Words: A Visual Journey through The Women's Movement.* New Delhi: Zubaan.

Mustafa, S. 1986. 'Behind the Veil'. *The Telegraph,* Calcutta, 2 March 1986.

Ranadive, V. 1990. 'Feminists and Women's Movement.' In *Feminism: Indian Debates*, edited by Krishna Maithreyi. New Delhi: Research Center for Women's Studies.

Sarkar, T., and U. Butalia. 1995. *Women and Right-Wing Movements: Indian Experiences.* New Delhi: Zed Books.

Sen, S. 2000. 'Toward a Feminist Politics? The Indian Women's Movement in Historical Perspective.' The World Bank Development Research Group/Poverty Reduction and Economic Management Network. Available at: https://asutoshcollege.in/Study_Material/towardsfeministpolitics.pdf (accessed on 18 February 2021).

Vaid, S., and K. Sangari. 1991. 'Institutions, Beliefs, Ideologies: Widow Immolation in Contemporary Rajasthan'. *Economic & Political Weekly* 26, no. 16: WS2–WS8.

CHAPTER 15

Ethnic Movements

LEARNING OUTCOMES

- To understand ethnicity as an identity
- To explore the development of ethnic identity in politics
- To study the Assam Movement as a special case of ethnic movement
- To recognize the dimensions of accommodation and confrontation in a diverse society

Keywords: Social movement, ethnicity, ethnic movement, mobilization, immigrants, ethnic politics

INTRODUCTION

Cultural differences are the markers of multi-ethnic existence. For a country like India, ethnicity has assumed an immense importance given the country's diverse linguistic, religious and racial composition. The nation-building process of post-Independence India has experienced ethnic assertions and often the process of development created a material condition for ethnic conflict. The differential sense of treatment and the benefits from the state by a multi-ethnic nation has given rise to collective action premised on ethnic identity.

Social movements for countries like India primarily aimed at achieving Independence. The thrust was to secure civil rights and political equality. The very accomplishment of Independence ensured a democratic space for social movement of various hues to prosper. Such a self-reproduction of democracy tends to expand its scope. Movements based on ethnic identity emerged in this historical context of post-colonial India. Intimately linked with the process of nation-building, ethnicity has offered a fertile undertaking to re-evaluate the gains of equal political opportunity and access to resources.

Major ethnic movements in India since Independence are prompted by sociocultural particularism with a distinct sense of economic discrimination. The political dimensions of these movements are varied, but they indicate that not all situations of powerlessness experienced by an ethnic group necessarily give rise to ethnic movements. An ethnic consolidation in terms of sharing the same sense of being discriminated is always provided by political leadership, with a political goal of maximizing the aspirations in a competitive political structure.

Social movements premised on ethnic identity have taken many forms in India. The sovereign state of India faces a threat when religion-based communal assertion takes a form of ethnic identity. Mutual mistrust between two communities gets aggravated recurrently in modern India due to a surge of nationalism with a religious connotation. On the other hand, India has seen linguistic consciousness leading to a distinct ethnic identity, resulting in the creation of linguistic regional states. Such movements have coexisted with the idea of unity of India as a multicultural society.

A major challenge for the Indian nation-state arises when ethnic identity takes the form of ethno-nationalism. Claims for separate nationalities by different ethnic groups from time to time (Kashmiris, Punjab of the 1970s and 1980s, and Naga movement in the north-east) have resulted in secessionist movements. Natives versus 'outsiders' strife in a plural society like India has given rise to regionalism. Some ethnic movements have given rise to a separate state within the union of India, for example, the creations of Jharkhand from Bihar, Telangana from Andhra Pradesh, Uttarakhand from Uttar Pradesh, or Chhattisgarh from Madhya Pradesh are instances of ethnic tension. Such regional aspirations couched on ethnicity may be due to the perceived threat of being assimilated into a dominant sociocultural order or the sense of being deprived from the gains of development. Another source of such regionalism is the nativistic drive which posits itself against immigrants. Assam, the north-eastern state, has been experiencing this kind of ethnic strife for a long time. For any multicultural society, the dynamics of ethnic identity and politics serves as a signifier of its political flexibility and persistence.

15.1. POLITICS OF ETHNICITY

15.1.1. Discourse on Ethnicity

Ethnicity is an expression of having a distinct ethnic identity. Conventionally, ethnic is understood as a timeless distinction of mankind based on race and descent. The existence of an ethnic group is a prior condition for such a sense to develop, but that does not mean that ethnicity will inevitably emanate whenever there is an ethnic group. It is only under certain conditions that the sense of ethnic identity finds its expression. One can understand ethnicity as follows: '...the process of formation and reformation of consciousness of identity (real or supposed) in terms of one or more social-cultural-political symbols of domination/subjugation of a group(s) or community by another that emerge out of the processes of assimilation, acculturation, interaction, competition and conflict' (Ghosh 2003, 223).

The term 'ethnicity' is derived from the Greek word *ethnos or ethnikos*. In Greek usage, ethnos means nation, whereas the adjectival form ethnikos refers to a people's collective, united on the basis of some shared living and common physical or sociocultural attributes. The term has acquired a new connotation to mean the native people in the context of a growing wave of ethnic politics across the world. Ethnic politics then is understood as a politics of assertion on the part of 'others' resisting their subordination/domination or exclusion by the nation. Although ethnicity may be used to analyse cultural politics of domination, liberating meaning is generally more in vogue in contemporary times. In post-colonial societies like India, where nation and state formation are coterminous, ethnicities can be better realized as follows:

> ...largely the product, rather than the foundation, of nation-states...The ever more powerful structures of central state control-be they colonial or autochthonous, imperial or national-are what germinate and motivate the new need for ethnic autonomy, and even, in many cases, the actual sense of ethnic identity on which the latter is predicated. (Guideri and Pellizi 1988, 7–8)

In contemporary academic studies, the concept of ethnicity is mainly dominated by American studies, due to its multicultural plural society. The elements that are highlighted by these studies as salient aspects of ethnicity are a sense of distinctiveness, a common descent and a shared culture. The studies are exploring the issues of assimilation and, later on, due to rising ethnic unrest in multicultural societies, the ethnic groups are examined as marginal and minority groups (Glazer and Moynihan 1963). Originally a sociologist and a social anthropologist, Edward Shils and Clifford Geertz, respectively, emphasized the primordial attributes of an ethnic group as a permanent feature of human nature, which helped the ethnic groups to self-perpetuate biologically. Primordialism, in a way, naturalizes ethnic groups with their strong loyalty to group solidarity.

Subsequently, against the primordialist and instrumentalist understanding, constructivist perspective tried to place ethnicity as a product of specific historical circumstances. Primordialism was thought to provide an essentialized model that could not account for the splurge of ethnic movements in recent times. In fact, political scientists like Paul Brass observes that certain attributes of ethnicity need not be fixed once for all. The fluidity of identity is becoming more evident in modern times when we encounter currents of immigration and subjective feelings of attachment that are developing among ethnic groups in a newer ecosystem.

The dynamics of ethnicity are best captured when understood as a relational concept, premised on the 'we and them'. Such ethnic identity is a product of social interactions, as identities are generated and transformed in the context of a new environment and circumstances of interaction (Barth 1969). In the new society, often designated as the 'network society', when identities become more open and less bounded by ascribed ones, a social constructionist perspective on ethnicity prevails. Such a society is also a knowledge society where knowledge is constituent of one's identity. Ethnic meanings and identity assertions become the function of sociopolitical contingencies. Nevertheless, there is no gainsaying in stretching the ideas of ethnic identity as free floating, free from social anchorage.

The conception of boundary as a defining criterion for self-definition by ethnic groups may not lead us to study the emergence of ethnic movements in modern times. In the South Asian context, drawing on his studies of the Shiv Sena Movement (1960s–1970s) in Maharashtra and the Akali politics of the 1980s in Punjab, Dipankar Gupta is dismissive of the 'boundary criterion' to understand ethnicity-based agitation. Cultural markers and ethnic identities are anthropological maxims but are insufficient to explain macro-structural ethnopolitical identities (Gupta 1991).

15.1.3. Ethnicity and Politics

Any social movement, historically, is a unified social action undertaken by a deprived group to transform or even revive a given social order. Sociologists such as Sidney Tarrow, Herbert Blumer, Neil Smelser, Porta Della and others have variously defined social movements. Since the middle of the 20th century, sociologist have analysed them as a response of the deprived or subjugated social groups against the very structure of such deprivations. Collective mobilization is the key concept to appreciate any social movement (Oommen 2010). In his two edited volumes on social movements, T. K. Oommen views mobilization as the crucial engagement and participation for achieving the goals pursued by any movement. Mobilization is a matter of crystallization of collective consciousness. Ethnicity provides a fertile vehicle for such 'crystallization of collective consciousness' leading to primordial collectivities that are different from civil collectivities. Civil collectivities are the result of workers, students, peasants and so on.

Contemporary studies on the linkage between ethnicity and politics emphasize on the constructed or invented nature of ethnicity. The essentializing model of identity politics is refuted by treating ethnicity as another form of resource mobilization. The very term of ethnicity is stretched to signify an imagined community. Ethnic politics in this sense is not a predetermined, fixed ones-for-all category.

> ...the mobilization of the assertion of the ethnic group in the political arena to defend and slash or sustain economic, political and cultural interests and wrest more concessions. In the process it becomes a device as well as a focus for mobilizing the members of the group into social and political action. (Phadnis 1989, 1)

Urmila Phadnis in her study has indicated that ethnicity is intrinsic in the South Asian sociopolitical context, but inter-ethnic groups relations are not inevitably conflictual. It is the politicization of ethnic communities as well as the ethnicization of politics that has given rise to ethnic consciousness and conflicts. Paul Brass has advanced an elite model of ethnicization. In terms of elite competition, he presents the politics of ethnic identity formation.

> 'The cultural forms, values, and practices of ethnic groups become political resources for elites in competition for political power and economic advantage...ethnic communities are created and transformed by particular elites in modernizing and in post-industrial societies undergoing dramatic social change' (Brass 1991, 15–25).

Such an exclusive reliance on the elite would be a simplistic explanation of ethnicization and its mobilization. Also, the way elites emerge as a result of in-group dynamics within ethnic groups needs to be examined. In a multi-ethnic situation, the common source of ethnic identification is caused by a failed assimilation, which in turn leads to ethnic mobilization. Eventually, the formation and mobilization of such an ethnic identity can be seen as a strategy to stake claim to resources and achieve it collectively. Commenting on the Indian situation, Rajni Kothari links ethnic movements with the aspiration of the marginalized people. The indigenous people whenever left out of the 'mainstream' gives rise to the problem of national integration. Kothari examines ethnic upsurges as cultural assertions. India's path of modernization, which has a centralizing and homogenizing tendency premised on techno-instrumental model, is considered as the primary reason for ethnic movements (Kothari 1988).

Political anthropologist Hamza Alavi's observation of ethnic politics in the Indian subcontinent is incisive. The idea of some 'pre-given' ethnic attributes to mark the boundaries is dismissed by him. Any given objective criterion, like religion, maybe replaced by some other like language in a changed situation with different sets of interests. Boundaries are always open to re-alignment (Alavi 1989). Ethnic grassroots discontents, according to Dipankar Gupta, are structurally caused. From his own study of ethnic movements in India, he poses some crucial questions as to why only some particular ethnic groups are politically invested and not all others. That too, at certain points of history, such conflicts are manifested (Gupta 1991).

Ethnic politics in India is a result of deliberate and calculated manipulation by political heads. Secular civic demands are converted over a period of time to ethnic demands. Like the demands for employment and jobs for the local youths of Maharashtra got communalized by the Shiv Sena Movement in Bombay. Nativism was invoked to whip up passion of Maratha identity in a metropolis like Bombay. Similarly, demands for better water distribution, territorial demarcation and the city of Chandigarh for Punjab were ethnicized in the Khalistan Movement in Punjab. Religious identity was fused with regional identity by some Sikh leaders to whip up the extreme position of ethno-nationalism in Punjab (Gupta 1982, 1985). Apparently timeless, pre-given objective criteria determining ethnic re-negotiated or re-drawn in terms of politics. By referring to the work of political anthropologist Stanley J. Tambiah, Gupta insisted on a processual perspective to analyse ethnic identities as they are fluid enough to accommodate new elements. Ethnic violence is located at the defects in the civil society (Tambiah 1989).

Ethnicity is finally an unstable category, at times constructed or imagined. Like the nation, it is an imagined community and therefore a social practice. Therefore, ethnic imageries are contextual. The context of particular stage of sociopolitical development shapes the modes of ethnicization. Ethnicity in politics is a matter of ethnicities in relation, it is implicated by the role of the state in such relations.

15.2. THE ASSAM MOVEMENT

15.2.1. Historical Background

As a plural society categorized by a diverse population exhibiting a multitude of ethnic identities, India has been subject to a variety of ethnic assertions. Historically, the nature of the politicization of ethnic identities has varied in terms of the conditions and context of such ethnic mobilization. While the feeling of insecurity among minority identities of being assimilated into the dominant culture has resulted in ethnic tension, there is also another dimension of ethnic turmoil. That is, the feeling of insecurity due to the loss of indigenous identity as a result of the continuous influx of immigrants from neighbouring countries. The partition of India in 1947 carries the germ of the problem of immigration from East Pakistan (now Bangladesh) leading to ethnic tension in the north-east region. They have taken violent political turns from time to time. The Assam Movement from 1979 is the most notable one which exhibits the interlinkages of ethnic diversity, electoral politics and ethnic mobilization.

Migration in different phases of time into the north-east created political instability in the region. Local communities were pitted against the migrants, who are considered as 'outsiders'. The immigrants from East Pakistan and also migrants from other parts of India are seen as encroachers. 'Outsiders' were seen as competitors on scarce resources, employment opportunities and even political power. The Assam Movement brought to the fore this issue of 'outsiders' in the national politics from 1971. Sanjiv Baruah's study of the Assam Movement (2010) shows the veracity of the theoretical contention that ethnicity as politics needs to be understood in terms of the fluidity of ethnic boundaries. More than the genuineness of grassroots sentiments, the mobilization of ethnic identities is the product of political manoeuvrings. The issue of 'outsiders', especially the immigration issue, could not emerge as a major political controversy since Independence till 1979. The ethnic Assamese leadership campaigned for a unilingual state. They also demanded preferential treatment from the government, but the state reorganization policy of the Government of India through the creation of the linguistic state of Assam contained doubts and insecurities of the ethnic Assamese.

The ethnic Assamese is constituted of many diverse ethnicities. The cultural policy issues of the ethnic Assamese were accepted by the Bengali Muslim immigrants, whereas they were opposed by the Hindu immigrants. Apart from an occasional burst of the issue of illegal immigration, the situation was under control as within all major political parties, especially the Congress, there was a sharing of the interest. There was an aggregation and sharing of interests given the diverse demographic character of Assam. The divisions ran through different axes. Overall, the Assamese population has two broad divisions: Hindus and Muslim, and the tribes. The tribes are of three types: hill tribes, plain tribes and tea plantation (workers) tribes. The Bengali community also has Hindus and Muslims. And Muslim Bengalis are of two categories: immigrants and non-immigrants.

The coalition of diverse ethnic groups provided stability to Assam. The slow and continuous demographic transformation showed up in a by-election in one parliamentary constituency where the concentration of immigrants was high. It indicated a huge increase in the number of voters. Large-scale illegal immigration has been a matter of fact and it led to the formation of the All Assam Students' Union (AASU), which was not affiliated to any party. The movement took shape as one against illegal migration, against faulty voter's list that included the names of illegal immigrants. The year 1979 could be taken as the watershed in Assam's ethnic tension-ridden history, with the formation of the AASU and the subsequent constitution of the Assam Gana Sangram Parishad (AGSP). AGSP is a coalition of all those favouring the agenda of 'detection, disenfranchisement and deportation' of foreigners (the immigrants of Bangladesh [the erstwhile East Bengal]). A series of protest movements started with a state-wide strike call. Popular support gathered momentum through various modes of protest.

15.2.2. Demands and Protest

Demographic transformation of Assam was the primary background for the Assam Movement. The movement for ethnic identity has gone through many phases. Initially, the nationalistic policies of the Assam Official Language Act of 1960 assured that the Assamese and local Muslims were part of the Assamese 'we feeling'. Later, the influx of immigrants from Bangladesh made the ethnic Assamese insecure and they demanded the deportation of illegal immigrants.

For the beginning, the AASU and the AGSP leadership demanded 1951 to be the cut-off year to deport 'foreigners'. Later on, they changed it to 1961. Hence, the revision of the electoral rolls was insisted on that basis, along with the reservation for the indigenous Assamese in education and employment. The AASU and AGSP successfully articulated the insecurity of the Assamese and other diverse ethnic communities in the face of the influx of immigrants and the changing ethno-demographic composition. The lopsided developmental model of India, whereby many north-eastern Indian states feel discriminated against, despite being rich in natural resources, acted as a catalyst in this scenario of insecurity, fear and distrust. Explicit Assamese chauvinism developed and found expression in popular mass movements. A major form of protest was disobedience of government orders.

The main plank of the Assam Movement was to disrupt the institution of education and governance. Existing political parties and their leadership was boycotted. Even elected state governments were not recognized as legitimate. However, the first phase of the movement, which lasted from mid-1979 to mid-1980, was not ostensibly violent. In fact, it was full of optimism with popular participation by every section of the ethnic Assamese. The technique of *Satyagraha* was adopted. During the initial years, the movement prospered under the Janata Party rule at the centre. Government offices and officials were all involved in the upsurge, as most of the executives were ethnic Assamese. The scope of the movement expanded further as the agitators stepped up the scale to economic blockade of all raw materials (crude oil, plywood and so on) from Assam to the rest of the country.

> With enthusiastic support for the demands of the movement by major sectors of Assamese intellectuals and cultural life—for example, literary societies, cultural associations, newspapers, magazines, and school and college teachers' associations...the Assam Movement had extremely broad support among the ethnic Assamese...with displays of distinctive Assamese cultural and historical symbols, acquired the appearance of a state-wide cultural festival. (Baruah 2010, 194–195)

As the movement stepped up, a sense of mistrust developed among other ethnic groups. First, all the East Bengali immigrants felt threatened, both Hindu and Muslim, irrespective of the historical context of immigration, all of them were marked as 'Bangladeshi'. Second, immigrants from other states of India too felt the brunt of the supposedly 'son of the soil' movement. Third, the tea plantation workers, mainly tribals from other states, who whole-heartedly supported the AASU and AGSP during the initial phase, started opposing the intermittent strikes of the tea gardens. Finally, the most significant development was the formation of the All Assam Minority Students' Union (AAMSU), a new organization, in 1980. To contest the AASU, both Hindu and Muslim East Bengali immigrant students came under the banner of AAMSU to ensure that all immigrants who came before 1971 be given citizenship status. They resisted the hounding of minorities by the Assam Movement. The AAMSU appeared as another party to negotiate ethnic demands with the central government.

The central government acknowledged the Assam Movement and its representative leaders. Solutions were sought on the negotiation table. The Indian government had to consider diplomatic relations with its friendly neighbour Bangladesh, which had denied any illegal immigrants from Bangladesh to India. It was a sensitive issue for the government to treat Hindu immigrants as illegal or to consider Hindus as 'refugees' and Muslims as 'immigrants'. These considerations were of national importance to the ruling government. So the government agreed in 1982, after many rounds of negotiations, to accept 1971 as the cut-off year, that is, all those who crossed over after 1971 were to be deported. Indian citizenship would be conferred to those who came between 1951 and 1961. The status of those who came between 1961 and 1971 continued to be the bone of contention as through a previous negotiation the government planned to rehabilitate without deporting them. The biggest issue remained: what kind of documents would be entertained to detect the year of immigration (Baruah 2010).

Not much headway could be made on the ground, and the leaders of the movement tried to intensify the agitation realizing the futility of negotiations. On the other hand, the government used strong arm tactics to retrieve the legitimacy of its institutions and strategically tried to wean away the other ethnic subgroups to destabilize the Assamese ethnic coalition. The ground was laid for the violent turn of the Assam Movement.

BOX 15.1
Criticality of Ethnicity

We should also bear in mind the fact that the ethnic option is one amongst many, and like other political options it has its swings-its ups and downs.' To believe that we are now firmly in the ethnic age is to seal off history with biography. There is a lot of vanity in this and a sense of self-importance in the raking of such a position. The Hungarian poet-philosopher Petofi had once said, 'despair...is vanity'.

Source: Gupta (1991).

15.2.3. Violent Phase and State Response

As the ethnic situation was becoming more conflict-ridden and communalized, some ethnic Assamese intellectuals and political personalities voiced their concerns. At the very indications of the ethnic cooperative life getting vitiated, many democratic and Left political parties clearly started opposing the Assam Movement. They reasoned in favour of 25 March 1971 for the detection of illegal immigrants. As a result, all the Left political parties and their frontal organizations came under murderous attacks by the Assam Movement agitators.

Time and again, in the face of continuous disobedience and defiance of state governments, president rule had to be imposed intermittently. First, under Anwara

Taimur in 1980, then under Keshab Gogoi's term in 1982 and finally under Hiteswar Saikia's rule in 1983, three Congress (I)-led state governments were formed. However, in the face of stiff opposition, the first two state assemblies had to be dissolved. The Saikia government was dissolved in 1985 as part of the Assam Accord of 1985.

With the escalating violence on the streets, the response of the state was multipronged. The nomination of Anwara Taimur, a Muslim elected from a heavily East Bengal immigrant constituency as chief minister in 1980, or the propping up of Keshab Gagoi or Hiteswar Saikia, both from the *Ahom* caste, was indication of the state policy to wreck in fissures in the Assamese ethnic consolidation. Historically, as a distinct ethnic Assamese caste, the *Ahoms* nourished a separate *Ahom* awareness form the rest of the ethnic Assamese identity. With Anwara Taimur as chief minister, the ethnic Assamese Muslims' attitude towards the movement altered. More so, the killings of Muslims during violence drew the Muslims out of the movement, who earlier wholeheartedly supported the movement. Whereas the ethnic upper caste of *Ahom* was identified by the state as the potential weak link in the ethnic coalitions, by making chief ministers from the same caste, it tried to weaken the ethnic coalition.

If weaning away ethnic groups from the coalition was a political manoeuvre, cocrcion and repressive measures were the other tools adopted by the Anwara Taimur government. From the government bureaucracy, all the sympathizers of the movement were identified and hounded off. By filling up with only Muslim gazetted officers, an apparent de-Assamization of state bureaucracy was resorted to by the state government as the Taimur government went for an offensive. The subsequent Gagoi administration was less repressive, but the President's rule virtually turned Assam into an armed zone of conflict. Cleansing the locals from administration and bringing the paramilitary forces from outside the state, the central government tried to assert its legitimacy.

Subsequently, the legitimacy exercise was insisted upon finally by the Saikia government by showing earnestness to remove from the electoral rolls all post-1971 immigrants and stopping the future influx of immigrants. It continued with its political manoeuvres as well. It created new administrative districts and subdivisions to upgrade small towns. Protest against all government moves fell to mobilize or inspire locals as they felt that government measures as enabling. From the Anglicized spelling of the capital city as Gauhati, the Saikia government changed its spelling to Guwahati to instil a symbolic sense of pride for the Assamese people.

The net result of state policies created cracks in the ethnic coalition while the Muslim members of the AASU demanded a clear understanding of foreign illegal immigration. Second, the tribals of the plains distanced themselves from the ethnic Assamese on the question of boycott of elections. The tribals insisted on their distinctiveness and the Bodos demanded their rights, which included the recognition of Bodo as an official associate language and the adoption of the Roman script in place of the Assamese script for writing. Demands for the creation of autonomous district regions for tribals of the plains were floated. The government patronized the Bodo Sahitya Sabha as a counter to the Assam Sahitya Sabha. The Assam Sahitya Sabha and other such cultural institutions realized the cost of involvement with the movement as government's patronage of such cultural fronts shrunk.

In the entire trajectory of the Assam Movement, the question of election took the centre stage. While the leaders of the Assam Movement always boycotted the election to prove the illegitimacy of the elected governments, the centre tried to conduct it somehow with the help of central forces and paramilitary to refute the claims of the movement. The 1983 election saw severe violence between the supporters of the election and the opponents of it. Every time, the centre confronted the 'power capability' of the movement's leadership by conducting the election.

The movement's power capability lay on the streets since it could mobilize the ethnic Assamese almost to a person, but the same power capability cannot be translated into electoral strength because of the state's ethnic diversity and transformed demographic reality. (Baruah 2010, 197)

Ethnic settlement patterns naturally had a bearing on the voter participation and election results. The voting percentage was high not only in such assemblies where Bengalis immigrant population was numerically more, but it was high in Assamese bastions also. The anti- and pro-election dimension was exhibited by other ethnic subgroups and disgruntled tribal groups too. The result was an internecine blood bath. The pattern of violence did not strictly follow any ethnic divisions because the nature of ethnic boundaries and coalitions was in a flux, not steady.

Of all the brutal killings, the massacre of Bengali Muslims in Nellie (a central Assam village) on 18 February 1983 by a rioting mob of Hindu Assamese shocked the nation. It had international repercussions too, as in a systematic manner Nellie and 13 other villages were surrounded by armed mobs, which massacred over 1,800 men, women and children, as per the official record. It was a total failure of the state which heavily deployed the CRPF, which had no idea of local terrains or language to avert the violence being let loose (Kimura 2013). In fact, reports by on-field journalists suggested that despite prior intelligence reports of the massacre, it was unheeded by the state administration. However, the Nellie mayhem was not the only one, but the most gruesome one. As the Assam Movement turned into a violent inter-ethnic one, a number of such incidents made Assam a killing ground. The state response was repressive, making Assam a battlefield zone.

15.2.4. Moderation and Accommodation—The Assam Accord

Taking note of all the angles that arose during the ethnic movement in Assam, constitutional and legal provisions, international relations, national priority and humanitarian values, on 15 August 1985, the historic Assam Accord was signed. After several rounds of talks between the Government of India and the movement leaders, the accord was signed at the behest of the then Prime Minister Rajiv Gandhi with the AASU and AAGSP leaders on the foreign national issue.

The salient points of the agreement are as follows:

1. On the condition of restoration of normalcy and cooperation by the agitating groups, the central government resolved to address the issue of the detection and deletion of foreigners from the electoral roll.
2. All immigrants from Bangladesh on or after 25 March 1971 shall continue to be detected and deleted from the electoral rolls and deported. This was an earlier central government offer too.
3. For the purpose of detection and deletion of illegal aliens, 1 January 1966 shall be the base data and year. All persons who came to Assam prior to 1 January 1966 shall be recognized with all citizenship rights.
4. Immigrants, who came to Assam after 1 January 1966 (inclusive) and up to 24 March 1971, shall be detected for deletion of names from the electoral

rolls in force. After their disenfranchisement, they are to be legitimized in phases after the expiry of 10 years following the date of detection.
5. Assam's international border with Bangladesh shall be made secure against all future infiltration by erection of physical barriers and so on.
6. Constitutional, legislative and administrative safeguards, as may be appropriate, shall be provided to protect, preserve and promote the culture, social, linguistic identity and heritage of the Assamese people (United Nations Peace Accord Archives 1985).

The agreement was a result of a hard-worked moderation exercise from both sides. The Assamese ethnic hardliners had to realistically assess the ground situation of wavering popular support for them and growing divisions in the movement. Since 1984, agitation leaders insisted in their National Conventions the need to regenerate the awareness of the Assamese identity. They realized the need to acknowledge the ethnic diversity of the state and to provide a united sociocultural–political platform. The intellectual input to the movement stressed the need to be inclusive and to shun narrow ethnocentrism as well as communalism.

The prospects for negotiation also brightened due to an accommodative stance of the government. It started with the Saikia government's gestures. The very act of the central government of leaving the state government out of the negotiation table and the decision to dissolve the state assembly during the agreement signing showed the earnestness of the central government. Further, the accommodative stance of the government was visible as sincere administrative steps were initiated to revise the electoral rolls on the basis of an earlier offer to disenfranchise all post-1971 immigrants. Finally, post Indira Gandhi (1984), the change of leadership in Delhi brought about a fresh air of goodwill and trust between the centre and the leadership of the movement.

Post accord, on the basis of a revised electoral roll, a fresh assembly election was held in December 1985. Although the revision was not all non-controversial, the development was significant. Two new parties came to the electoral contest along with Congress (I). The youth brigade of the AASU formed the Asom Gana Parishad (AGP) in a new avatar, claiming to represent all. Riding on the success of clinching an agreement from the central government, the AGP went to the election with the slogan 'Minorities Are Not Foreigners, AGP for All…'.

On the other hand, a new political outfit United Minorities Front (UMF) was formed by East Bengali Hindu and Muslim politicians who broke away from the Congress (I). The UMF fought the election by opposing the accord. The AGP's inclusive agenda, as well as its history of struggle, worked well as they secured 35.17 per cent of the popular vote with 64 seats. Congress (I) secured 23.43 per cent of votes to get 25 seats. The UMF could manage only 11.09 per cent votes and ended up with only 17 seats.

The election result showed an interesting pattern of ethnic voting.

1. The project of the UMF to bring all 'minorities'—immigrant Muslims, Hindu Bengalis, Assamese Muslims, Nepalis and tribals—under its umbrella did not work.
2. Only the Bengali Muslim concentrated constituencies voted for the UMF.
3. The Hindu Bengali areas voted for Congress (I).
4. The AGP won on an inclusive campaign. The ethnic Assamese, many ethnic subgroups and tribals of the plains stood by the AGP.

5. The AGP adapted its electoral appeal in sync with the transformed demographic reality of Assam.
6. Even some immigrant Muslims voted for the AGP to secure themselves prospectively.

The lesson driven home by the election result was that the imperatives of electoral politics constitute a hard reality, that is, electoral compulsions in a diverse multi-ethnic state are much harder than the boundaries of ethnic identities. The onset of election, post accord, gave rise to a clear ethnic polarization with two new political parties representing two views on the ethnic issue. The result showed that the AGP's accommodative avatar and agenda mediated the process of polarization. The ethnic polarization did not show up in the election result. The AGP secured wider support beyond its original ethnic Assamese positioning. It was expected after all those tumultuous years that an approach would emerge that would focus decisively on stopping future illegal immigration rather than deporting those who are already there, given the complication of international relations with Bangladesh. Towards that end, the AGP has shown flexibility to develop an approach that allows all disenfranchised non-citizens to enjoy all other citizen rights except voting rights. Ethnic accommodation is the key concept in any new approach to ensure political stability in a dyad of representative democracy (electoral) and multi-ethnic reality.

A nuanced historical analysis of the ethnic movement in the state of Assam by Sajal Nag throws light on how the ethnic conflict is built into the process of development of Assamese nationality (Nag 1990). Nag uses the term 'big nationalities' and 'small nationalities' to differentiate between groups that have developed languages and those that have not. The 'big nationalities' outsmarted the less advanced 'small nationalities' in their interaction with the British colonial order. During the colonial rule in India, the Bengalis turned out to be an adjunct to the power as a result of their advanced language and competence with the English education system. The domination, though conspicuous in the economic sphere, had sociocultural ramifications. As a result, 'small nationalities' were galvanized around their culture and language to build their resistance.

According to Nag, the natural evolution of the precolonial Assamese group was disrupted during the colonial rule. The local ethnic Assamese group lost out to the dominant Bengalis as the economy expanded and got integrated with the wider world. The influx of the Bengali settlers changed not only the demography of Assam but also its ethno-cultural composition. It became the fertile ground for a growing ethno-nationalism as the British purpose pitted the less developed 'nationality' against the advanced 'big nationality'. The development of a new middle class among the Assamese fuelled ethno-nationalism. An exclusive Assamese identity formation took hold in the face of the growing immigration of Bengalis from the hitherto East Pakistan in post-colonial times. An ideology of simmering conflict united the ethnic Assamese across all classes.

Leading Assamese intellectual Hiren Gohain also pointed out the deep-rooted sense of insecurity among the Assamese. He linked this insecurity to the condition of 'weak' nationality vis-a-vis the development process in the state since colonial rule.

> The different ethnic groups owing allegiance to the overall Assamese way of life were not welded into a cohesive national group strong enough to be able to withstand outside pressure...it is also a weak nationality in the sense that it is materially and culturally backward compared to some other national groups in India. (Gohain 1982, 58)

However, ethnic separation was fanned by the ruling classes in Delhi and Shillong after Independence. Gohain argues that a small and privileged section of the Assamese Hindus cornered the benefits of state-sponsored development by playing on the insecurities and anxieties of the Assamese people. The fear was genuine but was whipped up to give rise to ethnic separatism. There had been plots to tyrannize or enslave minorities, but the popularity of the Assam Movement rested on certain genuine issues. The issues were concerning the boundaries of the state with Bangladesh, official language policy and regional underdevelopment. The fear of being strangers in their own land has been a ground reality in Assam.

CONCLUSION

India has experienced the emergence of movements for regional autonomy in the last quarter of the 20th century. Such movements were mainly premised on ethnic identity and posed serious challenges to the Indian state. In a way, they questioned the very legitimacy of the process of nation-building in India. Of all the ethnic movements, the Assam Movement is unique in the sense that it placed the immigration issue firmly on the national political agenda.

Primordialism is an essentialist view of ethnicity, whereby ethnic groups are considered timeless and unchanging. Instead of taking ethnic groups as given in contemporary times in view of the trajectory of the world evolution of ethnic movements, a constructivist concept of ethnicity has proved to be analytically more useful. The ethnic identity formation is better addressed in relation to cultural hierarchies and the developmental policies of the state. Ethnicity, when stretched to politics, is understood as a fluctuating composition of differences, intersections and incommensurabilities.

The ethnic question in the state of Assam has a history. Post-Independence, the simmering ethnic tension was contained by the linguistic state formation exercise of the Government of India and the aggregation of interests within the dominant political parties. Much of the alienation experienced by an ethnically diverse population was absorbed by a delicate policy of accommodation. The demographic transformation and ethnic diversity, however, have been continuously fuelling an anxiety among the ethnic Assamese.

The gradual realization of an explosion of immigrants in the electoral roles of the state led to the formation of AASU in 1979, which led the movement for six years to clinch a favourable accord from the Government of India on 15 August 1985. The AASU, along with its fraternal organization AAGSP, organized and mobilized the ethnic Assamese as the original locals. They represented the insecurity and fear of the ethnic Assamese of being rendered a minority in their own homeland. They led a protracted struggle against the state demanding the detection, disenfranchisement and deporting of illegal immigrants. They also raised the issue of cultural domination and underdevelopment. The issues raised were genuine, the problem of immigrations being the central pivot. The bone of contention was how to define 'foreigners' or, in other words, fix the date of illegal immigration.

After an initial period of creative and enthusiastic all-round support, the Assam Movement started experiencing cracks in solidarity. The successive state government from 1979 was unrelenting and often resorted to repressive measures to curb the aggressive movement that continuously boycotted or defied the government administration. Sporadic attacks on the Muslim immigrants from Bangladesh and on minorities in general communalized the movement. The Muslim leaders of the AASU broke away, while many tribals of the plain, workers of tea plantations started withdrawing from the movement. On the one hand, the state measures became ruthless and, on the other hand, the movement also became violent. The economic blockade of all goods movement from Assam aggravated the situation more.

From 1984 onwards, a certain moderation from both sides created an atmosphere of optimism. While the then state government played its political cards well to create divisions in the movement, the intelligent Assam Movement leaders also gave up their hardline and reorganized themselves with an inclusive approach. After a series of negotiations, the Assam Accord was accomplished in 1985, which signalled a new phase of Assam politics. Two regional parties emerged: Asom Gana Parishad and UMF. The subsequent state assembly election showed that ethnic polarization has a limited scope in electoral success. The inclusive style of the AGP succeeded by adopting the policy of accommodation and moderation. The movement opened up a fresh understanding of the ethnic movement in India. It showed the fluidity of ethnic boundaries and their implication for political mobilization in electoral democracy.

Points for Classroom Discussion

- The concept of ethnicity in contemporary times
- Ethnic identity as a political construct
- The historical phases of the Assam Movement
- The lessons of the Assam Movement

GLOSSARY

Disenfranchisement: To take away and derive an individual the franchise, the right to vote.
Ethnic identity: Identities that are specific to an ethnic group in which membership is determined by attributes associated with or believed to be associated with descent.
Ethnicization: Often a political construct, it is the process of ascribing ethnic or racial identities to a relationship, social practice or group formation.
Plural society: A society composed of different ethnic groups or cultural traditions with a sense of coexistence.
Power capability: Among the various contenders of power, the measure of one's political resources.
Primordial: The attributes that exist since the very beginning, primeval.

REFERENCES

Alavi, H. 1989. 'Politics of Ethnicity in India and Pakistan'. In *Sociology of 'Developing Societies': South Asia*, edited by H. Alavi and J. Harris, 222–243, London: Macmillan.
Barth, F., ed. 1969. *Ethnic Groups and Boundaries: The Social Organisation of Cultural Differences.* Boston, MA: Little Brown.

Baruah, S. 2010. 'The Assam Movement'. In *Social Movements I: Issues of Identity*, edited by T. K. Oommen, 191–208. New Delhi: Oxford University Press.
Brass, P. 1991. *Ethnicity and Nationalism: Theory and Comparison*. New Delhi: SAGE Publications.
Ghosh, B. 2003. 'Ethnicity and Insurgency in Tripura'. *Sociological Bulletin* 52, no. 2: 221–243.
Glazer, N., and D. P. Moynihan. 1963. *Beyond the Melting Pot: The Negroes, Puerto Ricans, Jews, Italians, and Irish of New York City*. Cambridge, MA: MIT Press and Harvard University Press.
Gohain, H. 1982. 'Once More on the Assam Movement'. *Social Scientist* 10, no. 11: 58–62.
Guideri, R., and F. Pellizi. 1988. 'Smoking Mirrors—Modern Polity and Ethnicity'. In *Ethnicities and Nations: Processes of Interethnic Relations in Latin America, Southeast Asia and the Pacific*, edited by Pellizi Guideri and Stanley J. Tambiah, 24–34. Houston, TX: Rothko Chapel.
Gupta, D. 1982. *Nativism in Metropolis: The Shiv Sena in Bombay*. New Delhi: Manohar.
———. 1985. 'The Communalising of Punjab, 1980–85'. *Economic & Political Weekly* 20, no. 28: 1185–1190.
———. 1991. 'Communalism and Fundamentalism: Some Notes on the Nature of Ethnic Politics in India'. *Economic & Political Weekly* 26, no. 11/12: 573–582.
Kimura, M. 2013. 'The Nellie Massacre of 1983: Agency of Rioters'. In *The Bangladesh Reader: History, Culture, Politics*, edited by Meghna Guhathakurta and Willem van Schendel, 632–634. Durham, NC; London: Duke University Press.
Kothari, R. 1988. *State Against Democracy: In Search of Humane Governance*. New Delhi: Ajanta Publications.
Nag, S. 1990. *Roots of Ethnic Conflict: Nationality in Question in North East India*. New Delhi: Manohar.
Oommen, T. K. ed. 2010. *Social Movements I: Issues of Identity*. New Delhi: Oxford University Press.
Phadnis, U. 1989. *Ethnicity and Nation-Building in South Asia: A Case Study of Sri Lanka*. New Delhi: SAGE Publications.
Tambiah, S. J. 1989. 'Ethnic Conflict in the World Today'. *American Ethnologist* 16, no. 2: 335–349.
United Nations Peace Accord Archives. 1985. 'Assam Accord'. Available at https://peacemaker.un.org/sites/peacemaker.un.org/files/IN_850815_Assam%20Accord.pdf (accessed on 19 February 2021).

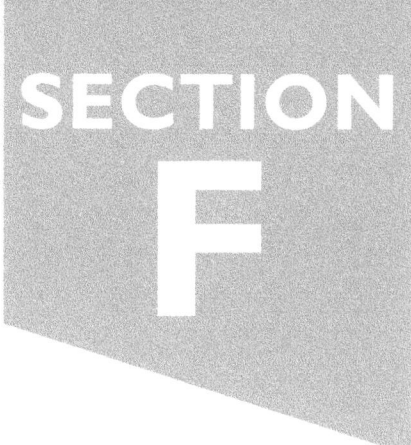

SOCIAL CHALLENGES

Chapter 16
Population, Poverty and Illiteracy

Chapter 17
Child Labour, Delinquency and Social Disorganization

Chapter 18
Violence against Women and Children

CHAPTER 16

Population, Poverty and Illiteracy

LEARNING OUTCOMES

- To critically analyse the problems of population, poverty and illiteracy and their linkages
- To introduce theoretical, interpretative and empirical aspects of the economic analysis of poverty and inequality
- To evaluate the problems of poverty and illiteracy, and initiatives undertaken to address them

Keywords: Population, birth rate, mortality rate, fertility rate, demographic dividend, poverty, poor, illiteracy

Poverty hence presents a unique sociological constellation: a number of individuals occupy specific organic positions within the social whole through purely personal fate; but it is not personal destiny or personal conditions that determine the position, but rather the fact that others, individuals, associations—or social totalities—attempt to correct this state of affairs.

—**George Simmel**

Children deprived of words become school dropouts; dropouts deprived of hope behave delinquently. Amateur censors blame delinquency on reading immoral books and magazines when, in fact, the inability to read anything is the basic trouble.

—**Peter S. Jennison**

INTRODUCTION

Population refers to a group of similar species inhabiting a particular area. Under this section, we grapple with the concept of population and society. Kingsley Davis believed that majorly because of elimination of war, banditry and control of famines and epidemics, mortality in India has been declining since 1921 and will continue to reduce further, but 'a continued low death rate without modern economy and civilized fertility is inconceivable'. Indian fertility is high, but not the highest in the world, or the maximum allowed by biology. However, its trend suggests that it will not decline soon. The current rate of population in India is growing at a steady rate, with statistics revealing the numbers to be around 135 crore in the month of April 2020. India is a unique and heterogenous country with regard to its topography and population, which are important prerequisites to assess its societal structures, economy and polity.

There are works by various scholars, each providing diverse approaches to understand the growth and pattern of population across the world. Malthus stated that the two laws which have been fixed laws of nature are as follows: (a) food is necessary for the existence of man and (b) the passion between the sexes is necessary and will remain nearly in its present state. These two laws exert power on individuals. He attempts to argue that the power of the population is indefinitely greater than the power of the earth to produce subsistence for man. Population, when unchecked, increases in a geometric ratio, and subsistence increases in an arithmetical ratio. And as numbers will rise, the first law will reflect more power than the second. The population cannot increase without means of subsistence, the population invariably increases when there are means of subsistence. For example, times of distress act as a deterrence to marriage, and the difficulty of rearing a family is so great that the population is at a standstill. Malthus had suggested two types of checks: preventive and positive. Preventive checks are applicable when men and women control birth rate through marriage, celibacy, moral restraint and foresight. And positive checks operate through famine, war, disease and pestilence. Positive checks are crude, and preventive checks are always in operation in a civilized society.

The other approach is the optimum population approach, which is concerned with the law of diminishing returns. It is concerned with the size of the population and the production of wealth; the population that makes the maximum returns possible is the optimum or the best population. Dalton and Robbins believed that there was a close relationship between the size of population and economic development.

The demographic transition model by Warren Thompson describes population change over time. Kirk (1996) attempted to reflect the stages of transition of population by analysing diverse approaches to causation: socio-economic, economic, institutional, cultural, ideational and so on. Interestingly, none of these meet the demand for specificity in regard to timing and speed of transition, in spite of the fact that this was a common criticism of the classic formulation of the theory.

According to Knodel and Van de Walle (1979):

1. Fertility declines took place under a wide variety of social, economic, and demographic conditions.
2. Family limitation was not practised (and was probably unknown) among broad sections of the population before the decline in fertility began, even though a substantial proportion of births may have been unwanted.

TABLE 16.1 Key Population Statistics of India 1901–1991

Census Year	Total Population (Million)	Average Annual Growth Rate (%)	Density (Persons per Sq. Km)	Sex Ratio (Males per 1,000 Females)	Per Cent of Urban Population
1901	238.3	0.3	77	1,029	10.8
1911	252.0	0.6	82	1,038	10.3
1921	251.2	N	81	1,047	11.2
1931	278.9	1.1	90	1,053	12.0
1941	318.5	1.3	103	1,058	13.9
1951	361.0	1.3	117	1,057	17.3
1961	439.1	2.0	141	1,063	18.0
1971	548.2	2.2[b]	178	1,075	19.9
1981	683.3	2.2[b]	221	1,071	23.3[a]
1991	846.3	2.1	267	1,076	25.7

Source: Census of India, 1961, Vol. 1, India, Parts II-A (i) General Population Tables, 1961 and II-C (i) social and cultural tables, 1964; Census of India, 1971, Series 1, India, Parts II-A (i), General Population Tables, 1975, and II-C (ii) Social and Cultural and Tables, 1977; Census of India, 1981, Series 1, India, Paper I of 1982, Final Population Tables; Part II- Special, Report and Tables Based on 5 per cent Sample Data, 1984, Part II-B (i) Primary Census Abstract General Population 1983; Census of India, 1991, Series 1, India, Paper 2 of 1992, Final Population Totals: Brief Analysis of Primary Census Abstract.
Notes: a = Includes only and estimate for Assam; b = Growth rate for 1961–1971 and 1971–1981 take account of the fact that the reference data of the 1971 Census was 1 April, whereas that of the 1981 Census (like the 1951 and 1961 Censuses) was 1 March.
N: Negligible.

3. Increases in the practice of family planning and the decline in marital fertility were essentially irreversible processes once under way.
4. Cultural settings influence the onset and spread of fertility decline independently of socio-economic conditions.

No two countries have followed the same path to transition, because there are so many possible combinations of nuptiality, fertility, mortality and migration at each stage of transition. Nonetheless, this diversity is not incompatible with the universality of the transition; as the differences in the above conditions may delay or accelerate the transition but cannot escape the transition. Therefore, there is a need for understanding the various factors responsible for limiting and proliferating the rate of population in India. Refer to Table 16.1 for the change in population growth and density in India over the years.

16.1. POPULATION

16.1.1. Population of India

As noted by Pravin Visaria and Leela Visaria (2006), post-Independence India avoided a sharp acceleration of the population rate as observed in Mexico, Kenya or even China. In India, the decennial rate of population growth has remained stable at around 2.1–2.2 per cent during 1961–1991. This stability of the growth rate is attributed to a relatively gradual decline in both the death rate and the birth rate. The growth rate of population during 1991–2001 was likely to be around 1.9 per cent; however, it is important to note that the large size of India's population reached by 1991 would mean that even with a relatively moderate rate of growth of about 2.0 per cent, the absolute addition to its population would be higher than any other country, including China. In order to understand the dynamics of the observed trend in the rate of growth of population, birth, fertility and death rates should be considered.

16.1.1.1. Birth and Fertility Rate

Birth rate refers to the number of live births per 1,000 population per year, whereas fertility rate is the number of live births per 1,000 women of reproductive ages (15 to 49 years) per year. This is a more refined way to measure fertility. Beginning in 1962–1963, the goal of reducing the birth rate through family planning was pursued on the advice of the Director of Family Planning, but the actual decline in the birth rate was much slower. This caused to introduce frustrating and impatient efforts of compulsory sterilization in some parts of the country during the 1975–1977 emergency. This step was a major setback in the family planning programme in India. Visaria and Visaria (2006) observed that the birth rate was lower in urban areas as compared to rural areas. Fertility has declined not only among the better educated but also among illiterates and disadvantaged groups of population. Factors contributing to this include both a rise in the age of marriage and control of fertility within marriage through contraception. Table 16.2 is crucial in understanding the trends of population growth, it represents vital statistics in India from the year 1901.

TABLE 16.2 Vital Rates per 1,000 Population in India 1901–1990

Year	Birth Rate	Death Rate	Rate of Natural Increase
1901–1910	49.2	42.6	6.6
1911–1920	48.1	47.2	0.9
1921–1930	46.2	36.3	9.9
1931–1940	45.2	31.2	14.0
1941–1950	39.9	27.4	12.5
1951–1960	40.9	22.8	18.1
1961–1970	40.0	17.8	22.2
1971–1980	37.8	15.4	22.4
1980–1982	33.8	12.3	21.5
1988–1990	30.8	10.3	20.5
1991–1993*	29.1	9.4	19.4
1994–1996*	27.4	8.9	18.5
1996–1998*	27.0	9.0	18.0

Source: Davis (1951); Registrar General India (1954, 1998b).
Note: *Excluding Jammu and Kashmir.

16.1.1.2. Mortality Rate

Mortality rate or death rate is a measure of the number of deaths in a particular population over a particular unit of time. Death rates in India have shown a continuous decline over the decades, which has brought about important changes in the estimated longevity or expected life span of an average Indian. An Indian born during the 1930s and 1940s could expect to live for only 32–33 years; females were disadvantaged with lower life expectancy at birth. Also, at the time of Independence, the infant mortality rate in the country was around 230–240 per 1,000 live births. The reason for higher mortality rates was due to uneven distribution and lack of medical and healthcare facilities across the country. Longevity was better in urban areas as compared to their rural counterparts (Visaria and Visaria 2006). Also, mortality rate is affected due to crisis such as natural calamities and pandemic. For instance, in 2020, the Coronavirus pandemic would have affected the rate of global and national population; however, this issue requires a rigorous analysis by demographers to arrive at precise statistics.

16.1.1.3. Deficit of Women

Sex ratio is defined as the number of females per 1,000 males. The sex ratio at birth is difficult to obtain because of the inadequacy of vital statistics. Therefore, there are not accurate figures of sex ratio at birth; in particular, where home births or unwanted or abandoned infants go unrecorded. In the 2011 census, it was observed that the population ratio in India 2011 is 940 females per 1,000 males.

The practice of disregarding the female girl child existed long before technological intervention, which made it possible to determine the sex of the foetus, the juvenile sex ratio favours the boys largely as a result of infanticide or neglect. Visaria (2007) had stated that the deficit of girls aged 0–6 increased considerably between 1981 and 2001 in several northern and western states. Patel (2007), on the basis of her own data from the states of Gujrat and Haryana, suggests that last births were disproportionately more likely to be male than female, and this finding reflected the practice of sex-selective abortion. In India, the Medical Termination of Pregnancy (MTP) Act became legal in 1971, and many women who entered marriage around that time heard that abortions were legal, and many of them themselves aborted foetuses since then. This act was washed of any moral criminality for several decades (Patel 2007). The deficit of females is attributed primarily to excess female mortality, which has declined but persists in rural India in certain states.

16.1.2. Demographic Dividend and Future

Since 2018, India's working population (aged between 15 and 64 years) has grown larger than its dependent population (children aged 14 years and below and people above 65 years of age), this youth bulge will last till 2055. The period of this 'demographic dividend' is usually 37 years; the demographic dividend, as defined by the United Nations Population Fund, means the economic growth potential that can result from shifts in a population's age structure. According to the Economic Survey, the country will enjoy the 'demographic dividend' phase despite some of its state transitioning into an ageing society by 2030. This is due to the declining fertility and mortality rates across the country, as discussed above. The country has witnessed a sharp decline in the total fertility rate (TFR) since the mid-1980s; from 1984, the TFR has halved from 4.5 to 2.3 as of 2016 and continues to decline. The government intends to harness the economic advantage of its large workforce by introducing several skill development and educational programmes. However, it will become challenging in another two to three decades from now, as the country will have an enlarged elderly population, which would require better investments in elderly care facilities.

The rapid growth of population is perhaps the major demographic force challenging development, environment, human well-being and international relations and security. This growth affects various sectors. Steep population growth retards the investment needed for higher consumption and exerts pressure on the available resources. Due to the increase in the number of family members, the expenses increase and there is a decline in the accumulation of capital. Sociologists, economists and demographers argue about the irrevocable impact that the increasing population will have on India's environment, natural resources and social structure. The subsequent sections discuss the problems of poverty and illiteracy faced by the Indian population.

16.2. POVERTY

16.2.1. Dimension of Poverty

In a continuously developing world, many people and families live and perish in conditions of absolute poverty. Poverty can be understood as a condition where economic means do not correspond to economic needs or ends. Poverty is a state of deprivation and can be defined as a social phenomenon where a particular section of society fails to meet even the basic requirement of living. Poverty is the condition and the individual negotiator is referred to as poor. Poverty may be understood as an aspect of unequal social status, inequitable social relationship, experienced as social exclusion, dependency and reduced ability to participate in social living. Sociologists have discussed two types of poverty: absolute and relative. The term 'absolute poverty' is based on the idea of survival; the basic conditions must be met in order to sustain a physically healthy existence. The concept of relative poverty is complex. As societies develop and become advanced, the standard of relative poverty is gradually adjusted. For instance, once consumer goods such as television, refrigerator and mobiles were a luxury, now they are a necessity. But the concept of relative poverty often diverts away attention from real deprivation of necessities such as nutritious food and healthcare.

Coser (1965) argued that historically the category of poor emerges when society elects to recognize poverty as a special status and also assigns a set of persons to this category. It is crucial to ascertain that personal references of being poor are irrelevant, and poverty is socially recognized condition as a social status. It can be examined as an aspect of the social structure. There has been a change in the medieval status of the poor. In modern society, the status of the poor is assigned to an individual or a household only when they receive assistance. However, the category of poor is wider than the category of assisted poor. Hence, he argued that it is not a personal need, but the sociological category of poverty emerges when those who are unable to meet their ends receive assistance. This status of being poor or the category of poverty always invokes negative emotions, such as pity, and is often marginalized or invisible, as they are believed to have little or no contribution towards the growth of society.

Each person's feelings and experiences of poverty are unique and different but, according to Qureshi (2004), a general conception that each one of them possesses is 'powerlessness' and 'resourcelessness'. Rein (1968) discussed three elements in poverty: subsistence, inequality and externality. Poverty is regarded as the root cause of all the evils in society and leads to multiple social, economic and cultural problems. And despite continuous efforts by the government agencies, India has a staggering rate of poverty.

16.2.2. Poor and Its Identity

In a competitive modern society, to receive assistance for survival is often stigmatized. Poor person is isolated from ordinary social life. Being poor is to possess a degraded status. According to Garfinkel (1956), 'public identity is transformed into something looked on as lower in the local schemes of social types'. The societal view of individuals becomes so prominent that it alters them. Once the status of the poor is assigned to an individual, their role changes. Societal members across all status groups can employ a variety of ways to shield their behaviours from being observed by others, and the right to privacy facilitates them to shield their role behaviour from public observance. But this right is denied to the poor. Even when money is provided to them through assistance, they do not have free disposition over its use. They are under scrutiny of donors who want to regulate how they spend their money, and the poor are infantilized through such procedures.

Identity of the poor is not defined by lack of money but also by lack of access to resources that allow for a minimum of living and participation in society. According to Ringen (1988), the emphasis on deprivation reflects theoretical concerns that low income provides an indirect measure of poverty rather than a direct measure. As discussed, their status may not be equivalent with the status of any other materially deprived section. Therefore, Atkinson (2002) argued that indicators of being poor or poverty should include inequalities, unemployment and worklessness. Further, there are certain categories of individuals who are more disadvantaged than others and are discriminated against in many aspects of social life.

16.2.2.1. Women

A substantial section of the poor comprises women. Women are poor due to cultural norms and values, unequal division of assets and power struggle between men and women. Social conventions in India continue to divide the workspace between men and women. Women bear the burden of unpaid domestic responsibilities and often comprise a large section in informal and precarious jobs, which has a negative effect on income growth and future security. The need to focus on category of women distinct from men among the poor is defended as women's unpaid and paid work is crucial for the survival of poor households. Women are social, political and economic actors; they produce and process food for the family. They are the primary caretakers of children, the elderly and the sick; and their income from paid labour is usually directed towards the well-being of their family. They fail to acquire equal access to productive forces in the economic market due to long working hours or long travel for jobs; they face significant constraint in maximizing their efficiency. Interventions by government often overlook the inherent knowledge possessed by women in their poverty reduction programmes.

16.2.2.2. Children

Another vulnerable category among the poor is children. Children who live under poverty face malnutrition, are at risk of disease and have higher chances of no or limited access to education. While growing up, they are subject to harsh living conditions, lack of food, no or dilapidated housing and no parks to play. These children are at a higher risk of child abuse and have early exposure to problems of substance abuse. According to the report by World Bank and UNICEF, titled 'Ending Extreme Poverty: A Focus on Children', India is home to nearly 30 per cent of almost 385 million children living under extreme poverty, the highest in South Asia.

16.2.2.3. Elderly

Poverty among the elderly is also one of the rising concerns in several countries, with many people retiring from jobs that provide less or no pension assistance. The elderly face the challenges of low income and require care. In India, by 2050, nearly 20 per cent of the population will be above 60 years of age. Pension covers only 35 per cent of senior citizens, this is a tantamount to the estimate that around 61.7 per cent of India's elderly population will be without any income security. The central government pays ₹200 per month under the Indira Gandhi National Old Age Pension Scheme to every Indian over the age of 60 and living BPL, but many still do not have access to this amount. Also, the states are encouraged to add to this sum and are free to expand its coverage.

16.2.2.4. Disabled

Disability is both the cause and consequence of poverty. It is a cause of concern as it leads to unemployment and reduced earnings. It acts as a barrier in acquiring education and skill development and also requires incurring expenses for healthcare. It is a consequence as poverty may lead to limited access to healthcare and other services. There have been some studies establishing the link between disability and poverty, each with distinct methodologies. Some studies signify the existence of a positive relationship between disability and income poverty, while others established that there is no indication of the rate of poverty between disabled and non-disabled persons.

16.2.2.5. Caste and Ethnicity

In India, caste hierarchies have created unequal access, and similarly STs have faced historic exclusion due to their religious/cultural diversities and geographic location. Several studies in India have divulged that the levels of poverty are higher among SCs and STs. Poverty is a visible manifestation of unseen social discrimination on the basis of the identity of caste, religion, ethnicity and gender. According to the National

Family Health Survey 2015–2016 (NFHS-4), 45.9 per cent of ST members were in the lowest wealth bracket compared to 26.6 per cent of SCs, 18.3 per cent of Other Backward Caste, 9.7 per cent of other castes and 25.3 per cent of those whose caste is unknown.

16.2.2.6. Rural Poor

Studies have shown that, in households, women and children often suffer more than men, and that, in a community, ethnic minorities or lower castes have higher chances of facing poverty due to inadequate opportunities. Similarly, it is argued that the rural poor suffer more; and among the rural poor, landless wage workers suffer more than landowners and tenants. It is essential to delineate that rural poor is not a homogenous category. The rural poor majorly depend on agriculture, fishing, forestry, animal husbandry and other related small-scale industries.

The causes of rural poverty are multidimensional; they comprise culture, climate, gender, markets and public policy. Similarly, the rural poor is quite diverse both in terms of problems they face and the possible solutions to those problems. The rural poor's association with economy is a considerable contrast to urban space, they face difficulty in their access to land and credit, education, healthcare, support services, such as availing subsidized food benefits through public distribution schemes. Increasing levels of rural poverty, without economic facilitation, have caused great population migration to urban areas. One-sided government policies that neglect agriculture sector and rural infrastructure have contributed to both rural and urban poverty.

16.2.3. Initiatives Undertaken

The central as well as state governments in India continuously attempt to address the crisis of poverty through several policies such as Pradhan Mantri Jan Dhan Yojana, a financial inclusion scheme, Pradhan Mantri Gramin Awaas Yojana, a housing scheme for the rural poor, the Atal Pension Yojana, aimed at increasing pension scheme beneficiaries in India, the SAGY, aimed at promoting infrastructure development in rural areas, Pradhan Mantri Fasal Bima Yojana, a scheme for crop insurance, the Pradhan Mantri Gram Sinchai Yojana, aimed at attracting irrigation investments and the DDUGKY for skill development of rural youth. These policies aim at improving the confidence and independence among the poor; however, their spread to beneficiaries has to be monitored for enumerating their efficiency. According to Krishna and Shariff (2010), in India, it is not the lack of resources or technical skills which are hindrances in our development, rather it is mainly due to the gap between policies and legislation. Elimination of poverty is not merely an economic upliftment, but it is related to politico-social awareness of people (Qureshi 2004, 65–112). Table 16.3 depicts state-wise poverty estimates.

The list reflects a decline in the poverty ratio over the years, but India's human development index, measured on the basis of health, education and standard of living, remained low and lagged behind other developing economies. Also, the reduction in national poverty between 1999 and 2006 was driven by the standard of living indicators, such as electricity, housing conditions, drinking water and sanitation facilities, rather than social indicators (Alkire and Seth 2013). Also, the reduction in poverty has not been uniform across different states or population subgroups.

TABLE 16.3 State-wise Poverty Estimates (% Below Poverty Line; 2004–2005, 2011–2012)

State	2004–2005	2011–2012	Decrease
Andhra Pradesh	29.9	9.2	20.7
Arunachal Pradesh	31.1	34.7	–3.6
Assam	34.4	32	2.4
Bihar	54.4	33.7	20.7
Chhattisgarh	49.4	39.9	9.5
Delhi	13.1	9.9	3.2
Goa	25	5.1	19.9
Gujarat	31.8	16.6	15.2
Haryana	24.1	11.2	12.9
Himachal Pradesh	22.9	8.1	14.8
Jammu and Kashmir	13.2	10.4	2.8
Jharkhand	45.3	37	8.3
Karnataka	33.4	20.9	12.5
Kerala	19.7	7.1	12.6
Madhya Pradesh	48.6	31.7	16.9
Maharashtra	38.1	17.4	20.7
Manipur	38	36.9	1.1
Meghalaya	16.1	11.9	4.2
Mizoram	15.3	20.4	–5.1
Nagaland	9	18.9	–9.9
Odisha	57.2	32.6	24.6
Puducherry	14.1	9.7	4.4
Punjab	20.9	8.3	12.6
Rajasthan	34.4	14.7	19.7
Sikkim	31.1	8.2	22.9
Tamil Nadu	28.9	11.3	17.6
Tripura	40.6	14.1	26.5
Uttar Pradesh	40.9	29.4	11.5
Uttarakhand	32.7	11.3	21.4
West Bengal	34.3	20	14.3
All India	37.2	21.9	15.3

Source: Planning Commission (2009, 2013).

16.3. ILLITERACY

16.3.1. Illiteracy in India

Illiteracy refers to the condition of incapacity to read, write and do simple mathematical calculations to carry out basic day-to-day functions with ease and awareness. According to UNESCO reports 2008, nearly 781 million adults across the world did not have basic literacy skills, and 64 per cent of this population were women. The diverse population of India has an unequal access to education. Where some regions and communities cannot think of remaining uneducated, others are struggling with social impediments to acquire basic education. It is observed through government and civil society reports that more number of individuals who reside in rural areas as compared to urban areas are illiterate. The ones who are at the receiving end of the inequalities, lack of education is one of the after effects. The impacts of illiteracy on an individual and society as a whole are immense and, more specifically, these impacts are negative. The inability to read and write hinders their economic emancipation as they are unable to open bank accounts and engage in any banking transactions without assistance, read documents or even have access to well-paying jobs in the market. Illiteracy is also argued to be a major cause of poverty; it impedes an individual from having better opportunities to earn a livelihood for sustenance. It is understood that far-reaching illiteracy is detrimental in the progress of the country. Education and literacy are indispensable to democracy and are essential for informed electoral participation. The UNESCO reveals that the income of a person with poor literacy stays about the same throughout their working life. It loses earnings and also limits employability avenues. The impact of illiteracy on personal income varies; however, illiterate earn relatively less than their literate counterparts, the latter have the literacy skills needed to undertake further vocational education or training to improve their earning capacity (Cree et al. 2012).

16.3.2. Understanding Literacy in India

According to Rao and Gupta (2006), literacy is the process that fosters rational thinking and is crucial for shaping individuals into responsible citizens. Literacy is a crucial parameter of socio-economic development. Studies have shown that higher levels of literacy are an indicator of better economic and social status and may depict human capital and their employment patterns. Increasing literacy will remove inequalities and function as a means of improving family status (Pathak and Gupta 2013). Literacy is essential due to several reasons; first, it allows for economic independence. It promotes technical learning and facilitates skill learning as per the demands of the industry. Second, it promotes confidence among the disadvantaged and enables them to sustain themselves through acquiring suitable jobs. Third, literacy helps to understand that increasing population exerts burden not only on the individual family but also on the society tussling with limited resources available. Literacy is the baseline of education, without which schooling cannot take place. Here, the lower economic section is the most disadvantaged since they cannot afford quality education, whereas children in high-income countries have better access to quality education. The difference in literacy levels in various countries is due to the reason of public expenditure on education. During the period of colonization, education was facilitated, which introduced and glorified the European curriculum instead of exploring native knowledge. It is observed that India continues to carry the burden of colonial legacy with regard to its education system.

16.3.3. Constitutional Provisions

The Indian Constitution recognizes the importance of education for all. Therefore, it has laid down various provisions to ascertain the right and effective implementation of educational rights in the country.

1. Article 21(A) of the Indian Constitution was amended to provide free and compulsory education as a fundamental right to all children aged between 6 and 14 years. The fundamental right here clearly signifies that nobody should be discriminated on the basis of status, caste, sex, class or creed and equal opportunities to be provided to everyone in the country.
2. Articles 15, 17 and 46 of the Indian Constitution safeguard the educational interests of weaker sections of the society, which include socially, economically and educationally backward families, along with those belonging to SCs and STs.
3. Article 30 of the Indian Constitution guarantees all minorities the right to establish and administer institutions of their choice.
4. The Constitution under Articles 41, 45 and 46 of the Directive Principles of state policy instructs the state to ensure that all citizens receive free education.

According to the reports of Census 2011, any person aged 7 years and above and who has the ability to read and write is considered to be literate. The average literacy rate in India stands at 74.04 per cent, while Kerala has the highest literacy rate in India at 93.91 per cent, Bihar has the lowest literacy rate at 63.82 per cent. Literacy levels in India are affected by several reasons such as gender disparity, economic deprivation, caste system, regional differences and quality of schools.

According to the last census, which was conducted in 2011, the literacy rates of the top and bottom five states are shown in Table 16.4.

16.3.4. Origins of Illiteracy

16.3.4.1. Gender Bias

A common notion in Indian households pertaining to female education is *padh likh kar bhi toh roti hi banani hai* (even after becoming literate, you only have to cook). Due to the hierarchal social order of the caste system in India, gender, caste, class and religion are crucial factors to determine the access to education (Deen 2014). Several women in India face discrimination since their birth and, especially in rural areas, gender becomes a negotiating factor to educate children. Deen (2015) stated that male children are preferred to be educated, which further widens the gender gap in education. There is a reverse relationship between literacy and gender in the context of women. Katiyar (2016), through a study, claimed that rural areas are unfavourable to female literacy. In contemporary India, among many communities, an illiterate daughter becomes a liability, as it is difficult to look for marriage prospects. Whereas even a very highly qualified daughter causes similar concern as there is a dearth of suitable match for her. Dreze (1997) explored how public campaigns can have a positive influence on social attitudes towards women's education. The perception of female literacy in India is largely a by-product of male literacy and may be depressing, but it is only historical patterns. Studies also reveal that women's illiteracy is a product of poverty and, in order to encourage literacy, free and inclusive programmes should be introduced. The literacy programmes are an integral part of national development. Government should also focus on mechanisms to incorporate vocational skill development that will facilitate income generation among women (Das and Singh 2002).

TABLE 16.4 The Literacy Rates of the Top and Bottom Five States

	Persons		Males		Females	
Rank	Name of State/UT	Literacy Rate	Name of State/UT	Literacy Rate	Name of State/UT	Literacy Rate
			Top 5 States/UTs			
	India	74.0	India	82.1	India	65.5
1	Kerala	93.9	Lakshadweep	96.1	Kerala	92.0
2	Lakshadweep	92.3	Kerala	96.0	Mizoram	89.4
3	Mizoram	91.6	Mizoram	93.7	Lakshadweep	88.2
4	Tripura	87.8	Goa	92.8	Tripura	83.1
5	Goa	87.4	Tripura	92.2	Andaman & Nicobar Islands	81.8
			Bottom 5 States/UTs			
	India	74.0	India	82.1	India	65.5
1	Bihar	63.8	Bihar	73.4	Rajasthan	52.7
2	Arunachal Pradesh	67.0	Arunachal Pradesh	73.7	Bihar	53.3
3	Rajasthan	67.1	Andhra Pradesh	75.6	Jharkhand	56.2
4	Jharkhand	67.6	Meghalaya	77.2	Jammu & Kashmir	58.0
5	Andhra Pradesh	67.7	Jammu & Kashmir	78.3	Uttar Pradesh	59.3

Source: Census of India 2011, literacy statistics.

16.3.4.2. Economic Deficit

Poverty is one of the major factors that restricts primary education among people. Several poor families struggle to meet their daily ends and procure meals in a day, education is distant luxury that is unaffordable due to reasons such as dependency on child labour for survival and inability to incur fixed and recurring costs of schooling. Kapadia (1997) observes that in rural Tamil Nadu, it is common to put children to work by their parents to keep them out of trouble as they have dropped out of an uninspiring and underfunded school system. Thus, child labour is an impediment to schooling, but poverty is its primary cause.

16.3.4.3. Caste Hierarchy and Tribes

The census and other reports have revealed that the literacy rates among disadvantaged castes, particularly SCs and STs, is much lower than the average. Customarily, Indian society is driven by the caste system featuring social exclusion and inequalities, which is the backbone of society (Deen 2015). Among SC there is high illiteracy rate and unemployment. Inequality among the castes is more than gender inequality in literacy, as there is more distinction between non-SCs and SCs (Raju 1988). Thorat (2009) states that education among SCs reflects low literacy levels, high dropout rates along with prevailing caste-based discrimination. And tribal society is unaware about the value of female education and hence devaluing non-formal education reducing enrolment (Swamy 2013). However, the basic cause of educational deprivation among tribal communities is not a fundamental lack of interest on their part, but rather a dismal condition of schooling facilities in most tribal areas.

16.3.4.4. Regional Differences

The table from 2011 census report above depicts the variation in the literacy levels across the country, and these variations are concomitant with the aspect of social development of these areas. Kerala is far ahead than the northern states of Rajasthan, Uttar Pradesh and Haryana. In some regions, such as Himachal Pradesh and Uttarakhand, topography becomes a limiting factor with scattered villages and poor connectivity. But it is important to explore the social causes of such variations across the state; social equality is an overriding principle to foster higher literacy rates through equal opportunity for schooling. In inegalitarian states, village leaders exercise greater control over the agencies of education which impedes universal access and participation.

16.3.4.5. Quality of Education

In many societies, the participation of young children in their family work is considered more essential than their enrolment in school. Education appears to have less or no relevance, as earning situation appears to be precarious. Also, when earning skills are taught at home through apprenticeship in family, there is less relevance of knowledge acquired through purchased books. Several children in India learn to speak and read in their mother tongue and may not be interested and well equipped to start learning in Hindi or English language at the early stage. Further, there is a shortage of simple and interesting reading material. The teachers at the regional level often lack enthusiasm for innovation. This is due to a reason that teachers are underpaid and there are limited training sessions for government elementary schools. The problem is further complicated through concerns of unyielding curriculum, which is less inclusive. These reasons cumulatively lead to apathy towards the education system in the country.

16.3.5. Initiatives and Transformations

The impediments discussed above affect literacy levels across regions. There are attempts to improve literacy through alleviation of poverty, mitigating gender, caste, class inequity and improving access to quality education. In recent years, developing countries are identifying shortcomings in curricula inherited from colonialism and are now redirecting several educational programmes towards rural poor. India has developed and developing many self-help educational programmes to engage communities. The government schemes of Sarva Shiksha Abhiyan and Beti Bachao Beti Padhao are encouraging communities towards the positive impact of education. The policy of Mid Day Meal Scheme launched in 1995 to provide students with free food to promote better enrolment, attendance and retention in government schools is continuing to expand its reach across remote areas of the country. But there are concerns regarding the quality of meals and the recurring occurrence of caste-based discrimination against mid-day meal cooks.

The education system and approach to literacy are changing, and the unparalleled proliferation of technology in people's lives is one of the major reasons for this change. The spread of information technology is influencing education in schools in several ways. Along with the ability to read and write, the knowledge-based economy necessitates computer- and technology-literate workforce. However, according to Giddens (2009), it again becomes a concern that causes a divide between IT-rich and IT-poor households. New information and communication technologies may serve to exacerbate existing divisions and create new ones.

CONCLUSION

In India, poverty and illiteracy are closely linked and, being the second largest population in the world, India is home to one-third of all-world poverty. India's current rapid population growth, on the one hand, is providing a demographic dividend whereas, on the other hand, it continues to hinder its progress and development. Unchecked population growth can impact the society adversely and can have serious implications. The rapid growth of population is the major demographic force challenging development, environment, human well-being and international relations and security. It is not possible to reduce the existing population, but it is feasible to check the rate of population growth. This can be achieved through higher rates of literacy across all states. Overpopulation adversely affects illiteracy, because a country that is struggling with a massive population fails to provide proper schooling and education system. Also, factors that contribute to ignorance towards education are parents with little or no proper schooling, lack of concentration, poverty, unemployment and difficult living conditions.

Literacy along with skill development programmes can generate opportunities for sustenance and alleviate the burden of poverty. Poverty and inadequate planning are also creating issues of underemployment and unemployment. It is important to recognize that only the formulation and implementation of government policies may not be enough to eradicate the problem from its roots. It is imperative to mobilize and involve a higher number of people, and youth should be encouraged for self-employment, which may provide employment to others too.

Points for Classroom Discussion

- Poverty and inequality reduction is a central objective of economic policies in both developed and developing countries
- Unchecked population growth is perhaps the major demographic force challenging development, environment, human well-being and international relations and security
- The spread of information technology is influencing education

GLOSSARY

Demographic dividend: It is a phenomenon related to the overall development of the country caused by reduced birth and death rates, thereby altering the age structure in a country.
Fertility rate: It helps in measuring the number of live births per 1,000 women of reproductive age (aged 15 to 49 years) per year.
Illiteracy: It refers to the inability of an individual to read, write and understand basic concepts, hampering their social and economic advancement.
Mortality rate: It measures the occurrence of frequency of deaths in the total population in a given period of time.
Poverty: A state or condition wherein an individual or a community lacks the necessary financial and economic resources required for maintaining a minimum standard of living.

REFERENCES

Alkire, S., and S. Seth. 2013. 'Selecting a Targeting Method to Identify BPL Households in India'. *Social Indicators Research.* doi:10.1007/s11205-013-0254-6.
Atkinson. T. 2002. *Social Indicators: The EU and Social Inclusion.* New York, NY: Oxford University Press.
Coser, L. 1965. 'The Sociology of Poverty: To the Memory of Georg Simmel'. *Social Problems* 13, no. 2: 140–148.
Cree. A., A. Kay, and J. Steward. 2012. 'The Economic and Social Cost of Illiteracy: A Snapshot of Illiteracy in a Global Context'. *World Literacy Foundation* 2&3.

Das, Y. L., and S. N. Singh. 2002. 'Literacy Campaign in Bihar: Problems and Prospects'. *Indian Journal of Adult Education* 63, no. 4 (October–December): 32.

Davis, K. 1951. *The Population of India and Pakistan*. Princeton, NJ: Princeton University Press.

Deen, S. 2014. 'Women in Higher Education: A Spatial-Temporal Analysis of Higher Education from Gender Perspective in India'. *Learning Community* 5, nos 2&3: 173–192.

———. 2015. 'Determinants of Higher Education for Scheduled Castes in Uttar Pradesh: A Socio-economic Analysis'. *Research Journal of Social Sciences & Management* 5, no. 3: 212–217.

Drèze, J., P. Lanjouw, and N. Sharma. 1997. 'Credit in Rural India: A Case Study'. Discussion Paper No. 6, Development Economics Research Programme, STICERD, London School of Economics.

Garfinkel, H. 1956. 'Conditions of Successful Degradation Ceremonies'. *American Journal of Sociology* 61, no. 5: 42.

Giddens, A. 2009. *Essential Concepts in Sociology*. Cambridge: Cambridge University Press.

Kapadia, K. 1997. 'Mediating the Meaning of Market Opportunities: Gender, Caste and Class in Rural South India'. *Economic & Political Weekly* 32, no. 52: 3329–35.

Katiyar, S. P. 2016. 'Gender Disparity in Literacy in India'. *Social Change* 46, no.1: 46–69.

Kirk, D. 1996. 'Demographic Transition Theory'. *Population Studies* 50, no. 3: 361–387.

Knodel, J., and E. van de Walle. 1979. 'Lessons from the Past. Policy Implications of Historical Fertility Studies'. *Population and Development Review* 2, no. 2: 217–245.

Krishna, A., and A. Shariff. 2010. 'The Irrelevance of National Strategies: Rural Poverty Dynamics in States and Regions of India, 1993–2005'. *Journal of Applied Economics* 13, no. 2: 181–120.

Patel, V. 2007. 'The Political Economy of Missing Girls in India, In *Sex Selective Abortion in India*, edited by Patel, T. 286–316. New Delhi: SAGE Publications.

Pathak, S., and A. Gupta. 2013. 'Status of Women in India with Particular Reference to Gap in Male-Female Literacy Rate in India. *International Journal of Environmental Engineering and Management* 4, no. 6: 549–552.

Planning Commission. 2009. *Report of the Expert Group to Review the Methodology for Estimation of Poverty*. New Delhi: Government of India.

———. 2013. *Press Note on Poverty Estimates, 2011–12*. New Delhi: Government of India.

Qureshi, M. U. 2004. *India's Social Problems in Twenty First Century*. New Delhi: Anmol Publications.

Raju, S. 1988. 'Female Literacy in India: The Urban Dimension'. *Economic & Political Weekly* 23, no. 44: 63.

Rao, B. S. B., and Gupta, P. V. 2006. Low Female Literacy: Factors and Strategies. *Australian Journal of Adult Learning* 46: 84-95.

Rein, M. 1968. 'Problems in the Definition and Measurement of Poverty'. In *Poverty in America*, edited by Louis A. Ferman, Joyce L. Kornbluh and Alan Haber, 116. Ann Arbor, MI: University of Michigan Press.

Ringen, S. 1988. 'Direct and Indirect Measures of Poverty'. *Journal of Social Policy* 17, no. 3: 351–356.

Swamy, R. N. 2013. 'A Bird's-eye View of Problems Plaguing Tribal Women's Literacy in India. *Indian Journal of Adult Education* 74, no. 4 (October–December): 31.

Thorat, S. 2009. *Dalits in India: Search for a Common Destiny*. New Delhi: SAGE Publications.

Visaria, L. 2007. 'Deficit of Girls in India: Can It be Attributed to Female Selective Abortion?'. In *Sex Selective Abortion in India*, edited by Patel, T. 61–80. New Delhi: SAGE Publications.

Visaria, P., and L. Visaria. 2006. 'India's Population: Its Growth and Key Characteristics'. In *Handbook of Indian Sociology*, edited by Veena Das, 61–77. New Delhi: Oxford University Press.

CHAPTER 17

Child Labour, Delinquency and Social Disorganization

LEARNING OUTCOMES

- To comprehend the social and economic aspects of child labour
- To explore childhood debates and intersections of gender, economy and polity
- To learn about the complexities, disparities and inequalities in social structures that lead to delinquency

Keywords: Child labour, delinquency, strain theory, social disorganization, drug abuse, cyberbullying

Child labour and poverty are inevitably bound together, and if you continue to use the labour of children as the treatment of for the social disease of poverty, you will have both poverty and child labour to the end of time.

—**Grace Abbott**

INTRODUCTION

The problem of child labour is of greater magnitude than other related problems concerning the development of individuals and society. It is widely accepted across societies that the children of today are going to be the citizens of tomorrow.

Society in general separates the ideology, needs and perspectives of children from the mainstream production of knowledge or value. The category of children is marginalized in society and reinforces their vulnerability to exploitation. The crisis of child labour, delinquency and social disorganization attracts attention as a global concern; and several countries in compliance with the International Labour Organization (ILO) have devised robust mechanisms to protect children from the caprices of labour market. Although what constitutes child labour may vary widely depending mainly on social, economic and environmental factors, child labour is a segment of the child population of a country that is found to have engaged in unpaid or paid employment in a given period of time.

Progressive legislation has facilitated the abolition of child labour across countries. While legislations defined child labour as waged work undertaken by a child under a certain age, it also establishes the borderline between morally desirable and pedagogically sensible activities on the one hand, and the exploitation of children on the other. While condemning the relatively uncommon forms of waged labour as exploitation, it authorized a broad range of other activities, including housekeeping, child tending, helping adults for no pay in family farms and shop, and also earning pockct money helping in domestic work and running errands. The latter activities are considered to be an important aspect of socialization across many cultures. Several countries have ratified the modified version of ILO's guidelines against child labour. Once celebrated as an antidote to poverty during the colonial period, child labour contributions to the family economy came to be perceived as an indicator of poverty, if not the cause.

Caldwell's (1982) study is influential in mapping the wider the setting of children's historical, social, and cultural roles in India. Research on intra-households relations also questioned the concept of the 'household', which can be a problematic unit where several inequalities persist, not only gendered but also age related.

The neoclassical belief that child labour is essentially a problem of household economics continues to be espoused in the studies of child labour published in UNICEF, WHO and ILO. Refer to Box 17.1 to understand what constitutes child labour. Morice and Schlemmer (1994) state that the continuous reference to Western moral values may supplant scientific analysis but create a conceptual confusion in which ill-grasped notions from diverse analytical fields are indiscriminately used. Reference to the broad and ahistorical causes of the oppression of children, such as poverty, illiteracy, backwardness, greed and cruelty, fail to go beyond the mere

---

BOX 17.1
Child Labour

In order to understand the extent of child labour, it is important to comprehend what constitutes child labour.

UNICEF's standard indicator for child labour includes the following:

- **Age 5 to 11 years:** At least 1 hour of economic work or 21 hours of unpaid household services per week.
- **Age 12 to 14 years:** At least 14 hours of economic work or 21 hours of unpaid household services per week.
- **Age 15 to 17 years:** At least 43 hours of economic work per week.

description of oppression and ignore the historical and social conditioning of exploitation (Sahoo 1995). As a global solution to eliminate child labour, several modern economies criminalize poverty; penalizing the ways poor bring up their children. This criminalization is made more malevolent as modern economies increasingly display their unwillingness to protect poor children from the adverse effects of neoliberal trade policies (Amin 1994).

17.1. CHILD LABOUR

17.1.1. Case of India

The Census of India defines child labour as any person under the age of 14 engaged in one of the 59 occupations or processes listed as hazardous under India's Child labour Act of 1986. The Constitution of India has provisions for this; Article 24 of the Constitution reads: 'No child below the age of 14 years shall be employed in work in any factory or mine or engaged in any other hazardous employment.' Similarly, Article 39 of the Constitution of India states:

> The State shall, in particular, direct its policy towards securing the health and strength of workers, men and women, and the tender age of children are not abused and that citizens are not forced by economic necessity to enter avocations unsuited to their age and strength, and the children are given opportunities and facilities to develop in a healthy manner and in conditions of freedom and dignity and that childhood and youth are protected against exploitation and against moral and material abandonment.

Direction for free and compulsory education for children has been provided under Article 45 of the Constitution. This Article states: 'The State shall endeavour to provide, within a period of 10 years from the commencement of this Constitution, for free and compulsory education for all children until they complete the age of 14 years.'

The Census of 2011 depicted some positive signs when the number of child labour reduced by 65 per cent from 1.26 crore to 82.2 lakh between Census 2001 and Census 2011. With policies to ensure the mandatory school participation of every child, India has made significant progress in the overall social development and has implemented necessary measures required for the protection of working children. There is still a need to expand the network of enforcement machinery required for enforcing the various existing laws on child labour in the country. One reason used to justify child labour is that the family economy would collapse if children do not contribute to the workload. This argument is usually justified in the agricultural and informal economic sector; there are industries such as *agarbattti* (incense), bidi and embroidery where payments are done on per-piece basis.

This will indeed go a long way in saving the treasurable future of millions of working children in India.

17.1.1.1. Gendered Labour

There are current debates around the need for education versus experiential learning for children. Feminists and women groups in India have argued considerably regarding the importance of formal education for girls versus their significant assistance to their mothers in household work. Tradition and customs do not allow equality and justice for women and girls. Traditional household structures have been skewed and favour male child. Stereotypes observe girl children as transient members of the family who will eventually marry and go to another household, whereas the sons will look after the ageing parents. Girl children who are denied formal education also lose out on the choices regarding their life and future. Nussbaum (2000) employed Gary Becker's model of family, stating that parents are not altruistic agents concerned with the interests of a female child. Amartya Sen points out that males are quite neglectful of the interests of females and make decisions that are inimical to those interests (Nussbaum 2000). Parents are reluctant to send their daughters to school for socio-economic and cultural reasons. The question of challenging mindsets and attempting to alter ideological perspectives is still a distant dream in Indian households. Cultural relativism is employed to maintain and uphold the practice of inequality to maintain status.

17.1.1.2. Concerns during Covid-19 Pandemic

The current global pandemic of Covid-19 will impact the integration of the global economy and may have a lasting socio-economic, financial and psychological impact on individuals and families. The situation is increasing economic insecurity causing disruption in the supply chains, falling commodity prices and halting many manufacturing industries. This will impact the standards of living across the lower and middle class as employment opportunities have been affected. It has also led to an increase in informal work, a reduction in remittances and migration due to the tightening of trade and foreign direct investment. The temporary closure of schools by governments and the unavailability of house helps due to reverse migration have created additional pressure on working middle-class households, especially among households where both partners are working, allowing for intermittent or continuous engagement of children in household labour. The situation is worse for female children as the burden of expectations and labour for them is higher than their male siblings. Schools besides fulfilling educational purpose also provide social protection and well-being among growing children. Another issue of concern is that many private schools are moving to online mode with facility of distance learning, but this leaves many children further behind as they struggle for independent devices and internet connectivity for online classes.

In the future, fewer opportunities and lower wages can drive people into informal or exploitative work, which can also contribute to child labour as many parents are not or will not be able to afford school fees, and this will have a significant impact on children's lives.

17.2. CHILDHOOD

17.2.1. Childhood and Its Debates

The detachment of childhood from the performance of valued work has been considered a yardstick of modernity. According to Nieuwenhyus (2004), the problem with this way of defining childhood is problematic as it denies children's agency in the creation and negotiation of value. Late modern experiences of childhood suggest that the basic source of trust in society lies in the child. Progress in children's rights and media campaigns against child labour or sex tourism would point to a growing sanctity of the child in late modernity (Jenks 1994). This sanctity is only symbolic and is contradicted by social and economic policies. As childhood becomes a contested domain, the legitimacy of directing children into economically useless activities is losing ground (Zelizer 1994). The need to direct children into these activities is linked to a system of parental authority and discipline of family that was instrumental in preserving the established bourgeois social order. The cost of sustaining this arrangement is quite high as it requires, among other obligations, money to support the institutions at the basis of childhood ideal, such as free education, housing, recreational activities, family welfare and healthcare. Developing economies lack infrastructure to support such institutions, and even developed economies become reluctant to continue to aide childhood institutions; the market has also begun to address children as consumers, linking their status with the possession of expensive goods, thereby inducing poor children to seek self-esteem through paid work (White 1994). Working children identify themselves to be in conflict with childhood ideology, which places higher value on the performance of economically useless work. Even though working for a pay chances self-esteem, it also involves sacrificing childhood, which exposes children to negative stereotyping.

The neoclassical perspective believes that schooling is the best antidote to child labour (Weiner 1991). Around the world, children undertake all kinds of odd jobs not only to help their families but also to contribute in the fast-rising costs of schooling. There are instances where schools and work can coexist as separate means of childhood, but such changes in schooling pattern may have a bearing on both children and parents.

17.2.2. Exploring the Concept of Delinquency

The term *delinquency* is employed to label improper petty criminal behaviour; however, in legal context, it is widely accepted as a disorderly and illegal action committed by an adolescent which is referred to as juvenile delinquency. It ranges from minor offenses such as substance abuse (drinking, smoking, drugs) to theft, property crimes to violent acts.

When societies become advanced and differentiated, the period of adolescence is extended. The sociological study of crime, deviance and delinquency emphasizes on structural factors, such as poverty and social disorganization, that are believed to generate such behaviour, or through socialization with primary (family) or secondary groups (school and peer groups). Both of these perspectives recognize implicitly and explicitly that some kind of learning takes place. But they have failed to explain the social process. According to Sutherland (1947), agencies such as cinema and newspapers play an important role in the initiation of criminal nature. A person becomes delinquent because there is accessibility of the definition of violation of law and mostly hostility against violation of is unknown. Differential association theory states that criminal behaviour is leaned from others through agents of communication and may vary in duration, priority, frequency and intensity.

17.2.2.1. Strain Theory

Merton (1957), on the other hand, explored anomie; he believed that anomie occurs due to a breakdown in the relationship or absence of social norms and value. He viewed anomie as a condition that arises when there is incongruity between the societal goals and the means available for their attainment. In reality, the means of achieving the goals are not accessible to everyone. Therefore, anomie or anti-social behaviour occurs due to the value system of society and encourages high material aspirations as a marker of individual success without adequately providing the required means for attaining these aspirational goals. This mismatch between goals and means produces strain and leads to 'modes of personality adaptation', different combinations of behaviour in accepting or rejecting means and goals. The inability to achieve one's goals may lead directly to delinquent behaviour among adolescents as they search for alternative means of goal achievement. This is often understood as 'strain theory' in the discipline of sociology.

The validity of the strain theory lies in the premise that delinquency is highest when aspirations are high and expectations are low. For instance, delinquency would be high when there was a strong desire for monetary success and a low expectation of fulfilling that desire. However, there are several studies which attempted to test this idea, focusing mainly on educational and occupational goals, but failed to support the strain theory (Elliott and Voss 1974; Hirschi 1969; Liska 1971). These studies have rather found that delinquency is highest when both aspirations and expectations are low, and delinquency is lowest when both aspirations and expectations are high.

The strain theory also predicts that there is a relationship between social class and delinquency. It predicts that delinquency is concentrated in the lower class, since low-class individuals mostly lack the means to achieve economic success or middle-class status. But this is a suggestion from the strain theory which has been contested by studies (Braithwaite 1981; Elliott and Ageton 1979; Elliott and Huizinga 1983) that indicate delinquency to be quite common among the middle class and that the relationship between class and certain types of delinquency is negligible.

Also, the strain theory has been criticised as it fails to explain the fact that most delinquents abandon crime in late adolescence; and why delinquents can go for long periods without committing delinquent acts.

17.2.2.2. Revised Strain Theory

Much research around the revision of the strain theory challenge the conjecture that the monetary success of middle-class status is the primary goal of adolescents. Adolescence is an era of transition between the ambiguously conceived statuses of childhood and adulthood. This is because whenever the rights and privileges of this group are discussed, there is general vagueness and disagreement. Adolescents may pursue a variety of goals and that goal commitment should be reconsidered as variable rather than prearranged criteria. If commitment to goal is variable, one can argue that the middle class has higher aspirations, and this balances any advantage they might have in achieving goals.

With goal commitment as a variable, some studies suggest that adolescents will be more interested in the achievement of immediate goals rather than long-range goals like monetary success. The immediate goals of adolescents may include things such as popularity with peers, good grades, winning a sport and getting along well with their parents. Here, immediate goal gratification is independent of the social class, and incoherence between immediate goals and the achievement of these goals leads to delinquency.

Therefore, both the strain theory and the revised strain theory are premised on the assumption that there is a rise in frustration due to an obstacle in goal-seeking behaviour. Adolescents and individuals both, however, not only seek certain goals but also try to avoid painful situations. According to Zillman (1979), individuals engage in both reward-seeking and punishment-escaping behaviours.

17.2.3. Delinquency among Children

The problem of juvenile delinquency has been the subject of increasing concern and attention in India since the last two decades, but there still persist many misconceptions regarding the same. There is no single explanation for the development of delinquent behaviour. In legal parlance, delinquency denotes acts of varying degrees of social consequence, from mere naughtiness to major assault, punishable under the aegis of law. In our society, the term *delinquency* is commonly used to describe the misdeeds of only juveniles that are detrimental to society.

Therefore, an adolescent is said to be a juvenile delinquent when he/she starts stealing, assaulting, indulging in sex offences and develops pathological symptoms of lying and truancy. Many of these offences are said to be criminal actions committed by a person who is beyond the age group sanctioned for juvenile courts. In India, the legal understanding for the delinquent age group is between 7 and 18 years of age for adolescents who can be tried as juveniles. Also, the Indian Penal Code uses the expression 'juvenile offence' rather than 'delinquency'. According to the Reformatory School Act, first passed in India in 1876 and later modified in 1897, a youthful offender is defined as a person below the age of 15 years who has been convicted of any offence punishable by imprisonment or transportation. There are special courts known as 'juvenile courts' established in some larger states of our country for the trial of these offenders.

There are several reasons and causes for delinquent behaviour, and it is not something which is inherited; delinquents are made, not born. It is the social environment which is responsible for delinquent behaviour.

The causes of delinquency could be classified under two categories: (a) social factors and (b) personal factors. Sociologists have stated factors such as poor housing, slum neighbourhood, lack of recreational and basic amenities, fragmented homes and disturbed family, unresolved mental issues, bad company, exposure to violence in real life and through popular media as the root cause of delinquency. Families and the site of home play a very important role in the primary socialization of children. The factor of broken homes or disturbed families due to high divorce rates, domestic violence and separation leads to lack or absence of parental affection and security.

17.2.4. Drug Abuse among Children

Drug or substance abuse is one of the most common delinquency problems among the children. The WHO defines drug addiction as a state of periodic and chronic intoxication produced by the consumption of drugs (natural or synthetic) that are detrimental to the individual and the society. A drug is a product that affects the way people feel, think, see, taste, smell, hear or behave. A substance can be a medicine or an industrial product, such as correction fluid, petrol, solution, alcohol, cigarette, bidi and cannabis. The harmful effects of the substance used by children lead to several medical problems such as lung problems, stomach ailments, cancer, blackening of teeth and psychological behavioural problems.

In India, children are victims of this problem of substance abuse. This problem affects all categories of children inhabiting both rural and urban India. Also, there are variations in the degree of the issue, with a higher prevalence rate among children inhabiting slums and streets compared to school-going children. There are reports from several studies that reflect that the prevalence of substance abuse is higher among boys compared to girls, and they also reflect higher substance abuse among children in urban areas as compared to children in rural areas. The children who go to school indulge in mostly tobacco and alcohol, whereas out-of-school children, especially street-based, slum-based and child laborers, are at risk of experimenting with the most dangerous substances, both licit and illicit in nature (Ahmad et al. 2007).

Early initiation of substance use is usually associated with poor prognosis and a more serious impact on health, education, familial or social relationships. Substance use may lead to behavioural problems, relationship difficulties and may cause disruption in studies and even dropping out of school. Substance abuse remains a critical problem in most countries and is associated with several social and economic consequences. At times, adolescents using substances may tend to engage in anti-social behaviour, for example, lying, stealing, pickpocketing and so on, and this may occur in association with early onset of substance use.

17.2.4.1. Cyberbullying and Children

Bullying is defined as an aggressive behaviour that is purposely and repeatedly targeted towards an individual who holds less power than the perpetuator. Bullying can take many forms, including physical (hitting, shoving), verbal (taunting, threatening) and social (spreading malicious rumours) exclusion. With the proliferation of the internet and mobile phone technology, new forms of bullying have emerged. The surge in global cases of cyberbullying has initiated worldwide attention and debate around the issue. With increased awareness and intervention of technology in our personal spaces, it is also perpetuating incidents of bullying which go beyond harmless ridicule and are now being categorized as criminal behaviour under cyber laws of various countries. Evidences from various studies has shown that cyberbullying victimization can result in severe emotional trauma as it is relentless, inescapable and has a wider reach. Further, it is pertinent to explore the link between bullying and cyberbullying, as well as the relationship between age and gender of victims.

17.2.5. Resolutions for Delinquency

There are two suggested approaches to deal with the problem of delinquency: preventive and rehabilitative. As the name suggests, under preventive measures, government along with the assistance of non-governmental agencies, participation of civil society and schools, encourages treatment towards any kind of early symptoms of maladjustment and disturbance that could contribute to the development of such tendencies among young children.

- Awareness is created through informing the parents about the responsibility towards a stable home environment that contributes to the development of

good citizens. Educating families helps parents to realize the importance of thorough care to the young children.
- Their awareness is disseminated through popular media, such as TV, radio and newspaper to instil positive social values. Such values promote a law-abiding attitude that is appreciated and rewarded.
- The government also introduces policies and programmes to alleviate property and improve the conditions of the slums and provide better educational, social and economic opportunities to the residents.
- Schools now have resident psychologists who periodically engage students in predictive tests to identify potential delinquents and suggest appropriate treatments and therapies.

Under a rehabilitative approach, the youth who have engaged in delinquent and criminal behaviour are sent to rehabilitation centres as punishing them is not a measure. The reason behind this approach is not to punish the delinquent, but to get them proper guidance and training to prevent them from committing crime again and to restore normal living. There are several legal measures through legislations that have been introduced as a practice in India to deal with delinquency.

- **Reformatory Schools Act, 1897:** This Act is considered as a landmark in the history of legal provisions towards delinquency in India. This is in force across all the states in India. Under this Act, the courts empower to send male youth offenders to detention to reformatory school for not more than three years, which could be extended to seven years depending on each delinquency case. However, no person can be detained after attaining 18 years of age. In compliance with this Act, the government may establish and maintain reformatory schools towards providing useful change.

17.3. SOCIAL DISORGANIZATION

17.3.1. Social Disorganization Theory

The social disorganization theory articulates the degrees of criminal offences and delinquency across the variables of time and space as a product of institutional disintegration (Akers 2008; Jensen 2003). Institutions of family, school, religion, peer groups and friendships are considered indispensable for fostering cooperative relationships in society. They provide individuals with a sense of belonging and enable the reduction in likelihood of any delinquent behaviour. Thus, social disorganization refers to the rupture, breakdown or dismantling of the social system and social institutions impacting the social order. Durkheim considered social disorganization as a state of social disequilibrium.

17.4.1. Dominant Theories

Durkheim (1897) explored that how Catholics, being homogenously practised, have lesser number of suicides, and he attributed strong religious social control for preventing deviance and suicidal tendency. Sutherland (1939) underlined the effects of industrialization and urbanization on individuals as inconsistency and conflict.

Further, Sutherland (1947), through his differential association theory, explained that criminal behaviour is acquired or learned through the process of interaction with other person in intimate small groups. Learning includes techniques of committing crime and the specific direction of motives, drives, rationalization and attitudes. Motives and drives are learnt from the understanding of legal codes, the chances of acquiring criminal modes are higher when there is an excess of favourable definitions to violation of law over unfavourable definitions to violation of law, that is, criminal behaviour is determined in a process of association with those who commit crime.

Differential association occurs as a society comprises various groups with different cultures. Cultural conflict is the underlying case of differential association. And cultural conflicts occur due to social disorganization.

Park et al. (1925) explored deviant and criminal behaviour through the ecological framework of their concentric zone theory. Their social ecological theory argued that residents inhabiting the city had varying propensities to engage in deviant behaviours on the basis of how close in social and spatial proximity the residents were to the transition zone. The transition zone is characterized as the part of the city that is assigned for industrial manufacturing and housing of low-income residents, particularly immigrants seeking economic activities. This zone has a high poverty rate, dysfunctional families, high rates of illiteracy, high crime rates, alcoholism and violence. These conditions are related with ecological conditions. But Shaw and McKay (1942) extended the ecological concentric zone theory and argued that social disorganization is a result of a lack of macro-level social controls on the community. Disorganized urban areas are lacking social control and have a high level of poverty and crime rate as well as a weakened control of institutions of family, schools and so on. Also, neighbourhoods with high rates of residential mobility and limited social capital produce the conditions for crime to emerge and persist.

On the basis of the discussed theories, the following are the characteristics of social disorganization:

1. Disagreement in values and institutions
2. Inconsistency between expectations and achievements

Further, the disorganization can be of three types: (a) individual/personal disorganization (drug abuse and juvenile delinquency), (b) family disorganization (divorce and separation) and (c) community disorganization (poverty, corruption, crime and collective violence).

Sampson and Groves (1989) presented an empirical model of social disorganization, wherein they highlighted 'external factors' beyond the variables of social class, residential mobility and family disruption. They included factors of community supervision of teenage gangs, informal friendship networks and participation in formal organizations that contribute towards social disorganization. Social disorganization theory, thus, enables us to predict youth violence and crime. The finding indicates that researchers need to take into consideration the association between economic deprivation and social disorganization while attempting to explain the genesis of crime and violence committed by youth.

CONCLUSION

The chapter initiated to highlight crucial debates and discourses around the problems of child labour, delinquency and social disorganization. In India, children are victims of problem of substance abuse. This problem affects all categories of children inhabiting both rural and urban India. Children, irrespective of what they do, think or believe, are excluded from the production of value. It is important to explore the mechanisms through which children create and negotiate the value of their work and how they impinge constraining structures of age and seniority are important aspects to explore the notion of agency among them. As discussed above, government and non-government organizations are working towards the emancipation and rehabilitation of children and are counselling children and their families; as one of the factors for child labour, delinquency and social disorganization is the reason of disturbed families due to high divorce rates and domestic violence separation and leads to lack or absence of parental affection and security.

Since children are at the growing and developing stage, they are more vulnerable than adults with respect to workplace hazards, and the consequences of unsafe and threatening work are more often devastating and lasting for them. They have special needs and require the requisite attention for their physical, cognitive and behavioural development and emotional well-being. A significant aspect of child labour literature suggests that it is considered essential in various households; however, economic conditions play a significant role in determining the degree of child's involvement in domestic or paid work. The sociological and economic dichotomy between creation of preference and choice becomes apparent with the literature discussed above. However, the socialization effect of youth employment may yield benefits in dimensions of crime reduction pertaining youth.

Points for Classroom Discussion

- Exploitation of childhood deprives society of any substantial development
- Delinquency is the by-product of social disorganization
- Cumulative and comprehensive resolutions can only combat the crisis of delinquency and child labour

GLOSSARY

Child labour: It refers to the exploitation of children through any form of work that deprives children of their childhood, interferes with their ability to attend regular school to develop their mental ability and competence.

Delinquency: An illegal and unacceptable behaviour especially carried out by a juvenile.

Drug abuse: It is excessive intake and dependence on illegal drugs and substances, which is detrimental to the well-being of individuals and society.

Social disorganization: Social disorganization theory is a widely used theory which renders explanation of criminal offences and delinquency as a result of institutional disintegration.

REFERENCES

Ahmad, M., C. D. Smith, and F. A. Schmitt. 2007. 'Prevalence of Psychosocial Problems among School Going Male Adolescents'. *Indian Journal of Community Medicine* 32, no. 3: 219–221.

Akers, R. L. 2008. *Criminology Theories. Introduction, Evaluation and Applications*. Los Angeles, CA: Roxbury Press.

Amin, A. A. 1994. 'The Socioeconomic Impact of Child labour in Cameroon'. *Labour Capital Society* 27, no. 2: 234–249.

Braithwaite, J. 1981. 'The Myth of Social Class and Criminality Reconsidered'. *American Sociological Review* 46, no. 1: 36–58.

Caldwell, J. 1982. *Theory of Fertility Decline*. New York, NY: Academic Press.

Durkheim, É. 1979 (1897). 'Suicide: A Study in Sociology'. (Translated by John A. Spaulding,) New York, NY: The Free Press.

Elliott, D., and D. Huizinga. 1983. 'Social Class and Delinquent Behavior in a National Youth Panel'. *Criminology* 21, no. 2: 149–177.

Elliott, D., and H. Voss. 1974. *Delinquency and Dropout*. Lanham, MD: Lexington Books.

Elliott, D., and S. Ageton. 1979. 'Reconciling Race and Class Differences in Self-reported and Official Estimates of Delinquency'. *American Sociological Review* 45, no. 1: 95–110.

Hirschi, T. 1969. *Causes of Delinquency*. Berkeley, CA: University of California Press.

Jenks, C. 1994. 'Child Abuse in the Post-modern Context: An Issue of Social Identity'. *Childhood* 2, no. 3: 111–121.

Jensen, G. F. 2003. 'Social Disorganization Theory'. In *Encyclopaedia of Criminology*, edited by R. A. Wright, 31–46. New York, NY: Fitzroy Dearborn Publishers.

Liska, A. 1971. 'Aspirations, Expectations, and Delinquency: Stress and Additive Models'. *Sociological Quarterly* 12, no. 1: 99–107.

Merton, R. 1957. *Social Theory and Social Structure*. Glencoe: Free Press.

Morice, A. 2000. 'Paternal Domination: The Typical Relationship Conditioning the Exploitation of Children'. In *The Exploited Child*, edited by B. Schlemmer, 195–213. London, New York: ZED.

Nieuwenhyus, O. 2004. *Doing Research with Children and Young People*. London: SAGE Publications.

Nussbaum, M. 2000. *Women and Human Development the Capabilities Approach*. New Delhi: Kali for Women.

Park, R., E. W. Burgess, and R. D. McKenzie. 1925. *The City: Suggestions for the Study of Human Nature in the Urban Environment*. Chicago, IL: University of Chicago Press.

Sahoo, U. C. 1995. *Child Labour in Agrarian Society*. Dordrecht: Reidel.

Sampson, R. J., and W. B. Groves. 1989. 'Community Structure and Crime: Testing Social Disorganization Theory'. *American Journal of Sociology* 94, no. 4: 774–802.

Shaw, C., and H. McKay. 1942. *Juvenile Delinquency and Urban Areas*. Chicago, IL: University of Chicago Press.

Sutherland, Edwin. H. (1939) 1947. *Principles of Criminology*. Philadelphia, PA: LippincottWeiner, M. 1991. *The Child and State in India: Child Labour and Educational Policy in Comparative Perspective*. Princeton, NJ: Princeton University Press.

White, B. 1994. 'Children, Work and Child Labour: Changing Responses to the Employment of Children.' (Inaugural address). The Hague, Institute of Social Studies.

Zelizer, V. 1994. *Pricing the Priceless Child: The Changing Social Value of Children*. Princeton, NJ: Princeton University Press.

Zillman, D. 1979. *Hostility and Aggression*. Mahwah, NJ: Erlbaum Associates.

CHAPTER 18

Violence against Women and Children

LEARNING OUTCOMES

- To sensitize towards power and subordination within the purview of gender and age
- To understand women and children in juxtaposition with other forms of stratification and identity such as class and family
- To explore various approaches to study violence and the categories and structures through which it is perpetuated

Keywords: Violence, child abuse, gender socialization, violence, family

Violence against children cuts across boundaries of geography, race, class, religion and culture. And no country is immune, whether rich or poor. Some children are particularly vulnerable because of gender, race, ethnic origin, disability or social status.

—**Pinheiro (2006)**

INTRODUCTION

This chapter attempts to explore the structures of violence against women and children. As discussed in the previous chapters, women, children, the elderly and the disabled are a vulnerable category because they often have fewer rights or lack appropriate means of protection.

According to United Nations Women, a global and regional database on violence against women in the year 2013 comprised nearly one third (35%) of all women who have been in a relationship have experienced physical and sexual violence by their intimate partner. The prevalent estimates of intimate partner violence (IPV) range from 23.2 per cent in high-income countries and 24.6 per cent in the WHO Western Pacific region to 37 per cent in the WHO Eastern Mediterranean region, and 37.7 per cent in the WHO South-East Asia region. Globally, as many as 38 per cent of all murders of women are committed by intimate partners. In addition to IPV, globally, 7 per cent of women report being sexually assaulted by someone other than a partner, although data for non-partner sexual violence are more limited. Intimate partner and sexual violence are mostly perpetrated by men against women. Violence against children includes all forms of violence against people under 18 years old, whether perpetrated by parents or other caregivers, peers, romantic partners or strangers. Globally, it is estimated that up to one billion children aged 2–17 years have experienced physical, sexual or emotional violence or neglect in the past year (Hillis et al. 2016). The experiences of violence impact lifelong mental and physical well-being. WHO's Target 16.2 of the 2030 Agenda for sustainable development is to 'end abuse, exploitation, trafficking and all forms of violence against, and torture of, children'.

The discipline of sociology, after years, is attempting to renew its attention towards violence and how to develop theoretical approaches to define, understand and explain violence. Ungar Bermanzohn and Worcester (2002) argue that as the new century opens, violence has been growing within many countries; fragile governments in Asia, Africa and Europe are weakening with civil wars, and rapid economic change is leading to rising levels of violence. Wallerstein (2005) claims that a high degree of violence erupts everywhere in smaller and larger doses and over relatively long periods. Violence carries the power of enforcement, and many regimes across the world were founded by violent acts of rebellion or exclusion. It is essential to allow an open definition of violence, which is crucial to maintain sensitivity. The change of nature of violence from interpersonal to mass, self-inflicted and revolutionary violence, this fluidity, according to Stanko (2003), allows to creatively think about disrupting violence as a social phenomenon. Violence is an essentially contested concept, which is why it is imperative to define it as a process where actions recursively follow each other and cannot be singled out without losing the identity (violence) of the process as a whole (Schinkel 2010). The temporal character of violence often makes it difficult for separating the causes and consequences.

Violence is an act of aggression, usually in interpersonal interaction or relations. Violence brings into question the concept of boundary maintenance (Nedelsky 1991) and sense of self as well as the perception of another's autonomy and identity. It can also be understood as when the body and the self is vulnerable to violation. In the field of women studies, there are studies that have emphasized the aspect of power and powerlessness involved in a violent act. It involves a coercive manner to assert oneself over the other to feel a sense of power (Litke 1992).

18.1. WOMEN AND VIOLENCE

18.1.1. Violence against Women

Violence finds resonance in a hierarchical society based on exploitative gender relations. It also becomes a tool for coercive socialization of family members according to the prescribed norms of male dominance and control. Some females fall prey to violence before they are born when expectant parents abort their unborn daughters, hoping for sons instead. In other societies, girls are subjected to such traditional practices as circumcision, which leave them maimed and traumatized. In other words, they are compelled to marry at an early age, before they are physically, mentally or emotionally mature.

The Declaration on the Elimination of Violence against Women is the first international human rights instrument to exclusively and explicitly address the issue of violence against women. It affirms that the phenomenon violates, impairs or nullifies women's human rights and their exercise of fundamental freedoms.

The declaration provides a definition of gender-based abuse, calling it 'any act of gender-based violence that results in, or is likely to result in, physical, sexual or psychological harm or suffering to women, including threats of such acts, coercion or arbitrary deprivation of liberty, whether occurring in public or in private life'.

The definition is amplified in Article 2 of the declaration, which identifies the following three areas in which violence commonly takes place:

- Physical, sexual and psychological violence that occurs in the family, including battering sexual abuse of female children in the household, dowry-related violence, marital rape, female genital mutilation and other traditional practices harmful to women, non-spousal violence and violence related to exploitation.
- Physical, sexual and psychological violence that occurs within the general community, including rape, sexual abuse, sexual harassment and intimidation at work, in educational institutions and elsewhere, trafficking in women and forced prostitution.
- Physical, sexual and psychological violence perpetuated or condoned by the state, wherever it occurs.

18.1.2. Family and Violence

Uberoi (1994) feels that though the 'family is also a site of exploitation and violence, many a times sociologists eschew the issues of social pathologies with regard to the family.' This may be due to the reason that family is a cultural ideal and a focus of identity, and its inviolability as an institution continues to be reaffirmed. Malavika Karlekar (2004) argued that the situation gets compounded by the familial concern with propriety, honour (izzat) and reputation, which makes it difficult for researchers (interested in violence in domestic spaces) to get access to those perceived as victims. Thus, it is not coincidental that a large percentage of available data on violence against women locates the family as a major cause of oppression and subsequent ill health and loss of identity (Karlekar 2004). Institutions of family and marriage often trigger anxiety among both women and men, and thus, it becomes essential to explore the violence of everyday life. But there exists silence and hesitation around subjecting intimate relationships to scrutiny.

Family as a basic or joint unit have a direct bearing on the status of married women, with regard to adaptation and allocation of resources. Joint or extended family imposes a certain emotional and physical burden on the daughter-in-law; at the same time, it provides much-needed support in child rearing and care (Gore 1968; Karlekar 1982). In India, the institution of the family is becoming unstructured across time and space through the process of development. But a household is the operational unit that continues to operate according to norms of family and kinship ideology, which includes rules of marriage, residence, property ownership, roles and functions determined according to age and gender. Moral rules operate to maintain a kind of gender-biased order internal to families and kinship systems. Patriarchy asserts, limits abortions and often seeks to deny them rights over their body. It compels women to be mothers and also determines the conditions of their motherhood. This ideology of motherhood is also considered one of the bases of women's oppression because it creates feminine and masculine character types which perpetuate patriarchy; it creates and strengthens the divide between private and public; it restricts women's mobility and growth, and it reproduces male dominance.

18.1.2.1. Intimate Partner Violence (IPV)

The news and the newspaper comprise many cases of suicide, murders and violence against women in India. There exists a skewed process of labelling dowry death or bride burning as kitchen accidents (refer to Box 18.1). The WHO defines IPV as 'any behaviour with in an intimate relationship that causes physical, psychological or sexual harm', such as slapping, hitting, forced sexual intercourse, insults, belittling, intimidation, life-threats, isolating children, restricting access of a partner to financial resources, education, employment or medical care (WHO 2002). Johnson (2008)

BOX 18.1
Dowry

In India, in several parts of the country, at the time of marriage, it is customary for the bride's parents to give gifts, namely dowry to their daughters, the groom and his family. In contemporary times, in some cases, however, dowry is no longer a gift but rather a demand for cash and/or goods made by the groom and his family on the bride's parents. Increasingly, it has become difficult to meet these demands, and many times, a young woman dies for not fulfilling this demand. Dowry demands are made both before marriage and at the time of marriage, but in most of these cases, they were made after marriage. Where demands were made after marriage, it was perceived either as an exercise of the rightful prerogative of the groom and his family or to express discontent at what was given at the time of marriage or in social comparison with neighbours; at a later date, the dowry was perceived as inadequate. When these demands were not met, it precipitated serious consequences for the young bride. Domestic violence related to dowry are reported in several cases; the violence is often initiated through shoving, kicking, quarrelling, taunting, harassment, blackmailing and mental torture and may, in some cases, lead to murder and death of the bride.

classifies IPV as intimate terrorism (unidirectional with male violence against women), situational couple violence or violent resistance. Researches in India have documented that gender inequality at home and outside is perpetuated by a sociolegal order where legal entitlements of women in intimate relationships maintain the power balance in favour of males, as legal relief was available only to married women in legally recognized marriages. Intimate relationships in India are regulated by a plurality of laws—personal and secular. The sexual violence experienced by women in intimate relationships has also been well-documented along with the limitations of seeking justice in law through the court system (Nair 1996; Sen 2010). The sexual violence perpetrated by intimate partners was ignored and the public along with legal discourse was preoccupied with sexual violence committed by strangers. Also, Sen (2010) has argued that the process of emotional violence suffered by women is insufficiently recognized. Feminist researchers working on violence against women in India have worked tirelessly to highlight the forms of violence perpetrated by intimate partners, which brought into legal framework the Protection of Women from Domestic Violence Act (PWDVA) in 2005. The Act underlines the fact that violence is not limited to marriage and occurs in different kinds of intimate relationships. The Act, however, may have served the interests of victims at times, while at other times have failed to serve the interest of the victims (Ghosh and Choudhuri 2011).

As per secondary data from courts, 71 per cent of women who filed cases under the PWDVA were aged between 18 and 35 years. Also, it emerged that within the first five years of marriage, women regularly experienced violence; in the majority of cases (98%), women experienced three or more types of violence as listed under PWDVA. It has also been noted that most women do not directly approach the court initially, but they attempt family or community interventions, and when these efforts yield no result, they approach the legal system. There was also low awareness amongst women about the right to free legal aid, despite provisions for free legal aid. But several women have reported that there are severe judicial delays, and there was a rather low rate of interim reliefs being granted.

18.1.2.2. Violence in the Natal Home

The rising interest in research around women has led to the availability of rich information and data on violence against women at every stage of their life cycle. In India, the violence against women begins at their natal homes; being a country where the dominating ideology prefers sons, it becomes rather difficult for girl children to survive and thrive. In India, the Medical Termination of Pregnancy Act empowers women to exercise abortion and have control over their bodies; however, it is abused as numerous abortions are often motivated through sex determination. Female foeticide became popular with amniocentesis, a medical technique to discover birth defects, but soon a sequence of sex-selective abortion followed. Another practice which devalues girl child is of female infanticide, due to distinct son preference in the northern parts of India. This is primarily not only due to the inheritance practices and patterns but also because of the prevalence of dowry practices, which exert pressure on parents during their daughter's marriage. Further, studies have revealed poverty, alcoholism, ignorance of family planning and the cost of child rearing are the possible causes of female infanticide. These practices reveal a negative attitude towards girl child, and even if they are fateful to survive, there is perpetual inequality in routine life, and domestic work pressures are also unequally divided among male and female children in many communities in India. In families, female children are socialized to uphold altruism, believed to be the symbol of being a woman and face the brunt by negating their education and quality of healthy life for their brothers. Data from the 2011 census reveal that relatively prosperous states such as Punjab, Haryana, Gujarat and Maharashtra have poor child sex ratio, as compared to lesser developed regions such as Chhattisgarh and Northeastern states, which have a much better child sex ratio. According to the Population Research Institute, around 15.8 million girls went missing in India due to prenatal sex-selective abortions. Although the government has passed laws banning the usage of ultrasound tests for determining a foetus' sex and sex-selective abortions, they have failed to put an end to the problem.

The skewed sex ratio means that men in some India states, like Haryana, already have a difficult time finding wives. Newspaper reports from years have divulged, out of desperation, men increasingly approach human smugglers, who supply them with women trafficked from poor families from other states and countries like Bangladesh. These women, in turn, face several problems in their marital homes, beginning from the inability to communicate and adjust to a new culture to being treated as sexual slaves, worsening the women rights in these communities and make women more vulnerable to sexual violence. [Refer to Box 18.2 to understand the practice of child marriage.] In 2015, a central scheme of Beti Bachao Beti Padhao was launched in the

BOX 18.2
Child Marriage

Child marriage was prevalent for centuries in many parts of India. This practice was found to be harmful for the growth of the girl child in particular and society in general. Child marriages are solemnized, especially in Rajasthan, on 'Akshay Trithiya' day (29 April) with great celebration and gaiety and without obstruction from the authorities or the public. There have been efforts to prevent child marriages; the Child Marriage Restraint Act was enacted in 1929. Child marriage is publishable under this law, but it is recognized as valid by the civil law of our country. The Act does not make a child marriage null and void or voidable. It only provides that this could be a valid ground for divorce. Law is an institution of social change. It should have made, therefore, child marriage null and void ab initio so that the abolition of child marriage altogether could have been made a reality. Every state government has a statutory obligation under the Child Marriage Restraint Act, 1929, to prevent child marriages and for taking appropriate proceedings in accordance. With the provisions of the Act. So legal action must be taken against the responsible persons for their failure to prevent child marriages. Effective enforcement of the law also depends on the awareness of the common people about the evil effects of child marriages. The cultural preferences for early marriage among children are seen as a means to cope with poverty. An International Center for Research on Women (2011) study in Rajasthan and Bihar outlines how some families with several daughters (sisters or cousins) marry them all off in one ceremony in order to save costs of the wedding, which means some girls are married while they are still children. Sociocultural preferences for child marriage should not be explored as fixed norms, as there has been enormous change in practice over time, which reflects changing norms concerning gender and the acceptability, desirability, the importance of education due to campaigns and initiatives towards community sensitization that have impacted marriageable age.

state of Haryana as the state suffers from a dismal child sex ratio, which was further applied in several districts of the country. The primary aim was to prevent female infanticide, develop new schemes and work collaboratively to ensure that every girl child is secured and protected, ensure every girl child gets a quality education. The other expectations from the programme were to promote women and child welfare, encourage women empowerment and improve the status of women. The reports of the impact of the programme are underway; however, it has managed to question the male child preference in a state obsessed with the male child.

18.1.3. Violence against Women in Public Spaces

Violence affects the lives of millions of women worldwide, in all socio-economic and educational classes. It cuts across cultural and religious barriers, impeding the right of women to participate fully in society. Violence against women takes a dismaying variety of forms, from domestic abuse and rape to child marriages and female circumcision. All are violations of the most fundamental human rights. Violence against women in public spaces, which includes eve-teasing, rape, molestation and sexual harassment, is generally understood in feminist theory to be an expression not of unbridled lust and desire but power. Eve-teasing is a form of sexual harassment indulged in by men, which is not an exclusive act of any class, caste or educational background.

Another horrific crime against women is rape, a type of sexual assault in which one or more individuals forces sexual contact on another individual without consent. It can cause devastating physical and psychological trauma; several victims develop post-traumatic stress disorders. Rape victims are often stigmatized and experience emotions associated with shame, powerlessness and self-blame. The understanding of rape is culturally and historically contingent upon societal mores and laws. Rape is being used as a weapon of war, a strategy used to subjugate and terrify entire communities. Women and girl children are frequently victims of gang-rape committed by soldiers from all sides during a conflict. Such acts are done mainly to trample the dignity of the victims. Rape has been used to reinforce the policy of ethnic cleansing in the war and conflict-ridden areas. Perpetrators see such cases of rape as the symbolic assault of the community, the destruction of the fundamental elements of society and culture and the ultimate humiliation of the 'male' enemy.

The violence also continues in the form of sexual harassment in the workplace, which is a growing concern for women. The employer abuses their authority to seek sexual favours from their female co-workers or subordinates, sometimes promising promotion or other forms of career advancement or simply creating an untenable and hostile work environment. Women who refuse to give in to such unwanted sexual advances often run the risk of anything from demotion to dismissal.

18.1.4. Prostitution

Trafficking of women and children is a universal issue that has greater gravity, and discussions and deliberations are going on around the globe to curb the menace. Largely, it involves sex and labour exploitation. As per the Immoral Traffic (Prevention)

Act, 1987, prostitution means 'sexual exploitation or abuse of persons for commercial purpose'. There is data available where several girls and women victims are being trafficked with ulterior motives of engaging them in prostitution. Further, there are instances, where many women are forced into prostitution, either by their parents, partners or friends as a result of the difficult economic and social conditions in which they find themselves. Women are promised a better life, but instead, what they receive is violations of their human rights. They also may be lured into prostitution, sometimes by 'mail-order bride' agencies that promise to find them a husband or a job in a foreign country. As a result, they very often find themselves illegally confined in brothels in slavery-like conditions where they are physically abused, and their passports are withheld. Since prostitution is illegal in many countries, it is difficult for prostitutes to come forward and ask for protection if they become victims of rape or want to escape from brothels. Another concern is pornography, which represents a form of violence against women that glamorizes the degradation and the maltreatment of women and asserts their subordinate function as mere receptacles for male lust.

There are several reasons due to which women are forced into prostitution —poverty, domestic violence, better prospects of a job, war or armed conflict. There are countries where prostitution is legalized, and the state apparatus ensures the implementation of legal provisions to safeguard prostitution. There are controls to check breaches on their registration, work permits, safety regulations (including any violations of drug usage, AIDS testing, regular check-ups for sexually transmitted diseases). Nonetheless, there is a relation of mistrust between prostitutes and other state agencies.

18.2. VIOLENCE AGAINST CHILDREN

18.2.1. Child Abuse

The previous section underlined the violence against female child through practices of female foeticide and infanticide in India. But there is limited research around violence against children or child abuse within the home in India. The child abuse of children within private space may include beating, sexual aggression as well as engaging them in several hours of domestic labour instead of school or play. There has been an increase in the numbers of child labour who work as marginal labours due to absolute poverty. The literature available around inadequate care of children includes children left alone or with young sibling caregivers while adults are away working, increased accidental risk around children. There are studies that have managed to divulge that children are victims of psychological, physical and emotional abuse at the hands of their caregivers.

18.2.1.1. Feminist Perspective

The early and crucial contribution of feminist literature has successfully drawn attention to intra-household dynamics and the degree of abuse of children that takes place within the sphere of households and families. The feminist analysis also highlights the role of violence in the social construction of masculinity and gendered power relations of sexual abuse. There are works that have focused on gendered time poverty, changing family norms and social norms of obligations or responsibility for caregiving. Although these aspects have gendered implications, some considerations have been made towards children (Palriwala and Neetha 2011). Children's experiences also differ according to their sex which also affects the risk of particular violations. There is a direct but not exclusive relationship between poverty and inadequate care to children and child abuse.

18.2.2. Factors Contributing to Child Abuse

This section attempted to focus on how poverty can increase the risk of sexual violence against children: engaging in sexual activities as a livelihood strategy and increase in the precariousness and insecurity of children's lives and their vulnerability to sexual abuse and exploitation. There are different attributes of poverty that affects children's protection. The insufficient means of livelihood impede families to meet their basic needs and risk their future security and well-being. They try to secure their well-being through alternative economic strategies, some of which increases children's risk of early marriage, sexual exploitation, physical violence or inadequate care. This may manifest in several ways.

18.2.2.1. Lack of Power

Poverty makes people experience helplessness and powerlessness; this state is exacerbated in the case of children, making them vulnerable to abuse and exploitation. They may face sexual abuse from landlord, patron or breadwinner, which makes it harder for the child to resist as they and their families are dependent on them. There are reports of abuse in schools where some teachers or employees abuse children physically or sexually. Here, teachers may also be exploiting the power differentials between themselves and poor community members to behave with impunity.

18.2.2.2. Unavailability of Time

The conditions of low-paid work, inflexible working conditions and the need to work long hours to generate sufficient income for basic needs, combined with the additional responsibility of extensive domestic chores and unavailability of technology can restrict the time available for the care of young children. The problem is aggravated in the case of women who frequently suffer due to the double burden of both income-generating work and domestic responsibilities. Constrained adult time can lead to young children being left alone unsupervised while adults are working and can limit parents' availability to guide and support their children. This, in turn, can increase their risk of physical and sexual violence.

18.2.2.3. Exposed Living Condition

The poor housing localities in urban areas are often characterized by high levels of physical and sexual violence, putting the children residing in such areas at a greater risk than their better-off counterparts of opportunistic physical or sexual violence. They are also at higher risk of witnessing serious violence, consequences of which include pervasive fear, injury or even death. Violence and perpetual intervention of police in such localities is a normalized course of life which may strain their future cohesion with the larger society. In poor–urban neighbourhoods, strained social cohesion is associated with rising violence levels, which put children at risk both as victims and as witnesses to physical and sexual violence. It may also mean people are less willing to care for and welfare other people's children living in the same locality.

18.2.2.4. Inadequate Access to Amenities and Information

The poor living conditions devoid of basic necessities contributes to child protection violation in several ways. Unavailability of sanitation and toilets may compel them to go to distant or secluded places, increasing the risk of sexual violations. Also, the absence of affordable daycare facility for working parents means young children are left unsupervised. The high cost of secondary education or higher studies and distance may lead adolescent girls dropping out and marrying early. Further, due to lower-education levels, there is limited access to media, social capital and moreover inadequate information regarding better pursuits. The limited information among young people and their parents of the nature of work at far off destinations can put them at risk of trafficking.

The lack of awareness regarding positive discipline methods can lead to the use of corporal punishment and violations of children's rights, undermining their capacity to defend or assert themselves. But it is important to understand that the children, however, are not simply victims in need of protection but actively negotiate strategies and resist violence and abuse in their capacity.

18.3. VIOLENCE AGAINST THE ELDERLY

18.3.1. Old Age and Abuse

The aspects of demography and population have been discussed in detail in the previous chapter. The Indian current demographic dividend and increased life expectancy provide insight into the future of its ageing population. Ageing and the existence of elderly people in society is a universal phenomenon; the age of the elderly in India is 60 and above but varies in other countries. The Gazette of India (2007) defines a senior citizen as a person who has attained the age of 60 years or above. The United Nations also treats persons aged 60 years or more as elderly. The challenges and problems faced by the elderly are considered to be one of the most important domestic and public issues in the current context. A section of the growing population of the elderly is also becoming a victim of abuse and crime. The elders are vulnerable and also constantly battling with their physical limitations, familial interrelationships and economic and social conditions. The psychological conditions or their mental well-being is also being affected due to their loneliness.

Based on WHO/International Network for the Prevention of Elder Abuse (WHO 2002), elderly abuse has been classified into three broad categories: first, neglect, including isolation, abandonment and social exclusion; second, violation of human, legal and medical rights, and third, deprivation of choices, decision, status, finances and respect. Elder abuse as physical abuse is any action by another that produces pain or injury to the older person; sexual abuse is any intimate behaviour that is undesired or lacks competent consent by the older person, and emotional abuse is the inducement of fear, intimidation or a lowering of self-esteem to punish or control the older person. It also includes financial exploitation of the elder such as using the elder's goods, income and assets for purposes other than the safety, benefit and enjoyment of that elderly person. It may also be in the form of intentional or unintentional neglect at the hands of another or by elders themselves.

CONCLUSION

Violence is a complex phenomenon that involves violation, suffering and a sense of loss; it necessitates sociology to explore it as a negative connotation prevalent in social life and is part of the social structure and institutions. The family structure and society are changing, and the same is true with the norms and values regarding gender violence and violence against children. Violence, whether on women or children, reflects a kind of abuse of power.

In addition to poverty, other key factors or characteristics increasing children's risk of protection violations are disability and orphanhood and, depending on the violation concerned, gender and age. Girl children are at greater risk of sexual violence; however, boys' risk is substantial and often underestimated, and boys are at greater risk of fatal physical violence. It is equally important to recognize the degree of sexual violence committed on children by their peers. The meaning of gender and sexuality and the balance of power between women and men at all levels of society must be reviewed. Combating violence against women requires challenging the way that gender roles and power relations are articulated in society. Sexual harassment at the workplace degrades women and reinforces and often reflects the idea that women are unfit to perform in professional space. But in recent years, more women have been coming forward to report such practices, some taking their cases to court. A recent example is of the 'Me Too' movement which had taken on the world.

Conflict and post-conflict situations witness greater sexual violence. This is partly because of the normalization of physical and sexual violence, where social controls on violent behaviour have broken down and girls may be abducted and raped with impunity. Victims frequently fear for their lives if they do not comply. Conflict is widely recognized to exacerbate poverty and may drive greater number of children and adolescents into sex work or transactional sexual relationships in order to survive the conditions. Further, the institutions set up to counter the effects of conflict, fail to alleviate the conditions of all the survivors.

Points for Classroom Discussion

- Families are a site of perpetuation and sustenance of violence
- The temporal nature of violence leads to the blurring of its causes and consequences
- Violence on women and children is due to patriarchal ideology, gaps in socialization and powerlessness among them
- Gender-based violence cuts across nationalities, class, caste and ethnicity

GLOSSARY

Child abuse: It refers to the maltreatment of children physically, emotionally and sexually.
Gender socialization: Every society has a set of expected roles and behaviours from both men and women; this becomes cause and mechanisms which creates unequal relations among the sexes.
Gender-based violence: The term is primarily used to describe violence against women since most gender-based violence is perpetrated by men against women, nonetheless, includes violence against men, boys, other sexual minorities.
Intimate partner violence (IPV): It is violence that occurs between individuals who maintain a romantic or sexual relationship. Individuals include unmarried, cohabiting, and same-sex couples as well as heterosexual married couples.
Violence: As per WHO, it is described as 'the intentional use of physical force or power, threatened or actual, against oneself, another person, or against a group or community that either results in or has a high likelihood of resulting in injury, death, psychological harm, maldevelopment or deprivation'.

REFERENCE

Bourgois, P. 2004. 'Gang Rape.' In *Violence in Times of War and Peace: An Anthology*, edited by N. Scheper-Hughes, and P. Bourgois. London: Blackwell.
Gazette of India. 2007. 'Maintenance and Welfare of Parents and Senior Citizens Act 2007'. New Delhi: Ministry of Law and Justice. Available at: https://www.indiacode.nic.in/bitstream/123456789/6831/1/maintenance_and_welfare_of_parents_and_senior_citizens_act.pdf (accessed on 22 February 2021).
Ghosh, B., and T. Choudhuri. 2011. 'Legal Protection against Domestic Violence in India: Scope and Limitations'. *Journal of Family Violence* 26, no. 4: 319–330.
Gore, M. S. 1968. *Urbanisation and Family Change.* Mumbai: Popular Prakashan.
Hillis, S., J. Mercy, A. Amobi, and H. Kress. 2016. 'Global Prevalence of Past-year Violence against Children: A Systematic Review and Minimum Estimates'. *Pediatrics* 137, no. 3: e20154079.
Johnson, M. P. 2008. *A Typology of Domestic Violence: Intimate Terrorism, Violent Resistance, and Situational Couple Violence.* Boston, MA: Northeastern University Press.
Karlekar, M. 1982. *Poverty and Women's Work: A Study of Sweeper Women in Delhi.* New Delhi. Vikas Publishing House.
———. 2004. ed. *Paradigms of Learning: The Total Literacy Campaign in India.* New Delhi: SAGE Publications.
Nair, J. 1996. 'Prohibited Marriage: State Protection and Child Wife'. In *Social Reform, Sexuality and the State*, edited Patricia Uberoi. New Delhi: SAGE Publications.
Nedelsky, J. 1991. 'Law, Boundaries and the Bounded Self. *Representations* 30, 162–189.
Litke, R. 1992. 'Violence and Power.' *International Social Science Journal* 132, 173–183.
Palriwala, R., and N. Neetha. 2011. 'Stratified Familialism: The Care Regime in India through the Lens of Childcare'. *Development and Change* 42, no. 4: 1049–1078.
Pinheiro, P. S. 2006. *World Report on Violence Against Children.* New York: UN. Available at: https://digitallibrary.un.org/record/587334?ln=en (accessed on 22 February 2021).
Schinkel, W. 2010. *Aspects of Violence.* Farnham: Ashgate.
Sen, R. 2010. 'Women's Subjectivities of Suffering and Legal Rhetoric on Domestic Violence'. *Indian Journal of Gender Studies* 17, no 3: 375–401.

Stanko, E., ed. 2003. *Meanings of Violence*. London: Routledge.
Uberoi, P. 1994. *Family, Kinship and Marriage in India*. New Delhi: Oxford University Press.
Ungar, M., S. A. Bermanzohn, and K. Worcester, ed. 2002. 'Introduction'. *Violence and Politics*, 1–12. London: Routledge.
Wallerstein, I. 2005. *World-Systems Analysis: An Introduction*. London: Duke University Press.
WHO. 2002. 'Abuse of the Elderly'. In *World Report on Violence and Health*, edited by Etienne G. Krug et al. 123–145. Available at: http://www.who.int/violence_injury_prevention/violence/global_campaign/en/chap5.pdf (accessed on 22 February 2021).

SECTION G

CHALLENGES TO CIVILIZATION AND SOCIETY

Chapter 19
Nationalism and Citizenship

Chapter 20
Communalism and Secularism

CHAPTER 19

Nationalism and Citizenship

LEARNING OUTCOMES

- To appreciate the historicity of nation-state as a concept
- To explore the contending theories of nationalism
- To examine the linkage between national identity and citizenship
- To identify the bases of nationality

Keywords: Nation, nationality, nationalism, citizenship, Hindu nationalism

Neither the colourless vagueness of cosmopolitanism, nor the fierce self-idolatry of nation-worship is the goal of human history.

—**Rabindranath Tagore on nationalism**

INTRODUCTION

Popularly, nationalism is understood as a consciousness or a feeling of one's own nationality. As a sentiment, nationalism is an expression of shared living in a well-defined geographical territory. In the classical European term, this shared living is based on speaking a common language; having a common history, culture and tradition; expressing the same aspirations and even, in some cases, having a common origin. As a derivative from this understanding, nationalism is an ideology of pronounced patriotism. The ideology of nationalism at different points of history across the world has guided and shaped up movements for attainment of national independence or self-governance. It helped to re-energize people of the same cultural and social unity to secure a common future of prosperity and dignity. On the other hand, nationalism can also instil a sense of exclusivity or superiority vis-à-vis other nations. This leads to a dogma of accepting one's own nation as end in itself.

We need to clear the casual usage of the two terms, nationality and citizenship, interchangeably. Nationality as the plinth of nationalism indicates the belongingness of a person to a particular nation. Nation is classically understood as a group of people united on the basis of certain attributes such as territory, history, language and choice. Whereas citizenship is understood as status which has a legal or juristic connotation. It is a legal status granted to any individual by the state, when one satisfies the legal formalities required for becoming a citizen of a country. Citizenship is not limited by consideration of one's place of birth or inheritance. A person can be a national of only one country, whereas one can become a citizen of more than one country.

Citizenship rights have developed historically in Europe along with the development of a modern capitalist society. Similarly, the development of nation state in Europe is linked with the development of modern industrial capitalism. Going by the historicity of the context, India as a nation is a political construct under the auspices of the colonial rule. It is not the paradigm of modernity as fostered by industrial capitalism that gave rise to Indian nation state. Nationalism developed in India as a reaction to colonialism in a multi-ethnic, multi-cultural, multi-lingual and multi-religious diverse society. The independence from the colonial rule, coupled with the Partition of the erstwhile country on the basis of religion, has continued to complicate the issue of national identity and citizenship rights in independent India.

As a diverse society, India presents a unique case of developing as a modern nation state. The idea of a modern state has from time to time grappled with the issue of nationality and the appropriate bases of claiming nationality. Citizenship has been a contentious issue in India as questions of citizenship and nationality frequently become fodder for identity and electoral politics. When used interchangeably, without realizing their differences, citizenship collapses into a kind of nationalism that promotes exclusionary politics for pursuit of power at the cost of the universal principles of equity and justice.

19.1. NATIONALISM

19.1.1. Nation and Nationality

Nation as a concept has evolved through a long history. As a corollary, nationhood or nationality has also substantially undergone transformation with regard to its content. Sticking to the original meaning of nation will be misleading to make sense of the dynamics of contemporary reality marked by the intricate triad of nation, national identity and nationalism. It is so, as in the modern times the terms nation and state are conflated. In its original classical Latin meaning of the term *nasci*, the political dimension was not attached to nation. It meant just a tribal-ethnic group who enjoys a common territory. L. Greenfield (1992) has shown that historically the term nation has the following five different connotations:

1. As a group of foreigners
2. As a community of opinion
3. As an elite group
4. As a sovereign people
5. As a unique people

The political dimension of nation is the result of the French Revolution, whereby it attained the modern connotation. Simultaneously, it meant a cultural entity—a group of people bound together by some timeless attributes obtained by birth. The attributes are that of descent, territory, history, language, custom, religion and so on. Also, as a political entity, nation meant a community which organizes itself as a state. Thus, having its own state allows a nation to protect its sentiment.

It is all too obvious that such a tribal-ethnic notion of nation is untenable in the modern world of politics. Across the world and historically more in the USA or South Asian states, we find enhanced movements of populations and shifting notion of homeland. With the formation of modern states, any collectivity claiming nationality may run into the very project of sovereignty of states. Unlike the European nation states, the post-colonial states are culturally plural. India has been a homeland of numerous collectivities with specific immutable attributes. As pointed out by T. K. Oommen, if such collectives or 'nations' asserted for their political entity as states, India could not have continued as a single sovereign state. The linear understanding that nationalism is the common sentiment of each 'nation' and it automatically results in the formation of its exclusive state is refuted by Oommen (2002).

Nation state is just a specific European historical sociopolitical formation. We find a fusion of citizenship and nationality in many West European sociopolitical formations. The German and Italian nation states are good examples of such collective-authoritarian states. This coexistence of nation with state is possible when a cultural entity is coterminous with a political entity. Even in Europe, the one-nation, one-state model pursued as an ideal or a pure type cannot be found everywhere. One such clear example is the case of Great Britain. When a nation could be understood as a collective of sovereign individuals, that is, individual members as rightful bearers of citizenship rights in the classical sense, an individualistic-libertarian concept of the state could be realized. That is the way Great Britain constituted a state with citizens drawn from different nations—England, Scotland, Wales and Ireland. Clearly, we can see the possibility of a multinational state given the heterogeneity of contemporary politics premised on the values of democracy, equality and justice (Oommen 1997).

The nation–state relation is a variable of historical formation of a society. State as a centralized political structure is best explained in classical political sociology of Max Weber. Put simply, it is an institution which claims successfully its rule over a specified territory having a monopoly on the legitimate use of force (Gerth and Mills 1948). Subsequently, contemporary theories of state have explored state both as having a structure and a system of ideas (Mitchell 1989). Essentially, it is being indicated that there is a spillover of society into what is ordinarily taken to be the state and it is the question of how a social and political order is maintained.

As against the English sense of individualistic-libertarian state, Western Europe experienced a different model of collectivistic-ethnic nation in many new sociopolitical formations. Citizenship is a conglomerate of civil, political and social rights, which has evolved over three centuries as a part of emergence of modern capitalist society. It is a condition as well as a consequence of capitalist development since the 18th century. The three sets of rights—civil, political and social—followed one another in the sequence in three centuries, though always not so strictly (Marshall 1950). The two contrasting notions of state, individualistic-libertarian and collectivistic-authoritarian point out two different kinds of citizenship. When the nation and state are not fused or coterminous, citizenship is open and voluntary. It is civic and can be acquired. Whereas when the model is that of 'one nation, one state', membership in the nation is inherent and citizenship is inherited.

Oommen talks about the process of 'Frenchification' to explain the French state as the third type. By 'Frenchification' he means learning the French ways (language, culture and education) irrespective of race and religion. Through this process, one can acquire nationality in France. He calls this third type a civic-collectivistic state. However, none of the three assures a true exposition to the principles of equality and justice. The three types as enumerated by Oommen are as follows:

1. **Individualist-libertarian state:** Ireland, Wales and Scotland are often treated as internal colonies of the dominant English nation, although the nationals of these 'colonies' are British citizens.
2. **Collectivistic-authoritarian state:** Those European nation states (German, Italian and so on) who have to negotiate the condition of equality on the face of contemporary enhanced movement of people, immigration and fluidity of the notion of homeland.
3. **Civic-collectivistic state:** France, apparently ensuring a community of citizens but practically experiencing a hierarchy of citizens with the White, Catholic, French-speaking citizens enjoying the top rungs, while the 'Frenchified' ones/Black Muslim immigrants are downgraded.

Having noted the conceptual and practical disconnect between nationality and citizenship, one can re-examine the pronounced and emotive content of nationalism in the processual dynamics of nation-building. Taking cue from the trajectory of Western history, nationalism most often has led to an intense emotive loyalty to one's nation. In different historical contexts, nationalism guided its loyalists at variance. At one extreme, it could lead to a fascist tendency like the Nazi terror of the 1930s in Germany. On the other, it could act as an anti-colonial binding force in any colonized country like India. So nationalism can act as a positive as well as a negative force—the perceptions change depending upon the context of its formation and expression. Historically contentious and tentative is the concept of nationalism:

> ...Thus nationalism was viewed as a positive force in the ex-colonial countries in the context of the anti-imperialist struggles, but if any of the constituent units of the multi-national colony were to assert its separateness as a nation and mobilise its national sentiment after the attainment of freedom, the rest of the constituents, particularly the dominant nation, would invariably dispute the claim and instantly condemn the mobilization as being anti-national! (Oommen 2002, 2)

Going by the original notion of nation, India represents a case of a poly-ethnic multinational state. A single sovereign state containing multiple nations has unevenly developed the Indian society. This is borne out by the development and formation of the Indian state resulting from the Partition of the subcontinent and preceded by the colonial rule. In such a poly-ethnic multinational state, the coexistence of its different nations or ethnic groups is coordinated and consolidated by the state. Such a polity is possible when the multi-nations and ethnic groups function without stress and strains on their territorial integrity. This is possible only on the conditions of equality, justice and multiculturalism. The poly-ethnic situation in India gets substantiated if one appreciates that historically ethnicity has been a product of conquest, colonization and immigration. So inherently, ethnie, nation and state relationships are dynamic.

19.1.2. Historical Understanding and New Nationalism

Quite early in Indian sociology, A. R. Desai in the 1940s took up the macro-sociological theme of Indian nationalism. He revisited the same theme after two decades to understand Indian nationalism as an indispensable function of the encroachment of capitalist forces that took place during the colonial period (Desai 1960, 1966). Using a historical method, Desai analysed Indian nationalism as an event. Every nation, according to him, is forged in a unique way as the conditions for such a formation differ across time and space. In the case of India, it is against the backdrop of colonialism that nationalism developed. As a dominant determinant of Indian politics, nationalism continues to be tentative even after Independence. As the political liberation was not accompanied by socio-economic freedom, the nationalist aspirations of various linguistic, ethnic, religious or regional groups remained unfulfilled. In the absence of a composite culture and aggravation of competitive interests of multiple classes and strata, nationalism failed as a homogenous perception. Hence, nationalism as a product of colonial development was not a natural development. It was argued that the emergence of nationalities was the result of such a lack of natural and spontaneous development of nationalism.

Accounts of historians on the development of nationalism in India show a change from the 1980s onwards. The pre-1980s historical studies show a fundamental linkage between nationalism, modernization and modern class formation. New historical researches are guided by theoretical frameworks of leading scholars of nationalism such as A. D. Smith, Ernest Gellner and Benedict Anderson. The pattern of modernization in India is correlated by historians with the pattern of nationalist development. The project of modernizing the traditional society was mainly a middle-class agenda. It was the politically conscious educated middle class who played the crucial role of mediating between the tradition and modernity.

The theoretical guidance of the classically developed notions of nationalism emphasized the breakdown of the old world of religions under the impact of the forces of capitalist production in Europe. The passing away of the old order was a prelude to the emergence of the modern world view of nationalism (Gellner 1983, 7). By introducing the concept of 'print capitalism', Benedict Anderson explains the growing importance of the middle class as related to 'vernacular thrust' of printing. The liberation of the literate classes from the limitations of religious truths and languages was made possible by the 'vernacularizing thrust' of print capitalism (Anderson 1991).

Post 1980s, Indian historiography changed its theoretical stance to move away from nationalist elite reconstruction of history and retrieve the agency of the masses in history making. So nationalism was not to be studied as the agenda and project of the middle class only. Instead, the subaltern classes were seen as the prime mover of nationalist consciousness which was evidently disparate, fragmented and subversive. The subversion was not only to the colonial state but to a variety of other forms of domination that constituted the colonial society. While it is true that subaltern perspective forwarded an alternative domain of politics, in the same breadth, one has to admit that there remains a substantial overlap between the elite/middle-class construction of nationalism and the fragmentary projects of the subaltern classes (Chatterjee 1993; Guha 1982).

T. K. Oommen talks about 'new nationalism' to examine the post-Independence tensions in Indian nationalism. He classifies two kinds of nationalism—state-centred and state-renouncing nationalism. State-centred nationalism privileges the existence of a sovereign state for a nation. It has two versions—the old state-seeking nationalism, which aspires for a national state from an external colonial power. The new state-seeking nationalism is the one which seeks to build its 'sovereign state' against 'internal colonizer'. The secessionist movements in India are the examples, which are reactions against cultural homogenization.

There is another kind of new state-centred nationalism. State-centred nationalism could also be built with reference to an 'other' as an alter to sustain itself. In terms of religion, language, race and so on, the 'other', even if not there in the real, has to be created to foster aggressive nationalism. State-centred nationalism of this kind prospers well when the 'other' is in the neighbourhood or having a disputed political boundary. The present-day Indian and Pakistani nationalisms are apt cases for such a type.

On the other hand, the state-renouncing nationalism operates within the framework of a federal structure. Without raising the question of a separate state, based on language, ethnicity or region, it demands cultural-fiscal autonomous status. In fact, India has seen many such autonomist movements, for example, the very reorganization of states on linguistic basis, then creation of many states such as Jharkhand, Uttarakhand, Telangana, Chhattisgarh and so on. Identity-seeking ethnic movements (Urdu or Sindhi) are also minor version of state-renouncing nationalism. Without any territorial congregation of the Urdu- or Sindhi-speaking collectivities, they could best be addressed as ethnic demands for protection of cultural rights (Oommen 2002).

The argument of T. K. Oommen is that the historical trajectory of nation and nationalism does not confirm a conflation between nation and state. Polity may be run in a new framework, where all nations need not have their exclusive sovereign states. A clear disjunction between citizenship and national identity is more probable in a world marked by an accelerated space of spatial movement of people.

19.1.3. Citizenship and National Identity

Thomas H. Marshall's foremost study on citizenship tells us that citizenship is an ensemble of three different sets of rights. It begins with civil rights—entailing freedom of speech, thought and faith—and fosters rights to justice. Civil rights are followed by political rights—the right of franchise and political participation. The culmination is social rights that ensure full share of the social heritage and the prevailing standard of living. It is premised on economic rights that provide social security (Marshall 1973).

The concept of citizenship is universal, but its context varies in terms of the relative salience of its component part in different socio-historical contexts. Also, the heterogeneity of contemporary state populations and commitment to the principles of democracy work against any direct linkage between citizenship and nationality, or for that matter with any primordial identity.

Jürgen Habermas's (1992) critical theory has examined the possibility of delinking democratic citizenship from the limitation of nationalist identity. Working towards a Universalist conception of human rights, Habermas puts the principles of democracy beyond a restrictive nationalist context. Analysing the stress on the European states in the emergent condition of immigration accelerated by forces of globalization, he posits 'republican citizenship' which is independent of any particular national or cultural form of life as its premise.

Historically, the linkages between citizenship and national identity, in other words, the relationship between the state and the citizens, have shown three distinct types. They are as follows:

1. **Hegemonic pattern—feature of feudal states:** Here, the culture of the dominant group is considered to be the national culture.
2. **Uniformity pattern—feature of bourgeois states:** Here, every nation has its own state as national and political boundaries coexist. This pattern also allows for several nations to coexist under one state.
3. **Pluralist pattern—feature of the socialist state:** Here, several 'historic' nations could coexist within one state by delinking citizenship with nationality. The fate of the 'non-historic' nations is very tenuous. The fate of such socialist multinational states ended up with national chauvinism, disintegration and break-up of the state (Worsley 1984).

T. K. Oommen finds that the Indian situation needs to be treated in terms of its historically evolved social formation marked by heterogeneity and hierarchy. It does not fit exactly into any of the above three models. The colonized years did not allow many of its primordial identities to raise head, except the political expression of Muslim nationalism from the 1920s onwards. Many identity questions and related issues of identification with a 'nation', which were subsumed by national freedom struggle, started gaining salience once the context changed post-Independence.

> That is the nationalist expectancy that all citizens of free India would enthusiastically involve themselves in the task of 'nation building' irrespectively of their socio-cultural background was flawed and could not be easily realized... the conceptualization of the relationship between state and citizen did not adequately account for the simplicity and complexity of the Indian situation. (Oommen 2006, 793)

The major factors, according to Oommen, that contributed to the troubled linkage between citizenship and national identity in terms of historical developments in India are as follows:

1. The present-day India claimed as a nation is essentially Aryan. The Indian society is a result of accretion of immigrants and dislocation of original inhabitants. The original inhabitants, the Dravidians, were dislocated by the Aryan invasion. The Aryans gave rise to distinct religion, language and order

of social life (Hinduism, Sanskrit and *Varnashrama*, respectively) to dislodge the native ways of life. Over a long period of time, this process got normalized as an ethnie transformed itself into a nation and claimed a territorial basis.

2. Series of Muslim conquests, beginning with the invasion of the Sindh in the 8th century AD, also led to cultural accretion. Only a very small section of the conquering group settled down, but as a result of proselytization, a big section of downgraded locals embraced Islam. The Muslim rule made Persian the official language, which in interaction with local North Indian languages gave rise to hybrid language of Urdu. Urdu is popularly associated with the large Muslim population in India.

3. The Western intrusion has led to major cultural change. Despite large-scale proselytization of Christianity, the Christian population is quite negligible but English as a language of learning and administration has emerged as a strong cultural component.

4. The wide diversity of language, religion, culture and so on, except the caste system, could not foster an all-India unity. The Independence movement achieved it much in a political sense. 'Indian consciousness' is more a totalistic response to a colonial rule.

5. The formation of the independent Indian state premised on the religion-based Partition left an indelible mark on its polity for years to come. A major transfer of population happened involving the Hindus, the Muslims and the Sikhs. The trouble spot was the Eastern boundary, where 'migration' continued beyond 1951. This created the issue of 'illegal immigrants' in Assam and north-eastern states. Whereas on the western front, the Sikh refugees were more enterprising as they settled not only in Punjab but spread all over. Over a period of time, an emotive demand for a separate homeland for Sikhs emerged which used language and culture to seek an independent sovereign Khalistan state.

6. The exclusivity of sociocultural identity is missing for a state like India, as it shares the same (also physical characteristics) with populations of neighbouring states. For example, Nepal shares a long Hindu religious-historical tradition

---

BOX 19.1
Citizenship and Autonomy

While this is unquestionably important, the whole relation of rights to the nation-state has itself become progressively more problematic in the twentieth century. For a gap has opened up, linked to processes of globalization, between the idea of membership of a national political community, that is, citizenship, and the development of international law which subjects individuals, non-governmental organizations and governments to new systems of regulation. Rights and duties are recognized in international law which transcend the claims of nation-states and which, whilst they may lack coercive powers of enforcement, have far-reaching consequences.

Source: Held (1998).

and sociocultural similarity with India. Bengali Muslims of Bangladesh and Bengali Hindus of India (Bengal, Tripura) share society and culture beyond their state boundaries. Same is the case of Tamils or Kashmiris.

The disjunctions between nation and state are so obvious in India that the linkage between citizenship and national identity is the most problematic. Interestingly, in every Indian language, the distinction between *desh* (homeland) and *videsh* (foreign land) has salience that *desh* is beyond a territory to mean people with a distinct way of life, in fact, a nation. Any political administrative state in India may have multiple 'nations' or parts of it. As the political-administrative units and national regions are not coexistent, belonging to *desh* confers a privileged identity of being a native, while those who do not belong become an outsider and ethnic. Thus, in many situations, the 'ethnicity' identity as an outsider complicates the issue of 'nationality' in India (Oommen 1997).

19.2. BASES OF NATIONALITY

19.2.1. Religion

An analytic detail is presented by T. K. Oommen to dismiss the claim of a Hindu nation state. Not only Hinduism but any religious basis of national identity is historically as well as conceptually a flawed one. Hinduism as a marker of Hindu identity exhibits no single ideal type. Present-day Hinduism is a mix of both—the old symbols and values are revived, and new ones are constructed to build its boundary vis-à-vis other Semitic religions. As a result, the energetic and emotive claims of nationalists are put to scrutiny in the following ways:

1. The literature of Hindu nationalists such as Desh Raj Goyal (*Rashtriya Swayamsevak Sangh*) and M. S. Golwalkar (*We or Our Nationhood Defined*) put Hindus as the original inhabitants of India. Hindus are considered as those who naturally own the homeland Hindustan as a collective. Such an understanding confers no religious content to Hindus.
2. Contention of other Hindu nationalists like Vinayak Damodar Savarkar (*Hindutva*) is that ipso facto Hinduism means the religion that is native to India. It attempts to be inclusive by suggesting all followers of religions of Indian origin are Hindus. And an essence of Hindu nation is thus forwarded, that is, the contiguity of the community of faith and the country of residence. This proposition falls flat on the evidence of 'non-Hindu' religions of the Indian origin (e.g., Sikhs).
3. Hinduism is also understood in a third way by invoking the variables of caste and language. It is a very exclusivist narrow understanding that excludes the ex-untouchables, the Adivasis and Dravidian Hindus of South India. It becomes a valid religion of only the upper castes like Brahmans, Kshatriyas, Vaishyas and at best ritually clean Shudras. Also, it renders many 'Hindus' as outsiders by restricting itself to upper castes of *Arya Bhumi* (North India). Not only the ambiguity is inbuilt in such a conceptualization of the Hindus, but by invoking the caste and linguistic factors, it takes away the saliency of religion.

> **BOX 19.2**
> **Hindu Nationalism**
>
> No sane man can question the proposition that Hindus are a nation. There will also be no difficulty to concede that the Hindus constitute the vast majority of the population. India is therefore pre-eminently a Hindu nation, Hindustan. The practical bearing of these conclusions on the problems that confront the politicians is immense and deserve to be very carefully and dispassionately considered.... Hindu Nation as a sovereign State is entirely a different entity from the Hindu nation as a cultural nationality. No modern State has denied the resident minorities of different nationalities rights of citizenship of the State if they are once naturalised either automatically or under the operation of a Statute.
>
> **Source:** Golwalkar (1939).

The very idea of India as a Hindu homeland is ridden with multiple problems. The very claim of India as a Hindu homeland was made at a time when undivided India had the largest Muslim population in the world. On the question of the nativity of the people, the claim of the Hindu nationalist is also weak with respect to what could be counted as the appropriate time record of settling in India. As at different points of history, many other religious faithful had settled in this land. Above all, the claim of nativity is much more valid of the original habitants of India—the dislocated outcastes and the Adivasi tribes who later on overwhelmingly converted to Christianity and Islam.

The assertion of Hindu nationalist is not uniform with respect to other religions. Only when the 'other' becomes a parallel contender of religious nationalism that Hindu nationalism raises its head. Hindu nationalists have antagonistic relation in independent India with Sikhs and Muslims as both of them claim themselves as nations or nationalities. With other 'migrant' religions (Jews, Bahaiis and Zoroastrians), Hindu nationalists have been tolerant or indifferent. But with proselytizing religions such as Christianity and Islam, the attitude is hostile. Since Christians never defined themselves as a nationality or sought any special benefits from the state, the interrelation with Hindu nationalists was moderated upon. For a number of reasons, the relationship between the Hindu nationalists and the Muslims is severely hostile. Some of the reasons are as follows:

1. The 14.2 per cent of Muslim population constitute a single most vote bank against Hindu nationalism, considered so rightly or wrongly.
2. The relationship is affected between the Hindu majority and the Muslim minority as the two neighbouring states of India, Pakistan and Bangladesh, are Muslim-majority states.
3. Hindu nationalists considered the Muslims responsible for the division of India, considered as their holy land.

4. Although Muslims are territorially dispersed in independent India, still there have been efforts to consolidate Muslims as a nationality by projecting Urdu as their exclusive language.
5. The secessionist ideas among Kashmiri Muslims, often abetted by Pakistan, and the claim over Kashmir as their exclusive homeland.

Finally, there are uneasy questions like what would be the status of the Hindus who have settled in large numbers outside the Indian subcontinent. The central homeland as the salient marker of national identity poses problem for Hinduism which is migratory. The Hindu nationalists' claim becomes more ludicrous as to where to put the agnostic rationalist or secularist in this frame. Also, the task will be to annex the neighbouring Hindu majority nation of Nepal to execute the scheme of religion-based Hindu nation. The religion-territory co-terminality is not tenable even if it is restricted to religions of the Indian origin, as Buddhism and Hinduism (both of the Indian origin) are the dominant religions of Sri Lanka. The case of native population getting dislocated and pushed out is true for Sri Lanka just like Aryanization in India.

19.2.2. Language

The Hindu nationalists' project of Sanskrit as the common ancient language of all Hindus and Hindi written in Devanagari script as the national language of India is also problematic. This linguistic project on their part has been to mitigate the fact of multiplicity of speech communities of Hindus. The uneasy issues are as follows:

1. Sanskrit is not a living language and has a very miniscule speech community.
2. Sanskrit is not the exclusive heritage of Hindus only.
3. Sanskrit is at best an exclusive possession of Aryan Hinduism.
4. Like Sanskrit, Pali and Tamil were ancient and highly developed languages, of which Tamil is a living language having a big speech community.
5. Pali is identified with Buddhism, while Tamil is identified with Dravidian Hinduism; hence, Sanskrit is not even the heritage language of all Hindus.
6. Hindi, even when projected as a unified language irrespective of the languages and dialects it consists of, is spoken by less than 40 per cent of the Indian population.
7. All the major Dravidian languages and several regional languages such as Marathi and Bengali compared to Hindi are no less developed, if not more, and will always rebel against any move to install Hindi as the national language.
8. To facilitate the installation of the Hindu nation premised on Hindi as the common language will be an anomaly for several developed speech communities in India.

The way Hindu nationalism is not sustainable in the Indian society, similarly the claims of the Muslims and the Sikhs for separate nations are refuted by T. K. Oommen. The use of argument that the Muslims are alien to this land is a poor one, as the majority of the population are actually original inhabitants who resorted to conversion to escape downgrading by the conquering Aryans. But the valid reasons are different as to why like the Hindu nationalism, the Muslim claim of nation on the religious basis is untenable:

1. In India, no territory as claimed by the Muslims is exclusively populated by them, so the claim of nativity and nationhood on that count is a flawed one.
2. Like many sections of the Hindus, Kashmiri Pundits, Maghi Brahmans and Rajputs, some Muslims are migrants to India, which happened several centuries ago. Nationality cannot be doubted on that count, but religious faiths or affiliation cannot be attached to nationhood.
3. Most importantly, Pakistan created on the basis of religion could not be sustained as a single nation state. The creation of Bangladesh (on the basis of language and territory) again points out the irrelevance of Islam or any religion in this subcontinent to give rise to a nation.
4. Muslim nationalists be it in Pakistan or Bangladesh refused to accept Hindi/Urdu-speaking Muslims of North India or Hindi-speaking Muslims from Bihar, respectively, as natives. So co-religionists are not accepted to share the nationality.
5. Faith communities are less acceptable than speech community to signify a homeland as the situation in multilingual Pakistan shows. Different linguistic groups such as Punjabis, Sindhis or Baluchis raise the issue of homeland on the basis of language.
6. Except the Kashmir valley, no region in India is dominantly populated by Muslims after the Partition. But Kashmiri Pundits (Hindu) too claimed Kashmir to be their homeland, for which they were hounded out of Kashmir. This violence again points out the negative consequence of any sense of co-terminality between religion and territory.
7. As such in post-Partition India, Muslims are dispersed all over the country. So they resort to using new symbols like Urdu to maintain a cultural specificity but the lack of geographical contiguity is a deterrent for any such claim of nationality.
8. There is a clear lack of link between Urdu and Islam as except in Bihar and Uttar Pradesh (that too some sections), Indian Muslims do not speak Urdu. This nullifies any possibility of Urdu nationalism in India.

In a similar vein, the Sikhs' claim to Punjab as their homeland is refuted by Oommen. Because of the clear disjuncture between religion and territory, any moral claim over a specific territory as a homeland cannot be sustained by any religious faithful. For the Sikhs claiming Punjab as their homeland is weak also on the ground that before the Partition, Punjab was a Muslim-dominated region. After the reallocation of the territory and migration/transfer of population, the Sikhs settled in Punjab but that too, Hindus were the majority. So Punjab as the homeland for Sikhs could not be entertained as they lacked a clear demographic majority. Language as the single criteria of claiming nationhood by Sikhs is quite a weak one.

19.2.3. Language Tribe

Like religion, language and tribe combination is also another dimension in defining a nation. It is true normally that languages and tribes enjoy common territory but the variations in the Indian context are as follows:

1. In the same territory, one finds more than one language or tribe groups so the combination of language tribes co-jointly claiming to constitute a nation is problematic.
2. In modern times, most language or tribe groups get so dispersed that no such exclusive territorial homeland can be identified.
3. A language or tribe or any segment of them, due to spatial mobility, may find a new homeland to claim a 'new nation'.
4. Sizes of many languages and tribes are too small to claim national identity.

Further, it is interesting to consider language tribe as a durable basis of national identity in a society like India, which is polyglot with numerous tribes. Language is a signifier of group loyalty as well as could be a matter of national identity; so denying any speech community and privileging some other linguistic group in the determination of national identity will invite divisions and disorder in the society. To make the matter worse, the language policy of independent India has sowed the seeds of disharmony. Some languages such as Sanskrit, Sindhi and Urdu are accorded the status of 'national' languages although they do not have any territorial anchorage. Whereas many subaltern speech communities having exclusive territorial enclaves are not conferred the same status. The hierarchy thus created has put Hindi at the top. The linguistic hierarchization is a continuum. The regional languages point out rightfully the domination of Hindi, whereas they in turn dominate and marginalize the languages of the subaltern groups. So a continuum of cultural hegemony of dominant nationalities designs the multilingual, multicultural Indian society.

Having identified the area of tension, the regional-linguistic map of India would still find it possible to acknowledge linguistic groups and tribes with territorial basis as nations, provided they have a minimum size with an accredited homeland, while those without homelands or those disassociated from their homelands as ethnies. This leads to conflict between nationals and ethnies expressed as insiders versus outsiders tension on the question of entitlements within nations. The Indian Constitution guarantees common citizenship entitlements to all legal inhabitants of this land irrespective of sociocultural differences. Any claim to entitlement based on nationality will be a contradiction in terms. Any attempts to factor in the sensitive issue of the religion, even in the context of resolving the vexed problem of illegal immigrants in some pockets of India, will basically damage the polity of democracy.

> To the extent national identity and citizenship entitlements are linked, democratic principles are likely to be endangered in a multi-national polity. This is particularly so when national identity is defined as the basis of religion. At any rate, religion cannot provide the basis of national identity because the two basic conditions of nation formation, namely common territory and language, are not common to a faith community. (Oommen 1997, 167)

What is very common in contemporary world of social and spatial mobility is the dispersal of people of one nation in the homelands of other nations. The conflict arising out of this could be mitigated with the ideal operation of market principles that ensure equal opportunities to all irrespective of any primordial identity. Oommen's proposition provides a fresh thinking on nation and nationalism which is sensitive to the changing face of the contemporary world.

CONCLUSION

For aeons, India has been a land of diverse religions, languages and cultures, whereas the very notion of nation demands a sense of commonality shared by the members of a community in terms of language, culture, ethnicity, history and aspiration for a common political destiny. It is amply clear that the meaning of Indian nationalism has always been fraught with difficulties. From time to time, Indian polity has faced the crucial question and challenge to the very idea of a nation state since its formation after the colonial rule.

Historically, the very concept of nation has been subjected to contending understanding. The coterminous existence of nation and state is only a specific socio-historical instance to be found in Europe. It involves a fusion of citizenship and nationality. Such a model need not be an ideal or universally valid and also socioculturally applicable in many societies marked by multi-religious, multilingual, multi-ethnic groups. Rather, the question of citizenship rights premised on modern values of democracy, equality and justice is more significant in contemporary politics.

A dispassionate understanding of nationalism takes note of the historical disconnect between nationality and citizenship. It is a crucial as well as critical proposition for a poly-ethnic, multinational state like India. The entire complex of India's socio-cultural-political development through different phases of history points to the coexistence of its different 'nations' or ethnic groups. The post-Independence crisis revolving around the question of Indian nationalism demands a theoretical innovation.

Within a single sovereign state, nationalities can thrive on a better public life of equality and justice. As suggested by T. K. Oommen, one needs to theorize beyond the assumed conflation between nation and state. The heterogeneity and hierarchy that characterize the Indian society make it necessary to reconsider the relevance of the markers of nationality. That is, whether religion or language–tribe combination could stand the test of marking a distinct nationality for a nation–state congruence in India. Moreover, the empirical reality has changed substantially due to the emergence of the New World. Changes are caused by dislocation of populations wrought by socialist states, the failure of the homogenization project initiated by nation states and the ongoing process of interstate migration. All these are results of a new form of globalization process at the auspices of a neoliberal world. With enhanced physical and social mobility in the contemporary globalized world, any fixed timeless markers are bound to keep the issue of disconnect between nationalism and citizenship alive. Against the slippery connotations and expressions of identities, only the principle of universality of justice, liberty and equality needs to be worked out.

Points for Classroom Discussion

- Nation–State relation as a variable of historical sociopolitical formation of any society
- The issues of linking citizenship with national identity
- The nature of disjunctions between nation and state in India
- Any claim of religious basis of national identity is historically and conceptually a flawed one

GLOSSARY

Authoritarian: Opposed to individual freedom of thought and action, a form of government that is centralizing and dominating.
Citizenship: A legal status and relation between an individual and a state that entails specific legal rights and duties.
Critical theory: Influenced by Marxist theory, also known as the Frankfurt School, stresses the critique of society and culture, drawing from knowledge across the social sciences and philosophy.
Hindutva: Coined by V. D. Savarkar in the early 20th century is the Right-wing ideology that promotes Hindu nationalism.
Libertarian: With a long intellectual tradition spanning hundreds of years, the philosophy to allow personal liberty and economic freedom with least governance.
Poly-ethnic: A condition where people who together represent multiple ethnicities coexist and interact harmoniously.
Rashtriya Swayamsevak Sangh: A Right-wing, Hindu nationalist, volunteer organization founded by K. B. Hedgewar in 1925.
Subaltern: The lower social classes and the downgraded social groups displaced to the margins of a society.

REFERENCES

Anderson, B. 1991. *Imagined Communities: Reflections on the Origins and Spread of Nationalism.* London: Verso.
Chatterjee, P. 1993. *The Nation and Its Fragments: Colonial and Post-colonial Histories.* Princeton, NJ: Princeton University Press.
Desai, A. R. 1960. *Recent Trends in Indian Nationalism.* Bombay: Popular Prakashan.
———. 1966. *Social Background of Indian Nationalism.* Bombay: Popular Prakashan.
Gellner, E. 1983. *Nation and Nationalism.* Ithaca, NY: Cornwell University Press.
Gerth, H., and C. W. Mills. 1948. *From Max Weber: Essays in Sociology.* London. Routledge & Kegan Paul.
Golwalkar, M. S. 1939. *We or Our Nationhood Defined.* Nagpur: Bharat Publications.
Greenfield, L. 1992. *Nationalism: Five Roads to Modernity.* Cambridge: Harvard University Press.
Guha, R. 1982. 'On Some Aspects of Historiography of Colonial India.' In *Subaltern Studies*, edited by R. Guha, Vol. I. New Delhi: Oxford University Press.
Habermas, J. 1992. 'Citizenship and National Identity: Some Reflections on the Future of Europe.' *Praxis International* 12, no.1: 1–19.
Held, D. 1998. *Political Theory and the Modern State.* Cambridge: Polity Press.
Marshall, T. H. 1950. *Citizenship and Social Class and Other Essays.* New York. Cambridge University Press.
———. 1973. *Citizenship and Social Class.* Cambridge: Cambridge University Press.
Mitchell, T. 1989, September 1–2. 'The Effect of State.' Paper presented at a workshop on State Creation and Transformation, SSRC/ACLS Joint Committee on the Near and Middle East, Istanbul.
Oommen, T. K. 1997. *Citizenship and National Identity: From Colonialism to Globalism*, 143–172. New Delhi: SAGE Publications.
———. 2002. 'Demystifying the Nation and Nationalism.' *India International Centre Quarterly* 29, no. 3–4 (Winter 2002–Spring 2003): 259–274.
———. 2006. 'Social Structure, Culture and Citizenship.' In *Soziale Ungleichheit, Kulturelle Untershiede*, edited by K. S. Rehberg, 785–795. Frankfurt am Main: Campus Verl.
Worsley, P. 1984. *The Three Worlds: Culture and World Development.* Chicago, IL: University of Chicago Press.

CHAPTER 20

Communalism and Secularism

LEARNING OUTCOMES

- To understand communalism in the Indian context
- To examine the ideology of communalism
- To explore secularism as a concept and its varieties
- To identify the challenges of secular practices in India

Keywords: Communal, nationalist sentiment, structuralist theory, ideology, religion, secular, nationalist movement, liberal plural, orthodox plural, radical socialist

Subject to public order, morality and health and to the other provisions of this Part, all persons are equally entitled to freedom of conscience and the right freely to profess, practise and propagate religion.

—Article 25(1), The Constitution of India (1949)

INTRODUCTION

As a diverse society, India presents a unique case of developing as a modern nation state. The idea of a modern state has from time to time faced issues of growing communalism. The project of modernity, largely sponsored by the colonial power, could not eliminate the role of religion in the India polity. Violence between communities based on religious identities developed in the early 20th century and continued to affect the Indian polity thereafter.

In the Indian context, communalism can be understood as an ideology that organizes people of a particular religious faith to pursue common social, political and economic interests. So religion facilitates such distinct communities with strong common identities. Communalism develops subsequently by emphasizing differences between such different communities. Ultimately, such mutual incompatibility leads to mutual hostility and antagonism. The question of communalism is special for societies like India, where religious minorities exist alongside a religious majority.

Over the years, social science scholarship has tried to understand communalism not simply as hostility between competing religious groups. Communalism has been examined at an ontological level by pointing out at the two distinct worldviews of the Western modern society and the tradition-bound Indian society. Communalism has been theorized as a part of the normative order of the Indian society in contrast to the modern structure of the Western society.

Secularism, on the other hand, as a concept has evolved and understood in India quite unlike the way it had developed in the West. As a project of modernity, secularism not only rationalized religion but ensured separation of the spheres of politics from religion in the West. The very adoption of such a concept for statecraft in independent India has met with challenges. Growing communalism and interpreting Indian nationalism on cultural foundation of Hindu provenance have run into the very concept of secularism, the way it was adopted as an essential organizing principle of the Indian polity. The debate has unfolded an uneasy question of whether without benchmarking an identity for India, can Indians still respect and acknowledge differences to share the same national identity. Sociologically, an evolving notion of secularism is being proposed by critiquing the Eurocentric meaning attached to the concept of secular.

In popular parlance, the three terms of nationalism, communalism and secularism feed into each other in any understanding of the contemporary Indian society. In the shadow of the stark reality of communal violence leading to the Partition of the Indian subcontinent, the Indian Constitution adopted the secular vision which set aside any politicization of religious identities, in other words, denying any legitimacy to religious politics. Much to the dismay of political observers, the expectations of rational ordering of the Indian society appear to be illusive. Side by side with noticeable breakdown of social relations among local communities as impacted by new forces of economic development, a revivalist tendency among religious groups found expressions in conflictual forms. Nehru held religion as an erroneous view of the cosmos. However, his idea of a scientific, rationalist interpretation of social life, could not make much headway. Instead, the Gandhian position of validating the role of religion as a system of faith that gives meaning to a moral and truthful life appeared to be more useful for India to function as a 'secular' sovereign state.

20.1. COMMUNALISM

20.1.1. Communalism in the Context of Indian Society

For a multi-religious society like India, communalism carries a negative meaning of rivalry and hostility practised by one community towards another. The communities are marked on exclusive religious identity to the exclusion of all other identities. The communal holds religion as the most important marker in the society to organize the community in a tight hold to create a boundary and develop a sense of 'otherness' to give rise to inter-community hostility. It takes an ideological turn which transforms a religiously plural society into religious communities; the interests of religious communities are posited as not only different but opposed to each other.

Definitely a distinct negative dimension is conveyed by the term communalism. This is so obvious as it is understood in contrast to an already established concept of secularism. With its negative connotation, communalism is in vogue in the India polity. The political aspect has been clearly the source of the challenges put up by communalism, which became visible in the 1920s, with the assertion of religion-based national identity.

The creation of sovereign independent state of India, in a way, legitimated religion as the basis of Partition of erstwhile India. The career of independent India shows the manifold application of communal identity in modern-day mobilization for realizing political ends. The salience of E. Thompson and G. T. Garrat's prognosis in their *Rise and Fulfillment of British Rule in India* (1966) is more than obvious—'communalism is an old India problem that time does little to solve' (Ahmad 1969).

The politics of religious appeal has been there for a long time in the Indian history, but the politics of communal appeal is a modern phenomenon. In the past, the legitimization of political power was less dependent on 'mass'. Modern politics is all about gaining legitimacy from the mass—a popular sanction has to be secured by moulding or influencing popular perceptions. Communalism exactly fits in the bill in the mobilization of the masses. For such societies which are multi-religious, where religious minorities exist side by side with the religious majority, religious collectivity flourishes in divisiveness and promotes bigotry. The colonialist thrived on such a situation and the British colonizers used the term 'communalism' to justify their 'noble' mission to civilize such parochial societies. Such a negative meaning was picked up by the Indian nationalists to see it as a British colonial agenda; so logically, the expectation was that in the post-colonial India, communalism would gradually fade away from state policy. However, the ground reality of aggressive communalism in post-Independencc India demands understanding at a deeper level, beyond an instrumentalist conception. Politics of religion definitely gives rise to communalism, but communalism is not just all about politics of religion.

Studying communalism takes us to the question of communal politics. Nationalist politics in pre-Independence time had to face the challenge of communal forces both from the Hindu nationalists and its Muslim counterpart. The glorified past of intimate interaction for centuries leading to a composite synthetic cultural past is quite a popular idea. However, many historians as well as sociologists have pointed out that such a view of India is an exaggerated one. Be it the Hindu kings or Muslim emperors, bigotry and fanaticism were regular in India's past (Smith 1963).

To unitedly contest the colonial rule in a sociocultural diverse society, nationalism and patriotism were invented and invoked. The lack of any indigenous notion of nationalism and patriotism prompted the leaders of anti-colonial movement to evoke the passion of deities from the Hindu pantheon to deify India (Ahmad 1969). Nationalist sentiments were not homologous; the disjuncture became more conspicuous as the freedom movement became more intense. A distinct Hindu nationalism asserted a communal interpretation of India's past—the notion of Hindustan as the *pitribhumi* and *punyabhumi* of the Hindus (Savarkar [1923] 1969). Sensing the danger of the divisive potentiality of religion, Gandhi made an innovation with mass politics shunning fanaticism and fundamentalist positions. A popular use of Hindu idioms was resorted to reach out to the masses. Growing Islamization was a parallel development, almost as an opposite reaction to Sanskritization among lower-caste Hindus. The nationalist project couched in Hinduism did not inspire much the Muslim leadership.

Consolidation of religious identity for group action set up an uneasy complex for the modernist leaders like Jawaharlal Nehru. Nehru found the Western concept of 'secular' as an antidote to communal passions in Indian polity. Having no anchorage in the Indian cultural history, the Nehruvian secular model failed to resist the religion-based Partition of the country, and post-Independence, the hope for communal amity has been under continuous stress and strain. A simplistic argument would suggest the British policy and Muslim League's demand for a separate nation as the root cause of communalism in the subcontinent. As an extension of that, in the post-Independence times, the onus of the discord is put on the Hindu and fundamentalist forces. There is no point denying that communalism in contemporary times has pitched for Hindu nationalism by reducing the varied and complex Indian history to a 'history of perpetual Hindu–Muslim conflict—Muslim aggression and Hindu resistance, Good versus Evil or the Pure versus the Impure' (Pandey 1993, 12). In the initial years after Independence, the sovereign state could withstand the active religious campaigns by any fundamentalist force, but the simmering revivalist tendencies dashed the Nehruvian dream of a secular order in the later years.

Communalism has been analysed as an ideology—as a false consciousness claiming to represent the interest of a religious community. This is the dominant strand of understanding among the Left nationalist historians (Chandra 1984). Although premised on the politics of religious identity, the phenomenon of communalism is much more than simple religious identity. A further elaboration of this primary understanding has been forwarded by orthodox Marxist school. It links the phenomenon of communalism with class and power relation. As an ideology and practice, it represents the interests of the ruling classes who are deeply embedded in feudal-colonial inheritance (Singh 1990). A qualified Marxist study focuses on both the religious and secular dimensions of communalism. It tries to probe non-political realms of social life. It is a competitive exercise among different religious communities to spread and imbricate religious tone and tenor in the wider spheres of life. This is creating more hardened boundaries and hostility among different religious groups (Vanaik 1990).

With the development of modern capitalist forces and ethos, there is a dwindling of primordial collective identity in favour of emergence of a 'free' individual. In this context, communalism in modern India is a clear case of anachronism. And overtly political explanation will be restrictive. Instead, the social anchorage of communalism in the Indian social structure demands a sociological explanation. A comparative sociological approach that contrasts the Western ideals with the Indian society, which is having a deep historical legacy of an encompassing hierarchical structure, as examined by Louis Dumont, might be holding a few clues to the vexed issue of communalism.

20.1.2. Louis Dumont on Communalism in India

Having adopted the definition of communalism from Wilfred C. Smith, *Modern Islam in India* (1943), as an 'ideology which emphasizes as the social, political and economic unit the group of adherence of each religion, and emphasizes the distinction, even the antagonism between such groups', Louis Dumont compares the traditional and modern types of society. In a traditional society, the allegiance is given to the community as designed by the communalist, whereas in the modern society, the nationalists owe their allegiance to the nation. Religion plays a role in the composition of communalism, but only as a distinguishing marker that separates one human group from another. The essence of religion is lacking in the term communalism.

> Communalism supposes the existence of a community, a group of adherence to the same religion, but it gets the edge of its meaning through the parallelism with the other term: it is something like nationalism, in which the nation so to speak, is replaced the community. In other words, communalism is the affirmation of the religious community as a political group. (Dumont 1997, 90)

In the modern society, the nation entails a secularized political life to the exclusion of religion; a sense of sharing of territory and history is attached with any other attributes of the choice of the individual. In the traditional society, dharma is sovereign—the king rules in the name of dharma. The autonomy of the political is absent. So between the two extreme worlds of the traditional and the modern, Dumont places communalism as an ambiguous intermediary, almost a transitory phenomenon. The group–religion claim as political is unlike the way nation emerged in the modern rational West. The delinking of religion from statecraft has been a strenuous process in the West. At times, it involved inter-religious hostility. Communalism is similarly a phase of transition for traditional societies like India on its journey towards emerging as a nation state where the hostility between opposing confessions (Hinduism and Islam) could be more intense. A genuine transition to a nation may not be actualized by communalism, as it could end up resisting the transformation due to its religious configuration and allowing only a modern state on appearance only.

Dumont's comparative study of two distinct systems rests on a systematic opposition of key concepts in their relation to one another and as parts of a constituted whole. Two kinds of belongingness—communalism and nationalism—are analysed as the key opposition in Dumont's scheme of understanding the Indian society. He resorts to an explanation of the Indian social structure as parallel to that of the West to substantiate the structural persistence and the failure of the emergence of basic tenets of secularization to shape the Indian society. In traditional India, both territory and people are subject to the rule of dharma. The king's authority subsumes both the territory and its people, rendering them as undifferentiated. The notions of nation, territory, religious values and people are experienced as holistic. The separation of territory and people as a precondition for the development of individualization is missing in the Indian history. The lack of territorial sovereignty has acted as a deterrent to the development of modern state in India.

Adopting a structuralist theory, Dumont advances social-cultural parameters of nationalism and communalism in logical sets of opposites or in binary terms. The connections between the opposites are not real but syntactic. Such an understanding refuses to see any possibility of interaction or exchanges between tradition and modernity. The basic opposition between equality and hierarchy is transposed in his opposition between nationalism and communalism. The tradition-bound India normatively stressed people and territory as undifferentiated or fused. Here, the ultimate values are found in the conformity of each element to the role assigned to it by the whole, as the parts take meanings from the whole. This is in contrast to the modern social structure of the West. The ultimate values are located in the concrete human individual element, who is taken as an end in itself. Individual is a source of all norms, rationality and order.

The political aspect of the two distinct social universes is contrasted by Dumont to account for the difficulty in transition to a modern nation for a traditional hierarchical society. While comparing the two, religion, as giving ultimate values to human activity, has been given analytical priority. The salience of a deep and continuing Hindu–Muslim divide has been indicated as follows:

1. Lack of any actual social fusion during the Mughal period. There were only reciprocal cultural exchanges and fusion.
2. Both the Hindus and the Muslims resorted to their past glories to withstand the Western colonial impact. It resulted in religious revivalism of the groups.
3. The nurture of democratic ideology was left to the Western educated middle class, where the Hindus had a lead. The Muslim middle class lagged behind, and as a consequence, the Muslim community was sceptical of the transfer of power from the British. The rivalry ensured a mistrust that the Independence would result in 'Hindu Raj'.
4. The proposal and institution of separate electorates aggravated the clearly divided community feelings.

The basic postulate of Dumont is that there is lasting social heterogeneity of the Hindus and the Muslims. Despite all the claims of coexistence for centuries, there was no general ideological synthesis. Power being the determinant parameter, the coexistence was all matters of compromise or contingencies. That is, in terms of values, different religious groups who lived together do not constitute a society. The British rule negatively affected the Muslims at the cost of the Hindu merchants and moneymen. The Muslim participation in the administration, army and judiciary also dwindled. The Hindus gained as they picked up the English education system promptly, while Persian was dropped as the official language. Moreover, for an active political struggle against the colonial power, the Hindus retrieved religious tradition while embracing modern Western values of democracy, freedom, justice and nationalism. A kind of 'Hindu nationalism' appeared as the common terrain of diverse strands of the freedom movement led by the Hindu leaders. The Muslims too picked up the clue to affirm their tradition. The parallel revivalism could not meet at a point to portray a united sentiment against the British.

The spectacular combination of religion and politics marked the nationalist movement led by Gandhi, who largely shaped the trajectory of resistance against the colonial British. The Muslim League complicated the picture. The insecurity and the uneasiness of the Muslim community found expression in demands for separate electorates, special representation or compensatory privileges which were duly attended by the British to deepen the disunion. The vexed issue with the Congress was that swearing by political modernism of not to consider religious consideration for political ends, they had to tap deeper emotional connect with Hindu idioms and tradition. The deep divisions that ran through the two communities made the Partition inevitable while securing Independence. Dumont considers that the way of creating a nation state in this manner abjures the reality of duality and separateness of the two distinct communities in the subcontinent. The contention of uni-national state is thus problematic in the Indian context.

Elements of ahistoricity and formalism can be seen in Dumont's contrast between communalism and nationalism. Yogendra Singh has observed that the contrast in operational terms rests on the dualism of 'rational' and 'basic'. The fundamental opposition rests in the value systems of traditional and Western societies. As against the modern and rational Western societies, the Indian society resting on the principle of hierarchy lacks rational value in social life. Communalism is theorized at this fundamental lack. The possibility of coexistence of the rational with the fundamental value or transformation of the tradition does not find a place in this framework.

20.2. SECULARISM

20.2.1. Secularism in India

Secularism is considered as a gift of modernity handed down to India by the West. Modernity promoted separation of different spheres of life, granting each one its autonomy. Such a historical tryst with modernity has been missing in India. Contending explanations are offered for the failure of secular ideals to govern inter-religious community behaviour, especially in the political matrix of modern India.

First, colonial power is considered as the villain that unscrupulously created the divisions between religious communities through blatant administrative moves. Second, the polarization of the two communities since the 1920s was attributed to the emergence of communal organizations representing the two communities. With the Partition, the hold of religion on politics was formally given legitimacy in the development of sovereign nation states in this subcontinent. The project of secularism remained tenuous since then (Chandhoke 2009). A third understanding for the fate of secularism is given by comparative sociologists like Louis Dumont, who find that the traditional societies like India are structured on values that are opposite to the values of rationality and equality of the modern West. The sociological studies for the lack of secular ideas follow such a theorization, as we find in the works of T. N. Madan or Ashis Nandy (Bhargava 1997). It is being argued that as a concept and practice, the very term secular is alien to the Indian masses. The vacuity of the secular in the Indian context has failed to deliver a rich public morality.

The interesting point is that secularism is not a uniform practice. One variety of secular politics clearly keeps away religious values and institutions from statecraft. Another type of secular politics would adopt a neutral position towards religious values. If these two indicate two extreme types, there are many variations of secularism in between the two. Evidently, secularism takes different meaning in different societies as religious values and practices are also different in different political societies. Ravinder Kumar examines the quality and nature of secularism that has taken shape in independent India through the politics of nationalism from the pre-Independence years (Kumar 1986). It is being suggested that India practises a kind of secularism which is neither abjuring religion nor acting neutrally with different religious faithful.

Basically, focusing on the two religious communities of the Hindus and the Muslims, Kumar studies the respective social structures and values governing such structures. First, Hinduism lacks a proper institutional structure; instead, it entails a wide range of beliefs and practices. The Hindu order is marked by divisions and hierarchy, so there is only a structural unity provided by the *jati* arrangement, but no common intellectual identity shared by all the *jatis*. Second, as per as the economic structure is concerned, the Hindu society is organized for a feudal agricultural production. Therefore, from both the angles, the material and the ideal (the economic and the normative), the Hindu social order essentially puts up a picture of a loosely bound society. Villages, the basic unit, were characterized by spatial dispersal of a dominant *jati* of village zamindars. It led to a federation of zamindars held together by tax-collecting bureaucracies and armies for defence and internal order. The British administrators by introducing a centralized system of administration changed this picture of political societies. The intermediaries between the villages and also with the bureaucratic representatives of the states were eliminated.

Apart from centralization of policies, the expansion of the scope of market economy along with the introduction of new legal system accelerated the separateness of village communities. On the other hand, the Western educational values broadened the thinking of both the religious communities. The erstwhile Muslim community was also heterogeneous. There was a great gap between the upper-class gentry and the lower classes who were the cultivators and the artisans. The lower classes of both the Hindus and the Muslims for simple economic reason interacted with less barriers between them. However, an important contrast with the Hindu society remained for the Muslims. Despite inner differentiations, they were united as one closely knit community, outlined as an ideal in the central religious text Quran.

Ravinder Kumar (1983) located within the matrix of the nationalist movement leading to the Independence in 1947, as well as in the politics of independent India, three different varieties of secularism:

1. **Liberal-plural secularism:** The liberal-plural approach was a product of modern political theories which shaped the overtly religio-cultural orientations of the Hindu intelligentsia of the second half of the 19th century. Towards the end of 19th century, they placed in the formal domain of politics the idea to put religion in the private sphere and keep politics free from religious tones. Only the Westernized and the upper-class intelligentsia could appreciate such a fresh idea, while the masses lagged behind in accepting and appreciating this vision.
2. **Orthodox-plural secularism:** The orthodox-plural version emerged due to the failure of the liberal-plural approach. It rested on a strategic use of religious idioms and symbols to mobilize masses for political interest. M. K. Gandhi was the forerunner of this approach, who campaigned for religious sensibility of all communities to forge a liberating sense of national identity. An enduring national identity was to be premised on religiosity of faith and commitment, instead of the formalism of institutionalized religion.

    The success of this approach was due to its popular appeal and its inclusive policies which united the rich powerful classes and the poorer classes for a common alliance. However, the lofty goals of healing religious fissures by appealing to the essence of religiosity failed. The British took full advantage of the religious tone of political agenda to create more division and the enhanced communitarian solidarities in post-Independence times often masked off class interests. Also, the policies to rope in the rich and powerful into the nationalist struggle were fully utilized by those classes to usurp dominance in post-Independence years.

3. **Radical-socialist secularism:** A radical-socialist version of secularism grew out of an ideology that underscored the causes of the poorer classes. This was an attempt by a new generation of nationalists which grew parallel to the orthodox version. This trend which addressed the question of redistribution of wealth and power appeared within and without the encompassing structure of the Indian National Congress. However, it failed before the overwhelming hold of Gandhi and his popular appeal.

The success of the orthodox plural-secular model of Gandhi was not only that it could touch the religious feeling of the different communities in a strategic political way, but also its powerful appeal for the lower classes did not challenge the distribution of power and wealth or the status of the dominant classes.

> A theory of nationalist politics which could rally the lowly classes around the demand for national self-determination, without raising any awkward question about the ownership and distribution of wealth in the community commended itself in no uncertain terms to the propertied classes. (Kumar 1983, 44–45)

The radical-socialist secular agenda failed as the task of uniting the poorer classes in a diverse country marked by layers of fragmentation on different counts of identities has been humongous. At the same time, the continuation of antagonistic communal solidarities makes one point very clear that any version of secular nationalism that rests on religious or communitarian basis cannot lead to a harmonious order in India.

Primarily, secular politics has to be based on separation of religion and politics. This can be either done by upholding the interests of the privileged classes or that of the poorer classes. The growth of an industrial commercial economy has united the national market in the post-Independence times. The structural insulations of traditional India are much removed. This offers a ground for unity of the poorer classes for radical politics on a secular theme. A truly secular agenda needs to ensure religious freedom with equity and justice. It ensures the freedom from irrationality and communal frenzies.

20.2.2. Crisis of Secularism

Religious discourse has taken political forms in post-Independence India and has posed serious challenge to the practice of secularism as envisioned in the India Constitution. The secular ideals, although uneasy, rode much on the shoulder of the modern politics of the first prime minister, Jawaharlal Nehru, in India. After the passing away of Nehru, slowly, the cleavages started showing on Indian politics. Stark dark days could be anticipated. There were apprehensions as slowly a decisive shift in the very discourse of 'secularism and communalism' started making inroads into the mainstream Indian polity. On the face of an aggressive cultural nationalism hinging on excluding minority communities, the very concept of secularism has been subjected to substantive scrutiny.

In simple words, the failure of secularism is the failure of the society and the state to move beyond the communal strives that resulted in the Partition of the subcontinent in 1947. The hostilities were not caused by religious differences as such, but the strategic use of them by politicians for secular ends, that is, political

> **BOX 20.1**
> **Nehru's Lamenting Voice**
>
> We talk about a secular state in India. It is perhaps not very easy to find a good word in Hindi for 'secular'. Some people think it means something opposed to religion. That, obviously, is not correct.... It is a state which honours all faiths equally and gives them equal opportunities.
>
> **Source:** Nehru as quoted by Madan (1993).

power (Madan 1987). Madan is unequivocal in his apprehension that the spirit of secularism as a shared credo of life is unrealizable, as it is impracticable as statecraft. Such a sceptical view of Indian secularism is located at the three basic assumptions which have gone wrong. First, it was thought that as an anti-religious or non-religious ideology, secularization has universal applicability. If it had succeeded in the West, it would experience the same success in India. Second, as it is based on rational plans for state action, secularism will be positively accepted by all. And third, the age of ideological secularism will overcome hurdles with necessary qualifications (Madan 1997).

The challenges to free the state action from religion is implicated with everyday life, which is much under the tutelage of religious values. While it is true that secularism, as enshrined in the Indian constitution, de-legitimizes any politicization of religious identities in Independent India, it has no anchorage in Indian cultural history. In the West, secularism initially meant the transfer of church properties to the exclusive control of the princes. After the French Revolution, it became a value statement denoting that all ecclesiastical goods were at the disposal of the nation. As a modern phenomenon, the term was coined by G. Jacob Holyoake in 1851, denoting a rational movement of protest in England. As a positive connotation, secularization was seen as a defining aspect of the ideology of progress. T. N. Madan refers to Peter Berger in his article, 'Secularism in Its Place' (1987), to examine the term secularism as it stands in contemporary times. Secularization is understood as a process by which society and culture are relieved from religious institutions and symbols. The modern Indian state has set its goal to the same purpose. For Madan, however, the problem is how far this avowed mission has contextual relevance and carries meanings for conducting everyday life.

20.2.3. Gandhi, Nehru and Indian Secularism

The differing perspectives of Gandhi and Nehru on secularism are sociologically important for J. P. S. Uberoi, as the two great minds of politics shaped India towards its Independence and beyond (Madan 1997). The provisions of the constitution and the expressions of intercommunity stress and strain in Indian polity are incisively commented upon by him.

Gandhian politics is unique in his project of spiritualizing and moralizing the world of public life and statecraft. Beyond the formalism and ritualism of religious faiths, Gandhi wanted to tap the emancipatory potential of every religion. He wanted to sacralize the domain of politics by acts of *ahimsa* and *Satyagraha*. It involved the spiritual realization of the unity of life—a holistic vision with religiosity as a constitutive principle. Religion is the faith that transcends reason. If *ahimsa* is the mode of existence, *Satyagraha* is the prayer of a political activist. It is a conscious striving to realize the spirit within. Religion is the source of ethics. So no one who trades the path of true religion can remain detached from politics. True religiosity harmonizes all different religions as it rests on the faith of moral governance (Rao 1968).

Referring to the Gandhian expert, Bhikhu Parekh's (1989) work, Madan contends that, the very concept of the state was altered by Gandhi. Instead of the conventional notion of the state as the proprietor of the legitimate use of force or coercion, he preferred morally awakened and spiritually enriched individuals constituting a civil society. When politics is sacralized, the state abdicates its coercive role. In the Western liberal democracy, Gandhi could trace the germ of hedonism and materialist pursuit. So even if Indian secularism entails the idea of equal respect for all religious faiths as a state ideology, it is incomplete as it is bound with the hedonistic ideology of socialism. He refuted the idea of a state religion or state promoting any religion but, at the same time, distanced himself from the Western colonial construct of secularism.

On the other hand, Jawaharlal Nehru had unambiguous confidence in the role of reason and rationality as promised by Western thought. A wide experience of Western liberal and socialist philosophy as well as encounters with the Indian masses during the freedom struggle shaped Nehru's thinking. He clearly denounced institutional religion, ritual and mysticism. In fact, at times, he abhorred Gandhi's approach to politics. While dismissing the role of religion and bigotry, he still admitted to the inner spiritual cravings of the people. In his *The Discovery of India* (1941) Nehru laid his strong conviction on the modern scientific way of interpreting the world and setting aside all that sentimentality and emotion around religion.

Dismissing the Gandhian vision as a diversion, Nehru proposed that by focusing on the strength of economic growth and development the religious differences would fade away. He was appalled at the creation of Pakistan or the division of India on a religious basis. He could acknowledge communalism as an expression of class interest. According to Madan, Nehru hailed onto ideal European enlightenment values, which were at variance from the ground reality of society, culture and politics in India. However, the compulsion of embeddedness of religion in the society made him climb down from the strict secular position to a qualified one, suitable for the Indian society. In the famous Karachi session, 1931, he was instrumental in inserting in the resolution on fundamental rights, the freedom to practice any religion. The cardinal change in his position was that in free India the state would exercise neutrality with respect to all religious groups. Madan considers that Nehru's change in stance, that is, opting for religious pluralism to characterize a secular state was a compromise. The compromise, as a strategy not a surrender, was in acknowledgement of the all-pervasive hold of religion in Indian society.

How to create a secular state in a religious society remained the central problem for Nehru as well as the delicate task of the Indian constitution. At an ideological level, Sarvepalli Radhakrishnan laid bare the problem as to how could the state be secular when its culture is deeply spiritual. Nehru held onto a state-centric centralized project of development to offset the religious sentiments but it was clearly an instrumentalist exercise.

The term 'secularism' did not figure in the Indian constitution originally, it was only through the 42nd Amendment in 1976 that the words 'secular' and 'socialist' were added to qualify India as a 'sovereign republic'. The Hindi vernacular uses *panth nirpeksha* as equivalent to secular, meaning neutral attitude towards all religious faiths. Madan finds crucially that the constitution retains a fundamental paradox between the fundamental rights and the directive principles. There are unresolved tensions between Article 25–30 and Article 44, as single out by Madan. Article 25–30 guarantees freedom and rights to all religious faiths with respect to different dimensions of practice and propagation (especially protection to minorities), whereas Article 44 pronounces the Directive Principles of effecting a uniform civil code throughout the Indian territory. It is true that the fundamental rights supersede the directive principles, but effectively, the rights guaranteed have led to the aggravation of communal feelings and attitudes among cultural minorities, always under the pressure of real or imagined loss of identity. So the spread of modern secular ideas is absent in such communities.

> The framers of the Constitution ... overlooked the possibility that in a democratic polity the State may reflect the character of the society, and that a communally divided society and a secular state could be mutually contradictory. On the one hand, there is the danger of majoritarianism and, on the other, that of vesting the religious minorities with the kind of veto power. (Madan 1997, 249)

There are other instances of inconsistencies, as noted by Madan. If Article 17 takes on the casteist practice of Hinduism by prohibiting the practice of untouchability, Article 48 assuages the feelings of high-caste Hindus by prohibiting cow slaughter and so on. Again, Article 48 is an out and out instance of caste Hindu appeasement, Article 47 does the same for Islam by directing a prohibition on consumption of intoxicant. Overall speaking, in the crucial decade of the 1950s, Nehru seemed to be bold enough to confront and get the obscurantist Hindu practices de-legitimized through various acts enacted in the parliament. It was possible for him to act as the 'benign elder brother' to mould or reform the Hindu practices but fell short of daring the other communities.

The central point was driven home by Madan after observing the performance of successive governments after Independence that steps that appear to be vacillating on the question of a steadfast secular attitude where actually contingent on the situations. Non-discrimination may not be the only response of an Indian secular state. Instead, the anxieties and insecurities of the minorities, which are not always perceived but under the real threat of the fundamentalists demands special attention and security. The conundrum of majority–minority is a pressing continuous problem for India. Historically, no religious community is internally undifferentiated. Instead, the majority-minority divide as religious monoliths has become a political gambit. It is the language of the communalists to compete for political power.

20.2.4. Fragility of Secularism in India

Indian history since the last quarter of the 20th century is replete with group antagonism of a subtler dimension, involving not only the Hindu–Muslim relationship but also Hindu–Sikh interactions. The profound search for the 'enemy within' as suggested by Sudipta Kaviraj (1990) in his article 'On the Discourse of Secularism' brings out the discontents in the secular practice in India. His analysis on the discourse of secularism shows how, although defined in opposition to each other, the secular discourse in the Indian context with the full support of the state-power since Independence failed to offset communalism. By the term secular discourse, he refers to the generally accepted modes of validation and arguing by which people construct political arguments in favour of secularism. He posits culture as an important agenda for political action, as a supplement to political–economic forces. In this framework, he examines how the argument for secularism is made up and what exactly does it mean to the people. The central problem is whether the claim to truth (as rationalist) and the communicative strategy of that truth are in sync.

According to Kaviraj, the secularists have failed to enhance the truth but enhanced the rhetoric of its reasonableness. The re-enactment of European modernity is a failure as the English-speaking middle-class intelligentsia could not possibly address the lower rungs of the Hindu society. The creation of a vernacular orbit of discourse is a must for attacking the religious ways of thinking. The structure of political structure as created by the nationalist discourse gave rise to vernacularism. This proved to be a better success than the stratagem of the nation-state which lacked such an authentic voice to converse with the lower-level social groups. The vernacular culture helped nationalist ideas to be communicated to the masses. As a precursor of secularism, the admissibility of nationalist criteria in discussions of religious beliefs served as a good starting point for a change. For ideas of secularism to be carried down to the masses, such a vernacularization was lacking.

Kaviraj's scrutiny of the voice of the secularists almost converges with T. N. Madan's scepticism of the idea of transferability of a concept like secularism, a Western social theorist's paradigm of modernization, in the Indian soil (Madan 1997). Privatization of religion is a futile exercise where religion is constitutive of social life. As an alien cultural ideology secularism is bound to fail in the Indian context as it is not as simple as the separation of the Church from the state, like the West. Like the West, Indian indigenous religions do not entail the dichotomy between the sacred and the secular. What is secular in Indian tradition is always encompassed by the sacred, in these religious traditions, the search for an autonomous ideology of secularism is thereby ruled out.

For Madan, secularism, as opposed to religion, is anathema to the Indian situation as religion confers people their place in society and gives meanings to their lives more than anything else. He does not propose a straight rejection of secularization but insists on a search for a proper means for its expression—the idea of self-emancipation of humankind. It involves the sacralization of the secular. Secularism is compatible with faith when religion is considered a way of life. Madan is closer to Gandhi to argue that rationalism is not the only motive force of a modern state. Indian secularism, as goodwill towards all religions, is understood as a rearguard action on the part of the state in the face of failure to separate politics from religion. Madan thinks this has trivialized religious differences as well as the notion of the unity of religions.

Madan, finally, contends that it is possible to tap India's own resources located in its indigenous Abrahamic religious traditions to evolve a notion of secularism, which fosters interreligious understanding. These traditions are more pliable and open to questioning from within and reformulation through interpretation. So the exploration has to be made away from the Brahmanical tradition and focus on the Indic religious traditions. These traditions are more pliable and open to questioning from within and reformulation through interpretation. The task to move beyond religious discord is the task of sociocultural reconciliation in an indigenous way. It has to be an ideological exercise to be premised on religion as tolerance. The very survival of the Indian state is dependent on the success of rigorous and concerted thinking as well as action.

Ashis Nandy points out at the epistemological issue by critiquing the concept of secularism as part of a hegemonic Western discourse. As a faith, religion does not serve the communal, but when it acts as an ideology, as a sub-national or even cross-national marker of exclusive populations geared towards non-religious, especially political or economic interests, it constitutes the axis of communalism (Nandy 1990). The Eurocentric notion of secularism directs itself against the ideology not the faith of religion. It fails in India because as an ideology religion is more resilient than faith which has shown more pliability and catholicity.

There is a twofold reception of the Eurocentric concept of secularism in India. First, restricted amongst the middle-class public consciousness is a pure scientific temper and rational meaning that keeps religion away from the public sphere. Second, for the majority as well as for all practising politicians, secularism meant equal treatment for all religions. Through this accommodative meaning, religion has entered public life through the backdoor. Side by side, modernity has emerged as the organizing principle of the dominant culture and politics. Growth, security and modernization are counter-posed by Nandy (1990) as the repertoire that displaces the triad of religion, fanaticism and violence. He is dismissive of the claim of secularism as opposed to communalism, as a better guide to political action to provide a more tolerant and stable political life. Statecraft based on secularism has failed to provide a richer public morality. An absurd search for a modern language of politics is all that secularism means to him. As a new justification of domination, secularism has been theorized by him.

CONCLUSION

Communalism is a 'modern' phenomenon in the Indian context with a negative connotation signifying a politics of communal appeal. The use of religious boundaries to mark distinctions and strive for power by using group antagonism premised on such distinctions is the hallmark of a communal ideology. It is, however, much more than a simple religious identity. It is used to mask off the 'secular' interest by the ruling classes in their pursuit of power. As a practice, communalism, then, signifies that state of affair where religion becomes the vehicle for the organization of political and economic life.

Despite the coming of a secular, sovereign independent state, the challenges put up by communalism have been a vexed one in India. As expected, the unleashing of the modern forces could not outdate the use of primordial identities from the public sphere. The very notion of belongingness to a community in the Indian context has been subjected to comparative sociological studies. One such study by social anthropologist Louis Dumont examines communalism in the matrix of the contrasting value system of two different kinds of society—the modern west vis-à-vis the traditional Indian. He traces the group antagonism based on religion within the framework of problems of social change in a traditional society like India. Contrasting the traditional structure with the West, he underscored the hierarchical principle and the absence of the development of an autonomous individual in Indian society. The difficulty in evolving into a modern nation is located in the lasting influence of encompassing religious values in India.

On the other hand, the secular, as a project for modern statecraft, has been an avowed path for Independent India, but it has been an uneasy journey so far. T. N. Madan, along with many other sociologists, has noted the impracticability of operationalization of a concept that lacks historical roots in a traditional society. Madan criticizes the imposition of secularization on India because it is essentially a Protestant idea. In Indian religions—Hinduism, Islam, Buddhism and Sikhism—secularism is 'encompassed' as a subordinate aspect of the religious world view. So 'secularism' cannot be 'translated' to India's culture.

The assumptions behind popular expectation for a successful operation of a secular state in Independent India turned out to be vacuous. Secularism is not simply an anti-religious ideology, but it is also a result of the process which talks about expanding human control over human lives. Essentially, it is opposed to any idea of revelation and unreason. Indian indigenous religions had never gone through such a process of secularization. So in certain protracted ways, the concept has been adapted to suit the Indian situation. Scholars, like Sudipta Kaviraj, point out the failure of the secular project as the lack of 'connect' of the elite with the masses. Vernacularization of the European concept is a daunting task to be successful in making secular a viable one in the Indian cultural context. Ashis Nandy considers the very agenda and paradigm of secularism as couched in the Western hegemonic post-colonial knowledge structure.

Madan, while admitting the incongruity of the two different world orders of meaning, hopes for reconsideration for a secular state. The regular definitional opposition between communalism and secularism conceals more than what it reveals in the Indian context. By retrieving resources from *Abrahamic* Indic religion, one can give secular an evolved meaning in the Indian context and work out a clear relation between religions with civil society. It is an ideological exercise premising on religion as tolerance.

Points for Classroom Discussion

- The historical context of communalism in India
- Louis Dumont's understanding that communalism as a phase of transition for traditional societies like India on its journey towards a nation state
- The meaning of secularism with special reference to India
- The challenges of secular practices in India

GLOSSARY

Communal: Belonging to a community but a negative connotation in the Indian context, meaning an ideology that rests on and uses religious differences.
Hierarchy: An arrangement that places one social group over the other to signify a ranking.
Nationalist sentiment: Belongingness to one's nation that is subjective.
Secularism: Essentially a European concept that calls for the separation of the Church from the state affairs.
Vernacularization: The promotion and propagation of vernacular language to highlight nativism.

REFERENCES

Ahmad, I. 1969. 'Secularism and Communalism.' *Economic & Political Weekly* 4, no. 28–30 (July).
Bhargava, R., ed. 1997. Secularism and Its Critics. New Delhi: Oxford University Press.
Chandhoke, N. 2009. 'Why Is Secularism Important for India.' In *Contemporary India: Economy, Society, Politics*, edited by Neera Chandhoke, and Praveen Priyadarshi. New Delhi: Pearson.
Chandra, B. 1984. Communalism in Modern India. New Delhi: Vikas Publishing House.
Dumont, L. 1997. 'Nationalism and Communalism.' In *Religion Politics and History in India*. Paris/The Hague: Mouton Publishers.
Gopal, S. 1980. *Jawaharlal Nehru: An Anthology*. New Delhi: Oxford University Press. Delhi.
Kaviraj, S. 1990. 'On the Discourse of Secularism.' In *Secularism and Indian Polity*, edited by Bidyut Chakrabarty. New Delhi: Segment Book Distributor.
Kumar, R. 1983. *Essays in the Social History of Modern India*. New Delhi. Oxford University Press.
———. 1986. 'The Varieties of Secular Experience.' In *Essays in the Social History of Modern India*, 31–46. Calcutta: Oxford University Press.
Madan, T. N. 1987. 'Secularism in Its Place.' *Journal of Asian Studies* 46, no. 4: 747–758.
———. 1993 'Whither Indian Nationalism'. *Modern Asian Studies* 27, no. 3: 667–697.
———. 1997. *Modern Myths, Locked Minds*. New Delhi: Oxford University Press.
Nandy, A. 1990. 'Politics of Secularism and the Recovery of Religious Tolerance.' In *Mirrors of Violence: Communities, Riots and Survivors in South Asia*, edited by V. Das, 69–93. New Delhi: Oxford University Press.
Nehru, J. 1941. *The Discovery of India*. New Delhi: Oxford University Press.
Pandey, G., ed. 1993. *Hindus and Others: The Question of Identity in India Today*. New Delhi: Viking.
Parekh, B. 1989. *Colonialism, Tradition and Reform: An Analysis of Gandhi's Political Discourse*. New Delhi: SAGE Publications.
Rao, Mohan U. S. 1968. *The Message of Mahatma Gandhi*. New Delhi: Publications Division Ministry of Information & Broadcasting.
Savarkar, V. D. 1923. *Hindutva: Who Is a Hindu?* Bombay: Veer Savarkar Prakashan.
Singh, R. 1990. 'Communalism and the Struggle against Communalism: A Marxist View.' *Social Scientist* 18, no. 8–9 (August–September): 4–21.
Smith, D. E. 1963. *India as a Secular State*. Princeton, NJ: Princeton University Press.
Vanaik, A. 1990. *The Painful Transition: Bourgeois Democracy in India*. London: Verso.

INDEX

acculturation, 160
agrarian society, 175
Akali politics of 1980s, in Punjab, 252
All Assam Students' Union (AASU), 254
alternative media theory, 188
Ambedkar, Babasaheb Bhimrao, 54, 216
  criticism of Hindu *shastras*, 60–62
  debate with Mahatma Gandhi, 64–65
  idea of India, 59–60
analytical models of caste system in India, 75–78
animism, 99
anthropologist in East, 46–47
Antyodaya Anna Yojana, 136
Arya Samaj, 171
Asiatic Society of Bengal, 6
Assam Gana Sangram Parishad (AGSP), 254
Assam Movement
  AASU and AGSP, demands of and protest by, 255–256
  and state response, 256–258
  Assam Accord (1985), 258–261
  historical background of, 253–254
  violent phase of, 256–258
Atal Pension Yojana, 275
authoritarian theory, 188

Bahujan Samaj Party (BSP), 225–226
Beti Bachao Beti Padhao, 281
Bhakti movements, 171
block panchayat or panchayat samiti, 128
Bonded Labour System (Abolition) Act, 218
Bose, Nirmal Kumar, 27
bourgeois anxieties, 147
bourgeois environmentalism, 147
Brahamanization, 160
Brahmo Samaj, 171
British social anthropological tradition, 5

Buddhism, 12
bullying, defined, 291

caste system in India
  Weberian perspective, 81
caste system in India and political system, 79–80
caste system in India and women, 80–81
caste system in India in rural and urban areas, 79
Chattopadhyay, K. P., 13
childhood, defined, 287–288
child labour in India
  and impact of Covid-19 pandemic, 287
  defined, 286
  gendered labour, 287
child labour, UNICEF's standard indicator for, 284–285
child marriage, 301
Child Marriage Restraint Act, 1929, 301
citizenship
  and autonomy, 319
  and national identity, 316–319
city
  and space, 150–151
  and urbanism, 146–150
  Simmel concept of, 140–141
civic-collectivistic state, 314
collectivistic-authoritarian state, 314
colonial conditioning, 6
colonial view of Indian society
  administrative approach and field view, 24–26
  and role of missionaries, 23–24
  Orientalist view, 21–23
communalism, defined, 330
communalism in Indian society
  development of, 327–329
  Louis Dumont on, 329–332

Comte, August, 158
concentric zone theory, 293
consumption, 145–146
contesting spaces, 147–148
Contributions journal, 37
culture structure, categories of, 159

Dalit movement in India
    post-Independent struggle, 223–224
Dalit movement in India
    and politics, 224–226
    and state action, 224–226
    constituted of competing ideologies, 217
    new phase of, 226–227
    pre-colonial and colonial era, 222–223
Dalit Panther Party, 223
dalits (untouchable) in India
    counter ideology, 220–222
    cultural consensus, 220–222
    defined, 217–218
    identity of, 218–219
    ideology of, 218–219
    impact of changes on, 227–228
    self-image of, 220
de-Ashrafization process, 95
Deen Dayal Upadhyaya Grameen Kaushalya Yojana (DDUGKY), 135, 275
delinquency, concept of
    among children, 290
    and cyberbullying, 291
    and drug abuse among children, 290–291
    defined, 288
    resolutions for, 291–292
demographic transition model, 269
Desai, A. R., 16
de-Sanskritization process, 162–163
development media theory, 188
dharma, 61, 92, 330
differential association theory, 292–293
disembeding of social system. concept of, 168
disenfranchisement, 254, 259, 261
dominant caste, 78
dominant peasantry in Indian rural society, concept of
    assessment of, 203–205
    features of, 202–203
double-edged phenomenon, 168

Dube, S. C., 16
Dumont, Louis, 38–40

eco-feminism, 244
egalitarianism, 92
ethnicity, concept of
    and politics, 252–253
    criticality of, 256
    defined, 250–252
    dynamics of, 251
ethnicization of politics, 252
ethnographic approach of sociology of India
    and theoretical informed fieldwork, 44–45
    applications of, 45–46
    field versus book view, 43–44
ethnography, 13, 18
ethnoscapes, 184
E.V. Ramaswamy Naicker, 222

family system in India
    and household, 108
    and women, 116
    changes in, 116
    structure of, 106–107
    types of, 109
features of caste system in India, 75
financescapes, 184
Frenchification process, 314
French Revolution, 313

Gandhi, Mohandas Karamchand (Mahatma Gandhi), 26, 28, 54
    Hind Swaraj, 55–57
    on untouchability, 57–59
    vision of India, 54–55
Gandhi, Rajiv, 258
Ghurye, G. S., 13
giant corporation, 181
globalization
    agents of, 183–184
    defined, 181–182
    elements of, 183
    impacts of, 186–187
    oldest form of, 182
    trajectories of, 183
Golwalkar, M. S., 319–320
Goyal, Desh Raj, 319
gram panchayat, 128
gram sansad, 128

Harijan, 218–219
Harijan journal, 66
heterogenetic change, 158
high net-worth individuals, 148
Hind Swaraj, 54, 56
Hinduization, 160
Hindu nationalism, 320–321
Hindutva, 170, 319
home, notion of, 149
homogenization, 185
hybridization, 185

ideoscapes, 184
illiteracy, defined, 277
illiteracy in India, reasons for
  caste hierarchy and tribes, 280
  economic deficit, 280
  gender bias, 278
  initiatives and transformations, 281
  quality of education, 281
  regional differences, 280
imagined communities, 189
Indian Council of Social Science Research, New Delhi, 7
Indian Sociologist, 8
Indira Awas Yojana (IAY), 128
individualist-liberatarian state, 314
Indology, 9, 11, 18, 21, 32
  debates for sociology of India, 40–42
  qualified use of, 42–43
  use of classical texts, 38
industrialization
  and industrialism, difference between, 179–180
  first phase of, 177
  fourth phase of, 177
  historical development of, 176–177
  second phase of, 177
  third industrial phase of, 177
industrialization in India
  developing federalism, 178–179
  development of, 177–178
industrial society, 175–176
institution of caste system in India, 74
Islamization, 171

Jat-Pat-Todak Mandal, 65
Jawaharlal Nehru, 217, 329
Jones, William, 6
Jyotiba Phule, 222

Kamla Bhasin, 231
Kanshi Ram, 225
karma, 92
Karve, Iravati, 12
Kashmiri Pandits, displacement of, 149
Kaviraj, Sudipta, 20
kinship
  and women, 116
  approaches to study, 112
  changes in, 116
  in India, patterns of, 112–115
Kshatriyaization, 160

literacy in India
  Constitutional provisions, 277–279
  importance of, 277
local–global dialect, concept of, 184–185

Madan, T. N., 14
magic bullet theory, 188
Mahatma Gandhi National Rural Employment Guarantee Scheme (MGNREGS), 136
Mahila Samitis, 236
Majumdar, D. N., 12
Malinowski, Bronislaw, 5, 12, 109
Mandal Commission, 226
marriage
  and legislations in India, 111–112
  and women, 116
  changes in, 116
  in different religions, 110
  rules of, 111
  types of, 109–110
Marxist theory, 200–202
Mayavati, 226
Medha Patkar, 102
media
  global debate on, 188–189
  role of, 188
  theories of, 188
mediascapes, 184
Mid Day Meal Scheme, 281
middle class
  and globalization, 211
  and Marxist theory of class, 205–206
  as a signifier, 206–208
  contemporary, 210–211
  Indian, 82–85

in post-colonial societies, 208–209
shallow, 210
middle peasantry, 200–202
M. N. Srinivas, 78
modernity
  and nationalism, 170–171
  critique of, 170
  elements of, 168–169
  in Indian scenario, 169–170
modernization
  agents of, 166–168
  defined, 165–166
  in India, 165–166
Mohandas Karamchand Gandhi (Mahatma Gandhi)
  feminization of politics, 236
monogamy, 109
Mukerjee, D. P., 12, 26
Mukerjee, Radhakamal, 12, 26
Mukherjee, D. P., 158
Mukherjee, Ramkrishna, 16

Narmada Bachao Andolan, 102
nationalist discourse of Indian society
  ideology of, 28–29
  indigenous knowledge, 26–27
nationality, bases of, 319
  languages, 321–323
  tribe groups, 323
National Rural Livelihoods Mission, 136
nation, notion of, 312–315
Nehruvian model of social democracy, 29
new nationalism, historical understanding of, 315–316

orthogenetic change, 158

Panchayati Raj system, 126–127
  73rd and 74th Constitutional Amendment Acts, 127
  structure of, 127–128
Panini, M. N., 7–8
peasant movement in India
  Andhra Delta movement, 199
  and peasantry, 197–198
  Bardoli agitation, 199
  Champaran movement, 198
  Kheda district movement, 198
  Oudh peasant movement, 199
  Tebhaga movement, 199
  Telangana movement in Hyderabad princely state, 200
  United Province rural agitations, 198
Phule, J.G., 8
pluralistic industrialism, 180
Pocock, David, 38–40
polyandry, 110
polygamy, 110
population
  defined, 268
  growth and pattern of, approaches, 268
population of India
  birth rate, 270
  deficit of women, 271
  demographic dividend and future, 272
  fertility rate, 270
  growth rate of, 270
  mortality rate, 271
post-Independence phase of sociology and social anthropology, 14–15
post-industrialism, 180–181
post-industrial society, 180–181
poverty
  and children, 274
  and disability, 274
  and elderly, 274
  and rural poor, 275
  and women, 274
  caste and ethnicity, 275
  defined, 272
  dimensions of, 273
  identity of poor, 273
  initiatives to eradicate, 275
poverty in India, estimation of, 150
Pradhan Mantri Fasal Bima Yojana, 275
Pradhan Mantri Gramin Awaas Yojana, 275
Pradhan Mantri Gram Sinchai Yojana, 275
Pradhan Mantri Jan Dhan Yojana, 275
professionalization of sociology and social anthropology, stages of, 10–11
proto-professional stage of sociology, 7
public space, 150–151

Ranade, M.G., 8
Rashtriya Swayamsevak Sangh, 319
Redfield, Robert, 5
religion in India
  Christianity, 97
  complexity and thoughts, 90–91

Hinduism, 91–93
Islam, 93–95
Sikhism, 95–96
Republican Party of India (RPI), 224
Roshni (a skill development scheme for tribals), 135
Roy, Ram Mohan, 8
rural development in Indian villages, 124–125
  Gandhi's notion of, 125–126
rural sociology, 140
rural–urban continuum process, 134–137, 142
rural–urban migration, 149

Saansad Adarsh Gram Yojana, 275
same-sex marriages, 110
Sanatan dharma, 64, 228
Sansad Adarsh Gram Yojana, 135
Sanskritization process
  act to perform to elevate social social status, 161
  defined, 160
  structural functional perspective, 161–162
Sant Ramji, 65
Sarkar, B. K., 6
Sarva Shiksha Abhiyan, 137, 281
Saubhagya Yojana, 135
Savarkar, Vinayak Damodar, 319
Seal, B. N., 6
secularism, 29, 92, 97
secularism in India
  and Jawaharlal Nehru, 335–337
  and Mahatma Gandhi, 335–337
  crisis of, 334–335
  fragility of, 337–339
  types of, 332–334
secular politics, 33
Shah Bano case (Muslim women's bill), 246
Shiv Sena Movement (1960s–1970s) in Maharashtra, 252
Shosit Samaj Sangharsh Samiti, 225
Singh, Yogendra, 3, 6–7
slum, 149–150
social anthropology
  alternative view, 7
  colonial interface, 8
  exploratory phase, 9
  foundation years, 7–8

Indian scenario, 6
professionalization of, 13
Western scenario, 4–5
social change, concept of
  approahces of, 158–159
  defined, 158
social conditioning of Indian sociology, 6
social disorganization theory, 292
social resposibility theory, 188
social structure
  approaches of, 73–74
  critical evaluation of, 72
  defined, 72
  elements of, 73
sociology
  as an academic discipline, 11–12
  diversification in, 15–17
  specializations in, 15–17
  Western and Indian scenario of development, 4–7
sororate marriage, 110
squatter settlements, 152
Srinivas, M. N., 7–8, 11, 16, 44, 160
strain theory
  defined, 289
  revised, 289–290
structural changes in caste system in India, 79
subaltern school of Indian nationalism
  alternative history, 29–31
  debates within, 31–32
Swachh Bharat Mission, 135
Swadeshi, 26
Swami Dayananda Saraswati, 8
Swami Vivekananda, 8
Swaraj, 26
symbolic order, 232

Tagore, Rabindranath, 26
Taoism, 12
technoscapes, 184
themes and issues, of Indian anthropology and sociology, 47–49
Thorstein Veblen, 146
Tilak, Bal Gangadhar, 26
T. N. Madan, 97
tribalization, 160
tribal society, 175
tribes in India
  and issues of identity, 101–102

and religion, 99–101
during British era, 98–99
tribes, defined, 98–99

Ujjwala Yojana, 135
United Nations International Women's Year (1975), 232
urban conflict, 149
urban, defined, 140
urbanization
  and consumption pattern, 145–146
  and education, 143–144
  and modernization, 143–144
  course of, 143
  defined, 140
  implications of, 143
  in India, history of, 143
  model of city, 140–141
  primary phase of, 142
  restructuring of urban space and middle class, 144–145
  secondary phase of, 142
urban poor, 150
urban sociology, 140

varna model, 72, 76
varnavyavastha, 65
Vedanta, 12
Verelst, Henry, 8
vernacularization, 48, 338, 340
Vidyasagar, Ishwar Chandra, 8
village republics, 55
villages in India
  agrarian structure, changes in, 131–132
  Green Revolution in, 133
  institutional credit system and CDP, 133
  political identity of Dalits and women, 130–131
  post-1991 changes, 134
villages in India, changes in power structure, 129–130
  unequal distribution of power, 130
violence against children
  child abuse, 303–304
  factors of child abuse, 304–305
violence against the elderly, 305–306
violence against women
  defined, 298
  in public spaces, 302–303
violence against women by family
  in natal home, 300–302
  intimate partner violence, 298–300

Wadia, A. R., 11
Westernization
  cultural structures, changes in, 164–165
  defined, 163
  phases of, 163–164
women in India
  and colonial era, 235–237
  cultural ideal of womanhood, 232–234
  Hindu girls in patrilineal Indian society, 234–235
women movement in India, 246–247
  campaigns by women and state, 238–243
  challenges of, 243–245
  history of, 237–238

zila panchayat, 127

Lightning Source UK Ltd.
Milton Keynes UK
UKHW030741250721
387700UK00005B/108